Praise for *An Unexpected Light*

"Humorous, honest, and wry . . . [Elliot's] literary talents are exceptional. His sonorous prose moves forward with the purposeful grace of a river."
—*Publishers Weekly* (starred review)

"*An Unexpected Light* is an unexpected gift. . . . Elliot's account is vivid and should broaden the reader's comprehension of an often misunderstood country."
—Jonathan   y, *Columbus Dispatch*

"*An Unexpected Light* thoughtfully lays out new and overlooked information that policy-makers in the U.S. and the West as a whole need when trying to decide what may work."
—Robert A. Lincoln, *Richmond Times-Dispatch*

"The author's impressive knowledge of Afghanistan's history, his seemingly boundless affection for its people, his understanding and respect for their culture and religion, and his flair for the language make this more than a casual travelogue. It is a plaintive love song whose discordant notes are provided by daily encounters with violence, hardship, and poverty."
—*Kirkus Reviews*

"In his skillful illumination of an ancient and noble history long obscured by war, Elliot has done service to a country rarely written about. But it's his lyrical   of beauty fro   ir that will resonate long after the last page has been turned."
—*Trips*

"Everything a travel book should be—truly memorable."
—Eric Newby

"A tour de force of travel and memory: vividly evocative, courageous, and self-aware."
—Colin Thubron

An Unexpected Light

JASON ELLIOT

An Unexpected Light

Travels in Afghanistan

Picador USA
New York

www.picadorusa.com

Picador® is a U.S. registered trademark and is used by St. Martin's Press under license from Pan Books Limited.

For information on Picador USA Reading Group Guides, as well as ordering, please contact the Trade Marketing department at St. Martin's Press.
Phone: 1-800-221-7945 extension 763
Fax: 212-677-7456
E-mail: trademarketing@stmartins.com

ISBN 0-312-27459-9 (hc)
ISBN 0-312-28846-8 (pbk)

First published in Great Britain by Picador, an imprint of Macmillan Publishers Ltd

First Picador USA Paperback Edition: November 2001

10 9 8 7 6 5 4 3 2 1

To my Mother and Father

for showing me which way the oxen go

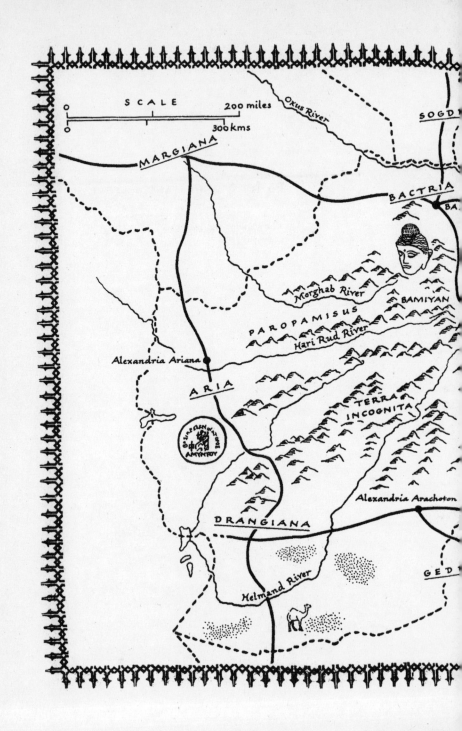

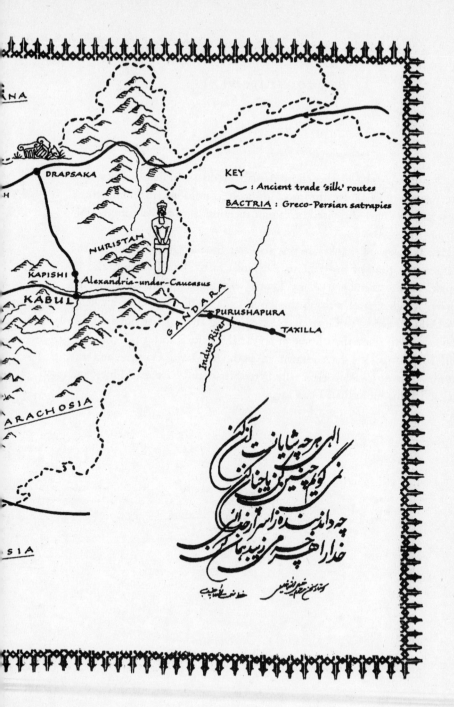

KEY

⌒ : Ancient trade 'silk' routes

BACTRIA : Greco-Persian satrapies

DRAPSAKA

NURISTAN

KAPISHI

Alexandria-under-Caucasus

KABUL

GANDARA

PURUSHAPURA

Indus River

TAXILLA

ARACHOSIA

الهی هر چه شایانت آکن

نمی گویم چنین کن یا چنان کن

چه داند بنده از اسرار خدائی

خدا را هر چه می زیبد همان کن

Acknowledgements

To the many Afghans who showed such kindness and hospitality to a burdensome guest under the most difficult conditions, including those whose names I have disguised or cannot mention, I owe a debt impossible to repay in words.

Late but sincere thanks are due to Peter Stocker and the staff of the ICRC at the time of my visit to Afghanistan; to Tim Johnston and to Ropate; to the members of my family who eased in various ways the different challenges of writing this book; to a small number of incorrigibly faithful friends; to Doris and Peter Lessing and the late Butchkin for allowing me to share their home at a crucial juncture; to former travellers from whose works I have drawn strength; to David Godwin and the editorial team at Picador, especially Peter Straus and Richard Milner; and to Claudia, for more than I can say.

A Note on Languages

The *lingua franca* of Afghanistan is Dari, the Afghan version of Persian (sometimes called Farsi), though over a third of the population, predominantly in the southern portion of the country, speaks Pashtu. Both belong to the Indo-European family of languages. Within the country as a whole as many as forty other languages are spoken.

Persian uses a modified form of the Arabic script, along with many assimilated Arabic words. There are a number of Persian words in this book, as well as a few Arabic terms, the pronunciation of which are not accurately conveyed by English spelling. Since this is not a technical work, I have aimed in transcription for a reasonable degree of consistency which will make sense to people familiar with the language and not weigh down those who are not.

Frequently used names such as Kabul, Herat and even Afghanistan (which in the country doesn't sound much like the English version) have been Anglicized. But Persian has three 'long' vowel sounds (as well as a few tricky consonants) distinct enough to deserve their own characters. These are the long 'a' sound (as in barn), the long 'i' (as in beet), and the long 'u' (as in boot). To distinguish them from their 'short' counterparts in English they are represented in the text by the characters ā, ī and ū respectively.

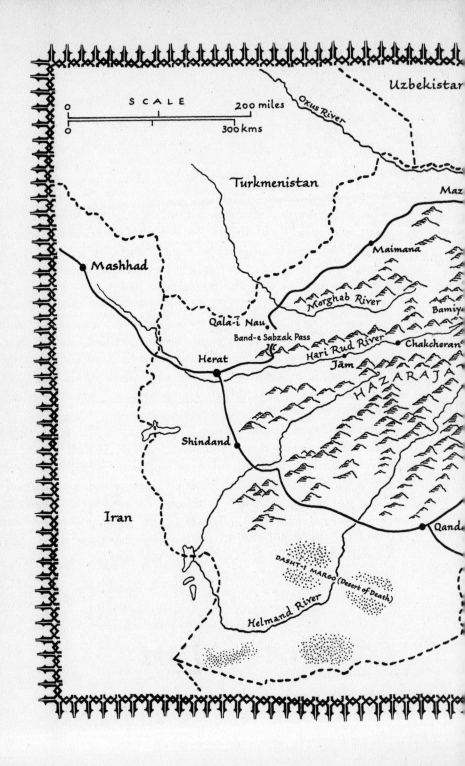

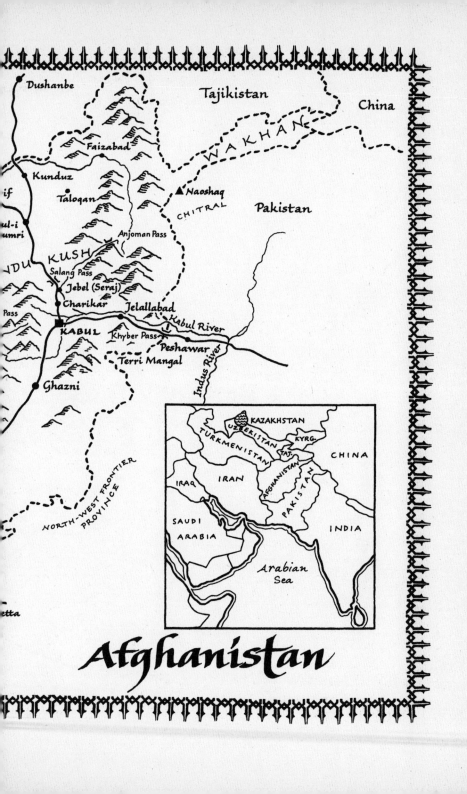

Afghanistan

The repentance of the common man is for his sins; the repentance of the elect, for their heedlessness.

Dhū'l-Nun Misri (d. 860)

Can you walk on water? You have done no better than a straw. Can you fly through the air? You are no better than a gnat. Conquer your heart — then you may become somebody.

Khwāja Abdullah Ansāri of Herat (1005–1090)

MULLA NASRUDDIN: I have met the king, and he spoke to me!
VILLAGERS: Incredible!
THE VILLAGE IDIOT: What did he say?
MULLA NASRUDDIN (whispering): He said: 'Get out of my way!'

An Unexpected Light

Wiltshire, England

Dear Ropate,

So much has happened in that part of the world where our paths first crossed that it's hard not to think of our time there, and of the time in which it was contained, as an island, now submerged. Perhaps the same is true of any journey you begin to look back on. But if comfort and distance have given this recollection of events the flavour of a tide-borne dream, the essential trouble remains. Once snared, as you so well know, one never fully leaves; a portion of one's heart is forever woven into the fabric of that place.

Here as promised is the account of the journey on which we met: an incomplete attempt to be true to that time. I have not been able to find any other way, given the nature of that journey, than to make it very personal. If what follows is now hampered by the clumsy thud of description, the recollection behind it is both fleet and fond. I need hardly say how much I cherish the memory, among many others, of our midnight strolls through the moon-silvered streets of the capital, or those light-filled days spent dreaming of the unclimbed summits of the Wakhān. Not only because to repeat such luxuries is for the moment so unthinkable, but because it was then, and with such satisfaction, that I discovered I was not the only outsider to have felt so at home among strangers, or so at peace amid the curious exigencies of war.

You ask me how the whole thing began. I am not sure if it is right — or even possible — to begin at the beginning. There are two reasons. One is that I'm reluctant to slow down the process with the weight of reminiscence. I'm as curious as you about what

3

originally set things in motion, but now that this albatross is finally ready to be flung overboard, it seems hardly to matter. The other is this: a seed, once it begins to grow, breaks from the shell that enclosed it and is lost — it's hard to find lasting traces. I've come to the conclusion that journeys are sparked from small and unlikely things rather than grand convictions; small things that strike a note which resonates beyond earshot of the rational. They wait quietly for the season of their birth until some correspondence in the visible world falls eventually into place, and after that, neither love nor money has much to do with it.

Did you ever read Thesiger, who, when the desert summers of Iraq got too hot, would tramp through the Hindu Kush and the Afghan Hazārajat for the pleasure of it? He put his wanderlust down to the thrill of seeing, at the age of three, his father shoot an Abyssinian oryx.

> What would ye, ladies? It was ever thus.
> Men are unwise and curiously planned.

This from one of your favourites, Flecker.

I've never seen an oryx, and admit I hadn't even discovered Kipling at the time of my first visit. In fact I'd read next to nothing about Afghanistan, which makes the impulse for that first journey seem so obscure. But there's one book I had read — which brings me to the oxen.

Perhaps I never told you.

If I must look for a beginning, I have to go back to when I was twelve years old, my mind spinning from a turn-of-the-century account I'd just read of an explorer's travels through what was then Turkestan, to which the northern portion of what is now Afghanistan belonged. The names meant very little to me then, but I felt the living image of them nonetheless, and longed to know if the descriptions I had read were real. In this spirit I had asked my father if he would be able to find such places.

'Perhaps,' he had mused. Then added, enigmatically: 'I know which way the oxen go.'

My imagination vaulted at this improbable intimation: *the oxen!* And a man, watching and waiting...

From then on I didn't have to try too hard to see, somewhere in a high and tangled tributary of the Paropamisus range, a man lying in wait beneath the incandescent lapis dome of a central Asian noon, watching from his hiding place a shimmering trail in the valley far below. I had followed him there in my mind's eye, in disguise, from the desert shores of the Amu Darya to the forests of Kafiristan, along a route of great hardship, danger and, I fancied, unutterable solitude. It led over wind-haunted passes where there was no sound but the fluttering of votive pennants tied to withered sticks, through echoing gorges on a raft buoyed by inflated skins, and across slatted bridges no wider than a man, which swung, horribly high, over furious mountain torrents.

He had no map or compass but was waiting for a rumble of hooves to lead him to his destination: he was listening for the oxen. At the sight of them he would follow the course of their annual migration towards a hidden breeding-ground and thence to a mountain-shrouded temple, where his trials would be rewarded with the gift of secrets known to few other living souls ...

Well, for several years that was that, until I took up the trail more diligently myself, and realized I'd misheard my father. There are, as you know, no oxen in central Asia. There are yaks and camels and fat-tailed sheep and ibex and snow leopards, bears, caracals, corsacs, rhesus monkeys, markhors, wild pigs, long-eared desert hedgehogs and three-toed dwarf jerboas, but no oxen. My father had said Oxus, the old name for the Amu Darya river, which runs all the way from the Pamirs to the ailing Aral Sea and for a thousand miles or so forms the northern border of Afghanistan. Conceivably, the direction of its flow might help a lonely traveller find his way about, but not much more than the knowledge, say, that it gets hotter as you approach the equator; a map and compass would have been more useful after all. If my imaginary explorer had set off for his temple knowing only which way the Oxus flowed, he would have had a rough go of it.

But that is not really the point: the seed was already sown.

✣

To give you the gist of what happened next: it was the Russians' fault. They invaded Afghanistan a few years later and I remember hearing about it while I was still in school. The Afghans seemed to belong to a different world, for which I was developing an inarticulate hunger; a people of prototypical human dignity with Old Testament faces, who with guns almost as ancient as themselves were trying (and with some success) to shoot down the latest in helicopter gunships. From reports at the time it was difficult to know whether, at the one extreme, the Afghans were indeed born fighters inured to bloodshed and somehow managing to hold whole armoured divisions at bay, or, at the other, whether the Soviets were pretty much slaughtering anyone who put up a fight.

The exile of nearly a third of the country's population pointed grimly to the latter. But the whole idea of a modern army invading that poor and dusty country disagreed with me deeply (I had older brothers, and a certain sympathy for the oppressed). I knew I had to see the place for myself.

I was nineteen. When you told me about your own efforts at the same age to track down Che Guevara, I knew you'd tasted that same blinkered confidence, which, looking back at it, is fairly baffling. In my case it led, as soon as the orbit of my summer holidays was finally unrestrained, to Peshawar, not far from the Afghan border. I filled out my university application forms on the night train from Lahore.

Life had never changed quite so swiftly, and I remember feeling even then that it would never really be quite the same. A few months earlier my worst fear in life was being made to stack chairs after class; now I was trying to get myself smuggled into what had become one of the most inaccessible countries in the world. Within a week or so I had met, and explained myself to a bemused but kindly Massoud Khalili, whose difficult job it was at the time to sort through the foreigners hoping for 'picnics' with the mujaheddin, and steer the more deranged supplicants towards more fitting pursuits. I have no words to describe the thrill at hearing him approve my first trip 'inside'. He was a great charmer. 'Who knows?' he said. 'Maybe one day you'll write a book about Afghanistan.'

You would have liked Peshawar in those days: it was awful, but it was never dull. The war had lifted it, as a new conflict rouses an old mercenary, to an unforgettably disagreeable pitch of infamy. Five years into the war across the border, the sleepy frontier town had been transformed. The place was bursting with Afghan refugees, alongside whom had descended, like vultures around a wounded beast, an ignoble assortment of outsiders. Some came to play, others to watch, others to do unpleasant business. The scent of war drew a steady stream of journalists, photographers, deranged do-gooders, smugglers, poseurs of various stripes, arms dealers, missionaries, mercenaries, spies and a handful of the genuinely well intentioned. For years the city's few modern hotels were reborn into theatres of high intrigue, of farce, of dreams realized and broken.

I stayed at the notorious Green's, where cloak and dagger had become the order of the day. Tended by a duo of somnambulant waiters, foreigners would gather in its inexpressibly gloomy restaurant to voice endless opinions about the war. Rumour and counter-rumour flew across the tables. Conversations were charged with the reckless conviction of the uninformed. At the arrival of unfamiliar faces, an almost comic hush would settle over the room, gradually dispelled by a tide of speculative murmurs.

No one spoke openly of their plans or dealings; the idea was to find out as much about others as possible while revealing nothing of oneself. It was part of the morbid etiquette of the time not to enquire too deeply into others' affairs, and information was exchanged on a titbit-for-titbit basis. Whispers were exchanged in ill-lit corridors or unventilated rooms fetid with conspiracy. There were, literally, thumps in the night. Telephone conversations were inexplicably interrupted by third parties, and if you spoke in a foreign language the line would go dead until whoever was listening could find an interpreter. Mail arrived opened and carelessly resealed, or never arrived at all (at least the money my family had to send me never did) and notes appeared under doors: warnings from complete strangers to 'be careful of X'. The funniest characters were the few bona fide tourists who had no interest in the war, whose lack of obsessive secrecy made them the most conspicuous.

I killed time learning backgammon with an Afghan carpet dealer called Jāmal, and gambled away half my possessions in the process; there came a sinking moment when I returned to his shop with an armful of my things, and laid them out in front of him. It was only then I learned how much the Afghans like to play.

He chuckled and said he didn't want my things but my friendship – and shook the dice for another game. When I told him I was going to Afghanistan, he said I'd need some Afghan clothes, and took off his shirt – a silk-embroidered *shalwar* that had taken his wife three months to make – and tried to give it to me. I thought: if this is how Afghans are, I will get to like the place.

Afghanistan was barely forty miles away. Rumours from the war buzzed through the streets like shrapnel, and the lure of the place was irresistible. I got to know my first Afghans in the smoke-wreathed alleys of the old city: mujaheddin who had come to Pakistan to wait for shipments of arms or to visit their relatives among the three and a half million Afghans who had been given refuge there. They looked a stern but beautiful people – almost unapproachable at first – but after I'd discovered how astonishingly companionable they were, I felt quickly as though I was among friends. They would uncover their wounds with all the glee of schoolboys showing off grazed knees. I can never forget the Pushtun fighter, nearly seven feet tall, who showed me three olive-shaped scars from Russian bullets: one from a bullet that had passed neatly between the bones of his wrist, one in the fleshy part of his thigh, and another, barely healed, from a bullet that had gone cleanly through the very edge of his waist. He put his thumb and finger like a pair of calipers over the entry and exit wounds and, when I asked if he was afraid to go back to the fighting, roared with laughter.

Apart from the occasional bomb blast, the drug dealers, the spies and the food at the hotel, there was another hazard I couldn't have foreseen – prompted, I was told, by my pale skin and the freshness of my features. A one-eyed kebab seller whose shop I passed regularly let his intentions be known with a single repulsive gesture. Another hoped to lure me to his home with illicit supplies of whisky. Nothing in the world could have been less enticing. A very fat man from the tribal territories with a bulbous neck and lizard eyes who lurked in the lobby of the hotel, trailed by obsequious underlings, pressed me daily to accept a 'local speciality' in his bedroom. I dubbed him the 'lizard king', moved about with extra vigilance, and stopped shaving. Alas, my fugitive behaviour attracted added attention and my beard grew in wispy patches that heightened the ardour of my would-be suitors.

By day it was too hot to wander about, and at night I wallowed in sweat. The air above the city was suffocating, immovable, and reeked of diesel fumes and human waste. I never saw clouds but the sky was never blue; it was obscured by an almost tangible yellow malaise. In the restaurant I found a cockroach embalmed in my breakfast omelette; in the evenings the live ones would scuttle in vigorous circles around the edge of the plate. I caught dysentery, developed a raging fever, and my insides came to resemble a hollow watery tube. For several days I lay in bed nibbling Kendal mint cake and staring at the fan which swung by its bare wires overhead, knowing that if it dropped I lacked the strength to move.

It was a desperate time. The whole of life seemed to be sweating away to the dreadful thud of the fan, and with it all ambition and capacity for action seeping drop by drop, hour after hour, into the dank sheets. I couldn't wait to get across the border, whatever the risks.

On the eve of my departure I staggered into the lobby to answer a phone call. Over the crackle of the line I heard a voice I recognized.

'DON'T GO,' it said.

It was a well-meaning friend calling from England. He had just heard the news that a French television reporter venturing across the border had been captured by paratroopers and sentenced to fifteen years in a dreadful Kabul prison. Questioned about the event in Pakistan, the Soviet ambassador had warned that 'bandits and so-called journalists' trying to penetrate Afghanistan with the mujaheddin would be killed by Soviet forces. But my mind was made up.

'I'M GOING,' I said, little guessing at the troublesome

persistence with which that first foolhardy act of trespass would reverberate down the years.

*

It wasn't the moment to hesitate. They came the next morning. Two stern-faced, booted and bearded guerrillas appeared at my door, handed me a note, and left without a word. Through sleep-laden eyes I read: 'These are the brothers of Commander A——. They will return at five o'clock. Be ready.'

I scribbled farewell letters, daubed myself with potassium permanganate until my face was the colour of a walnut, and hoped the stuff wouldn't run if I started to sweat. Then I put on the Afghan clothes I'd bought in the bazaar, and gave myself up to the journey.

I was passed like a human baton in a relay race out of the city and towards the frontier, and slept in a different house each night in the care of men I didn't know and would never see again. We seemed to be moving backwards through time; at each stage the trappings of the modern world grew fewer, the countryside wilder, and the characters that moved across it less and less encumbered by the twentieth century.

There was a big storm just as we had passed the final police checkpoints and were bumping towards our last stop in Terri Mangal. I heard the first explosions echoing in the hills and felt the presence of the war like an electric charge. The sky turned yellow and filled with dust as the clouds opened over us: I still see the smiling faces of the men opposite me as the rain poured over their eyebrows. I'd never seen such faces. I crossed the frontier the next day, with a taciturn Afghan guide and a letter from Khalili instructing me to trust totally in God. He underlined that part.

And that is how the seed began to grow.

*

The decision to return twice more in the intervening years grew directly out of that first trip. During those later visits I felt I saw the innocence go out of the conflict and, in some parallel way, out of myself.

10

This last time was the hardest — comfort and distance again — and I agonized for ages. I was tied down in all the usual ways, the flirtation with danger had run its natural course, and with the war over I wondered if the country might somehow not measure up to my hopes for writing about it. I was afraid too, now it was no longer a forbidden place which one had to risk one's life to reach, that my feelings towards it would be correspondingly dulled.

There's an ignominy to modern air travel that I'd come to dread. There's no arousing sense of passage towards your destination: no slowly changing landscape reaches back along the line of your motion, adding usefully to an awareness of where you will end up. The quantitative measure of the distance you are travelling loses all relevance; miles mean nothing as you leap, in a single, stratospheric bound, across the barriers that have guided, ever since humankind stood vertical enough to get over them, the very passage of civilizations.

But I leaped, eventually; and ten years on, I was back again in Peshawar. The lizard king no longer prowled the lobby of Green's hotel, there was a surfeit of Land Cruisers in the streets, satellite TV in my room, and everyone had mobile phones. There were very few Afghans about, and I wandered along the dusty teeming streets of the old city half-hoping to meet up again with friends among the mujaheddin. They were all gone, of course, and I couldn't escape a sense of longing for the electric atmosphere of the days of the war.

A few things hadn't changed. The air was still chokingly thick with diesel fumes, and the taxi drivers still offered you heroin with the same cheerful smiles. And there was still that improbable range of foreign visitors, all hoping vaguely to get across the border. At the hotel I met a beautiful Japanese girl called Keiko who wanted to photograph desert flowers inside Afghanistan (I suffered a momentary impulse to throw up earlier plans and help smuggle her into the country), a pair of Polish film-makers following the trail of a young compatriot who had disappeared in Nuristan during the war, an ex-SAS parachutist with a limp who was hoping to jump with what was left of the Afghan Air Force, and a Dutch journalist who taught me Japanese swordplay on the roof at dawn.

Soon things were gathering delicious momentum. Two of my biggest worries — how to get inside the country, and where to stay — were quickly solved. With the kind permission of Peter Stocker,* I was allowed to join a relief flight across the border. And on it I was lucky enough to meet an American photographer on assignment to the capital, who offered to put me up at his agency's headquarters in Kabul.

I left Peshawar in high spirits and flew to Bagram airport just north of Kabul — where it's about time I threw you into the story — a few days later, on a brilliant November morning. It was the strangest thing, but as soon as we'd stepped out of the little plane onto Afghan soil, I felt as though some inner clock of mine, which had stopped since I had last been there, began to tick again: it was like going into a room which has stayed locked while the rest of the house has been lived in. I realized then, with a familiar mixture of longing and relief, I had a lot of catching up to do.

With love,

J.

---

* Director, at the time, of the delegation in Afghanistan of the International Committee of the Red Cross (ICRC).

One

Asia is a living body, and Afghanistan its heart
In the ruin of the heart lies the ruin of the body
So long as the heart is free, the body remains free
If not, it becomes a straw adrift in the wind

Mohammed Iqbal (1876–1938)

FROM THE BEGINNING we became the captives of an unexpected light. Even as we stepped into its unaccustomed brightness that first morning, it seemed probable we had entered a world in some way enchanted, for which we lacked the proper measure.

We were soon lost but happy to be lost. For an hour or more we had been wandering a grid of broad streets flanked by slender pine and plane trees, hoping for a remembered landmark. The winter sun pressed like a warm hand against our chests. Our packs were heavy and we sweated under their loads, slightly breathless from the unaccustomed altitude, and felt the thrill of strangeness at every step.

The light was as delicate as crystal; I had forgotten its tricks. It stripped far-off shapes and colours of the usual vagaries of distance and played havoc with space, luring the mountains from beyond the city to within arm's reach and catapulting forward the expressions on faces two hundred yards away. Under its spell the landscape seemed to dance on the very edge of materiality. The light was joined in a gentle conspiracy with the air itself, which whispered in the leaves above our heads, tinged with a faint scent of balsam. Already our experience was drawing on the luminosity of our surroundings, and the boundary between them growing less substantial; already the ordinary rule of things seemed less likely to apply.

*

It was calm that first morning. I felt utterly removed from the haste and clamour of home. There was a trickle of bicycles and, moving barely faster, a few veteran taxis. Some elderly turbaned men, striding at an untroubled pace with hands clasped behind their backs, passed us in the opposite direction and broke into courteous smiles at the unlikely sight of two overburdened foreigners asking for directions. We heard the cries of merchants hawking fruit from their roadside barrows, and from behind the high walls on either side the sound of families: women scolding children and their children's laughter. Swooping through a lapis-coloured sky were dozens of tiny homemade kites, their strings worked passionately from the walls and rooftops by agile masters. Occasionally an incongruous grumble would roll like thunder from the enclosing mountains and we would stop, under the guise of shifting our loads, to catch our breath and gauge each other's reaction to the unnatural sound.

*

A week earlier I had been to see the ambassador in London, to ask his advice on getting into the country. For a man whose homeland was in ruins and whose government clung to power in a capital besieged by rival claimants, he was refreshingly cheerful. We drank tea together beneath twenty-foot-high ceilings and spoke of the faraway beauty of the valley which was his home. Beyond the windows the traffic roared into Hyde Park.

There was a large framed map of Afghanistan on the wall. We walked over to it and together traced names and roads like a pair of generals. Beneath our fingertips places I had hardly dared hope to reach flickered momentarily into life.

I saw the famous circular route by which an earlier generation of visitors had come to know the country in happier times, linking Kabul, the capital, with Mazar-i Sharīf in the north, Herat in the west and Qandahar in the south. It hardly mattered that in many places the road no longer existed.

My eye was drawn to a dotted red line creeping northeast from the capital into Badakhshān: this was Alexander's route on his brilliant outflanking of Bessus, the Achaemenid satrap. It thinned as it trickled north, towards Faizābād and Keshm: Marco Polo's route to China. I would need a horse there, and a guide.

'That is no problem,' the ambassador said, matter-of-factly.

Another red line wound westwards towards the megalithic Buddhas

16

of Bamiyan, the turquoise lakes of Band-i Amir, the lonely minaret of Jām and the springs and shrines of Chesht-i Sharīf; a manageable route by jeep, if the roads were not blocked by snow.

'You can find one easily,' he said.

A great dark mountainous wedge stretched from one side of the map to the other, and I thought of the winter that had just begun.

'It will not be too cold.'

I would remember this comment. Over the north and west he had swept his hand in a broad benevolent arc.

'Here is fine,' he said, smiling broadly. 'You can go anywhere! Here is fine too. *Here . . .*' he hesitated, waving with dismissive affection over the southern tier of the country, '. . . just some small problems,' he said, 'some – *opposition.*'

This was Afghan for civil war.

*

I had in mind a quietly epic sort of journey, the kind you no longer hear of much; no tailored expedition, but a route guided by events themselves. Things could change quickly and plans made in advance become impossible to follow; faced with the caprices of winter and the war it seemed the only sensible approach. I had given up on earlier and more ambitious schemes and was prepared to make an ally of uncertainty, with which luck so often finds a partnership. I was hoping also to keep faith with a kind of vision set in motion a decade before by my first visit to the place, the experience of which had long ago acquired a troublesome momentum beyond my control. To translate the longing that stemmed from it seemed to require no less than a long and solitary journey with every attendant danger, a journey to make quite sure my vision of the place was not some private hallucination that the time had come to outgrow. But already things had begun to unfold with unexpected facility, confirming a personal notion that the moment you commit to a journey it takes on a unique life of its own, which no amount of agonizing in advance can foresee.

*

The ambassador had talked over the least life-threatening route into the country with his secretary, Shirin. She was from Iran: her name meant 'sweetness' and her voice had the charming lilt of the Khorassanian plateau. She did her best to discourage me from going, pointing out that there was a civil war in Tajikistan to the north, that the western frontier with Iran was said to be closed to foreigners, and that the eastern border with China was a frozen wasteland at fifteen thousand feet. I asked about the overland route from Pakistan, to the south.

'It would be better to fly directly to Kabul,' said the ambassador. 'Sometimes the route by road can be –' he winced slightly – 'difficult.' The road from the south, I already knew, passed through the lawless territory of the opposition, and travellers' tales from the region were less than encouraging. At the very least one could expect to be robbed at gunpoint.

'*If they find you they will*—' began Shirin, but was swiftly checked by an admonitory glance from the ambassador.

'We feel responsible,' said the ambassador, with a kindly smile.

'We want you back,' said Shirin.

'That's nice,' I said.

'Why don't you go somewhere safer, like Bosnia?' said Shirin, with a strange but tender logic. 'Or you could wait until spring.' She rose from her desk as I turned to leave.

'Whatever you do, *don't go into the mountains!*'

But at this point the ambassador interposed himself between us, putting a stop to this very un-Afghan show of sentimentality. He was, besides, from the mountains himself. Smiling broadly, he escorted me to the door. I thanked him and we shook hands.

'*Safar-e khosh,*' he said. It meant 'happy travels'.

*

From the beginning we felt the touch of the war, which came to form the backdrop to our feelings and broke into life in unexpected ways. It threw everything into sharper focus and brought such immediacy to the present that the world of home took on at times a dreamlike quality. It pushed our feelings into uncharted orbits and challenged our ordinary logic in ways that would have been easier to ignore. Like vines that prosper on the slopes of a volcano we thrived nonetheless under its influence until we felt the whole of life more keenly, both in its joys and in its griefs. We found luxury in small things and in friendships discovered bonds we felt might last for life. There was bitterness too: not at what we found there but, in the end, at having to leave it.

*

We had walked in a mile-wide circle and realized we were in the same place as we had started: my new friend Craig had no sense of direction. Each time we turned down a new street, he would say: 'I have a feeling we're quite close now.' We trudged along for hours, knocking finally at a gate in a street where six-foot walls on both sides enclosed modern villas. Opposite, a guard was basking in the sun with an automatic rifle across his lap.

The gate swung open. A lean and fair-haired man wearing round gold-framed glasses appeared from behind it and led us across a yellowing patch of lawn to a verandah. We shed our packs and collapsed into low wicker chairs.

'Jān,' he called into the house, 'can we have some *chai*?'

He introduced himself with a nonchalant handshake. His name was Tim Johnston, and he was one of only three reporters living in the capital. A wheat-coloured beard covered his weary-looking face, and his exhaustion expressed itself in a laconic and offhand manner. I recognized the look. He caught up on news with Craig, who was a fellow reporter, as we sat in the afternoon sunshine, then turned to me and mentioned there was a spare room in the house if I wanted it, but that he'd have to charge me. I had a tiny budget and asked how much.

'Ten thousand Afghanis a day.'

It sounded a huge amount, and my heart sank. I was afraid I had met a lonely exile stranded grudgingly in an alien culture, scornful of outsiders who took a personal interest in it. I was very wrong.

'That's about fifty pence,' he added. 'For food.'

There were no hotels, he explained, and no tourists for that matter, no casual visitors beyond a trickle of other correspondents or photographers on brief assignments to the city. The exception, he told us, had been an obese American lady the year before. Armed with some photocopied pages of an out-of-print travel guide she had arrived in Kabul unaware that the country was in its seventeenth year of war. Hysterical at the revelation and furious at having been duped, she was wrestled out of the country by baffled officials, never to be heard of again. There was talk, too, of a pair of Englishmen who had entered the country recently from China on horseback. Rumour had it they had been arrested in the north, and thrown into prison by soldiers who took a dim view of the foreigners in native dress who carried a portable satellite navigation unit with them.

We swapped news and stories, mostly of close shaves, the calling cards of war correspondents in every troubled capital. The windows of the house were cracked by blast, and a bullet half an inch thick was lodged in the wall behind Tim's chair. It was fairly quiet at the moment, he said.

His staff of three obviously adored him and had become close friends. They sat outside with us in the sunshine and listened attentively to Tim's every word. Jān was a stocky, handsome Panjshīri of irrepressible cheerfulness, a guerrilla turned housekeeper. Rashīd, a lean and sullen, broken-toothed Tajik with a permanent cynical smile, was a former soldier in the Afghan army and now Tim's driver and translator. And there was Amān the cook, a round-faced Hazāra with the distinctively high cheekbones and narrow eyes of his people; six foot tall and as gentle as a kitten. They were all in their thirties and looked ten years older.

I began to warm to their solitary employer. The Afghans were a difficult people to know and he spoke of them with a jocular and irreverent familiarity. It was obvious he admired them. As a journalist he enjoyed the respect and close co-operation of government officials; as a friend he knew many of them on first name terms. His manner disguised enormous diligence under conditions the majority of correspondents abhorred. He loved Afghanistan but by his own admission was exhausted; he had been in Kabul for eighteen months with hardly a day of genuine rest. The visits to the front lines were the hardest, he explained, and the serious wounding of a colleague a few weeks earlier had left him shaken. He wore white trousers for the front-line days, which he hoped in the confusion of battle might increase his chances of being recognized as a non-combatant.

'They're the wrong colour though,' he added, 'when the dysentery kicks in.'

As he spoke there was an explosion that shook the ground as if a cannon had been fired in the garden. Craig and I ducked violently in our chairs and the plastic sheeting over the windows ballooned inwards under the shock wave. When we looked up the others were grinning broadly. Tim was calmly returning his glass to the table, and gestured casually over his shoulder to the hillside behind the house.

'Outgoing tank fire,' he said. 'On the hill. Makes a fuck of a noise but not very often.'

All this time we had been hearing a variety of grumbles from the hills to the south. There were bangs and thumps of various intensities: muffled, sharp, solitary or in rapid salvoes, and others like long, rolling peals of thunder, only the sky was clear. At each, the ground trembled or shook like the skin of a drum, and our bodies with it. I felt old feelings rekindled at the sounds; feelings of wonder and surprise and of an obscure longing I could not properly describe to myself; but mostly of fear. Tim translated from the catalogue of unnatural sounds, cocking his head between phrases to listen.

'That's outgoing ... that's artillery ... that sounds like a tank ... don't know what that is.'

There was an occasional burst of automatic gunfire from somewhere in the city, and I wondered if there was actually fighting in the streets.

'Probably a wedding,' he said gloomily, and lit another cigarette. We all smoked. It was impossible not to smoke.

He briefed us on the situation. It was a jigsaw we put together only gradually, turning and re-turning the pieces to make sense of our new and unsettling surroundings. A week ago the names and places had seemed distant things, of which there was only occasional news, the terminology of which evoked remote and troubled images of guns, turbans and mountains. Suddenly the focus of our world had shifted and the images taken on new life.

Kabul was under siege. To the north and west, the government's front lines were locked in uneasy standoffs with rival claimants to the city. But all eyes in the capital faced south, to the battlefields where the government was fighting daily with the latest contenders for power.

The year before, the southern provinces had been swept by an enigmatic militia force which had brought peace and a relative stability to areas formerly plagued by banditry and lawlessness. Its soldiers had begun by executing rogue commanders or paying for their peace with large sums of money. Roads had been cleared of mines by the crusading black-turbaned troops, and hijacked vehicles returned to foreign relief agencies. Order had been restored in the cities, which had been disarmed and brought under control. It was said that the general population, weary from years of anarchy, had welcomed them.

Astonishing as these victories were, they were disturbing. With peace, the new rulers brought with them an Islamicist fervour previously unknown in Afghanistan, traditionally a place of religious moderation. In the regions under their control, men had been ordered to shave their heads and grow beards in accordance with a fierce interpretation of Islamic law; thieves suffered amputations and women were banned from working and forbidden to show their faces in public places. A religious police force called the Department for Promoting Virtue and Prohibiting Vice was enforcing a growing catalogue of decrees as alien to Afghans as the rhetoric of the communists before them. Televisions were hanged from lampposts, kite-flying banned, sport and music prohibited.

They called themselves the Tālebān,* which meant students of religion, and their leader was said to be a one-eyed *mullā*, inspired by divine prompting to take up arms. No mention was made of how between Qur'ān-reading lessons the young men claiming to be students had learned to drive tanks and fly jets, or how they had come by the satellite telephones installed in their new headquarters.

A few months earlier the whirlwind militia had seized the major

---

* From the Arabic verb *talaba*, to seek. The Arabic plural is *Tulub*, the Persian *Tālebān*. Similarly, a *madrasseh* is a religious school, with the plural *maddaress*. Purists will rail at Anglicized Arabic plurals: 'Tālebs', 'madrassehs', 'kebabs', etc.

western city of Herat with hardly a shot fired; its defenders had melted away without trace. Bolstered by the unexpected victory, the Tālebān charged to the outskirts of the capital, where they were violently repulsed by the government's seasoned fighters. The commander of the government forces, the charismatic guerrilla veteran Ahmed Shah Massoud, had no intention of allowing Kabul, at peace for the first time in years, to fall into the zealots' hands.

Few in Kabul believed that an ill-trained force of mostly young and idealistic men could seize the well-defended capital. Many undoubtedly no longer cared. Yet this latest turn in the conflict had imposed new strains on the fabric of the region. The embers of ethnic rivalry had been fanned anew; and relations with neighbouring Pakistan had turned more bitter than ever. The government claimed their neighbours were supporting the Tālebān as a means to an old dream: installing a malleable client in Kabul, and securing in the process the vital overland routes to the central Asian republics to the north.

Pakistani military advisers, along with fighters they had trained, had been captured in recent skirmishes; the world seemed oblivious to this obvious violation. Accusations flew from either side. In the local newspaper that morning a cartoon depicted Pakistan's prime minister, Benazir Bhutto, stooping over a young Tāleb fighter and handing him a rifle above the caption: 'Now, dear Tāleb, go and fulfil your duty for Pakistan.'

Recently the fighting had reached the eastern suburbs and the daily echo of artillery duels could be heard in the hills. The Tālebān held the roads to the southern border, which like an artery to the country's heart they could squeeze or sever at their will. Food prices had already risen fivefold and fuel used for heating was even scarcer, its cost growing steadily beyond the reach of ordinary homes. It was a time of desperate negotiation between the government and the commanders of formerly rival parties, now tentatively united by a wariness of their new and enigmatic opponent.

*

I had not visited the south, the heartland of the Tālebān, and wondered if perhaps the reports of their extremism were exaggerated. It was easy to demonize a phenomenon outside its cultural context. Were they really as backward, I asked Tim, as stories seemed to indicate?

'On the contrary,' he said. 'They're the finest minds of the fourteenth century.'

Now all talk was of whether they would be able to take, and hold, Kabul. The most likely scenario was a government alliance with the forces of the north, although it was anybody's guess how long such a Faustian pact might last.

In the meantime the powers in the capital had looked outside for support, finding Iran, India and, not without irony, their former invaders in Russia all willing to enter the fray in an effort to bring the Tālebān to heel. Of the key players only America, whose influence in Pakistan was seen as pivotal in avoiding further carnage, appeared to be hedging its bets. The Americans had washed their hands of Afghanistan in the wake of the Soviet withdrawal and left ordinary Afghans with a widespread feeling of having been abandoned; and now they felt betrayed too by Pakistan, whose claim to have no favourite in the conflict had an increasingly hollow ring. We kept our cynicism in check, knowing nothing of the American pipelines then.

As rumours of a Tālebān offensive grew, the weary city waited, impoverished and bracing itself for winter. But it had been impossible to drive its besiegers beyond the range of their rockets and artillery, which took a daily toll of lives with terrifying unpredictability. Rockets and high-explosive shells fell in market places and busy streets, sailed through the windows of homes extinguishing whole families at a stroke, delivering tiny parcels of death without warning to their long-suffering victims all over the city. It seemed an extreme way to enlist popular support.

'Actually,' said Tim, 'they're being quite restrained.'

*

Out of the hills we heard three thumps in quick succession like the slamming of far-off doors. Tim straightened in his chair and said in a different tone:

'Now *that* is incoming,' and put down his glass.

I counted, instinctively. For seven seconds there was nothing. Then, the sound that would brand itself on our senses; a rolling, crunching sound like the felling of a great tree, which trailed to a splintered echo.

'That's down by the presidential palace,' said Tim, and reached for his bag. 'Rashīd, get the car. Jān – the gate, please.' As we watched, bewildered, the others sprang into life like pilots scrambled to the alert. Tim turned to us from the open door of the car.

'Want to come?'

We hurtled through the streets. Rashīd yelled from the window to pedestrians who pointed us towards the fallen rockets.

'Got to get there quickly,' said Tim, 'or they take the dead away. Saves going to the hospitals.'

Yet when we lurched onto the pavement and parked nearby there was no crowd, only a handful of dazed onlookers long accustomed to the sight of the random attacks. A solitary man was standing over a shallow crater where one of the rockets had struck – miraculously, it seemed – an empty plot of ground in a quiet street near the presidential palace.

With a notebook at the ready Tim walked calmly over to the men, who were picking at the shards of shrapnel, and confirmed through his interpreter that there had been no casualties. Craig wandered over to the crater and took a picture. I stayed by the car. In the open I felt acutely vulnerable and struggled with the fear of a second strike in the same place. My mouth had gone dry and my imagination was racing. Above the sound of nearby traffic we would never hear the thump of further rockets … I looked around for a ditch in which to throw myself at the last moment, and heard the shallowness of my breath. It was the equivalent of walking through a parking lot knowing that somewhere in a car there was a ticking bomb.

The moment passed. We drove back to the house and Tim wrote up a report of the strike. From his office, an untidy room upstairs with a computer and satellite telephone, scattered with books and papers and rolls of film, he maintained a tenuous lifeline to the outside world. We all knew the news he sent was unlikely to be widely heard, and from our sense of isolation grew a warm complicity. The keys on his computer were sticking, and he cursed the dust as he typed.

'You could close the window,' I suggested.

'Can't hear the rockets coming if you do.'

He had given me the room next door. I went in to arrange my things, and opened the window.

*

It was an unsettling beginning. I had not come to investigate the war, the sanguinary momentum of which was sure to exhaust itself sooner or later, but to explore what I could of the culture and its people. 'Culture?' the ambassador's secretary had asked me back in London. 'What's left of the culture?' That, I had said, was what I wanted to find out. I felt certain that beyond the cruel radius of the conflict I would be able to find evidence of the old Afghanistan which had so captivated earlier travellers; the home of a noble and chivalrous people who understood the needs of both body and soul and craved for little more.

It was still a difficult place to explore. There were far more tourists in Antarctica. And for twenty years now Afghanistan had sunk, Atlantis-like, beneath the modern traveller's horizon.

There was some irony to this. A hundred years earlier, when the country was arguably a far more dangerous place to travel, a host of European explorers was quietly mapping its lakes and passes with all the fastidiousness of the age, their solitudes and hardships unsoftened by Gore-tex and antibiotics. But these days there were no casual visitors. Perhaps the modern notion that there is nowhere left in the world to explore permits a fickleness to modern travel that dilutes the spirit of discovery; perhaps the window through which far-off places are glimpsed, although more informatively framed today, is as narrow as ever.

I had followed the recent news reports from Afghanistan; they tended to portray little more than a ruined and anarchic place, ravaged by fanatical warlords. Seldom were such images balanced by insights into ordinary life. Even when it is accurate, news can be skewed: it is itself a product of the way it is gathered. Countries at war are described by correspondents who tend, especially in dangerous places, to be pack animals, reporting on isolated events en masse. In Kabul, visiting television crews invariably asked to be taken to the worst-hit parts of the city; someone had even written of Kabul as 'ninety per cent destroyed'.

Wars complicate matters: there is a fascinating aspect to war which tends to drown out less inflammatory news. Conflict is a notoriously difficult thing to convey accurately. Fighting comes and goes; and modern conflicts can be peculiarly sullen and capricious beasts, moving with an unpredictable will of their own. Key battles are fought over-night and absorbed into the landscape. Even a so-called war zone is not necessarily a dangerous place; seldom is a war as all-encompassing as the majority of reports suggest. Countries and cultures do not simply draw to a halt in a period of conflict; there are the falls of shells, and there is the silence between them.

Yet there was a deeper obstacle to discovering the place: Afghani-stan did not really exist. It was, more accurately, a fractured jewel, yielding a spectrum as broad or narrow as the onlooker's gaze. Even in peacetime Afghanistan had been open to outsiders for only a brief chapter in modern history, that ruined island in time from the 1960s until the catastrophe of the Soviet occupation. To outsiders it had seemed more of a fairytale than a real place: it had never been a single country but a historically improbable amalgam of races and cultures, each with its own treasuries of custom, languages and visions of the world; its own saints, heroes and outlaws, an impossible place to understand as a whole.

For the generation of sandalled, bangled wanderers that made up the vanguard of travellers of the era, Afghanistan was the farthest-out place on earth, a no-rules, dirt-cheap trip of a place where you could get turned on and strung out − permanently, if that was your thing − on inexhaustible supplies of the world's purest hashish and opium, and nobody would seem to mind.

The effect on archaeologists was hardly less mind-boggling: the entire country was an unexplored treasure-trove. Ruined Greek cities were discovered far beyond what were formerly thought to be the limits of the Hellenized world, and hoards of garbled artefacts suggesting unlikely fusions and cross-fertilizations of culture were unearthed by the thousand. The place had no parallel. Greek, Persian, Indian and central Asian gods mingled in divine historical collusion.

Even Afghanistan's Paleolithic toolmakers were described as the Michelangelos of the prehistoric age.

Across the harsh and beautiful backdrop of the land historians traced the staging-posts of the world's empire-builders and their undoers, while philologists marvelled over the abundance of arcane languages and their dialects, many undeciphered to this day.

Seekers of wisdom too, both the serious and the starry-eyed, sought the counsel of Sufi mystics or their imitators. Afghanistan was the spiritual heartland of Asia, the historical nexus of converging streams of mystical knowledge: Buddhist, Islamic, Zoroastrian and Shamanic. There was an otherworldly character to Afghanistan, reflected in the pleasant anarchy of life, the medieval civility of its people's manners and their self-conscious but unaffected aloofness from the modern world. Its landscape was protohistoric, untamed, lit by a purifying light, a world that had escaped from time.

*

True to its troubled past it was also the instrument of outside forces. Notwithstanding its attachment to independence, Afghanistan had from the 1950s onwards become a cold war pawn courted by superpowers. The Soviets, with a thousand-mile border to the north, pictured a loyal ally in a widening arc of communist influence, and wooed Afghanistan with raw materials at exchange rates no capitalist country could afford. America had designs on refuelling bases for its long-range nuclear bombers, and financed massive aid projects. While the Soviets built factories and bridges in the north, the Americans constructed airports and dams in the south.

In time-honoured fashion the Afghans played both sides. A giant wheat silo in the capital, symbol of Soviet friendship, was full of American wheat. The roads were built of cement from Soviet factories; the cars that cruised them were Chevrolets.

There were some promising experiments with democracy under the constitutional monarchy of King Zāher Shāh but, impatient with the slow pace of change, the king's own cousin and brother-in-law pushed him aside to establish the Republic of Afghanistan in 1973. But like a river undermining the foundations of an ancient city, a new force was even more diligently at work. It carried with it a now defunct ideology that spread quietly among a small but ambitious cadre of urban politicians, hungry for change and for power.

Encouraged by their northern neighbours, its leaders came bloodily to the fore in 1978, proclaiming a new Democratic Republic. They claimed non-alignment with their Soviet mentors, and many in Kabul welcomed the demise of the old regime's authoritarianism, which was associated with the royal lineage of the Mohammadzai elite. Their enthusiasm was swiftly checked.

The country's new leaders spouted the arrogant and unfamiliar rhetoric of revolution, and the violence of their reforms proved too sudden for the deeply traditional population. In a foreshadowing of blood, the Afghan flag was redesigned in red. Efforts of urban party loyalists venturing into the countryside to strike at the heart of tradition proved disastrous. The widespread recalcitrance of the rural population was met with brutal force. In Kabul, opponents of the regime were kidnapped and executed and the city's jails filled to bursting point. Tens of thousands disappeared. The leadership was violently divided. Blunder followed blunder, and armed resistance to the new regime spread like fire.

The ailing government looked north for help. In the spring of 1978, there were some three hundrd and fifty Soviet military advisers in the country; within a year there were three thousand. Soviet staff appeared in Afghan ministries and in key defence and security organizations; fresh supplies of arms and equipment rumbled into Kabul in an effort to stem the rising tide of resistance in the countryside. Month by month the military commitment deepened as opposition grew.

Angry and deeply anxious at the sight of their southern satellite spiralling dangerously out of control, disturbed by the unreliability of its leadership and the growing threat of foreign intervention in what was seen as a local crisis, the Soviets assembled the largest military formation since the Second World War and, heedless of the fate of former invaders, moved it swiftly onto Afghan soil. In a brilliantly executed night-time takeover of the capital, the Afghan army was disarmed, the disobedient (and American-educated) president was assassinated and a former Afghan minister, plucked from exile in

Eastern Europe, was spirited into the stunned capital and installed as head of state. This was Christmas 1979. But the new year lifted not over a promised era of Soviet–Afghan friendship but over the catastrophe of what would become a decade-long war. It would be the empire's last.

Afghanistan was quickly sealed from outsiders by an increasingly brutal and sophisticated occupying force. From the first day the Soviets were dogged by a resistance movement of completely unexpected determination. In 1980, the head of Soviet military intelligence announced 'the final and irrevocable defeat of the counterrevolutionary bandits'. Soviet newspapers reported on the warmth that the labouring people of Afghanistan felt for the Soviet soldier and the noble international mission of their army. Nine years of war would follow. In the process five million souls were forced into a miserable exile on the country's borders. For the Afghans it was a war of liberation; for the enemies of communism, an exceptional opportunity. Vast quantities of weapons, purchased with American, Middle Eastern, European and Chinese funds, flowed covertly into the country among a complex network of resistance groups. CIA officials vowed to 'fight the Soviets to the last Afghan', and teams of guerrillas were trained by foreign instructors as far apart as China and Scotland. By 1989, the invading wave was finally driven back, stained with the blood of as many as fifty thousand Soviet troops.

By the time the Afghan communists were chased from power three years later, abandoned by a disintegrating Soviet Union, as many as two million people had died. The Americans rolled up their maps and let the Afghans fight it out among themselves. The country was in ruins and its new government clung to power in a capital savaged by rival claimants.

*

It was during the Soviet occupation that I had first seen Afghanistan. At nineteen I was captivated as much by its harsh and breathtaking beauty as by the mystifying tenacity of its people. Yet among the kindly Afghans who agreed to shelter me it was impossible to recognize the violent, drug-crazed mercenaries the Soviets claimed to be fighting.

I knew them instead as men of restraint and dignity whose profound attachment to freedom expressed itself neither in fanaticism nor in the fearlessness in battle with which they were said to be born, but in a quiet and painful incredulity at the presumptuousness of their invaders. These were the mujaheddin: ordinary Afghans. They were farmers, businessmen, merchants, university teachers, shepherds, or soldiers who had fled the army; rich and poor, educated and illiterate. The name meant 'those who struggle', but was invariably, and misleadingly, translated in the West as 'holy warriors'.

Of this long and bitterly fought conflict the Russian public knew nothing at first. The conflict in Afghanistan was portrayed as a crusade against foreign intervention. Smiling soldiers were photographed planting trees with friendly villagers and presiding over the opening of schools. The 'limited contingent' of a hundred thousand troops was said to be fulfilling its 'internationalist duty' in Afghanistan to protect the country from British, Chinese and American mercenaries. But the bodies of its nineteen-year-old conscripts were shipped home in sealed metal coffins, and their gravestones made no mention of the manner of their deaths.

Elsewhere news of the conflict was scattered; for the majority of news-gatherers it was simply too dangerous a place. The Soviets had put a price on the heads of foreigners entering the country with the mujaheddin, closing off even the capital from foreign eyes. A Soviet-run secret police trained children to infiltrate mujaheddin groups to report on the presence of foreigners. The risks for transgressors were high. Perhaps thirty foreigners were killed trying to cover the war, and a small number were captured and sentenced to prison in Kabul under terrible conditions. Almost all of them were young freelance correspondents hoping to cut their journalistic teeth on a conflict few staff reporters dared cover.

I had arrived in the final period of what outsiders sometimes called the 'golden age' of the war. The Afghans, though brutalized by the conflict, were still convinced of their eventual victory. Their struggle was full of unlikely heroes, women and children among them, their battles waged in a mischievous spirit of defiance, their ranks imbued with a pleasant anarchy. They took little interest in the internecine quarrels of politicians in the capital or the rhetoric of their so-called representatives abroad. Pitifully under-equipped in both *matériel* and training to cope with a twentieth-century war, they faced seemingly hopeless odds. Confronted by the enemy's awesome firepower their almost reckless enthusiasm for resistance was, for those who had the privilege to witness it, unforgettable.

For an aspiring war correspondent it was perhaps the most romantic destination on earth. But after sharing in the thrill and terror of life among the mujaheddin, observing at first hand the destruction caused by the conflict and the obvious afflictions visited on the country's population, it was hard to know which was more difficult to bear: the dangers and privations of the conflict or the general indifference to it back home. I was among many outsiders who had been touched by the place during those years, and who were left with the feeling of having participated in an epic and secret affair against which the lack of interest of the outside world seemed incomprehensible. The Afghan tragedy was enormous; and it was virtually untold. Back home I settled into a private grief, returning twice when the distance became too much.

*

That was a different time: now the scale, the intrigue and the moral clarity had gone out of the conflict, along with the menace of a foreign occupier's brutality. Gone too, was the heroic certitude of the mujaheddin. The *jehād* ended when the Soviets withdrew their demoralized army in 1989, leaving a shattered country and two million dead. Outlying communist posts fell like winter leaves, and the war moved to the cities, especially to Kabul, where the communists held out doggedly for three more years, crushing hopes of a swift return to peace.

Greater trials lay ahead for the city, which had escaped ten years of conflict relatively unscathed. Symbol of the government's legitimacy, Kabul was fiercely contested by rival groups after the communists fled in 1992. The city had been seized in a brilliant takeover by forces under Massoud, the celebrated commander whose mujaheddin had repulsed ten major Soviet offensives in the Panjshīr valley. It was fought for in turn by the notorious Gulbuddin Hekmatyar, Massoud's arch rival, whose forces controlled the southern tier of the country and whose rockets subsequently laid whole sections of the city to dust; by Rashīd Dostum, a former general under the Soviets, who had carved out a miniature state of his own to the north; by a powerful Shi'ite mujaheddin force from the interior of the country; and now, the Tālebān.

That it had survived at all seemed miraculous.

*

It was our first day in Kabul and despite the obvious dangers we were anxious to explore, to get the feel of the city and the measure, such as we might be able, of its people. Craig and I joked about the risks to keep our spirits up, and headed on a rough mental bearing for the city centre near the river, beyond which we had been warned not to go.

In that gentle afternoon light the caution seemed unnecessarily stern. We soon passed the stately and incongruously European-looking ministries set in once-tended gardens, relics of happier times. French and German architects had designed many of the city's official buildings in the 1920s. The grandiose neoclassical structure of the British embassy had made it one of the most luxurious postings in the empire. We saw one ministry, across a yellowing lawn, that resembled an *hôtel de ville* on the Côte d'Azur, and another that looked like a Bavarian country mansion.

In one of the long avenues of the 'new city' near the presidential palace, we passed a solid metal gate peppered with shrapnel holes, its top laced with concertina wire. Through a crack we could make out an abandoned building in an overgrown garden: this was the American embassy. The Chinese embassy was further on, and had fared little better.

We came to a crossroads where a traffic policeman in Ruritanian costume was directing trucks between bollards made from painted artillery casings. He waved to us, grinning broadly, and nearly caused an accident.

Soon we had reached one of the busiest sections of Kabul close to the river. The buildings here were on a more humble scale, like those of a provincial town from the 1960s, but had suffered from years of neglect and their raggedness gave the impression that they had been recently excavated. The exception was the cement-coloured post office, the only tall structure in the city, which at fifteen stories resembled a scaled-down version of the Knightsbridge Barracks. It was scored by rocket blasts, and from the holes hung chunks of concrete like severed flesh dangling from metal tendons.

At its base the streets were lined with open markets, a sea of merchant's barrows and tightly packed stalls. We wandered through the crowds, thrilled at the sight of so much life and industry in a place we had half-expected to find deserted.

Yet this was a capital without electricity, running water or any of the ordinary amenities that elsewhere seem so essential. There were no skyscrapers or screaming trains, no subways or escalators, no traffic lights or traffic jams, parking meters, billboards, banners or advertising of any sort – and the effect was strangely uplifting. Here it seemed that all the modern Western contributions to life had been reduced to irrelevance, without the slightest interruption in daily affairs.

Even in a country at war, it struck us suddenly, life goes on. People were still shopping, planting, collecting firewood, flying kites, sending their kids to school and running their businesses. The whole panoply of human endeavour was striving to assert its rightful continuation, even as windows rattled to the thump of shells.

Visually there was nothing to dull the eye, no routine of design to hypnotize the senses. Every face was different. We saw none of the vacant stares one meets on ordinary city streets; no neurotic malingering, no trace of the afflictions of urban lassitude. Craig was wearing jeans and taking photographs, and privately I was on the lookout for signs of resentment at this doubly foreign display; Kabul was, after all, a city deeply traumatized by years of war and unaccustomed to visitors. We attracted plenty of attention, but none of it was hostile.

Men strode purposefully in every direction, vigorous and watchful, dressed in a bewildering variety of costume. And women too, another sight we had hardly expected, accustomed as we were to images of timid creatures scurrying between the shadows and shrouded from head to foot. They were modestly clad to the Western eye but many wore high heels and only the most diaphanous of head coverings; tall, fine-boned women, with intense eyes and – it was impossible not to notice, despite the faint sense of trespass implicit in the act of staring – often very beautiful.

Everywhere there was an infectious enthusiasm for life, and we felt richer for it. The volume of activity around us made us feel safe, even though it was a false comfort: above the noise of the streets it was impossible to hear incoming artillery. Emboldened, we crossed the river by the Pul-i Khishti bridge near the money-changers' bazaar on the southern bank, and walked a little further, knowing that we had been warned not to go this far.

I was hoping to find the street of the carpetsellers. With a slightly sick feeling I realized I could see an open skyline where the carpet market had once been; it no longer existed. We walked on, thinking perhaps we were in the wrong spot, while a small sea of smiling children gathered behind us, daring one another to step closer. Then we came to a long avenue running east to west: this was the Jāde-ye Maiwand.

A little more than a hundred years before, across a burning plain not far from the city of Qandahar, British troops had suffered one of the most disastrous defeats in their imperial history. A thousand men and two hundred horses were killed by Afghan tribesmen rallied, it was said, by a Pathan heroine named Malalai, who used her veil as a battle standard and heaped shame on those afraid to die. The street was named after Maiwand where the battle was fought, and until recently had been one of the city's busiest commercial thoroughfares. Now, as we turned into it, we saw an avenue of ruin.

This was the place, we later found out, that photographers and visiting camera crews always asked to see: the street by which Kabul was represented to the outside world. It looked like Hiroshima after the atomic bomb. Not a building had been left standing. We had both heard about it, but the sight was something different.

It was late afternoon. Through hollow doorways suspended use-lessly in columns of broken wall the sun shot long sloping lances of golden light. We walked along in stunned silence as the desolation grew, past what had once been a cinema where the scorched carcass of

35

a crippled tank listed at a crazy angle against a mound of rubble. A few men were pulling carts of precious firewood or sacks piled piteously high, heaving at loads fit for animals. All along its half-mile length the street was lined with the skeletons of what had been homes and shops, their every inch of surface scarred by bullet and shrapnel holes. Not even the slenderest of metal telephone poles had escaped. They were twisted, torn and punctured, and their severed wires swayed in the breeze. Behind them, acres of homes had been reduced to a muddy wasteland of rubble, from which ragged tendrils of brick rose like weeds from the floor of a poisoned lake. Out of the ruins ran children on winding mud trails, greeting us in pockets of laughter: we both felt curiously oppressed by their cheerfulness.

A cold wind began to whip up the dust along the street and, like animals that have wandered too far from their lairs, we knew instinctively it was a bad place to be lost as the sun went down. It had a lawless air. The shadows thickened as the golden light retreated, and at last its touch slipped upwards, first from the city itself and then from the mountains beyond.

In a darkening doorway we glimpsed a one-legged man, rising on his crutches at the sight of us. He was young, perhaps thirty, with a rich black beard, and lured us nearer with an uncanny brightness in his eyes. Beckoning, and with a smile of improbable vigour, he asked if we would join him for a glass of tea.

We followed him to a half-ruined room between mounds of fallen brickwork. Inside three desperate souls were huddled around a sweet-smelling hookah. The room was thick with the intoxicating smoke and the men had racking coughs, but rose in turn as we greeted them with a customary embrace. We exchanged the usual Afghan courtesies, which fell strangely on our ears like the language of a different era.

'Peace to you, brothers,' I said.

'And to you. Welcome.'

'Thanks be given. Are you well?' It was obvious they were utterly destitute.

'Praise God, well enough. And you — your souls are happy?'

'We are happy. And yours?'

'*Fazl-i khodā*,' by God's grace. 'Please, sit, and be our guests.'

We had never expected to find men living among the ruins. Somehow even here they managed to eke out an unimaginably difficult existence. The one-legged man took off his shawl and, balancing on his good leg, laid it over the dusty floor for us to sit on.

'Rest and be comfortable.'

He disappeared for a few moments, then returned to pour us glasses of tea from a blackened kettle, smiling all the while. We spoke for a few minutes in Persian, and he asked us where we were from.

'England,' I said.

'And is it peaceful there,' he asked, 'or is there war, like this?'

There was movement from the back of the room and an old, turbaned man loomed from the darkness and sat beside us.

'*Inglestān*,' he murmured, as if the word was working its way towards something in his memory. '*Inglestān*. The English, yes. They came to Afghanistan,' he said slowly, fixing us with an Ancient Mariner's gaze, 'and we fought them *man to man!*' His hand flew suddenly upwards through the arc of a drawn sword and we started at the vehemence of the gesture. His eyes were half-maddened with grief and his forehead lined with a deep tracery of misery.

'Not like the Russians! They tried to take away our freedom too ...'

There was a rumble of artillery and we flinched involuntarily but the old man bore at us without blinking. He described, with growing defiance, the wretchedness his nation had been forced to endure, the helplessness of his people against rockets, and their love of freedom that could never be destroyed ... but soon I could no longer understand as his speech, driven to greater heights of desperation at each shake of his phantom sword, vaulted to a plea heavy with bitterness, then collapsed as he waved to the destruction beyond the doorway.

'Look!' His voice trailed miserably. 'Look what they have done. Afghanistan is ruined.'

There was nothing theatrical about his performance; it was obvious he had lost everything. One could photograph a ruined street: but not this ruin.

By now the sun had set and we dared not linger.

'With your permission...'

Our host jumped upwards with astonishing agility and led us back to the entrance of the desolate chamber, entreating us to return another day for a meal.

'We are poor but you will be our guests,' he said with a transparently earnest smile. Yet his look was filled with such grief that I found it hard to bear.

'We have caused you trouble,' I said.

'On the contrary.' I met his eyes as we embraced and for a moment our worlds were bridged. 'God protect you, brother,' he said, and waved us back into the ruined street.

'And you in His safety.'

We walked on, both relieved and shaken by the intensity of the encounter. Yet ahead of me I saw only the vision of the man's eyes, and in them, two tiny crescents of tears.

*

Afghanistan simply means 'land of the Afghans', although the true identity and the provenance of the Afghans themselves are mysterious. Before the term 'Afghan' came to denote anyone living within the borders of the country, it was used by outsiders to describe the ethnic group that today makes up roughly a third of its population – the famous Pushtuns, anglicized to 'Pathan'. These 'original' Afghans have been known as a particular people for several centuries, but they are only one of many who inhabit the area to which the modern name Afghanistan applies.*

---

* More strictly, the word 'Afghan', as it was originally coined, refers to a specific grouping within a multiplicity of Pushtun tribes. Just as 'British' can refer to at least four different nationalities, different Pushtun groups preserve strongly independent identities. The two largest tribes are the Ghilzai and the Durrani. The royal family of Afghanistan, which gained prominence in the early eighteenth century (the final branch of which, in the person of King Zāher Shāh's nephew and usurper Mohammad Daoud, survived in power until 1978), derived from the Barakzai line of the Durrani (formerly Abdali) of southwestern Afghanistan.

Pushtun legend, in fact, traces its people's origins to the Bani Israel, a tribe of wandering Israelites expelled from Jerusalem by Nebuchadnezzar and who embraced Islam, considering it a reforming extension of their own beliefs, in the seventh century. But there are only a handful of references to the Afghan people in written sources, and the etymology of the name itself leads down some tenuously lit historical alleys.*

I thought of some of the other peoples that made up the jigsaw of Afghanistan's inhabitants. The fair-skinned, blue-eyed farmer from the remote mountains of Nuristan, and his strikingly beautiful wife, who wears a black felt hat sown with tiny cowrie shells, consider themselves as Afghan as the Tekke Turcoman from near the northern border. He wears a hat with long, spiralling woollen tresses like a sheep's hide, and his wife, whose eyes slope gently downwards towards proud

---

* According to Pathan legend, Afghanah was a grandson of Saul, born in the time of Solomon, who led (with his forty sons) the tribe's exodus from Jerusalem to the central mountains of what is now Afghanistan, in around 600 BC. The discovery in the 1960s of a Jewish cemetery dating from the twelfth century testifies to a well-established community in the Hazārajāt; there was a Jewish presence in Balkh at least as early as the Arab invasions. But the genealogy is considered fanciful. Early references to the Afghans are scattered, comprising little more than a third-century Sassanian mention of the *Abgan*, a sixth-century Indian reference to the *Avagana*, and an account by the Chinese monk Hsien-Tsang, who trekked across the country in AD 632, of an independent state called A-po'kien between the Indus and the Helmand rivers; the earliest reference in a Moslem source is from the tenth century AD. A modern Persian interpretation has *afghan* as meaning wailing or moaning; for a most ingenious derivation, see H. W. Bellew's *An Inquiry into the Ethnography of Afghanistan* (1891): 'The name Albania, it seems clear, was given to the country by the Romans. Albania means "mountainous country", and its inhabitants were called Albani, "mountaineers" ... the Latin Albán is apparently the source of the Armenian Alwan, which is their name for these Albáni. The Armenian Alwán, Alván or Albán, though ordinarily pronounced indifferently, is written in the Armenian character with letters which, being transliterated, read as Aghván or Aghwán; and this word, pronounced Alván, etc. in Armenia, in the colloquial dialect of their eastern neighbours is changed to Aoghán, Avghán, and Afghán.'

cheekbones, wears a conical creation two feet high decorated with silver coins and braids of metallic thread. They are as Afghan as the Behsūd Hazāra from the central highlands, whose broad, flat and clean-shaven face is planted with a wide nose between eyes as narrow as slits. Likewise the plain-dwelling Nurzai Pathan, whose eyes resemble black olives and are framed by long curly tresses and a flowing beard . . .

Within the country, the intensity of the distinctions between peoples – linguistic, tribal, ethnic, religious – has varied according to the times. But beyond the country's borders, the label 'Afghan' has traditionally subsumed all these differences – identifying a spiritual rather than physical provenance. I wondered whether this still held true.

The country's borders have never been too reliable; here the English are partly to blame for the confusion. Afghanistan itself is a relatively modern word, an imperial term of convenience hardly used much more than a hundred years ago by Afghans themselves. The Afghan king Abdur Rahman Khan, who ruled from Kabul until 1900, called his land Yaghistan, 'Land of the Rebellious', and his country was all that remained of what in the mid-eighteenth century had been the greatest Moslem empire after the Ottomans. It stretched from Mashad in today's Iran to Agra (including Delhi), and from the Amu Darya river to the Arabian Sea; the Punjāb, Kashmir, Baluchistan and Sind were all ceded to Kabul.

But by the beginning of the nineteenth century the Russians had eaten it away to the north and the British with equal appetite to the south, until the two empires' jaws locked on the gnawed bone in the region of the Hindu Kush. The stakes were high: Russian and English armies were mobilized for war. In a bitter imperial stalemate and with characteristically scant regard for the well-established logic of ethnic and linguistic frontiers, the Anglo-Russian commissions went to work in London and Moscow and drew up the borders that have lasted to the present day.

Before all this, before these hated and contentious demarcations – which divided villages into different countries and severed traditional patterns of migration – were grudgingly accepted, Afghans divided their land into three or four different territories. South of the great Hindu Kush massif, including the capital and the region as far as the river Indus in what is today Pakistan, was called Kabulistan. The territories further south and west along the Iranian frontier were called Zabulistan or Khorassan. Turkestan was the name to given to the region east of the city of Herat, the northern foothills of the Hindu Kush, and the plains that stretch from their bases to Amu Darya, bordering Russia. Until the Second World War the old names were still in common use and they echo down to the present, as do the many problems associated with them.

These violent tugs-of-war were nothing new, and over the ages have made Afghanistan what it is: a patchwork quilt of ethnic groups and tribal kingdoms enmeshed in a web of history, whose filaments stretch broadly in every direction.

No other territory in ancient times was more thoroughly traversed. No other on earth grew into such a complex melting-pot. Slavic, Indian, Persian, Turkish, Arab, central Asian and European* bloods were spilled and blended, both generously, on Afghan soil; civilizations both sublime and barbarous left their mark.

Time and again the tides of upheaval have clashed in its valleys and high passes, sometimes fusing into a harmonious swell, at others driven by the storm of warfare, shattering and scattering peoples like flotsam into barely accessible mountain coves. Generations of migration and miscegenation have woven strands old and new into a complex tapestry of micro-countries. Twenty languages from four major language groups

---

* Not only from Greece and Rome. The Victorian British contribution to the gene pool was considerable: 'temptations which are most difficult to withstand were not withstood by our British officers, the attractions of the women of Caubul they did not know how to resist' (J. Kaye, *History of the War in Afghanistan*, 1874). There were other consequences arising from soldiers' 'acts under their own control'. Kipling wrote (somewhere – alas, I have lost the source of this titbit): 'It was counted impious that bazaar prostitutes should be inspected; or that men should be taught elementary precautions in their dealings with them. This official virtue cost our Army in India nine thousand expensive white men a year laid up from venereal disease.' The most common affliction was nicknamed 'the shrieking sister'.

and a multitude of adventitious dialects are represented among them, many of which – even within the borders of their relatively small land – became aware of each other's existences almost yesterday.

The reason lies in its geography; what is today Afghanistan has been a natural crossroads for as long as history has been recorded, straddling the volatile tetrad of Far Eastern, Indian, central Asian and Persian civilizations. The earliest recorded names for the region date from the sixth century BC, when Afghanistan formed the eastern reaches of the Achaemenid empire under Darius the Great.

To Greek writers such as Eratosthenes writing two hundred years before Christ, and who took their knowledge from the Persians, it was known as Ariana. Given the intervening two thousand years of upheaval, the classical divisions of the region into seven provinces are mirrored with remarkable fidelity in today's Afghanistan: Bactriana, corresponding roughly with today's Balkh and Badakhshān provinces; Margiana, the northwestern portion of the country around Murghāb now represented by the provinces of Baghdīs and Faryiāb; Aria, the region around Herat (possibly the Hairava of the *Avestas*) and the western end of the Paropamisus range; Gandara, embracing Kabul, Jelallabad and Peshawar; Sattagydia, from Ghazni to the Indus; and Drangiana and Gadrosia, comprising modern Baluchistan and Sistan and on to the south, as far as the home of the *Ikthyiophagoi* – the fish-eaters – of the coastlands around Makran.

Time has not rushed things there. The names of tribes both European and native, described twenty-five centuries ago by Herodotus, have stubbornly resisted, or else have not been subject to the usual transforming pressures. Today's Afridi (of British topee-sniping noto-riety) have been found, echo-like, in Herodotus's *Apyratai*, the ancient inhabitants of the seventh satrapy or the region around today's southeastern frontier – just as the *Hygenni* have crossed two and a half millennia to become the Khugiani of today, and the hardy *Thyraioi* braved the gulfs of time to succeed their distant ancestors as the modern Tirahi; we find too, like flies preserved in the amber of history, the *Thamanai* of antiquity in today's Taimani, the *Zarangai* in the Sarangai, the *Sattagyadai* in the Shattak, and the *Maionoi* in the Mayani; even perhaps, in the village of Barakai (68° E 34° N), the very Bactrian site given by Darius to the Barakaian slaves seized from the Libyan Greek territories during his Egyptian campaign...

*

I had dozed off, reading Louis Dupree's encyclopaedic work about Afghanistan. Now it was cold and there was no heating. I went downstairs to the room where Jān had installed a stove made locally from an oil drum, and was stoking it with cupfuls of diesel. Tim was flicking through a collection of grisly photographs he had taken on a recent front-line visit, turning the pictures sideways as he tried to distinguish body parts. Craig was huddled near the stove, mouthing sentences from a phrase book I had lent him.

'*Chotor hastī* ... how are you?'

'It's not *chotor*,' I corrected him, 'it's *chetūr*. People might think you're saying *shotor*, which would mean "you are a camel".'

It was not a difficult language but he was struggling.

'*Bad ast* ... it is bad. *Hoop ast* ... it is good.'

'It's not *hoop*, it's *khūb*. But the Afghans say *kho*.'

'*Who you callin' a ho', white boy?*' shot back Craig, lapsing into the gangland banter of his native Los Angeles.

'*Yo' mamma, tha's who.*'

We kept this up until it was time to leave: we had all been invited to a party at the Turkish embassy.

There was a strict curfew at nine o'clock, and by eight the streets were already deserted. Only government cars and foreigners were exempted from the rule. Foreigners took advantage of this unusual liberty to drive themselves to private watering-holes around the city. The price for such forays was the ritual braving of night-time checkpoints. These came and went according to the situation and consisted of temporary sentry-boxes at main intersections, manned by shaven-headed conscripts not known for their mental flexibility.

The result was that in the darkness it was impossible to know from inside a vehicle quite when to expect the blood-chilling cry of challenge from a soldier. This would be followed by the sight, looming in the headlights, of automatic rifles pointing at the heads of the occupants.

By day we grew accustomed to the sight of guns, which soon lost

43

their sinister novelty. A gun pointed towards you was a different matter, especially at night, when to the soldier upon whose reactions your life rested you were nothing more than a pair of headlights. I had known – briefly – an Italian cameraman, who was shot through the head after his driver failed to stop at such a checkpoint. It was why no one used cassette players in their vehicles at night or drove too fast, and why I was personally never entirely free of the urge to duck whenever we approached a crossroads.

Somewhere I had heard a story from the great corpus of traditional tales surrounding the bumbling sage and *mullā*, Nasruddin. The *mullā's* antics, known in endless variety throughout the Islamic world and beyond, seemed torn from a page in daily Afghan life. The tale I had heard must have grown out of the war, for in it the *mullā's* ancient wisdom had found a modern setting. Nasruddin had become a soldier in Kabul, and he was on curfew duty at a quarter to nine. He spots a man crossing the street a hundred yards away and, to the astonishment of his fellow soldier, shoots the man dead.

'Are you mad?' protests the other in disbelief. 'Curfew doesn't begin until nine o'clock!'

'Ah,' replies the *mullā*, with a satisfied grin. 'I knew that man and I also knew where he lived. I knew therefore that he could not possibly have reached his home before curfew begins. *That* is why I shot him.'

I consoled myself by trying to focus on the story's psychological rather than literal interpretation. But it ran with horrid vividness through my mind as we left the house for the Turkish embassy, and drove through the unlit streets.

Sure enough, a few minutes from the house we heard a long, high shout like a cry of battle, and into the lights ran a soldier in a thick felt coat, cocking his rifle and levelling it to our heads in a motion of terrifying suddenness. Tim was driving, but it was a borrowed car, and his free hand was scrabbling frantically over the dashboard as the headlights dazzled the soldier ahead of us.

'Can't find the fucking dip switch,' he muttered. It was a bad moment for this news.

From the blackness to our side the muzzle of a Kalashnikov appeared at the window, then a grizzled face, its dark eyes filling suddenly with relief as they glimpsed the pale and anxious faces inside.

'*Salaam* ... Peace.'

'And to you.'

'Foreigners? Go on ...'

An arm went up, the soldier shouted a deafening all clear, and the rifle ahead of us, which had never for a moment wavered from our heads, swung back onto a shoulder. The pair of them disappeared into the night and we breathed again.

Like most official buildings the embassy was hidden from the street in a walled compound at whose gates we hammered until a guard appeared. It was a medieval ritual. We were guided with an oil lantern across a courtyard to a door protected by high sandbags. After the cold and suspense of the car ride, inside I had the feeling of having again slipped beyond a magic veil.

Waistcoated attendants took our hats and gloves and glided over thick carpets to serve us wine from silver trays. There was a table piled with steaming dishes, and we helped ourselves to Turkish specialities served on gold-rimmed china plates.

I had expected for my time in Kabul to stay in a dusty hostel somewhere and was unprepared for such luxury. The dashing young ambassador, who saw personally to each of his guests in turn, took in my scruffy down vest and tennis shoes with magnanimity, saying he was always delighted to see new faces. I wondered who his guests were and eavesdropped on a handful of diplomats, United Nations officials and a few relief workers from the small number of private agencies that had chosen to ride out the trouble in the capital. There was an Australian correspondent researching the history of the war, whose knowledge of the various battles, their chronologies and commanders, was encyclopaedic; an Englishman, hoping to open a Land Rover outlet in Kabul, and an American member of a little-known chivalric order who had come to Afghanistan to search for the remains of Soviet soldiers listed missing in action.

Not for the first time I began to run up against the difficulty of explaining my own intentions. Mention of writing a book about Afghanistan prompted some sceptical raising of eyebrows.

'Are you quite sure you're not doing anything — you know — *else*?' asked someone in a voice honeyed with conspiracy. There were no casual travellers to Afghanistan and imaginations run riot in lonely places. (I do not mean among the Afghans, who were delighted at the thought of a foreign spy in their midst.) I was having trouble, for conversation's sake, reducing the endeavour to recognizable themes.

I had no sponsor for the trip and my plans lacked the respectable convention of a motif on which to base a story: retracing the silk route through Afghanistan, say, or the eastern campaigns of Alexander. Or, more interesting to my mind, an investigation into one of Asia's most enigmatic kings, Kanishka, the Kushan ruler whose ancient summer capital lay just to the north of Kabul; or a search for the vanished metropolis of the Firozkuh, the Purple Mountain, in the virtual *terra incognita* of the central Ghorid highlands.

Afghanistan was still fertile ground for all manner of unlikely — yet not entirely incredible — searches, of which there were scattered accounts from before the war; for Bactrian gold and buried Zoroastrian temples; for doctors still said to practise the healing sciences of Alexander's physicians, twenty-five centuries later; for the legendary schools of esoteric science overlooking the Hindu Kush, from which Gurdjieff himself was said to have built his immensely influential teaching; and for the 'secret' Christian communities which believed Jesus had settled quietly in Afghanistan after the Resurrection, and where his teaching caused less of a stir among natives accustomed to solitary men close to God. For now the war made any such ventures virtually impossible.

The guests began to trickle away, thinned by concerns over safety, which disappeared with daylight. Tim had no such reservations and I took my cue from him: we were the last to leave. Ample wine had drawn out our long and friendly discussions and at one in the morning the ambassador showed us out into the icy moonlight. Our breath steamed like clouds and the cypress trees were gilded with the silvery light.

Tim's motorbike, an indestructible relic of the Russian military, was waiting for us in the compound, its sidecar glazed with frost. It refused to start and the ambassador had to push us, slipping over the concrete in his polished brogues until the engine throbbed into life. He shouted a breathless cheer after us as we roared from the gates with a noise to wake the dead.

It was an unforgettable ride. The roads, built from cement blocks by the Soviets forty years earlier, were spine-shattering. Within minutes our faces were numb, and Tim took the corners at such speed the sidecar would lift off the ground. The road raced under us like a torrent in the headlamp and around it reared a spectral, silent world.

We seemed to have broken from the limits of the earth into a dream of the moon itself, from which all life had been consumed by the ghostly whiteness. Gripping the sidecar's lurching sides I looked upwards to a luminous canopy of stars beyond the streaking peaks of tall pine trees and thought how strange life had become so very quickly. I wondered how hard my family would take the news of my death; not at the hands of the unruly Afghans, but in a motorcycle accident with a fellow Englishman.

Then suddenly it seemed likely we would in any case be shot. Up ahead there was a checkpoint, where I looked forward to the chance to thaw my face. But instead of slowing down, Tim jerked into a lower gear with a burst of throttle, and drove the engine up to full power.

Bewildered, I looked up at him. His hair and scarf were trailing madly, his head and shoulders braced forward against the freezing air. He looked possessed, but over the roar it was impossible to protest. We tore through the checkpoint at high speed and, disappointed at the likelihood of dying on this, my first day in Kabul, I pictured the soldiers behind us tumbling into the road, their rifles levelled at our backs. Briefly I wondered if ducking would increase my chances and whether in the darkness the first volley might pass above our heads, but to hell with it ... we were kings of the night in our wild chariot and I never looked back to see: in the madness of the moment it hardly seemed to matter.

We reached the house and slipped quietly inside. In a beam of torchlight we caught Jān uncocking his pistol with a grin of relief as he realized who it was. Tim threw his gloves on a table, wiped the mist from his glasses and swept a hand through his hair.

'Good night,' he said.

I had already forgiven him his recklessness. In it I recognized something that our moment of folly had reawoken. I had tasted it again and found it sweet. We were witnesses to a world that had fallen beyond the bounds of ordinary rules, and reason proved a poor refuge for the urge to comprehend it. Something deeper was required to match the pitch of feeling, and in such small acts of insanity as that evening we sought a natural antidote for the greater insanity around us, hoping thereby to immunize the longing for which all other avenues of expression seemed blocked. It followed an unreasonable logic of its own, taking odd moments prisoner when the chance arose. A strange and potent medicine.

It had been a long day. I lit a candle and went upstairs.

Two

I can never forget the delights of Kabul, nor express the depth of my longing to return.

Zahiruddīn Mohammed 'Bābūr', founder of the
Moghul Empire, in a letter to his son Homayoun

KABUL IS A MOUNTAIN-RINGED HISTORY BOOK written in the faces of its people. Walking through the streets of the city you read the traces of the millennia in the features of its men and women and remember you have entered an unrivalled meeting-place of bloods.

In Afghanistan as a whole there are twenty different ethnic groups, and in Kabul they mingle more than elsewhere – perhaps anywhere. It is the faces of the inhabitants, light-stricken and intense, which tell more vividly of the nation's past than any written account.

History has assigned to these peoples a kind of hierarchy, which is not so much social but ethnic. Here as elsewhere, the inertia of tradition has hijacked the egalitarian spirit of Islam. Convention has put the Pushtuns at the head of the list, partly because they are the most populous ethnic group and because the country's rulers have been predominantly from Pushtun backgrounds since the eighteenth century. The Pushtuns themselves are a mixture of peoples; some say they are of Indian origin, others that they are descended from the nomadic Sakai of the central Asian steppes, who overwhelmed the Greeks in the second century BC.

'If you were to roam the world from the arctic goldfields of Kotzebue Sound to the pearl-fisheries of Thursday Island,' wrote Lowell Thomas when he visited the region in the 1920s, 'you could find no men more worthy of the title "desperado" than the Pushtuns who live among these jagged, saw-tooth mountains of the Afghan frontier.' The Pushtuns are none other than the 'Afghans' associated with the British campaigns in Afghanistan around the end of the nineteenth century. They were the thorns in the side of three periods of British occupation, and their martial traditions were immortalized in Victorian minds by Kipling, who spent time in the Frontier Provinces. They are a tall, dark-skinned and to the Western eye an often fierce-looking people, legendary for their marksmanship, love of poetry, women of savage beauty, hospitality, outspoken pride and complex inter-tribal rivalries. Their language is Pashtu – a difficult branch of the Indo-European family of tongues which the English nicknamed 'the language that would be spoken in hell' – and their home is roughly the southern tier of the country, of which Kabul marks the upper limit. Almost an equal number live in the North West Frontier Province of Pakistan. 'Firstly we are Pushtuns,' one tribesman told me with an emphatic wag of his finger, 'and secondly we are Moslems. Lastly we are either' (this with a dismissive wave) 'Afghans or Pakistanis.'

More European in appearance, often slighter in build, are the Tajiks of Persian descent. Historically they are a less controversial, though no less influential people. Their traditional homeland is the northeast of the country and their language Dari, the Afghan version of Farsi. In the old scheme of things the Tajiks came next in the ethnic pecking order. Tajiks who lived in Kabul were known as peaceful traders and administrators, drivers and domestic servants.

Next in the traditional hierarchy came the Nuristanis, from the region which until a hundred years ago was called the 'Land of the Idolators' and whose people traditionally claim descent from the armies of Alexander. Kipling wrote *The Man Who Would Be King* based on legends about the remote northeast province, the majority of whose villages are even today accessible only by foot. Like the Tajiks they are a fairer-skinned people than the Pushtuns, and a third of Nuristanis are reckoned to be blond. You see plenty of fair and ginger-haired men in Kabul; occasionally I would glimpse a young girl with skin the colour of ivory, blue or green eyes, and features Botticelli would have doted on. The pagan tribes of Nuristan, who spoke their own language, made their own wine and worshipped a complex pantheon of gods unknown elsewhere, were converted forcibly to Islam by King Abdur Rahman in the final years of the nineteenth century. Mystery still hangs over their origins like a cloud in one of their high narrow valleys; it is generally agreed they are the most ancient of the country's inhabitants, protected over the ages by the sheer remoteness of their mountain communities.

They are not the only people in Kabul popularly thought to be descended from former invaders. The high-cheeked, narrow-eyed Hazāras of central Afghanistan are said to be the distant offspring of the armies of Chingiz Khan. More likely they came as peaceful settlers in the fourteenth century; their widespread appearance in Kabul is relatively recent. Their distinctive features and language, as well as their adherence to the minority Shī'ite sect of Islam, placed them at the bottom of the social ladder, and makes them the object of continued persecution. There are also Turcomans and Uzbeks in the city, with sweeping moustaches and far-eastern features. Both are originally from the northernmost border areas, but are rarely seen outside the north today.

With history on their side the Pushtuns consider themselves rightful rulers of the country; at the other end of the scale the Hazāras still do the heaviest manual work in Kabul and seldom rise to official posts. In a country where affiliations of blood, rather than social and political factors, have traditionally determined the range and depth of human relations, the old mould has proven hard to break.

Until recently. Afghan society was so drastically altered by the Soviet presence that in the wake of their withdrawal, much that had been well established was turned suddenly on its head. Within a few years a Tajik leader, Massoud, was one of the most influential men in the country; the Uzbek warlord Dostum had carved out a semi-autonomous kingdom in the north, which had surpassed the capital as a commercial centre; the humble Hazāras had become a military force to be reckoned with, and the traditional Pushtun leadership was deeply divided. Ethnic divisions traditionally held in check exacerbated the differences. Pushtun representation in the government led by Massoud and Prime Minister Rabbāni — or rather the confusion over just which Pushtun groups should be included — had become the most contentious issue of the day.

*

53

Aside from the social upheavals, the natural setting for all these peoples remains spectacular. At nearly seven thousand feet above sea level Kabul* is one of the world's highest capitals, and for the first few days you feel slightly short of breath. The city lies in a broad plain fringed with blade-like ridges of mountains that tower to ten thousand feet or more. Its centre is clustered around three ragged peaks: Aliābād, Azāmai and Sher Darwāzah, the Lion Gate. The river Kabul snakes between them. A dozen lesser hills occupied by old forts (and, more recently, artillery, tank and anti-aircraft batteries) bump upwards from the low sprawl of buildings.

Before the Soviet invasion Kabul was home to roughly half a million people, but years of war wrought havoc on its population. In the 1980s refugees from the surrounding countryside swelled the capital's numbers to perhaps three million, and the city began to creep up the surrounding hillsides in colonies of mud-coloured homes linked by precipitous trails. The majority of residences are built in traditional fashion from timber frames and walls of baked mud bricks. More recent construction is in concrete and follows the old pattern in form, but not in character.

Beyond the city centre buildings are seldom more than two stories high, and spread in every direction in a sea of rectangular rooftops punctured occasionally by the dome of a mosque or a tall, solitary pine tree. The newest, tallest and unquestionably ugliest buildings were put up by the Soviets; smokestacks and silos and apartment blocks. The most conspicuous are the Nādir Shāh Mīnā complex, the eastern residential suburb called Microrayon and the now ruined area around the former Soviet embassy. Heinously out of keeping with traditional architecture, they seem to have attracted a greater than usual quota of bullets and rockets.

The northern suburbs are relatively intact and reach for miles,

---

* Kabul is pronounced 'car-bull'. The 'Caubul' of British literary coinage still persists, 'k'bull' is usual; both evoke puzzled looks inside the country. An *Afghan* is someone from Afghanistan; an *Afghani* is a unit of currency; the official national language is *Dari*.

lapping against the hills beyond the airport. To the west and south they peter out in ravaged ruins. The east, with deep regret, I never saw.

There are few ancient monuments. The seventeenth century covered bazaar was dynamited by English sappers a hundred and fifty years ago and the most famous historical building of all, the Bālā Hissār or High Castle, was left in ruins by the retreating army.* Ancient crenellated walls still run from the castle up to the summit of the Sher Darwāza hill, and down again towards the river. There was a cannon on the hillside which used to be fired daily at midday, and before sunrise during Ramadan, the month of fasting in the hours of daylight; I am not sure when the custom stopped.

The Bālā Hissār is interesting because its excavation may one day answer the question of whether Kabul was ever an important Greek city. The oldest walls appear to date from the sixth century AD but like so many of the country's important monuments these may have been raised on a much older structure. Kabul may conceal a lost city called Ortospana founded by Strabo. Alexander founded a number of important cities in Afghanistan along his bloody route to India, but Kabul does not seem to have been one of them. The closest of Alexander's cities to Kabul, Alexandria-ad-Caucasum, lies in a similarly contested site near the junction of the Panjshīr and Kabul rivers about fifty miles north of Kabul, next to the modern town of Jebel as-Serāj. Kabul itself lay off the main trade routes and became the seat of power in Afghanistan only in the sixteenth century. Certainly Greek rulers squabbled over control of the Kabul valley and beyond after Alexander's departure, and the names on the coins they minted are resoundingly Greek: Diodotus, Antimachus, Demetrius, Menander, Hippostratus, Straton. The famous collection of Greek coins found nearby — the only source of knowledge about the Hellenic rulers of

---

* 'Having thus re-established the prestige of British invincibility ... there followed the blowing up of the bazaars, the burning of the chief's houses, the destruction of the city gates and, last of all, a conflagration which spread everywhere till the waters of the river stayed it' (G. R. Gleig, *Sale's Brigade in Afghanistan*, 1879).

the region — was looted by art dealers' henchmen from the Kabul museum, along with 30,000 others, in 1993.

For years Kabul was the only city in the country to have paved streets. Paving began in the 1920s but was not completed until the 1950s, when the Soviets finished the job with indestructible cement blocks. Unlike the smooth and softer surface of macadamed roads, concrete is unaffected by the weight of tracked military vehicles and I often wondered if this was a coincidence or just bad road-building. The gaps between the blocks widen over time and driving is always a spine-jarring affair. In parts of the countryside, where Soviet-built roads have not been maintained for years, these blocks shift and sink, leaving gaps into which cars driving at night are said to disappear.

Then there are the old streets; tiny passages hemmed in by high mud-brick walls, where you hear the echo of your own footsteps and walk with a sense of trespass. But the Afghan love of both privacy and gardens means that countless homes, featureless from their exteriors, enclose relatively spacious gardens for a city centre, and from a dusty or muddy street you enter a tiny haven of cultivation with a sense of delight and surprise.

*

In those first days of exploring the city, I had a mission of sorts. I had promised an Afghan friend now living abroad to deliver a present, along with some news, to a relative in Kabul. I had an address but after a few days had still not found it, and had the idea of visiting the relative's place of work.

The news from my friend was that he would return to Afghanistan but didn't know when; the present was a bottle of aftershave I had bought en route, and the relative was an army general. I set off one morning with what was probably the only bottle of Issey Miyake in the country and headed for the Ministry of Defence.

It was on one of the long avenues of the new city, where the majority of rockets had the habit of falling. Armed men were coming and going in battered Russian-built jeeps. A small crowd of soldiers gathered around me at the entrance to a compound ringed with high gates. I said I had news for the general from abroad; it had a medieval ring. I played dumb and listened to the debate that followed. It was always like this with soldiers; unlike the mujaheddin they had been robbed for years of the ability to make quick decisions, and floundered over the problem of how to treat a foreign visitor. I couldn't be allowed inside, one of them said, foreigners had no business there. Another interjected: I should be let in, but searched and escorted. No, another of them said, I was a guest, and that wouldn't be right. Where was I from? England? Where was that?

I handed out some cigarettes, smiled broadly in every direction, and the matter was resolved; they had not lost their instinctive sense of courtesy. I was led into a broad and dusty courtyard hemmed in by the custard-painted walls of rocket-scarred and bullet-chipped buildings. Soldiers in thick woollen khaki scurried like ants in and out of doors, saluting officers in huge red-rimmed caps and uniforms studded with glinting brass buttons.

Murmurs and all eyes followed me to a building where dust trickled from between the floorboards overhead, up a flight of creaking wooden stairs and into a tiny room. There were two chairs and a bare desk by a window and here I was asked to wait. Some tea arrived and, a few minutes later, the general himself.

He was a bear of a man; six foot tall, barrel-chested, with a jet-black beard and piercing eyes. Red tabs flashed on his neck and shoulders. He greeted me like a long-lost brother with a spine-crunching hug, and we sat in silence for a few moments, until we were alone.

I hadn't much to tell him; only that his brother would be returning in the spring. He was delighted with the news, sent for grapes, and plied me with questions and compliments. As we talked a constant stream of soldiers appeared at the door, presenting thick sheaves of crude paper for the general's signature. They were scored with grids of handwritten lists and numbers like medieval ledgers. He signed them in turn, muttered instructions, and apologized for the interruptions.

Did I need a place to stay? he asked. Was there anything he could do?

Outside there was a thump of artillery which shook the building and I flinched. He turned to the window and waved his hand to the world beyond in a slow gesture of despair, raised his eyes to the ceiling and sighed deeply. Then he looked at me with an expression both sad and serene, and said:

'War!'

I didn't want to take up more of his time — he had a campaign to see to. I left him, and suffered another crushing hug. Having seen us part, a ripple of deference spread through the soldiers as I left them at the gates.

I walked away along the river with a feeling of regret that I'd never seen the city at peace or, at least, as the general had lamented, during springtime when the fruit trees were in blossom. Would the sights have really been any different? I was full of such questions in those first few days. As I walked further it seemed likely the answer was no: in a dusty public garden near the tomb of Abdur Rahman, men were praying on shawls laid out across the bare earth in the same manner as men had done for more than a thousand years. Their outer world was in chaos and ruin, but their fundamental orientation to the world, what was in it and what was beyond it, and from which the kernel of the culture was nourished, was not subject to the same forces of change.

I walked to the post office, curious to see if the postal system still functioned. The city's airport had been closed by the fighting and I wondered how letters could possibly reach the outside world. Beneath the blast-cracked windows of the huge, deserted central room, two young women managed fifty-foot-long counters and giggled coyly as I bought some airmail letters. There was a picture of a tank printed on the envelopes. I asked to see the box marked poste restante and looked at the stamps on the envelopes. They came from all over the world. Some were years old and still unopened, addressed to names in English, French, Russian, Polish, German and Afghan. I wondered at the tales behind each of them; the lives they had tried to touch and failed, ending up like little fallen arrows of hope, gathering dust.

I turned south, walked towards the river and watched the bustle of the markets, then headed west towards the mosque of the King of Two Swords. On a low wall above the riverbank, carpet sellers had draped their wares in long rows of colours. Opposite them stretched the crumbling façades in brick and plaster of a line of shops, each a tiny focus of endeavour. There were tailors at work on hand-powered sewing machines, hat and clothes makers with fox and leopard skins dangling from their ceilings, bookshops, barbers and photographic studios where the cameras resembled shoeboxes on tripods and the pictures were developed by hand, in the camera itself, under a long black cape.

I had seen photographs of Kabul in guidebooks from the 1960s and the sights had hardly changed. Years of conflict had paralysed the hand of modernization. In the side streets time's touch was lighter. The roads grew more dusty; here shops and homes made from mud brick and timber bore the neglect less visibly than modern buildings. Shrouded women carried water in earthen vases on their heads and venerable, turbaned shepherds prodded their flocks forward at a timeless pace. Spice sellers sat between multicoloured mounds or weighed out flour and grain on scales balanced with stones, and at the butchers' stalls men hacked with iron axes at carcasses on wooden stumps polished and gently concave from years of use, and laid out severed heads in long rows like the grisly trophies of medieval conflicts.

The mosque at the end of the road had been recently repainted in bright shades of yellow and blue. I had read that it marked the site of an earlier mosque built at the entry of Islam into Kabul in the seventh century. According to early Moslem historians, this first mosque had been raised in turn on the ruins of a much more ancient Hindu temple.

The latest structure dated from the 1920s and the reign of the amir Amānullah: architecturally it was a strange amalgam. It had a distinctly European flavour that made me think of a Bavarian train station, and its top looked like the peak of a Kaiser's helmet. Weighed down by two rectangular stories of Doric arcades and an oversized entrance resembling a neoclassical pavilion, its Islamic identity struggled to express itself in two stubby minarets. It was one of the many mutant fruits of Amānullah's feverish efforts to modernize Kabul in the 1920s, and the result was dubious and ultimately tragic. Amānullah was fascinated by Europe, and it was on a royal tour of the European capitals in 1925 that he found his inspiration for the transformation of Afghanistan into a modern state. While in Berlin, the story goes, he was given a luxurious model of the latest Mercedes by the Kaiser. He moved on to London where, not wishing to be outdone, the British offered him an even more beautiful Rolls-Royce. As was the Afghan custom, Amānullah offered to pay, and not wishing to offend either king, officials at Buckingham Palace agreed to charge the sum of one pound.

'At that price,' mused the wily Amānullah, 'I should like to have two.'

Back in Kabul he commissioned the rebuilding of the capital, opened co-educational schools, forced the city's inhabitants to wear Western clothes and outlawed the women's veil. The suddenness of his reforms led to widespread outrage and he was forced to abdicate and flee the country in 1928. Exactly fifty years later the communist government made the same mistake; their rule, and their architecture too, was even more disastrous. It was not a place to rush things.

The mosque was at a junction. The road beyond, running between the hills towards Deh Mazang, had a decrepit air and I was instinctively reluctant to follow it. Above the road was a hillside of ruined houses linked by narrow paths which children ran along like mountain goats. To the south the bustle of people dropped off as the desolation grew. For the moment I felt it was too dangerous to explore alone. I was especially sad because across the river on a nearby slope was the shrine of one of Afghanistan's most memorable rulers, Zahiruddīn Mohammed, later known as Bābūr the Tiger.

Bābūr is special. In a sense he is the last truly original ruler of Afghanistan, although it was not Afghanistan in Bābūr's time, but a wild patchwork of kingdoms linking east and west which Bābūr sought to unify. He was born in 1483 in central Asian Ferghana, the region of the upper basin of the Syr Daria, or Jaxartes river, between Tashkent and Kashgar. He was descended from Tīmūr, the West's Tamberlaine, on his mother's side and from Chingiz Khan on his father's by five generations. His father had been a king in the valley of his homeland but at the age of twelve Bābūr was deprived of his inheritance by invading Turkic Uzbek tribes. A prince by birth and training, he set out to recapture the territories lost by his father, captured and held Samarqand briefly when he was nineteen years old, but in the end was beaten back by the notorious Shaybaq Khan, the Uzbek chieftain.

So Bābūr wandered, landless and ashamed of his poverty, taking refuge with his Tīmūrid relatives in the western Afghan city of Herat, where the converging streams of central Asian and Persian culture had fused in a brilliant and final efflorescence during the fifteenth century.

With horror and deep sadness he watched the bright Tīmūrid flame gutter and die as the Uzbeks took Herat in 1506. Bābūr was driven eastwards with a struggling band of loyal followers. Weary of living out of a tent and rustling sheep to survive, he was driven east, and took Kabul, his most enduring prize, at the age of twenty-two. For the next thirty years he tried hard to regain his cherished Ferghana without success. Then in later life he turned his attention south to India, which he invaded to become the first of the Moghul emperors. India was transformed. At its height, the dynasty he founded ruled from Kabul to Calcutta, and among its descendants were the famous Akbar, Shah Jehān and Aurangzeb; Moghul rule survived until the English took control of the government in the nineteenth century.

We know about Bābūr from his memoirs, collectively called the *Bābūrnāmeh*. Written in Chagatay Turkish over a period of nearly forty years, they are a uniquely intimate portrait of the age. They are foremost a chronicle of his campaigns, both successful and unsuccessful, composed in a lucid and unpretentious language entirely free of the lushness of Persian prose of the period. He is a plain writer but for this his troubles and personal passions are all the more vivid. The descriptions of his early battles, when he was always outnumbered and on the run, are gripping. The later, matter-of-fact tone recounting his accomplishments as conqueror reveal a hard but not brutal ruler:

> If one goes into Hindustan the Jats and Gujars always pour down in countless hordes from hill and plain for loot in bullock and buffalo. These ill-omened people are just senseless oppressors. Formerly their doing did not concern us much because the country was an enemy's, but they began the same senseless work after we had taken it. When we reached Sialkot, they fell in tumult on poor and needy folks who were coming out of the town to our camp,

and stripped them bare. I had the silly thieves sought for, and ordered two or three of them cut to pieces.

The *Bābūrnāmeh* is also a catalogue of the personalities that surrounded its author. Through Bābūr, and especially his account of time spent at the court of the Tīmūrid Sultan Husain Baiqara in Herat, we know what they looked like, what they wore, what their hobbies were, the kinds of wine they liked to drink and even the jokes they made. The wealth of detail lends a human face to the empire-builder who weathered the upheavals of the era and opens a window onto the troubles and achievements of the age. Bābūr writes about politics, allegiances, his dealings with friends and enemies; he passes comment on the literature of the day, its poetry, music, architecture and the merits of different vintages.

Of all things natural he is a tireless and fastidious observer. There is an almost boyish enthusiasm to his observations. He records his fascination at seeing a rhinoceros for the first time, marvels at the configuration of leaves on fruit trees, and carefully compares the taste of pomegranates from different regions. On the hillsides around Kabul he counts thirty-three varieties of wild tulip, measures the distance frogs can jump, observes the migration patterns of birds, records the removal of a live mouse from the stomach of a snake killed during a picnic, and even details the characteristics of different types of firewood.

He devotes fifty pages to the flora and fauna of India and describes it as a place of natural wonders and fabulous wealth, but bemoans its lack of water and orchards, and overall judges it as a place 'of few charms':

Its people have no good looks; of social intercourse, paying and receiving visits there is none; of genius and capacity none; of manners none; in handicraft and work there is no form or symmetry, method or quality; there are no good horses, no good dogs, grapes, musk-melons or first-rate fruits, no ice or cold water, no good bread or cooked food in the bazaars, no hot baths, no colleges.

And between raising armies and quelling rebellions he draws on the models of high standards and love of civilization of his Tīmūrid ancestors and commissions gardens and parks at every turn, the planting of trees and the construction of wells, reservoirs and watercourses.

As a personality it is obvious Bābūr is deeply scornful of excess, meanness, vanity, rudeness of speech, narrowness of learning and incompetence. He cherishes loyalty, order and excellence in any activity from the catching of fish to miniature-painting. In statecraft he shows restraint, is often admiring of the bravery of his enemies and generous with pardons and the bestowal of gifts and favours. When his son Homayoun offers him the Koh-e Nūr diamond, the largest in the world, he hands it back.*

Bābūr's love of loyalty is born from the hardships of his early years as a wandering prince, and never lessens. In his winter crossing of the country he sleeps outside with his men rather than shelter in a cave. It pains him to describe an incidence of familial distrust. He has no patience for outright treachery. After a near-fatal poisoning attempt in India, he has his taster cut into pieces, the cook skinned alive, one of the women accomplices thrown under an elephant and the other shot with a matchlock.

There are only occasional moments of introspection. During his visit to Herat he praises the accomplishments of the Sultan's court but is disapproving of their love of wine, and when pressed by the notables of the city to drink wine at a party expresses a prudishness incongruous in the founder of a world empire:

> Though up till then I had not committed the sin of wine-drinking and known the cheering sensation of comfortable drunkenness, I was inclined to drink wine and my heart was drawn to cross that stream. I had no inclination for wine in my childhood, I knew nothing of its cheer and pleasure ... later on when, with the young

---

* The Persians looted it from the Moghuls; the Afghans stole it back; the British appropriated it in 1849, and three British queens have worn it in their crowns.

man's lusts and the prompting of sensual passion, desire for wine arose though there was no one to press it on me and no one aware of my leaning towards it; so that, inclined as my heart was, it was difficult for me to do such a thing, one hitherto undone.

Later in life Bābūr relinquishes wine, but without forgetting his own earlier hesitations, and pardons those in his own company who choose, contrary to royal custom, not to drink. The heady days of his early rule are filled with descriptions of wine parties and picnics, as well as the characters that enlivened them. There is detail enough in his memoirs for us to picture the young prince with his closest followers riding for a day's outing north of Kabul to the villages of the Shomāli plain. Sometimes they would go to Gulbāhār, at the mouth of the Panjshīr river, and take a trio of rafts downstream; occasionally the current would sweep them against the rocks and everyone would be thrown into the water. A favourite spot was the village of Istalif, a picturesque settlement nestling in the foothills at the edge of the plain, where they would set up camp in the orchards and watch the harvest being gathered in the fields below.

Their horses were left to graze; guards and scouts were posted, and a messenger sent to fetch wine from the household of a royal acquaintance. Meanwhile tents were swiftly erected among the trees, and carpets and cushions laid out beneath their billowing embroidered canopies. From here they would look down to the haze settling across the plain and watch the mountains deepen to the colour of purple as the sun began to sink, gilding the leaves of the fruit trees with luminous gold. Then fires would be lit and attendants return with freshly diced mutton brochettes. And then – wine! And calls of 'Let he who speaks like a Turk, drink a cup!' and 'Let he who speaks like a Persian, drink another!' and the evening would take flight like a dream on news of battles and tribes loyal and disloyal; of petitions granted and denied; of gifts of land or orchards or jewels or gowns to favoured men; of impromptu poems (these with chuckles of approbation and mock-reprovals) and mournful airs and the stirring *ghazāls* of Sufi poets composed to the music of slender-necked tambours inlaid with ivory and mother-of-pearl. And the wine would flow and flow, decanted from skins into gold and silver goblets, until even the crackling of holly-oak branches thrown into the flames failed to rouse those who hadn't the head for it, and whose heavy sleep would be broken only by the sound of the midnight drum.

Then comes the sudden news, delivered from a breathless scout, and a hush descends at the raised hand of the prince himself: a party of Afghans has been seen further along the valley. Quivers and bows are quickly readied and a team of soldiers sent forward, buckling their swords and leather chestplates as they run to the waiting horses before clattering into the night . . .

*

Bābūr's last act was to offer his own life for that of his son Homayoun, who was struck by fever at Agra. Accounts testify to his belief in the rite: a saint was summoned to recite the prayers, while Bābūr called on God for his life to be taken and his son's spared. Homayoun recovered the same day; Bābūr fell ill and died a few weeks later.

In his eventful lifetime he had known an enormous range of fortunes, from destitution to all the beauties and high living of Samarqand, Herat and, later, Delhi. But Kabul remained his greatest love. The inscription above his tomb reads:

> Only this mosque of beauty, this temple of nobility, constructed for the prayer of saints and the epiphany of cherubs, was fit to stand in so venerable a sanctuary as this highway of archangels, this theatre of heaven, this light-garden of the God-forgiven angel king whose rest is in the garden of heaven, Zahiruddin Mohammed Bābūr the Conqueror.*

I never saw it: the area was said to have been mined. I wandered back towards the house and found myself in the *kūche-ye murghā* – Chicken Street – a narrow, dusty avenue of stores dealing in antiques and curios, dear to the hearts of Western travellers from twenty years ago.

---

* I rely for this translation on the version recorded in Peter Levi's *The Light Garden of the Angel King*, Penguin, 1984.

I had visited it briefly at the end of communist rule, when for the first time in fifteen years outsiders were suddenly free to roam the city. I had bought a lapis necklace and a wolfskin hat as luxuriant as a guardsman's busby. Since then the street had suffered visibly from the effects of looting, stray gunfire and rockets, and many of the shops were shuttered and barred. One rocket had struck a high white wall and left an imprint of vapourized paint which had captured the shape of the explosion.

Here I recognized an old friend: it was Kayhān. I had met him at a more hopeful time, a day after the city's fall in 1992, and he had shown me with mischievous pride letters written to friends in America with the return address 'Islamic Republic of Afghanistan'. We had met by chance in an antique shop, where he was trying to get through to his wife on the telephone, but the line had been busy for an hour and he was exasperated.

'What does she talk about? How can anyone talk for an hour on the telephone? I mean, do you have this kind of problem?' Finally he had called a relative at the telephone exchange to disconnect the line. He spoke fluent English from university. Here in Kabul? I'd asked. No – Arizona, where his deepest regret had been failing to meet the height requirement for the football team.

But when I reminded him of our meeting the memory of it surfaced with only a wistful smile. He had aged visibly in the meantime and he seemed dazed by the grief of it all. I hardly recognized the jovial and articulate man I had met at that brief junction of promise when it seemed just possible that the country would be granted the gift of peace.

I asked after some others; they had gone to Pakistan, he said wearily, all gone. I declined an offer to return home with him, feeling sure we would meet again, and walked on.

Outside a stall a bearded man with a sad smile beckoned me inside. We sat and drank tea together as he brushed the dust off the forlorn collection of curios that made up the sum of his shop. He had an air of profound melancholy that I knew at once from former government soldiers. Men who under the Soviets had been forced to fight against their own people retained in their eyes a grief that betrayed suffering of a terrible magnitude. It was the same look that Vietnam veterans had nicknamed the 'thousand yard stare', and it was unmistakable.

He had been a soldier throughout the Soviet period, he said, and his duty was counting the dead on the battlefields. The years had taken a heavy toll. Under Soviet rule, he said, Afghan soldiers had been virtual prisoners, treated little better than dogs. He told me the story of his commanding officer, one of whose soldiers had defected to the mujaheddin. As punishment the officer was sent by his Soviet overseers to an area of heavy fighting; the Afghan guard who had allowed the man to escape was executed. I had heard similar accounts and didn't disbelieve him. But I was shocked when he said that over ten years he had counted, one by one, the bodies of twenty-eight thousand fellow soldiers.

✻

Life fell into a routine. In the early mornings, when it was warmer outside the house than in, we would sit on the verandah and soak up the sunshine like reptiles. Over glasses of tea we would listen for the sounds of the hour as if from them we might decode the events of the coming day; the weary call of an old man pushing a barrow of vegetables, the triple-toned blare of a truck horn, the ringing of old-fashioned bicycle bells, the roar of a distant military jet, and the shouts of children playing in the street just beyond the wall. Then, as the sky began to lighten under the crystalline gaze of the sun, the air would warm and plans were made for the day.

For the next few hours I would wander off to explore corners of the city which for years I had only heard or read about, following a mental jigsaw of names whose pieces I could at last, and with great delight, finally fit together. There was nothing to compare with this: every minute was a pleasure and a discovery. It was like walking through the landscape of a dream, finding it concrete and alive. I walked for miles those first days, taking the pulse of the streets on walks lasting hours. I had learned how to move unnoticed by others a long time ago and I soaked up the sights in my spare time for as long as the daylight would allow. Then at mealtimes like one of Pavlov's dogs I would head back to the house.

We ate simply but well. Jān cooked our dinners; by his own admission he was no cook, and laid out food with a sheepish grin and an apology before tucking in with us.

But lunch was worth walking for. Amān the Hazāra prepared our most delicious midday staples: *qābli pilau*, meat buried in mounds of rice cooked with raisins, almonds, pistachios and shredded carrot; *shorwā*, mutton soup; *mantū*, steamed meat-filled dumplings of Tibetan origin, and *samosas*, crescents of fried pastry stuffed with leeks and spice and served with a yoghurt and mint sauce.

What our diet lacked in variety it made up for by the attention given to its preparation. I had never seen food prepared with such meticulous care. Amān would arrive in the morning with a bag of supplies from the market and spend the next four hours preparing the meal. Occasionally he would labour an equal time over dinner. He chopped vegetables with the precision of a jeweller mending a watch, and rolled pastry with the delicacy of an archaeologist deciphering a Dead Sea scroll. He cooked not merely to fulfil the task but with the whole of himself and with great humility, claiming nothing for his efforts in word or thought. He would serve us these culinary treasures with a hesitant smile, wait silently and alone in the kitchen for us to finish, then prepare a pot of tea with which to end the meal. Then he would slip quietly from the house until it was time to repeat the process early the next morning.

A few times I would watch him at work in the kitchen. He was shy at first and couldn't decide whether to ignore me or not, but we made friends quickly after I expressed an interest in Afghan dishes. His face would light up like a child's as he spoke of how, were I to visit his home in Bamiyan where his brothers and father still lived, we would slaughter a sheep and hold a great feast. Then I would know Afghan cooking, he said … But when he came out of the kitchen and was among the others he spoke in a near whisper and padded between the rooms with an almost furtive motion.

Jān was more talkative. The jovial Panjshīri lived with his wife and children in one of the hardest-hit parts of town, on the slopes of the Azāmai hill. His family home in Panjshīr had been destroyed by Soviet bombing. We talked about the time Kabul had nearly been overrun the year before by Uzbek fighters under the northern warlord Dostum, and he pointed out the various bullet holes in the rooms the way other people point out family photographs. At the height of the fighting he had lived in the basement and hadn't eaten for five days.

We talked about the situation in Kabul. 'It's very difficult,' he said, shaking his head. 'Who gets killed when they fire rockets? Women and kids, mostly. It doesn't hurt the government. What if a rocket hit my house? That would be *kolān moshkel!*' Really difficult! But he would say this with a grin that would lessen its gravity, the same way the light seemed to lessen the terribleness of the conflict.

Compared to the majority of the city we had an easy life. The obvious inconveniences of waiting a hour for a bucket of water to boil over a feeble paraffin stove, or reading by candlelight, seemed forgotten; we knew that elsewhere in the city people lacked even these basic necessities. In the absence of a reliable telephone system, meetings had to be arranged in person. Visitors came on foot and by car at unexpected moments, and brought a natural spontaneity to every encounter.

It was a quality that extended even to meetings with government officials. There was a changing population of visiting correspondents in the city, and together we called on officials in a pack: the journalists overlooked the traditional rivalry between their different agencies, and pooled their resources in a manner uncharacteristic of their colleagues elsewhere.

The first of these visits was to the Ministry of Foreign Affairs, to get identity cards. To my delight I was mistaken for an Afghan and passed over at first. Other favoured ports of call during the day were at the homes of a small number of officials who spoke fluent English and who gave us news of recent fighting, negotiations, and upcoming visits from foreign diplomats. The majority were young men our own age on whose shoulders fell the task of representing their government to the world beyond. We would meet regularly with Amrullah for news of developments in the war; with a fiery and strikingly handsome young diplomat called Hāroun, recently returned from California to work under Massoud, and Dr Abdullah, Massoud's closest adviser, a widely travelled man impeccable in both dress and speech who during the war had given up his medical studies in America to fight the Soviets.

We did not believe these men were saints but their openness and hospitality nurtured an inevitable sympathy. Their willingness to tend to the trifling requests of foreign visitors, while the security of their capital hung by a thread, was impressive. Pressures on the government grew daily greater from the state of siege; prices were rising steadily, fuel was scarce, and all the while the winter tightened its grip on the city.

Under such circumstances we were granted extraordinary liberties. We were entirely free to travel in areas under government control, and beyond it if we chose. There were no obvious rules. We were exempt from curfew and from the traditional prohibition of alcohol in our homes, and were granted meetings at short notice and with unfailing courtesy.

To each of these encounters the conflict added a dimension of intimacy. Visitors found themselves in a city stripped of social pretence. This was as true for relations between foreigners and their Afghan friends as it was between foreigners themselves, where I fancied the effect was more noticeable. The expatriate world was small; there were perhaps fifty outsiders in Kabul and the atmosphere between individuals and their organizations was uncommonly warm.

The most visible foreign presence was the International Committee of the Red Cross, whose offices were in a nearby street of the new city. From this miniature enclave of Swiss industry, the huge task of lightening the burdens of war for the population was organized with tireless efficiency. The duties of the Red Cross, I had only recently discovered, went far beyond the emergency treatment of the wounded. A small nucleus of foreign staff, assisted by several hundred local employees around the country, co-ordinated a huge range of medical and supporting activities.

In and around the main cities they ran mobile clinics, first-aid posts and orthopaedic centres for the victims of mines, distributed water, food and desperately needed supplies to thousands of displaced families, forwarded messages between prisoners of war and their loved ones, and sent representatives to the leaders of the warring factions to promote the rules of war. The Red Cross offices also served as a message and information centre for visiting officials and journalists. And in keeping with its reputation for fearless humanitarianism, its headquarters stood firmly in the heart of the conflict. This was a bold contrast to the policy of the United Nations, whose operations in Afghanistan were run — absurdly, its opponents maintained — from Pakistan.

I went to meet the Red Cross's director, Peter Stocker, who had kindly allowed me to join a relief flight to Kabul. I stepped one afternoon from a dusty street into a compound filled with gleaming white jeeps emblazoned with red crosses. In tended flower-beds the last rose petals of the season were falling in splashes of white and crimson. A generator purred in a shed; in the offices there were flickering computer screens and two-way radios crackling with the urgent dispatches of the day. I asked an Afghan secretary if I could send a message to my family and she led me to the radio room in the basement of the building. The radio operator, a former Afghan pilot who had trained in America, offered me tea. We sat as if in a cockpit, surrounded by blinking consoles, and he fed my letter into the fax machine with such care it might have been a sheet of gold leaf.

We shook hands as it went through and I marvelled at the technologies that made its passage possible. The greater one's isolation the more miraculous they seem. It was impossible not to experience a sense of wonder at the thought of a handwritten message bouncing off a satellite in the freezing depths of space and, without a hint of its trials en route, onwards into a cosy home ten thousand miles away.

I went upstairs and was shown into the director's office. Peter Stocker had the build and gravitas of an opera singer and his face, broad and tanned and suggestive of an authoritative melancholy reminded me of a bloodhound's. His eyes were dark and alert. He wore a colourful silk kerchief around his neck and on a hook behind his desk there hung an expensive dark green trilby and cashmere overcoat. I thought of Orson Welles in *The Third Man*.

I told him where I was staying and he asked after Tim. I said I thought Tim was a man who had reached his limit and needed a rest.

'Ah,' he replied solemnly, as if I had hit on a notion of key importance. Then he lit a cigarette, and a coil of smoke spiralled upwards before his face. 'If a man does not reach his limit,' he pronounced, a flicker of enquiry surfacing into his eyes as if released from a great depth, 'how can he discover the way to go beyond it?'

I warmed to him at once. I had half-expected to hear lists of statistics which I wouldn't understand, not a man who delivered truths in the manner of an oracle. He asked me what kind of book I was planning to write and I explained that it would depend very much on events themselves. Here too I was prepared for the usual puzzled looks, but he was immediately sympathetic and said he thought it a excellent plan.

'It's time somebody did,' he said. With characteristic magnanimity he added that, if I needed a place on a Red Cross flight elsewhere in the country he would be happy to oblige. We agreed to have dinner later in the week. I left both charmed and impressed by the man whose admirers nicknamed him the 'Pope of Kabul', who dressed like an eighteenth-century European nobleman and offered his help unconditionally to scruffy-looking visitors.

*

This spirit of openness and generosity seemed entirely in keeping with things. It was partly the infectious goodwill of Afghans in general: foreigners felt vulnerable and isolated, but were brought out of themselves by the friendliness of their hosts. And partly, I supposed, there was a natural reaching-out between souls caught in the net of the war. I was reminded of studies revealing that the incidence of mental disease in a society drops during wartime to a tiny proportion of its peacetime figure.

The lie of the land, psychologically speaking, was measured against two inescapable reference points: that the city might at any moment be overrun, and that no one was exempt from truant rockets. There wasn't a day when they didn't strike, harpoon-like, somewhere in the city. The tight weft of traditional Afghan society meant that there was always someone we knew who, in turn, had known one or more of the victims, and each loss touched us with an almost personal intensity.

The experience of dodging rockets became an accepted, if terrifying, part of daily life. Everyone had close calls, and our private brushes with mortality were hardly ever mentioned. But they were never forgotten.

Often I would be walking along one of the broad streets of the new city, exchanging smiles with passers-by or fending off a little crowd of children, who knew my route and would ambush me gaily with cries for small change, when the muffled thump of incoming rockets would pounce from the hills.

At that instant a sort of internal spotlight was triggered and I found my thoughts caught rabbit-like in its beam. It was strange; the world took on a dream-like quality, and I could detect a variety of interior voices at work, each clamouring for a different vote. The first was an instinctive fear: an instantaneous urge to find a ditch, doorway or tree wide enough to shelter behind. Then, looking around, half expecting to see my own impulse to hide mirrored in other people, I would feel a stab of shame. Not a soul had given in to the urge to run, much less hide. Men and women continued to walk at an unchanging pace, greeting friends or chatting as if they had heard nothing. Seeing this it became almost impossible to do otherwise.

Out of these contradictory urges a third would surface, this one the voice of intellect, striving in the minuscule time allowed to find some compromise between the others, like a lasso thrown at the last minute across a widening fault-line. It went something like this: 'If you stand here and a rocket lands nearby you will be killed. But you are too proud to run to shelter. At the same time you are not as proud as these Afghans. What about turning into an east–west street where at least the risk will be less? You have four seconds left...' Fear, pride, calculation; and all this in a few seconds of terrible suspense: it was unreal.

Then came the crunch of explosions. Sometimes they were far off, sometimes nearer; once, in the centre of the city, as I paused in a doorway under the pretext of retying my shoelace with slightly trembling fingers, a plume of smoke and debris hurtled upwards from a stricken building thirty yards away. A few men fell off their bicycles, brushed themselves down and went on again. But they never cowered.

I was astonished at how quickly the wave of life would close over again after death had been meted out in public places. Within minutes the ordinary bustle of affairs would return to normal. People sank back into their business the way wet sand sinks back into a hole in a beach. All that was different was a crater somewhere, and a life or two extinguished.

In the flood of relief that followed these encounters I would wonder just what made it possible for these people to meet their fate so squarely. I couldn't help thinking of the rehabilitation centres that had been set up in America the year before for civilian victims of the bombing of the Federal Building in Oklahoma City. Not for the injured themselves, but for those who had been traumatized by the sight of the ruined building after the event.

I was not the only one to ask: what sustained these people? And I went through the usual lists: was it a collective spirit of defiance written so deeply into the culture that no room was left for ordinary fear? Was it the fatalism of a people who believed all things were written from Above, and who were willing to accept their own extinction in accordance with His will? Was it merely the indifference of the war-weary? Or was it the economics of sheer poverty that drove people back into the streets, the relentless pressure of having to strive ceaselessly in order to survive, to earn, to feed their children?

It may have been all or none, but it was impossible not to be infected by it. One morning, as I sat writing on the verandah of the house, an explosion shook the ground with such violence that we knew at once a heavy-calibre shell had struck nearby. I piled into the car with Tim and Craig and we found the site a few minutes later, in an ordinarily quiet street a few blocks behind the house.

In the middle of the road a dozen men were standing over a crater ten feet across. Fragments of glass and thick chunks of asphalt were scattered all around. There were stalls on either side, their windows blasted inwards. Someone had sprinkled a handful of dust over a patch of blood. From the wall behind me I pulled a twisted sliver of thick shrapnel. We heard two children had been killed, another injured. Tim drove to the hospital with the others, and I walked back to the house.

Instinctively I hugged the kerb on the southern side of the road, longing to dissolve into the shadow of the wall at my side, nursing a confusion of feelings. Then up ahead, a hundred yards away, I saw a man waving.

It was the young fighter who stood guard at the house opposite. Rifle over his shoulder, he was gesturing furiously at me. I stopped, puzzled. Then I saw his white teeth beaming from a broad smile, and realized: he was imploring me to step out from the shadows and walk in the road, back straight and shoulders squared...

Later, emboldened by his show of defiance, I left the protection of the garden and sat on the upstairs balcony to write my diary in the sunshine. He saw me from the street, lifted his upturned hands to the sun in a celebratory gesture, then to me, and to the sky above us, and gave me a double thumbs up, as if to say: 'That's it, you've got it now!'

*

The nights were long and growing colder. In the evenings we took advantage of our relative freedom to visit the homes of colleagues, usually following rumours of whisky. Huddled around stoves or open fires we would spend hours speculating on the military situation with all the authority of field-marshals.

'Massoud has to open a second front in the west.'

'He hasn't got the men for it – unless Dostum agrees to join the fight.'

'If the Tālebs take Kabul they'll be in Mazar a week later.'

'They can take Kabul but they'll never get Panjshīr...'

We would swap stories, the more irreverent the better, about recent events. Tim was adept at the art and that evening told us his latest. An ace pilot from the rival territory of the north had been sent on a mission to destroy a government construction project in the mountains, near the border with Tajikistan. Spying from his cockpit some recently excavated ground, a bulldozer and lines of men at work, he swooped down to deliver several direct hits. Back at base he recounted the successful strike, received a hero's welcome, and was put up for a medal – until the next day, when the apoplectic ambassador of Tajikistan telephoned to find out why an Afghan jet had bombed a civilian roadbuilding team.

Then there was the incredible but just possible tale of Massoud and one of his commanders, who had recently been to inspect the southern front lines by jeep. Somehow they had taken a wrong turn, lost the route, and driven unarmed into the heart of a Tālebān stronghold.

Massoud, instantly recognized and facing almost certain death, demanded confidently to see their leader. So baffled were his hosts at the sudden appearance of their arch-enemy, they obliged, and a cordial exchange was reported between the rival leaders. Their meeting was just long enough not to offend custom, but short enough to prevent the Tālebān from realizing that Massoud's appearance in their midst was nothing more than a one-in-a-million mistake.

Someone else mentioned the recent visit of the American Secretary of State, who was so ill-informed about events she had turned to him to ask the names of the different Afghan parties. Another mentioned his trip to Qandahar, the Tālebān's headquarters in the south. He had gone to make a documentary, but since cameras had been banned the only thing he was allowed to film was a blank patch of wall. And did anyone remember that Italian photographer seen in Kabul a few years back? He had gone on a training seminar for journalists about personal safety in war zones, and been killed when he fell out of his instructor's jeep. There was no need to invent improbable stories: just the day before, a colleague had tried to light a fire in the grate there in the house, discovering after several tries that the chimney was blocked by a cache of live grenades ...

It was an unexpectedly social time; on different evenings we clutched glasses around a fire at the house of the BBC correspondent, and shared cocktails with a duo of pukka-voiced English soldiers working for a de-mining outfit. (They called cars 'vehicles', and bombs 'ordnance'.) I told one of them, a former Guards officer, about my plans to write about Afghanistan.

'Fascinating,' he said. 'But *why?*'

We managed an all-night poker session with American colleagues at the United Nations, warmed bottles of the Turkish ambassador's claret in front of his electric heater, and were plied with tropical-tasting cocktails at a rowdy gathering of expatriate staff hosted by French doctors, where wreaths of cannabis-laden smoke coiled in layers around the assembly until the small hours.

All this was unforeseen and a source of delight, but I felt myself softening mentally under its influence. I was beginning to feel pulled from my own plans and weakened by luxuries whose sudden absence would only make the next stages harder to manage. Walking back one night through the silent streets, utterly still in the freezing clasp of the moonlight, I felt a longing to break free of the familiar and head as soon as possible into the countryside. It was time to trade in some pleasures, and to plan a route.

*

There was really only one way out: north. I spread out my maps in my room. The ordinary road was blocked at the famous Salang Tunnel by Dostum's troops. The alternative lay through the mountains, following the far more ancient route along the Panjshīr, Monjān and Kochkā valleys. Alexander had been this way, as had Marco Polo, Tīmūr, Bābur, and the ill-fated convoys of the Red Army. Historically at least, I would be in interesting company.

Somehow I would have to get to Panjshīr, which began fifty miles north of Kabul, then continue on foot all the way to the northernmost town of Faizābād. Then I could cut to the west and reach Mazar-i Sharīf, the regional capital near the border of Uzbekistan. This would involve crossing a front line; Mazar was in rival hands, and somewhere in the tangle of mountains the government's forces were locked in a standoff with the Uzbek 'wolves'. But how did you cross a front line? Ask permission? Wander across? Would I need some kind of *laissez passer?* Nobody I asked seemed to know more than I did, which was not much.

No two maps agreed on the place names along the route. On

Afghan maps I found names that didn't appear on my own. And on my own maps — extravagant topographic maps marked DESTROY AFTER USE — appeared names of which no Afghan had ever heard.

I had no guide as yet. There were no hotels or hostels to stay in along the way. No one would speak English. It would be cold and the passes were high. Then there was the war, and the utter lack of civil law ... factors perfect for a spirited expedition. In need of advice, I was directed to pay a visit to a man called Commander Moslem.

I found him buying vegetables at a stall in a nearby street. He was wearing flip-flops and a US army jacket over his *shalwar*, carried a crackling walkie-talkie, and greeted me with the usual Afghan bear-hug of an embrace. He was a stocky man with a big round face which broke into such a wholesome smile you would never guess he had spent most of his adult life killing Russian soldiers. Now in his early forties, he was one of Massoud's few surviving senior commanders and had lived through ten years of almost daily fighting in his home territory of the Panjshīr.

Panjshīr — it had become an almost legendary place for its resistance during the Soviet occupation. In accounts of the war written by Soviet soldiers its name rings today with the same grim emphasis as do Tet and Da Nang in American minds. In the 1980s the Soviets launched ten major offensives into the valley, involving thousands of troops and hundreds of tanks and armoured vehicles; these were the most extensive and bloody engagements fought by the Red Army since the Second World War. Commander Moslem's speciality during those years was said to have been planting anti-tank mines to divide the enemy convoys into sections small enough to attack with lightly armed teams of mujaheddin. Over the years these original fighting teams, led by men who had known Afghanistan as adults before the war, had been cruelly reduced. Now only a handful of the old warriors survived, and the present fighting was for the most part left to younger men.

He showed us into his house, shooing children into various rooms, and listened attentively to my plans. A four year-old child brought us glasses of mango juice. We talked about different routes and the time it would take to get to the north as far as Faizābād — ten days, he reckoned. He said he would ask around for a local guide, request letters of introduction to be written on my behalf, and he reassured me that things would work out; it was the perfect time of year for travel there, he said. I left him feeling touched that this unsung warrior who dealt daily in matters of life and death was able to step back from the harsh demands of his world, and occupy himself with the trivial requests of an ignorant foreign visitor.

A candidate arrived the following morning; he was a small, wiry Tajik about forty years old who spoke no English. By chance his face reminded me of a boy who had bullied me in school, and looking at this kindly Afghan I could think only of Geoffrey Cox, a six-year-old tyrant I had lived in fear of nearly twenty-five years before. He stood nervously to attention as I tried to make light of things.

'So, you want to go to Faizābād?'

'Yes, sāhib,' he said, looking far too serious.

'Get out of the city a bit.'

'Yes, sāhib.' His enthusiasm was unconvincing.

'Well then – what do we do about this thing?' I hauled out my rucksack. It was almost as big as him and as heavy as a fridge. He looked at it for a moment, then levered it heroically onto his back.

'Khūb ast, it's fine,' he said. But this was what Afghans always said when things were particularly bad. I tried to picture him on the Anjoman Pass at fifteen thousand feet.

'You don't think it's too heavy?'

He patted his spindly legs and tried to convince me it was nothing for him. I had the feeling he would rather die under it than admit it was too much, which it so obviously was.

Then there was the business of money. I disliked this part. What was a fair price to offer a grown man willing to drag himself, under the weight of an unbeliever's useless possessions, across two hundred miles of one of the world's most forbidding landscapes?

If I offered too much he would have no respect for me for the length of the trip, and consider me a fool. If I offered too little he would be insulted; I would lose him and word would get around. And if I offered the right amount by local standards he would probably be disappointed after having his hopes raised by the promise of Western riches.

'So what would be a fair price?' I asked him.

'It is for you to say.'

'How much do you want per day?'

'It is your choice, *sāhib*.'

This was the wrong approach, and I knew it. But I was hoping with such blunt attempts to gauge the motivation of a man on whom my safety might depend. I had no idea what challenges the journey might throw up; I knew only that, if I had the slightest instinctive doubts about a potential guide, I would make the effort to find another. I named a price, knowing it was fair, but that it would disappoint him.

'That is too little, *sāhib*.'

Word had got round of my intended trip. There was another visitor the next day; a gentle but confident young man in his early twenties. We could take a bus to Panjshīr, he suggested, then walk the rest of the way. He was hoping for the equivalent of ten dollars a day. But my budget was horribly tight. What if we got held up and the trip took three weeks? That would mean nearly three hundred dollars. A civil servant earned twenty dollars a month. I said I would think about it.

I was tempted by this young man's cheerfulness, but discouraged by his age. I knew too that I hadn't the heart to make another human being haul my things over a mountain range in winter, no matter how willing or tough they might be. I would need a horse, and we couldn't put a horse on a bus all the way to Panjshīr.

I wanted to travel with an experienced man who would know how to deal with difficulties, and for whom money was not the heart of the matter. These men from the city seemed too gentle and too preoccupied with cost. How would they behave if we got lost, or were held up by bandits? I felt ungrateful as I turned them down as gently as possible and left the decision to instinct, which led me back to an original plan: to strike north alone and try to find a guide en route. It was the riskier option and I thought about it deeply that night. It called for a strange weighing-up of things and, in the end, a kind of trust in the spirit of the journey to which I had set myself to be true;

a submission to fate. *Tasleem*: submission. It was, it struck me then, a derivation of the word 'Islam'.

Later in the day, as I was passing the house where I had earlier met the young Amrullah, our liaison with the Ministry of Defence, I was waved inside and invited to lunch. We ate together, in traditional fashion, on the floor. Over mounds of pilau he asked how the plans for my trip to the north were going. I told him I was having some minor difficulties preparing things, not knowing what to prepare for.

'It makes me think of a line of poetry from Hafez,' I said, 'which might apply as much to your own struggle as to mine.' And I shamelessly quoted the couplet that I had memorized a long time before for use in just such a situation:

Though the way is full of perils, and the goal far out of sight
There is no road to which there is no end: do not despair.

He was silent for a few seconds, then over his face crept a gentle smile like a tide of recognition. The distance between us had been suddenly shortened, and his formal manner softened.

'You know,' he said, 'the saddest thing about this war is that we have lost the old way of travelling in Afghanistan. Before, a Hazāra could travel in a Pushtun area without any fear whatsoever. A Pushtun could travel in Panjshīr and be sure of real hospitality. It was the same with the Uzbeks, and the peoples in the north. Nowadays none of that is possible. The tension between these peoples is too great. But before the war there was none of this. There were tribal differences, ethnic differences, yes – but they were secondary. We were all Afghans, and that was the important thing. The war has changed all that.'

He found a map and we moved to the table to study it. We traced the route from Kabul as far as Faizābād. Then he took a piece of paper and wrote out the names of villages along the way, the travelling times between them, and the prices I could expect to pay for a guide. It was exactly the information I needed.

I would need to get to Khawak, he said, nearly halfway up the Panjshīr valley and a day's travel from Kabul. There was a horse market there and I could ask around for a guide. Then from Khawak, which marked the end of the motorable road, I would go to Kūrpetāb. From here, the following day, I would reach Shalzor, at the foot of the Anjoman pass. From the pass it would take another day to Wūshtī, then on to Eskāzar the next day, where the valley divided. One route led to Nuristan, another to China, another to Tajikistan. I would take the northern route the following day, through the region of the famous lapis mines, as far as Jurm, where the road began again. From there it would be easy to get to Baharak, and on to Faizābād. After Faizābād I would have to enter the territory of a rival government; he couldn't help me after that, he said. It would take about a week, perhaps ten days. He made it sound very straightforward.

The names wheeled like swallows in my imagination. I had so often wondered if I might ever really reach such places; now it seemed possible after all, even likely.

'I'm glad you're making this trip,' he said, folding up the map. 'You may get a taste of the real Afghanistan.'

I thanked him for all his advice, but his tone changed as I got up to leave.

'You should be careful in the north,' he added, explaining that Russian jets had recently bombed a number of settlements around Faizābād. Certain mujaheddin groups had allied themselves with the Tajiks across the border in Tajikistan, and were causing trouble for the ex-communists. When the Russians wanted to make their disapproval known they sent jets from Dushanbe, the Tajik capital across the border, to destroy some likely targets. I was not so much listening to his explanation as wondering just how one was supposed to 'be careful'.

'And there is one other thing,' he added.

'Yes?'

'We have heard rumours of some other foreigners in the area.'

'Oh good,' I said, 'perhaps I'll meet them.'

'We think they may have been——' He hesitated.

'English?'

'. . . kidnapped.'

'Ah.'

'But you should be all right.'
'Yes.'

*

After this things fell almost magically into place. I met another man from Panjshīr who gave me the name of a friend in his village; if I could get there, he said, I would get help with finding a guide. Later the same day I met a young Frenchman working for the medical group Médicins du Monde. One of their doctors was leaving for Panjshīr in a few days, and might be able to give me a lift. I hurried to the French mission; a truck was leaving in a day or two. The doctor in charge, who was called Guillaume, said he'd be delighted if I came along. He was very charming and invited me back for an *apéritif* at six.

The next morning, just as it seemed possible to slip away from the city, came the opportunity I had been hoping privately to avoid: a visit to the front lines in the west. I was curious about the fronts but not curious enough to flirt with the attendant risks. Yet to have baulked at the suggestion would have been to go against the spirit of things by which we were already governed.

It was another brilliant morning. Beyond the mountains, on whose upper rims a dusting of snow had fallen in the night, roamed a scattering of cotton-wool clouds. Kites danced in the sky as we headed to the west in a dilapidated Russian Volga.

I was with Craig and the Australian correspondent Tony Davies. Leaving the familiar grid of streets with which by day we had become familiar, our sense of safety began to dwindle. We joked nervously the whole way, stopping once to buy diesel sold in jerrycans at roadside stalls. The cost of diesel was so high, and the car so decrepit, we proposed buying a donkey instead. Hearing our laughter the driver guffawed with us, though we knew he couldn't have understood. He was nervous, as were we all, about the route ahead. A jeep full of heavily armed, intense-looking mujaheddin pulled up alongside, and we noticed a bullet hole through its windscreen, exactly in line with the driver's head.

The road to the west was lined on both sides with corrugated container units from trucks converted into tiny shops, which stretched for several forlorn miles. Crowds swarmed along the roadsides. We saw women walking in *burqas* the colour of mustard, light blue and violet. Behind the cracked rear window of a thirty-year-old Mercedes bus, I saw a painting of a European-looking five-year-old girl holding a kitten. The sides of the bus were lavishly painted with garlands of roses, a Mercedes logo, and along the top was written in big letters KING OF THE ROAD and TRUST IN GOD. Riveted into the bodywork were long tiered necklaces made from scrap metal in the fashion of nomad jewellery, which dangled musically as it drove past.

At a junction, where a traffic policeman stood with his hands in his pockets, we turned west, weaving through a sea of battered taxis and bicycles, along the road towards Paghmān, once a favourite royal playground and picnic spot. We crept along at about fifteen miles an hour. The traffic thinned out as the city fell behind us, and the crowds faded as our distance from the centre grew.

Soon we were surrounded by the ruined western suburbs, meeting only the occasional car coming from the opposite direction. Then there was no traffic; we passed a final checkpoint where the soldiers' faces were unsmiling, and were waved forward. My compass read 280°. Gradually the ruins fell behind us, and we saw the first villages nestling in the folds of the chocolate-coloured hills, their terraces dotted with bursts of autumn blossom.

The road was climbing now, on an embankment pitted unrelentingly with shell craters. Only a few traces remained of its original surface. On either side lay the burned-out carcasses of tanks and armoured vehicles. Two elderly men with white beards, turbans and sacks over their shoulders, walked along the verge in the opposite direction, oblivious to the passing car. We were the only vehicle on the only road and began to feel uncomfortably exposed. The driver asked one of us for a cigarette. The smile had gone from his face. In his anxiety he had speeded up and the tools in the boot began to clatter at every bump.

We pulled off the road by a ruined house, beyond which he refused to drive. He crouched, smoking, under the shadow of a broken wall, as we started walking up the rise. It was a straight dusty road still heading directly west, and after only a few paces we heard the first explosions — thumps and cracks of incoming artillery about six hundred yards away. The air had a vitreous purity. There were dug-in tanks strung along the hillside five hundred yards to our left, and a puff of smoke from a striken target was rising a thousand yards away.

Two hundred yards on, just before the crest of the ridge, we turned off the road towards a nearby tank and a cluster of about a dozen men, and heard another crack and the owl-like howl of a truant shell. Tony called it 'stay awake boys' fire. Awake we were.

Then we were walking over a carpet of spent tank shells towards the men, who welcomed us to their miserable position. There was no natural protection to the site, only a long mound a few feet high which the younger men stood up on to point out cheerfully that the Tālebān were just beyond the next ridge. Their only shelter was a tiny earthen bunker with a roof made from young willow trunks. The roof was three feet high and a single oil lantern hung from the ceiling. My heart went out to them. The youngest were about sixteen years old; they had never known peace.

There was another angry crunch, followed by the musical buzz of shrapnel. Its echo rolled through the mountains like the breath of an angry god. The others paid no attention. Their commander was dressed in heavy khaki, calling into a hand-held radio over and over again: *Palang shīr palang, mishenāwi?* Snow leopard, are you receiving?

I could hear my breathing getting shallow again.

'How are things out here?' I asked one of the men.

'*Injā khūb ast*, this is a good place,' replied one of the younger ones.

'*Arām ast?* Is it calm here?'

'*Arām ast, arām!*' They replied in unison, and chuckled as I flinched at the sound of a shell exploding across the valley. We shared cigarettes; they scrutinized the twirling wheels of my tape recorder, and suggested I take a few pictures of them posing on the tank.

There was yet another thump, and a plume of phosphorus smoke billowed upwards a few hundred yards away. I felt slightly sick. I wanted only to go back: we were completely exposed. The enemy's shells were falling all over the place, and we had not the slightest protection.

The boys gathered cheerfully around me.

'How much money do you make?' asked one of them. 'How much does your government pay you to be here?' There was a deep thump on a nearby hilltop.

'*Dūr ast*,' said one of the boys with a grin as I flinched – a long way off. '*Natars!*' Don't worry!

And at the instant the meaning of his words registered there was a deafening crack, and our bodies buckled as the shock rippled through us.

'*Awān ast!*' cried one of the boys. '*Awān!*'

At that moment I saw the Australian scrabbling towards the entrance of the bunker.

'What does *awān* mean?' I yelled.

'Incoming mortar.'

'Where?'

'Just behind you.'

'Well what the fuck are we doing here?'

'Being shelled, mate.'

This was only funny much later. A curtain of dust was drifting down the hillside from a spot about twenty feet away, just beyond the mound where I had been standing a few moments before.

We crept into the bunker. The boys joined us, looking as scared as us now. The older commanders squeezed inside, yelling into their radios between bursts of static.

Snow leopard, snow leopard, this is unit five, are you receiving?

There were a few more thumps on the slope above us and the sharper crack of half a dozen outgoing tank rounds. I wondered if the bunker could possibly withstand a direct hit and asked the tank commander to say a few words for the record. He was attached to the 80th mechanized division and had been in charge of the position for nine months, during which the enemy, he said, had failed to make any progress.

'. . . and we will defend our position,' he said with stiff bravado, 'our region, and Afghanistan, to the utmost.'

Nine months! I had been there half an hour, and wanted nothing more to do with it.

*

All day I was shaken by our brush at the front. I had lost an earlier taste for such things. My mind would go back later to the friendliness of the boys and men we had met that day and their life in that hellish spot. Such moments were a reminder of how insulated we were from the sharp end of the conflict. I felt ashamed of the frivolity with which we treated it from the relative safety of our home in the city, and a pang of guilt at the ease with which I could turn my back on it and leave.

I had been in Kabul for ten days. At the Red Cross I found a message waiting for me from home. It had arrived by fax: my sister had found new curtains to match her carpet. It was snowing and miserable in England. And what was I up to?

It was like a message from another planet.

*

There were some last-minute preparations. I bought a woollen *pattū*, and some *keshmesh*, a mixture of nuts and raisins, wrapped in the pages of an old Farsi–Russian dictionary. I heard two men mutter from nearby guessing at my identity: one thought I must be an Iranian; no, said the other, I looked like a Tajik. I smelled a faint wave of hashish as I passed a narrow alley. On the way back a child was guiding a dozen goats through the street by the house, followed by a man leading a cow by a frayed rope.

I repacked my bags, studied my maps, wrote a final batch of letters, and fell asleep.

It was dark when I heard the slamming of a car door in the street. A black Mercedes had pulled up outside the gate. An armed fighter stepped from the front of the car and stood guard, and from the back, Hāroun, the young diplomat we had met a few days before. Seeing me at the window he called up in faultless English and told me to open the door. He sounded anxious.

'Get Tim,' he said abruptly, as I let him in. 'We have to leave right away. The Tālebān have broken into the city and we have orders to evacuate all foreigners.'

So it had finally happened, I thought: it was for real after all.

'I'll get my things,' I said, and turned to go upstairs.

'Forget your things. There's no time. Just get Tim.'

We bundled into the back of the car, and tore through the streets at speed. Armed guards loomed up in the headlights, rifles levelled at our heads. Hāroun whispered a password at each checkpoint, his breath steaming in the icy air. I exchanged a few glances with Tim but we never spoke, pondering only this sudden twist in our fates and those of friends. I was wondering what would happen to the others, how much time we really had, and where they would send us. The car raced on.

Somewhere in the eastern suburbs we pulled up outside a modern villa. There was a cluster of cars and the place was teeming with armed, bearded mujaheddin. Hāroun ushered us inside into a house full of men, who greeted us with a flurry of handshakes amid broad smiles.

In the central room a long table was decked with platters of steaming food. I recognized a number of senior government officials. Men were helping themselves from rows of drinks, snacks, pastries and a selection of cooked meats, and wandering with their plates and glasses into the adjoining room to sit on couches and chat amicably together. In their midst a man was singing poetry to tunes plucked on an inlaid lyre.

Dumbfounded, I looked at Hāroun. The serious look on his face had gone, replaced with a mischievous smile. He put his arm over my shoulders and guided me towards the tables. It was not an evacuation that was under way but a party, at which we were the guests of honour.

'Welcome to Afghanistan,' he chuckled.

It was an expression I had heard somewhere before.

Three

Only a madman will tell you the whole truth about what
went on there.

Soviet 'Afghansty' veteran

'WELCOME TO AFGHANISTAN.' It was a little more than ten years before, in fact, on an August afternoon about a thousand feet above the border village of Terri Mangal – that I had first heard the greeting. It must have been nearly midday because I remember the sun was hanging like a polished blade above the back of our necks, and already we were sweating from the climb.

I had, for the first time, just crossed the frontier into Afghanistan. There were five of us in all. Tired from our ascent, we sat down among some boulders to rest and watch the spectacle of life flowing over the trail beside us.

The sights were new to me and the manner of their unfolding unfamiliar; yet things had changed so swiftly over the past few days it already seemed in keeping with the curious exigencies of the time that a turbaned man on horseback, automatic rifle dangling from one shoulder, should have emerged from the confusion of men and animals, to address me by the Afghan name I had agreed to travel under.

He was tall and lean and his wavy hair fell to his shoulders. His eyes gleamed like chestnuts and his teeth were pearl-white as he smiled, reached into an inside pocket of his jacket, and leaned down to hand me a letter.

He watched me as I unfolded it. I have it now in front of me, although I still remember it word for word. Beneath a printed green insignia of crossed sabres, it was written on an old typewriter in misspelled English and signed with a cursive scrawl. It shook in the breeze as I read:

Dear Elliot,

You are now on the way to Kabul. One mountain pass (not all high) is welcoming you.

Mujahiddin do not know English but they can understand if you say: *Aab* (water) *Nan* (food) *Man manda astam* (I am tired). Or you can show them this letter* which means What time I should wake up. They are very friendly. Sometimes they look at you and may laugh, but this does not mean at all that they laugh at you.

When ever you are tired and cannot walk then tell the Commander of the road. Sometimes they walk slowly, sometimes very fast. Of course it depends on the situation.

When you reach to Chakaray (Dost Mohammed HQ) you will meet the commander who will be totally responsible. Do not take photos of the ladies and sometimes even old people do not want to be a camera target.

The only advice is to rely *totally on God*. He is the real protector.

A special instruction has been give to the people taking you.

I wish all the best.

Massoud Khalili

I refolded the letter, tucked it into a pocket, and looked up at the horseman as a broad grin spread over his face.

'Welcome to Afghanistan,' he said in English. Then with one hand he drew the tail of his turban across his face just below his eyes and with the other pulled gently on the reins. The horse wheeled and he was gone.

It was a satisfying moment. Looking back, I confess to being slightly baffled at my own choice of destination. In a rucksack not much bigger than a handbag, I carried my entire possessions for the journey: notebooks, camera, film, socks, compass, water bottle, field dressing and a bag of sugar; no money, documents or medicines. Nor had I much idea where we would eventually end up. I had met my travelling companions that same morning; there was a price on our

---

* The Persian script is: ساعت چند از خواب بر بخیزم

heads; I spoke precisely half a dozen words of their language; and our only way out was the same as the way in: on foot and over what looked like a sea of mountains. But I was amply supplied with the enthusiasm of one who has breached the threshold of a dream and found it real.

I walked to the edge of the plateau and looked down over the plain that stretched from its base, across a sulky expanse of mud-coloured land sweltering beneath bands of summer haze. We had not climbed far that morning but already the heavy and humid air of the lower ground was forgotten. The light, too, had been purified by the height, and was capable of subtleties unseen in the no-man's-land below us. The sky was clear and lit a bright horizon in the direction of the route ahead, which disappeared into a ragged mountain world.

A hundred yards away on a rocky outcrop was the ruined border post where, a few years before, we would have had to pass customs. Over it was assembled a weird array of life. Refugees from the interior of the country were streaming like blood from a wound, the few possessions of their salvaged lives dangling from the backs of skeletal animals. In the opposite direction, trains of dozens of animals were being led to mujaheddin bases inside the country. Horses and donkeys strained under the weight of ammunition crates or sacks brimming with the ungainly shapes of anti-tank mines. Rocket-propelled grenades, piled and bound like firewood, teetered on the humps of sullen camels. There were armed men everywhere, old and young, all vigorous and never idle, straining at ropes and bridles and entreating their overburdened beasts to their feet with whips and cries and whistles, charging the air with the intensity of their purpose.

I feasted on these sights: we were surrounded by characters forgotten by time, conjured from a page of Scheherazade. Venerable, straight-backed old men with furrowed and noble faces strolled boldly past in turbans, curly-toed sandals and striped silk gowns, daggers and swords at their sides. Others carried long-barrelled *jezails* inlaid with elaborate lattices of mother-of-pearl. A wild man with long, tousled black hair sported a blunderbuss. Younger men wearing cloaks or tattered overcoats carried British Lee Enfield rifles, lovingly preserved from wars that had ended nearly a century before, their bullets gleaming like polished teeth from double bandoliers. A few men, my new guide among them, shouldered Russian Kalashnikov rifles which, having been captured in combat, were invested with almost talismanic status.

*

I guessed he was in his forties, although he was probably younger. His face was dark and already deeply lined, framed in a black beard and curly locks that fell to his shoulders. He was strikingly handsome. His eyes were lit with an intelligence transmitted easily into a physical deftness that was comforting to see in a man on whom my life might depend. He wore running shoes and, over his loosely fitting *shalwar*, a faded army jacket. I liked him at once, and christened him Blackbeard.

It was not so much a meeting as a wordless acknowledgement of our responsibilities; his to protect me and mine to obey him without question, and the whole thing solemnized with no more than a glance and a nod. But what a glance and what a nod! He was the complete stranger in whom I was to trust my life and I the foreigner for whom he had agreed to risk his. We were not and did not become friends and I never even thought to ask his real name, yet across these distances the orbit of our feelings fell into some unaccountable sympathy.

I watched him as he stripped and cleaned his rifle with gentle and precise movements and, noting my curiosity, replaced the detached pieces of the gun with exaggerated clarity of gesture. Then he checked the spare magazines in the webbing across his chest — six in all — folded the metal stock with a satisfying click and swung the weapon over his arm with a motion as familiar as a schoolboy shouldering a load of books. He signalled for me to wait, disappeared for a few minutes, and returned leading a thin horse loaded with sacks of ammunition and supplies.

'*Harakat*,' he said, let's move: and it began.

He never looked back at me. No half measures were allowed to dilute our pace. We walked at a forced march which Blackbeard led with the unwavering rhythm of a human metronome. I could keep up if I tried, but the effort had to be constant and when my attention slipped towards our surroundings the gap between us would quickly widen and I had to run to catch up, thinking again and again: this cannot last.

It was a short trip, by local standards, at only three days. But the days stretched from before dawn to after midnight and our efforts broken by periods of rest as brutally short as they were sweet, and between these extremes we followed a route I lived so vividly I've often thought I could retrace it today without a guide. I had no experience of such extremes: of physical pain I knew must stop eventually but which violated all sense of hope by continuing far, far past the point of what I took for the limits of my endurance, and on into that inner place of dislocation where the ordinary senses seem to have abandoned their habitual allegiance to the mind; of beauty that seemed to draw from beyond the threshold of time; of the newly conflicting emotions of sadness and fascination at my first glimpses of the effects of war.

Blackbeard led me without a word and from his silence I drew a certain strength which I had not yet made my own. Often I was afraid and looked to him for some wordless reassurance, and took his actions as the measure for my own. Half an hour's walk from the border we heard a deep and resonant grumble of artillery followed by a cackling of automatic gunfire. It was the first time I had heard the voice of the war, which until then had seemed a distant and unknowable force. I felt a deep spasm of fear and a momentary longing to be done with it and return as quickly as possible to the border. Blackbeard, too, was momentarily transfixed, but he turned to me and for the first time smiled broadly and my fear was eased, although not lifted. Looking back, it was a gentle introduction.

Then he was still, his gaze locked in the direction of the dying echo. He saw me watching him, and nodded towards the sound.

'*Jaji*,' he said solemnly, and knelt down in the track, drew a circle in the dust with the tip of his finger and a dot in its centre.

'*Shorāvi.*' He pointed to the dot. Then he pointed to the circle: '*Mujāheddīn.*'

It was the communist base at Jaji: they had been besieged for over a month. It seemed a good moment to try out the only proper sentence I knew in Persian.

'*Shorāvī pedar la'natt.*'

Blackbeard paused for a moment in disbelief, then burst into a smile. His solemn face lit up with delight and he wagged his finger at me with emphatic relish as he repeated the words.

'*Shorāvī pedar la'natt! Pedar la'natt!*' Curse the Russians!

This was, in three days of walking, the sum of our conversation.

We walked on, and within half an hour reached a village destroyed by an earlier battle that showed how close the war had been brought to the border. Everywhere there were ruined buildings, their doors and windows ripped from their frames, their mud walls peppered with bullet holes. Around them were scattered the hulks of half a dozen crippled tanks, their scorched metallic corpses listing at crazy angles where in their last moments they had veered into ditches or against the surrounding slopes. I had never seen such things; I was awestruck and intensely curious, but never allowed a moment to linger.

My feet paid quickly for the pace and a generous crop of blisters was soon begging for attention. They would burst untended and a new generation of bloodier and more tender ones form underneath. But the pace would never vary. The landscape was cruelly beautiful. It would be wrong to call it countryside; there was no softness for the eye to caress along the route, no fields studded with grazing livestock or shady coppices of tended farmland. Instead, stretching in every direction towards an unreachable horizon were vaulting ridges of purple rock fractured by infinite corrugations, their bases piled with boulders swept like dust by a primeval hand, their peaks flayed by the heavens.

We threaded through ravines hemmed in by cataracts of stone and across parched riverbeds where the track weaved like a lost braid searching for release from its stony exile. We were nursed by cool shadows where the path dropped into gullies carved from soft shale and tortured by the steepness of sun-bleached slopes. But we never stopped.

Only the numbing hypnosis of the rhythm of my footsteps and the knowledge that without Blackbeard I would be lost kept me going. Where there was human life in that landscape it was made sweeter by the harshness of its surroundings. When, sweating and exhausted after a long stretch of climbing, I glimpsed a village in the valley beyond, flanked by a patchwork of meticulously tended fields, I felt I had glimpsed a tiny corner of paradise.

We would enter villages of Arcadian charm on dusty paths beside low mud walls bordered by glittering streams. Lines of poplars whispered overhead and threw their mottled shade over the dust thrown up by our feet. Against this natural accord between the elements the destruction was more acute. There was not a single village where half or more of the houses had not been destroyed by bombing, their shattered mud walls strewn like grain from broken sacks into the fields and their timbers twisted and snapped like the masts of ruined ships.

Our pace was barely changed by night, punctured only by sharp moments of moonlit terror when at some, to me inaudible, sound of alarm, Blackbeard would drop to the ground with cat-like agility, cock his rifle in the same lightning motion and scream a deafening shout of challenge into the darkness. These moments of suspense always passed but left their mark. For a few hours we rested in a tiny alpine clearing where mujaheddin, wrapped mummy-like in their *pattūs*,* slept beside their animals around a stone hut. I remember from a delirium of fatigue collapsing against a rocky mound that turned out to be a sleeping camel, and an old man bringing me tea and pressing fragments of bread from his hand into mine with a muttered blessing.

Blackbeard woke me before dawn and we were off in the freezing air without a word. I was hobbling visibly now and he had lost the status of warrior I had earlier assigned him and become a callous peasant, heartless and obsessed. Around midday we followed a steep and narrow trail downwards into a valley filled with fields the colour of polished malachite and kissed with the pink and white blossoms of fruit orchards. After the barrenness of the route we had covered, it was an oasis of colour. At its head a cluster of mud-brick buildings

---

*   The ubiquitous and indispensable item of Afghan attire: a cloak, blanket, towel, turban, picnic-mat, prayer-carpet, carrier-bag, dust-mask and camou-flage covering all in one.

grew organically from the soil, clinging to the base of an immense slope.

It was the most beautiful place I had ever seen. We stopped and joined a dozen other men sitting cross-legged and drinking tea from blue and green enamelled teapots and with the sunshine and the heavenly sweetness of the tea I collapsed against a wall and woke to see Blackbeard undoing my boots without a word. I was too exhausted to protest. He wrapped a bandage around each bloody foot, retied the boots and lifted me, smiling for the second time now, onto the horse and I felt deeply ashamed for the hastiness of my judgement.

As night fell the temperature dropped like a stone and I breathed into my jacket in a hopeless attempt to stay warm. The moon rose as we trudged forward, filling the clouds above us with light. I still remember their shapes; in the extremes of fatigue they seemed by turns both benevolent and evil, parading silently, hour after hour, in luminous processions overhead. The track was a white snake retreating into a lair of darkness ahead, and the night returned us nothing. There was not even a pinprick of light in the distance on which to fix our hopes.

In that state it seemed all life beyond our own had ceased, and our own had shrunk to the significance of a cryptic dream. I slept as I walked, stumbling, too exhausted even to cry in the paralysing cold. On the edge of collapse I remember hands imploring me to go on a little further until, with a relief too delicious to describe, I found myself being guided into a tiny hut. When I woke up the next day Blackbeard was gone and I never saw him again.

*

I was among strangers. The first person I saw when I opened my eyes was a boy of about fifteen wearing a red sequinned hat and a brown woollen waistcoat. He was peering at me with an expression of tender concern; in one hand he had a steaming kettle, and he held out a glass of tea in the other. It was a few minutes before I could make much sense of the new surroundings. Huge spiders gave the ceiling a mottled look; dazed, I watched them, wondering if they were the type that fell when they smelled blood. A dozen rifles were hanging from sticks in cracks between the stones of the wall, the floor was covered with overlapping canvas sheets, and the hut itself was built of black stone.

As I sipped my tea alone, mentally adjusting to the setting, a face appeared at the door. I remember it well enough although I saw it for only a few moments. It was narrow and dark, surrounded by a sweeping flow of black curly hair; the eyes were big and strangely luminous, the nose sharp like a rocky crag.

A choked voice mumbled at me in words I couldn't follow. Then for an instant the side of the face from which it came was caught in the morning sunlight from beyond the doorway and I saw it was wet with tears. The man was deranged with grief. Then I caught a word, and understood: *shaheed*. It meant, literally, 'witness' – the word used to describe someone killed in battle.

Sobbing, he was led away by the others, who sat with him on the ground outside, where I saw new horses and men, their faces tense and grave. I felt suddenly excluded from the intimacy of the crisis and was wondering what had happened when a young man, clearly not Afghan, approached the hut from the track below. He sat down on the canvas outside the door and had begun hurriedly unpacking a small nylon rucksack when he saw me watching him.

'Speak English?' He sounded American, and there was panic in his voice.

'Yes. What's going on?'

'They attacked the post at Chakaray last night.'

I wondered where Chakaray was; and who 'they' were. He was rummaging through his bag as he spoke, without looking at me.

'I was with them. Osman was up front and I was right behind him. There was an explosion and I didn't know *what* had happened. Something landed next to me. I thought it was Osman's boot, so I picked it up.' He looked up at me, his eyes suddenly full of anguish.

'It was his leg, man, his whole leg. His *leg*.'

He nodded towards the base of the track where, several hundred yards away, I could make out a small group of men and animals.

'He's down there,' he gestured, 'and he's dead.'

The world began to swim.

'I'm Bill, by the way.' We shook hands hurriedly. A bundle of cards, printed with the profiles and names of Russian military jets, fell to the ground as he reached up. He gathered them up in a flurry. I was about to speak but he had already fastened his bag and swung it over his shoulder before the words reached my lips. Then he was hurrying down the track, calling back to me as the distance between us grew.

'The headquarters is a few hours down the valley. They shot down a helicopter a few days ago. Qādeer speaks English. You'll see.'

His voice faded.

'Where are you going now?' I shouted after him.

'I'm getting the *fuckouttahere* . . .' He waved, without looking back.

In the opposite direction a man was labouring up the track towards the hut. He stopped beside me, caught his breath, smiled, and introduced himself in English. His name was Qādeer. He was a stocky, handsome Afghan in his early forties with short, jet-black hair and a neatly trimmed beard. His voice had a soft and weary melody, and his dark eyes looked out from a world of enormous melancholy. He carried an automatic rifle over his shoulder and, in his arms, what looked like a bundle of clothes.

'You are welcome here,' he said gently. 'Sadly — you have heard — one of our mujaheddin became *shaheed* last night. You know this word?'

I nodded. He studied me with friendly intensity, then without menace said: 'Others have come to visit our country. They make many promises to us. But when they leave, they forget us.' He let the words settle before lightening his tone, and we talked for a few minutes. Feeling doubly inadequate as a stranger at a time of grief and sensitive to this scarcely veiled admonition to outsiders, I asked if there was any way I could help. He smiled and then, as if he had forgotten it, looked at the bundle in his hands.

'Well, there is one thing, if you want.'

'Then tell me.'

'Only if you *want*.' A grave smile flickered in his eyes as he emphasized the word, then receded as he looked down again.

'This is the *pattū* that belonged to our *shaheed*. It has his blood on it.' He held out the bundle and measured my reaction at the sight. I recoiled inwardly at a cluster of dark spots on the brown wool.

'You could wash it, in the stream,' he said, and held it out towards me, then withdrew it slightly.

'But only if you *want*,' he repeated.

By taking it I knew I was accepting more than the task itself. It was a timely initiation: I was eager to prove myself to Qādeer and happy for the test. Yet I had no measure against which to fix the experience that followed; it struck, like a clean and unexpected wound, more deeply than I could have predicted.

I walked to the head of the stream and lowered the bundle into the water. Thinking I would wash out a few tiny stains, I had not noticed that its hidden folds were drenched with the dead man's blood. As I pushed it beneath the surface the fugitive colour was suddenly released, and swirled over my hands and wrists in curling crimson spirals until their whiteness was obscured. The world seemed to fall away like a leaf severed from a tree, and for a moment I was paralysed by the sight. Only the darkened water, which seemed suddenly to contain the essence of all grief, existed. I heard a cry go up inside me, not for the dead man alone, but for all those who had died in all wars.

The stream ran red, lapped over my boots, and sped downwards along the ravine. I rinsed the *pattū* until the water was clear again, then laid it out over some nearby rocks to dry.

*

Qādeer had poured two glasses of tea and I sat down beside him in silence.

'You can keep the *pattū*, if you want,' he said, and studied me again with that grave look of affection.

We talked. He told me he had taught English at Kabul University before the Soviets arrived, when he was arrested and taken to the city's notorious Pol-i Charkhi prison. In the presence of Soviet advisers he was beaten and tortured with electric shocks, 'down there,' he nodded towards his groin, and forced to swear allegiance to the communist party. After several months of further humiliations, he was released, and soon afterwards joined the mujaheddin.

'After what happened it was not a difficult decision,' he said, and considered himself fortunate to have been freed at all; many of his other friends were never released.

The dead man, he explained, was being taken to his village for the funeral. Qādeer would go with the others and return in three days: in the meantime I was to rest and stay close to the hut.

Half a dozen men came and went according to a logic I hadn't the means to question. They greeted me warmly, accepted the limits of my language without fuss, and left me in peace to explore the perimeter of my new territory.

At mealtimes a *pattū* was spread on the ground outside. We ate cross-legged from a single platter, and dipped into the mound of rice with our hands. I soon learned the knack of scooping it into neat handfuls and transferring it to my mouth with a thumb. After we ate, the boy who had first brought me tea would pour warm water over our hands from the kettle and pat them dry with a cloth. As night fell a fire was lit outside around which we sat for long hours; I in silence, watching the shadows play on the sunburned faces beside me, longing to understand the tales being told by the men whose eyes were fixed upon the flames.

By day the grip of time began to loosen. My blisters were healing and the trials of the journey with Blackbeard were displaced by the simple delights of ample food and shelter. Looking back I realize how little the men with whom I shared life knew of my world and I of theirs but the distance between them seemed hardly relevant: I was happy and at peace and gave hardly a thought to the future.

At the very head of the ravine was a cliff and a narrow waterfall which plunged into a shallow basin where we washed. Nearby was a track which I scrambled up to a ledge and a small cave where a heavy-calibre machine gun nestled on a tripod. From the ridge above it the hut was virtually invisible. There were bare mountains in every direction, yet even in this remote spot I came across a dozen unexploded bombs. They were scattered on the slopes and there was even one lying in the stream; I could see the black Cyrillic characters printed on its barrel-like sides. There were fat, thousand-pound bombs; long, thin bombs that resembled torpedoes; bombs that contained other bombs, and smaller bombs the size of cucumbers, painted blue with silver propellers on their tips. I was astonished at their numbers. I had seen others like them on the way, lying in fields or beside the track or stuck in the ground like so many milestones. What proportion had failed to do their designated work of destruction? For every unexploded bomb, how many had actually exploded? One out of a hundred? Fifty? Ten? Still and seemingly inert, these sinister gifts from above were irresistible to me. I gathered up half a dozen of the smaller ones and laid them out to photograph; a folly I shudder at today.

In the mornings the youngest of the men swept out the hut; I helped and, with nothing better to do, got carried away. I shook out the bedding of old army sleeping bags and dusted the tarantula-sized spiders from the ceiling. At the far end of the room was a wooden chest: it was full of papers, old clothes, some cartons of cigarettes and, most bizarrely of all, a copy of Lawrence's *Seven Pillars of Wisdom*.

In another corner there was an untidy pile of cardboard boxes. I lifted the canvas cover and looked inside the uppermost box: it was full of yellowish packets the size of bricks, each wrapped in waterproof paper. I undid one and sniffed at the marzipan-like substance inside. Did they know what this was? I asked two of the men, who had come to peer into the box.

'Butter,' said one of them, 'for cooking.'

It was plastic explosive, enough to blow up a small mountain. Beneath the box, to my horror, was a container the size of a cigarette case. I opened it gently. Inside were twelve detonators. These extremely sensitive sticks of high explosive had been stored, against the most elementary rules of safety, alongside the main charges. There were several men outside; I summoned them into the hut, took out one of the detonators, and tried to impress upon them, with a variety of exaggerated gestures, just how dangerous the devices were. One of the men stepped forward, took the detonator from my hand, opened his mouth, and pretended to bite down on it. The others roared with laughter.

We were sleeping, it turned out, in a tiny armoury. There were reels of detonating cord, blasting caps, time pencils for delayed explosions and what looked like switches for setting booby-traps. Another box was filled with grenades, and another with ammunition.

Yet another, which I wished I had never discovered, was filled with medicines.

Inside it was a strange assortment of pills, ointments and tonics, some of them for animal use and none with useful instructions. Most distressing of all was the sight of several plastic bottles of sterile plasma solution, unopened packets of needles, bandages and painkillers – exactly the supplies that might have saved the life of the wounded man. I felt rocked by despair and pity for the others; they were fighting a war but lacked the most rudimentary military or medical knowledge.

Later in the afternoon one of them came to me complaining of pain in his stomach and head. He motioned in turn to the box of medicines and his mouth, pursing his fingers like a beggar signalling hunger. There seemed no harm in giving him a spoonful of vitamin tonic, which I dispensed with all the gravity appropriate to the role. Word travelled fast and soon a line of men had gathered outside the hut, waving with pained expressions over their stomachs and heads. I gave them aspirins and capfuls of tonic, and they giggled like schoolboys as they left the hut in turn.

I was my own most conspicuous failure as a patient. Whatever bug I had acquired in Peshawar was still at large, and had caused my stomach to swell up like a medicine ball. At night I could hardly sleep and for hours I would sit outside in the moonlight, clutching my abdomen by the edge of the stream, while beside me a skeletal horse whinnied in its sleep.

*

Qādeer returned as promised three days later and led me with a handful of others to the headquarters in the village of Chakaray, three hours' walk away. The track wound gradually downward and emerged on a mountain-ringed escarpment which crumbled on one side into a broad ravine. We rested at its edge and Qādeer, wiping the sweat from his forehead, asked why I had been walking so fast. I told him I was only following the pace that Blackbeard had set on my earlier route.

'He must have been a crazy man,' said Qādeer, and I was comforted to hear this from an Afghan. We skirted downwards into the ravine, following a glittering stream lined with tall poplars at the edge of a large cornfield, then snaked upwards towards a hundred-foot-high wall of eroded stone. I looked up and saw houses rising vertically from its edge. Tottering on top of one another they seemed to grow out of the rock. It was late afternoon; the sky was the colour of lapis and the stone the colour of red gold.

The slope was studded with acacia trees, and the headquarters carved from the stone beneath the village itself. The main cave was fifty feet across and the ceiling equally high; behind it there was a further cave, slightly smaller, which was used as a storage area. Here, from a long wooden pole, hung a line draped with automatic rifles and two grenade launchers. Several more caves perforated the cliffs, served by narrow and branching trails that linked the village above and the valley floor below, where the stream snaked beyond the poplars. It was a beautiful setting, and for now it was home.

I settled in quickly with a changing population of about fifty men, who accepted the presence of an outsider with friendly curiosity. The days were charted by the small but meaningful pleasures of the moment. I was allowed to wander freely from the cave but not to go above to the village and risk being recognized as a foreigner. I thought of the captured Frenchman I had heard about languishing in prison in Kabul, and was never tempted.

At the base of the slope, along a path shaded by high walls of wild cannabis, there was an orchard of apricot, apple and walnut trees. I had the habit of wandering there and writing my diary by the stream. The place had a timeless quality, where man and nature had entered into an untroubled exchange of gifts. The trees had never known the indignity of pesticides or fertilizers and were tended by a single ancient farmer, who trimmed the orchard's borders with a primitive scythe and nursed the flow of water through tiny irrigation channels with imperturbable devotion.

With Qādeer's approval a young fighter called Mohammed Omar took me on nearby forays, carrying the heaviest machine gun he could manage each time we left the cave and making a great show of putting on a double bandolier studded with bullets. The village had been heavily bombed the year before. We made a tour one day of the ruined buildings, among them the local school, and others whose significance

I didn't catch. At the village mill, a tiny structure atop a diverted section of the river a mile upstream from the headquarters, we were greeted by a pair of elderly men dusted from head to toe with flour. One of them would pour the grain into a kind of hopper; the flour would sprinkle out from between two prehistoric millstones along a hand-hewn wooden channel, and at its end the other man guided it into waiting sacks.

We went to inspect the wreckage of a helicopter that had been shot down on the plain beyond the village. Wild camels grazed amid metallic debris scattered over half a mile. A helicopter was the greatest of mujaheddin trophies; of all the enemy's weapons it was the most unpredictable and the most feared. Helicopter gunships could land troops on a high ridge, swoop onto an exposed convoy or devastate a village with rockets. They could hover at the mouth of an otherwise inaccessible valley, picking off targets at will, and pour half-inch-calibre bullets into mujaheddin hiding places. Teams of half a dozen gunships were used to close in on their prey in a noose-like formation: Soviet pilots called it 'the circle of death'. Their slowness, prehistoric hugeness and bulbous perspex windows lent them the look of demonic dragonflies, and the faintest throb of rotors set the men in the camp on edge. We saw them sometimes in the distance. Even far away they evoked a feeling of terror, and the hair goes up on the back of my neck at the sound of a helicopter even today.

I ambled through the fragments, while Omar looked on with a scornful air at the debris of the fallen idol, all useful remains of which had been picked clean by human scavengers. Nothing substantial was left but the cabin door with its red star, and the central motor, from which spread four vast and crippled rotor blades. I photographed what remained of an instrument panel, and nearby found a severed, blackened hand, its fingers clenched over the palm. Omar gave a shout, and poked the tip of his rifle into something on the ground: it was the long, tangled black hair of a woman's scalp.

I told Qādeer about it afterwards. He said it was not uncommon for the officers in a military post to have women brought to them from Kabul for their 'entertainment'. The mention was visibly troubling to him.

I admired Qādeer enormously, and was secretly comforted by his protective and frequently didactic manner. At times the difference in our ages seemed a catalyst rather than an obstacle to our friendship. In his face was all the beauty, in his voice all the mischief, and in his eyes all the sadness of the country. Once he asked me how old I was; with all the oversensitivity of the age, I asked him what it could matter.

'You are afraid to tell me?'

'I am just a child,' I said, 'and no matter what my age I would hope to remain one.' Embarrassed by my own pomposity I turned and went out of the cave, but looked back as I heard him call my name. He was beaming.

'Why? You mean so that we could love, and laugh, like children too?'

'Yes, Qādeer-*jān*, that's exactly what I meant.' And so it was.

✻

Another foray took us to the nearby headquarters of a different mujaheddin group, where the local commander gave us tea. His men were preparing an operation against a nearby military post. One man caught my eye and invited me to watch as he linked charges of explosives with detonating cord and packed them gently into his rucksack. As he trotted away he gave me a wave and a mischievous parting glance, and I felt sorry not to be leaving with him. A man was going to wage war as cheerfully as other men went shopping, and seeing him leave, my feelings swelled with an unexpected yearning to draw closer to the conflict.

The war was still a distant and unknowable presence. There was little on a normal day to remind us that our sylvan hideaway and its surroundings belonged to a corner of a country at war. My own experience of it was limited to what I could see and hear, and it broke into our world in three ways.

The first was the sound of aircraft, to which our ears were unnaturally sensitive. Knowing that our fates might depend on what we could decode from the sounds of their engines brought enormous meaning to the act of listening. If a man was seen to stop what he was doing and cock his head skyward it was impossible not to do the same; we were on a perpetual and instinctive alert for such tell-tale gestures of alarm. However distant the sound, a few moments' scrutiny of pitch and intensity would tell us whether it was approaching or not. There was no front line in our area; we considered ourselves as likely a target as anywhere else. We could not help but fear the worst — although the worst, in fact, was never knowing; a fear that is known, quantified by the intellect, can be grappled with. It was the uncertainty of what might happen within the next few minutes that was hard to bear; sometimes, like the crew of a submarine waiting for the blast of a depth charge, the whole camp would freeze in suspense, all eyes searching the sky. In unguarded moments I could see the strain this pendulum of fear and relief caused among the others, and felt deeply for them.

I often glimpsed jets in the distance, flying in pairs on their lethal missions, and wondered, with a childlike sense of awe that has long since passed, just what went on inside the pilots' minds as the roar of their engines echoed through the mountains like a mechanical cry of war. I felt somehow that if I could only understand the pilots and their thinking, my fractured vision of the conflict would be made complete. This curiosity was only made more acute by the impossibility of its satisfaction. It was as persistent as it was naive, but whenever I saw those tiny flecks of silver, racing like sharks through the clear sky, as terrifying as they were beautiful, I was filled with a longing I could not explain to myself.

A more immediate reminder was the presence of the local military post, a fortified collection of mud-walled structures enclosed by high walls and minefields about two miles from the village. It was posts like these that occupied most mujaheddin groups, and provided a local focus to a given region's conflict. Small groups lacked the means both in resolve and *matériel* to mount more broadly co-ordinated operations over larger areas; that came later in the war. Often a local commander's sense of waging war would be satisfied by an occasional attack against the local post. It was in just such a recent attack that the villager whose *pattū* I wore had lost his life, after which, demoralized and short of ammunition, the mujaheddin had called off the operation.

Many posts changed hands several times over the course of the war.

The majority were manned by Afghan soldiers conscripted under the communists; they were miserably treated and lived like prisoners within the walls of their garrisons. In an old Soviet tradition, at least one member of the secret police figured among them. They terrorized the local populations, gathered intelligence on resistance activities and were resupplied by armoured convoys or helicopter.

Every day the post fired its artillery into the surrounding countryside, altering the range and direction of its guns with disturbing unpredictability. Here too I was amazed at the subtleties which our ears were able to distinguish from the most tenuous of clues. Even in conversation we never failed to hear the muffled bang of outgoing shells, and strained over the long seconds to calculate their likely trajectory.

I soon learned their telltale sounds as intimately as the other men. Fired away from us, we heard nothing after the thump of the outgoing shells until the faraway crunch of their explosions. If the target was nearer, there would be a rustling in the air like wind in the leaves of a high tree, and the explosions would shake the ground. Nearer still, and for about two seconds we would hear an owl-like whistling, growing at the last instant to an ugly whine. With a terrifying crash they would land within fifty yards. There was a final gradation: when a shell landed so close it gave virtually no warning at all. At most, there was a metallic scream a second or two before impact: hearing it we lay down and thought of nothing. Once, as I was dozing in the orchard by the stream, a pair of shells landed so close the apples were shaken from the trees. At nineteen the shadow of mortality passes quickly, and I was thrilled, not worried, to have survived. There was nothing to compare, after the feeling of having been dissolved by the shock wave of an explosion, to rediscovering one's original quotient of limbs, in place again and in working order.

The third reminder of the war was the sight and sound of explosions in the mountains that ringed Kabul, thirty miles away to our northwest. By day their outlines were barely visible through the summer haze, and after dark the horizon was black. But the nights were spectacular. From batteries around the city, rockets and artillery poured into their slopes, and every few seconds a burst of orange, yellow or incandescent white flame would give sudden shape to the profiles of the outlying ranges. I would watch from the mouth of the cave, waiting for the hypnotic sight of a sustained salvo of fire, when the explosions came so hard on one another that for several seconds the sky itself seemed to burn, and the silhouettes of the mountains rose through the night like an anguished hand reaching upwards through a flame. A few seconds later, a thunderous roll would sweep through the mountains towards us like the cry of a preternatural beast, prowling restlessly through the darkness.

There was in its scale alone a grandeur and beauty to the spectacle. I was never really able to believe that men were responsible for the sight; it was more like watching a far-off electrical storm. That its beauty was not only deadly but deliberately carried out by others filled me with powerful and opposing feelings. On the one hand there was comfort in our distance from the destruction. Yet I never failed to be captivated by the sight.

I felt the war was conspiring to remain beyond my reach, and the distance grew unbearable. I was too innocent to know any better. I knew only that the flashes on the horizon were endowed with an almost supernatural allure; the flames were the enchanted glances from the eyes of a cosmic temptress, and the grumble of artillery, her sighs. Heavy with anticipation, and draped in the seductive shroud of the night, they grew more irresistible at each moment.

I took this youthful malady to Qādeer, and asked him when I would be able to join the others on one of their operations. He fixed me with his sad eyes.

'War *is* dangerous, you know,' he said gently, and reminded me of the shelling in the orchard. He would ask the commander, he said, for permission on my behalf: the men were just then planning a mission to capture enemy deserters from a nearby military post.

My heart leaped. Deserters! Perhaps they would bring with them the maps of the minefield, and we would be able to launch a further surprise attack on the post. At last my longing had received the promise of an answer. And two days later, as night fell, men I had never seen before came streaming into the cave, sat in a wide circle on the floor, took the magazines from their rifles and began to fill them, bullet by bullet, from a mound of ammunition in their centre.

We left as the moon rose, dropped from the escarpment along a stony track and followed the valley floor alongside the river. Soon it dwindled to a trickle in a broad bed of gravel and boulders, lit a ghostly white as the moonlight tumbled from the surrounding hills. There were fifteen of us in all, and one man led a donkey – our ambulance, I assumed, to transport any wounded. There was not so much as a sticking plaster at the caves, much less the friendly and ubiquitous medics associated with modern military campaigns.

We were forbidden to smoke and talked in whispers. In the riverbed our feet crunched against stone; on soft ground there was nothing but the metallic rustle of swaying guns. For an hour we walked in a loose file and were crossing a patch of open ground in a wide gully bordered on one side by a small grove of trees when we heard the double thump of outgoing shells.

Frozen in mid-pace, we listened. The first shell screamed earthward and exploded before there was time to react. Our silent moonscape burst into orange flame, scattering the men in every direction. Engraved for an instant against the incandescence of the flash I saw their crazed shapes, black against the orange, and in their midst, the pathetic silhouette of the donkey. A second shell was on its way. I dived to the ground, but it seemed to take for ever. I was moving as fast as I could but I had fallen into the kind of dream where you try to run or scream but nothing happens. Time had stretched into a broad embrace through which I seemed to be idly wandering: I could only think how silly the whole thing was. Then the second blast swept over us. The ground bounced like the skin of a drum. And then – silence again. The world returned. We got up, brushed ourselves off and regrouped. To my astonishment, from all around I heard muffled fits of giggles.

We walked on through forest, open fields and the eerie ruins of a deserted village. I was worried now: was it a coincidence that the shells had fallen so close to us? Did the post have motion sensors on its perimeter? Perhaps one of the men had secretly passed on our position.

Of all the times and places to fire; why had we been so close? The possibility of a traitor could not be ruled out. Was the post equipped with infra-red vision systems? We would have been easy enough to spot...

I had twisted my ankle painfully in an irrigation stream and was beginning to feel the cold. I was hungry too. I heard the faint whistling of a shell and crouched involuntarily. Incredibly, the two young fighters behind me were convulsed in giggles: one of them had whistled the sound of the imaginary shell for a joke. I swore at him volubly in English, but my incomprehensible whispers only doubled his amusement.

We had walked for several hours when in the early hours of the morning we stopped at the edge of a cornfield. The donkey, refusing to sit, was wrestled noisily to the ground by three men. There was a ripple of hushed exchanges, and two scouts were dispatched into a dark line of trees ahead of us. This must be the place, I reasoned, where the deserters had agreed to meet them. The insistence on silence meant we must be close to a military post. I wondered how many deserters there would be and how quickly their superiors would discover their escape. Perhaps they would come after them. How long would we wait for them to show themselves? Then a dark possibility began to loom: what if they had been forced under torture to reveal their plans? What if the whole thing was a ruse, a trick to surround an isolated group of lightly armed mujaheddin? There was no way of knowing...

I slapped at mosquitoes. A fighter signalled to me not to move. I told him rudely in English what I thought; he grinned uncomprehendingly and his teeth flared in the moonlight. The others checked their weapons and all but two went forward into the patch of forest ahead.

My mind was overflowing with cheerless thoughts. There was no natural cover and our position was utterly indefensible. I wondered: if we were overrun and I managed to escape, would I be able to find my way back to our headquarters? No – I would be captured at gunpoint by some thirteen-year-old conscript and interrogated by the secret police. It would be months, if ever, before my family heard news of me. In prison they would torture me as they had Qādeer until I told them about the mujaheddin. Far away I could see the war grumbling beyond the hills above Kabul, its deadly corona erupting in bursts above the peaks. Then, more than ever, I felt impossibly far from home.

Half an hour passed. The suspense was too much to bear, and I crawled through the flattened corn to one of the remaining men, who lay with his rifle like a sharpshooter, staring into the blackness of the trees. Our moonlit exchange, conducted half in sign language, half in words whispered in a language I didn't understand, had a quality of the surreal. I wanted to ask him where the deserting soldiers would be coming from, and whether ours was the best defensive position; whether, if there was a problem, we would stay there, and if not, where the hell we *would* go – but the best I could manage was: 'Enemy – him – where?' I cupped my hands enquiringly towards the moon.

'*Unjā, unjā,*' he whispered, with a furious nodding towards the trees, where nothing stirred.

'Where?'

'*Unjā, unjā.*'

He smiled and nodded repeatedly as if by doing so he would lift my confusion. But the blackness ahead was ominously still. It was an orchard, and peering forward I could just make out the faint gleam of countless apples, hanging like Christmas decorations from the branches of the trees.

I knew then that I lacked the qualities necessary for guerrilla warfare. I wanted to go home. My hands and neck were ravaged by mosquito bites. So what if we captured a few deserters? So what, in fact, if the communists stayed in Kabul for ever? Was it really worth risking our lives for?

There was movement; the men were returning. There had been no shooting – that meant the deserters had escaped successfully. A dozen shapes loomed out of the trees and hurried towards us. But there were no shaven-headed conscripts. Instead, the returning men gathered around the donkey and began scrabbling through their clothes as if plagued by fleas. I could not quite see what they were doing, and crept closer, until I realized they were filling a huge pair of saddlebags with – yes, I was sure of it now – apples. As soon as their pockets were empty they disappeared into the orchard in a second wave, returning with their pockets stuffed with fruit. The saddlebags were so big and so full that the donkey had to be forced to its feet, tottering pitifully as it was led from the field. A happy fighter handed me an apple.

So this was war.

We trudged back, our mouths full of the apples, which were delicious and softened my sense of despair. The men chattered quietly as they munched. Our return took a different route, and we found ourselves wading in water up to our knees through a ditch like a canal. It was lined with trees. The leaves whispered in the breeze, and the moonlight danced over us in luminous beams to the music of the water rippling gently around our legs. I was trying to make sense of the whole deserter story. Surely the theft of the apples was no fortuitous distraction. Qādeer must have known all along. Why the charade? And if he had known, why had he told me—

Without the slightest warning, the night exploded. Volleys of bullets ripped through the trees above our heads as the air was split apart by the clatter of automatic gunfire. Red and white tracer spat into the undergrowth. The men fled in every direction, shouting madly to one another, hauling themselves through the water and up the muddy banks to return the fire.

I ran forward, fighting the water, kicking my legs out sideways to avoid its drag. Again time played its cruel trick of retardation; it pressed like a tangible weight, thickening horribly at each instant. I saw myself as if from above, running wildly through the water, hearing the heaving of my own breath as I struggled forward, the thump of my heartbeat, watching myself all the while from a place a few yards ahead, where the world was curiously quiet, like a film with the sound turned down.

There was a bend in the channel and I scrambled up the slope and slithered onto the flat ground. Gunfire spewed from every direction. I could hear the high-pitched cackle of automatic rifles and the chugging of heavy machine guns. Lines of red tracer streaked all around, there were strange flashes and whines and explosions as bullets exploded against rock, and I was hypnotized. It did not seem real at all, and I wandered through the hail of bullets as if in a dream.

Then two loud cracks that left my ears ringing prompted the sudden thought that I had been shot. I felt my legs buckle under me and my body hit the ground with unexpected force. Yet it was painless and my only feeling was one of intense curiosity. Something was wriggling underneath me, and I wondered whether it was my own legs kicking in the throes of death, until the face of a man I recognized appeared by my knees, glistening with sweat in the moonlight.

He had tackled me, rugby-style, and dragged me into cover, where my senses caught up with the world and I realized he had probably saved my life. Suddenly the spell was broken, and I cowered behind a line of boulders, cursing my stupidity, pressed hard up against a bundle of three other men, one of whom I could feel trembling next to me. These poor men, I thought, were even more terrified than me.

I turned to look at their faces: they were convulsed in laughter.

As suddenly as it had started, the firing stopped. No one was hurt. The donkey, mute and still, stood where we had abandoned it in the middle of the canal, surrounded by a flotilla of gently bobbing apples. After the apples had been recaptured we trudged back, reaching the headquarters four hours later just as the purple shroud of the dawn was drawn back and a great sheet of golden light began to unroll over the surrounding peaks.

I stumbled towards the cave. Qādeer emerged with an anxious look hidden by a smile as he caught sight of me. We embraced and he stood back like a father greeting a son returning home from his first day at school.

'So, how was it? You look a little – *tired.*'

I could barely stand and I wanted to cry.

'Yes, Qādeer-*jan*,' I said, 'I am tired. And the operation...'

What could I tell him? I had walked all night, I had nearly been killed, I was furious. Now that the dangers had passed, all the contradictory emotions suppressed in the act of survival were returning with unexpected force, swelling into a single, overwhelming tidal wave of feeling. I had never experienced such extremes: it was all too much.

'I didn't see any enemy deserters, but we did manage to capture several hundred apples,' I told him.

'Well, we have to *eat*, you know.' He put a consoling hand on my shoulder. 'I can see you are disappointed, but don't worry. Next time you will go on a proper operation.'

'You mean we will risk our lives again to capture more apples?'

'No, no, a *proper* operation.' But there was mischief in his eyes. 'Pumpkins!'

*

In the afternoon the valley filled with the menacing throb of a helicopter. For half an hour the giant machine circled in a mile-wide arc, hovering sometimes, a thousand feet above us. There was endless and nervous speculation.

Three puffs of white smoke appeared at the edge of the plain to our south, and another on a ridge beyond a cluster of houses on the outskirts of the village. Then, as we heard the sound of approaching jets, we understood. The helicopter had dropped smoke beacons for the pilots, whose aircraft flashed into the sky from nowhere, the engines so loud they shook the ground. The noise was indescribable. I tried to photograph them as they attacked. My fingers trembled at the controls of my camera as I tried to follow their shapes, certain that the pilots had seen me.

Two MiG fighter-bombers screamed over us, dived, swooped and leaped vertically upwards above the ridges, scattering clusters of magnesium flares that trailed from their bellies like comets. They banked and swooped again, glinting, deadly, silver, in long, roaring dives out of the west, pulled up suddenly in tandem, and then dived again, beyond the village, as a thunderous explosion rolled over and through us and we saw the first bombs detonate. Then they were gone and all that was left was the ringing in our ears and two widening stains of brown earth against the sky, hundreds of feet high.

It was punishment for the theft of the apples, some said. No, it was an effort to destroy secret mujaheddin bases in the area, said others. It was a random attack, according to another. We would never know for sure. The attack was typical of so much of what I witnessed; unexpected, purposeless and terrifying. It had significance but made no sense, a tiny fragment chipped from the mosaic of the war, the more of which I saw, the less I understood.

*

It was what you might expect from life in a cave. Our routine defined a narrow and uncomplicated world whose limits it seldom occurred to me to question. I lived an instinctive and sensual kind of existence that was satisfied by the fulfilment of simple concerns of shelter and food and rest. With the innocent selfishness of the time I vaguely assumed the whole of Afghanistan lived much as we did.

This experience of the war imposed a simplistic polarity on the world; there was life in our little headquarters and there was, beyond it, only the enemy, unknowable and sinister. I knew little of the complexities of the society outside our immediate territory – that there were regions entirely untouched by the conflict and others in an almost constant state of war; that in the cities a government and its administration were attempting to function; that there were cars and buses and schools and cinemas.

From the cave the idea of a civilian population striving to adhere to an ordinary way of life seemed too incredibly distant a thing to dwell on. I knew nothing of the lives of the men with whom I shared life, of their pasts, of their homes or families. I admired them: for their hardiness, their friendliness, and tenacity against the odds. But at the time they were merely characters who fitted the design of my adventure. Only much later did I wonder about them as human beings, when they appeared like stowaways in my dreams, long after I had abandoned them for the safety of home.

I did sense the incompleteness of this vision of things when visitors arrived and delivered their news to the others in animated tales; of battles and of journeys and all manner of trials I couldn't grasp, wishing more than anything that I spoke the language. I experienced a similar pang of isolation when, wandering near the cave, I discovered an abandoned house set among the trees on the slope beneath its entrance. I went in through an unlatched gate in a mud-brick wall and walked across dusty floors. A withered calendar, two years out of date, hung forlornly from a nail. Beneath a bare shelf I found some children's exercise books, full of the tentative but determined script of a young hand. I felt like a trespasser in the broken world of someone else's grief. The empty rooms, which had once contained all the passion and endeavour of family life, were suddenly and cruelly silent.

I was disturbed by the folly that propelled men on both sides of an artificial line to engage so wholeheartedly in killing one another and believing in the rightness of their actions; these were the privileged feelings of a non-combatant. I hadn't had my village bombed; or seen my best friend plough into the dust beside me as a guerrilla's bullet drilled through his head.

'To kill or not to kill? That's a post-war question,' wrote a Soviet veteran. 'The Afghans weren't people to us, and vice versa.' Life as a Soviet conscript must have been a deeply painful and traumatic affair. It often struck me at the time that a war was under way not only between two nations and cultures but between two ages, and the manner of their suffering correspondingly different.

The suffering of the general Afghan populace sprang from concrete sources in all the obvious ways that a war falls on a people. The resulting burden of grief was shared by an entire nation and firmly underpinned by a vigorous cultural and religious sense of identity; in such a way, ordinary Afghans were far less vulnerable to the spiritual crisis which increasingly afflicted their enemy.

The Soviet soldier, apart from the obvious horrors of warfare, suffered terrible privations. The use of drugs was widespread; disease rampant, and the most basic provisions frequently lacking. But the greatest problem was the mental affliction resulting from being forced to fight against an elusive and apparently fanatical enemy, in a war that made less and less sense. There was intense camaraderie between experienced soldiers, who took pride in carrying out orders but shared a loathing for the officers who gave them and for the political machinery that had forced war upon them. They would return home, not to build their homes anew, but to a society which, knowing so little of the conflict from which its soldiers had returned, was reluctant to recognize them as heroes, or even as soldiers who had fought in a 'real' war.

*

Our group was joined by a young Norwegian, an officer in the reserve army, who like me was making his first clandestine visit on Afghan soil. His name was Pål Refsdal. He spoke fluent English, was twenty-one and seemed very old to me. He was appalled by the lack of military discipline among the mujaheddin and accused me of being far too diplomatic towards them; I chastised him daily for his intolerance, and we became good friends. Occasionally we would tire of each other's company and sit at opposite ends of the orchard writing up our diaries like an old couple after a quarrel. From the day of his arrival we shared endless jokes about our plight and that of our hosts, and the value of a joke in English had never seemed greater.

There was one time of day I remember more vividly than all others. This was the moment just after sunset, as the day surrendered to the dusk and the final traces of golden drapery were lifted from the highest ridges. At this serene signal a young fighter would climb to a stone ledge above the cave, and with his hands cupped to his lips recite the call to evening prayers in a high and sonorous chant. The long drawn-out syllables, taking flight across the final breath of the day, seemed sculpted for their purpose. Then, magically, like the bearers of an invisible flame, his cries would ignite a second and third distant call somewhere further along the cliffs, until the entire valley seemed lit by a chain of antiphonal beacons of faith.

> *Allāhū Akbār, Allāhū Akbār, Allāhū Akbār, Allāhū Akbār,*
> *Ash'hadū an lā īllāha īll'allāh, Ash'hadū an lā īllāha īll'allāh,*
> *Ash'hadū anna Mohammed ar-rasūl Allāh,*
> *Ash'hadū anna Mohammed ar-rasūl Allāh,*
> *Hāyā al salāh, Hāyā al salāh,*
> *Hāyā al falāh, Hāyā al falāh,*
> *Allāhū Akbār, Allāhū Akbār,*
> *Lā īllāha īll'allāh.*

(God is most Great
I testify that there is no God but God
And that Mohammed is his Prophet
Come to prayer
Come to prosperity
God is most Great
There is no God but God)

Like travellers finding sanctuary from the encroaching night, the men would leave behind the things of the world and file wordlessly into the cave, drawing themselves into lines in readiness for prayer.

I never failed to be moved by this summoning of the faithful. In the silences between the verses of the call stretched a stillness in which time itself dissolved. They were haunting moments, which brought gradually to life a stirring in some inner territory where I was still a stranger to myself. One evening, the lure of the call seemed to find its mark and, responding to a spontaneous voice of consent from within, I joined the other men as they gathered in the cave.

There was no fuss; the line parted and I found myself ushered gently into place. The prayers began, and a few minutes later I heard the muffled bang of guns from the post. It was a heartless moment to threaten our lives. The shells crept up the valley in a slow, steady barrage, lighting up the cave with bursts of flame as the explosions grew nearer. The ground shuddered and a shower of dust fell over us from the ceiling. I imagined at any moment the others would break from the ritual and shelter deeper in the cave, and I stole a glance around me to see if my fears were shared. But if they were, there was no visible trace. As the world beyond continued its terrifying turmoil of blast and flame, inside, their foreheads pressed gently against the earth in voiceless obeisance, the men were still.

Inevitably these moments of collective worship were more highly charged when the threat of danger was near, and the whisper of mortality in the air. And although my own participation in prayers was quantitatively no more than an imitation of the formal ritual, it was the extension of a natural impulse made sharper by the precarious-ness of our existence. There was no mention of the exclusivity of belief from the other men, who were delighted at a foreigner's presence at prayer; Qādeer supported me with friendly scepticism; Pål suggested I put myself forward for the position of village *mullā*, and never fully forgave what he took for my apostasy.

This common sense of feeling was especially intense when we were preparing to leave the relative safety of the cave for night-time operations, which were always insanely risky. When I was told there would be an attack on a Soviet garrison on the outskirts of Kabul, I found it impossible to resist; I felt uncomfortable sharing in other aspects of life without also sharing in the risks. And on the evening that we were preparing to leave, Qādeer presented me solemnly with the dead man's rifle, saying: 'You know why this is a *special* gun?' and twisted the strap to show me where a tiny dark stain had set in the stiff fabric. I had no intention of using it but grew accustomed to its presence at my side, and before long it felt unnatural to be separated from it.

We left before dawn to avoid being seen from the post, walked until dawn, and slept wrapped in our *pattūs* in a field of boulders until late morning. I was pleased at how my body found comfort on a bed of uneven rock. Strips of cold bread were distributed for breakfast, and we walked on.

Late in the afternoon we stopped in a narrow ravine scattered with the scorched hulks of trucks from an ambushed convoy. A fighter asked to borrow my compass to establish the direction of prayer and asked if I would kindly hold his rocket-propelled grenades while he prayed. It was then I discovered that by shaking them you could hear the contents rattling inside, like rice inside a maraca; amusing myself in this way I suddenly realized I had no idea what it took to set them off, and laid them gently down.

We marched through the hills towards the capital and at sunset stopped on the banks of a river near a cluster of nomads' tents. An unsmiling, eight-year-old child brought us a blackened kettle of tea from one of the tents, and we shared sips from a single tiny bowl.

Waiting, we were joined by twenty other men from a different group, heavily armed with grenades and rocket launchers. Their commander was a slight and inexperienced fighter who wore a black leather jacket and carried a Heckler & Koch machine gun. It was a splendid but, on account of the rarity of its ammunition, useless weapon.

The one reliable distraction from the walking was fantasy; the more defiant the better. Nothing was more consoling than the idea I might still be back in school in England. I was on my way to attack a Red Army garrison with the automatic rifle of a martyred guerrilla dangling from my shoulder: who was going to challenge me now for leaving my top button undone? With relish I revisited former teachers in my new guise to settle old scores; but the most essential of longings were the most vivid, and I conjured hot meals and wines in endless variety, concluding with the most luxurious thing of all I could imagine: a bed to lie in, with sheets and pillows.

Exhaustion and fear played strange tricks on the senses. Together with the moonlight the combination was intoxicating. I heard the rushing of a nearby stream and mistook it for the sound of enemy vehicles. I saw a bright corona of orange light from above a ridge and thought there must be a giant fire burning ahead of us – an ammunition dump perhaps – which turned out to be the streetlamps of Kabul. When we finally rounded the crest of the hill on the outskirts of the city and saw the lines of orange lamps, I felt myself recoil from the sight. I had become so accustomed to the medieval simplicity of life at the cave that seeing electric lights for the first and only time of the journey evoked an animal-like sense of dread.

Stray tracer bullets streaked across the land; parachute flares dangled earthward under meandering trails of smoke. There was a searchlight on top of one of the city's peaks which swung over the hills with a terrifying and cyclopean intensity; I was convinced, when the beam passed over us in the course of its sinister roaming, that it would quickly return, lock onto us, and all the firepower of the city would begin to pour in our direction. The mujaheddin seemed indifferent to it; whether out of defiance, ignorance or indifference I never knew.

There was a cacophony of gunfire as we attacked. Pâl and I huddled in the ruins of a broken house as bullets ricocheted from the walls behind in a chorus of deadly musical whines. Volleys of incandescent tracer scarred the air in every direction. At intervals a fighter called Taj

Mohammed, a Russian from Tajikistan who had defected from his armoured unit to join the mujaheddin, would leap out of the shadows, ignoring the loaded rifle I trained at his body, and jump down beside me, his eyes aflame with the relish of the battle.

'Aks nemīgīrīd? Aren't you taking pictures?' he would yell over the clatter of bullets. 'Jang nemīkonīd? Aren't you going to fight a bit?' Then by way of encouragement he would stand up, lean his rifle on the wall above and fire a deafening burst. Before the spent bullet casings that scattered around us had cooled, he would bound away again over the rubble and into the blackness.

The volume of gunfire, punctuated periodically by the blast of rocket-propelled grenades, was incredible. I resigned myself to the notion that we would soon be surrounded by a retaliatory Russian force and waited only for the sound of enemy tanks or helicopters, glumly rehearsing the one line of Russian that I had learned from a mercenary in Peshawar. It was a common joke at the time that CIA officials working with the mujaheddin were taught to memorize it in case they were ever caught by Russian soldiers: nye strayu, ya znaya sikrety – Don't shoot, I know secrets!

They never came. We fell back in a ragged line across open ground as fountains of tracer erupted from nearby positions and arched through the sky towards us with terrifying beauty. The men sauntered beneath the rain of bullets as if returning home from a satisfying day's work. We walked through the night; the route back was long and cold and we never once stopped. At dawn, long after the exhilaration of the fight – it could hardly be called a battle – had passed, we left the track and waded through a freezing river, on the far side of which the group broke up into smaller groups, and the men began arguing in fierce whispers.

The wind chilled to the bone. Pål and I sat in the shelter of an outcrop of rock and shared a cigarette with a fighter, and asked what the hold-up was. He explained in sounds and sign-language: now that the dawn had come, it was too late to take the planned route to our headquarters. We would be visible and within range of the local post, he said, and traced the rattling arc of the enemy gunner's sights with a leathery forefinger and a duk duk duk duk duk!

So what would we do? I asked.

We would have to take the longer route, up the slope and around the far side of the hill we were sheltering against. There was just one problem.

'*Boom!*' The ash fell from his cigarette as his hands mimicked the explosion of a mine and his face a pantomime death which at another time might have been funny. His eyes rolled shut, his head lurched to one side and his tongue stuck from a corner of his mouth. The slope was mined.

But we would have to cross it. As the dawn began to swell, like a dam of light behind the hills, we headed for a saddle of land between the ridges above us, half a mile away. The ground was scored by tank treads and we knew the enemy had passed not long ago. At the crest we formed a hurried queue, and looked across the gentle slope to the road and the bank of trees alongside it, about two hundred yards beyond.

Somehow I had become second in line. It had happened so quickly there had been no time to follow the natural urge to join the line at its farthest end. The first man stepped forward onto the slope and began to walk. I had hardly realized it was my turn to follow him when already a fighter was at my side, instructing me (a gratuitous refinement, I felt at the time) to step exactly in the first man's footsteps.

For about twenty yards this was, relatively speaking, fine. But beyond this the ground was covered with a layer of wild heather, and the imprints of the other man's footsteps were impossible to make out. I took a few more steps, studying the ground ahead with growing distress until I heard a yell which made me look up.

The man in front of me had lost patience with tiptoeing across the slope and simply run downwards to the far side at full speed, letting out a kind of battle cry along the way. A hundred yards from me now, he turned around and with a flashing grin waved me forward. At the same time the others behind were urging me on with faintly vexed expressions of sympathy, and I knew that to turn back was impossible.

When I remember the ridiculousness of this moment I sometimes wonder if it wasn't all a ruse to test the mettle of a visitor for fun.

Perhaps the slope wasn't mined at all, or perhaps, as it turned out, we were just lucky. So I walked forward, studying the ground between each step, wondering ... and just then the sun breached the hills in the east and the light poured like a liquid flame over the slope. I watched it creep up the hillside on my right and saw the grey rock turn to purple and the plain beyond it transformed from the colour of dust to gold, and the air was suddenly fragrant with the energy of the new day, as if the earth itself were drawing a life-giving breath.

I had never known a sunrise quite so beautiful, and walking down the slope felt so overtaken by the splendour of the new day that the danger underfoot seemed only vaguely troubling. Wherever my mind turned, it seemed to find its mark more keenly than ever before; without an effort I could see the white teeth of the smiling fighter on the far side of the slope more than a hundred yards away; I could feel the shrubs underfoot compressing like tiny springs, and a breeze dancing over my face in minuscule currents. The colours too were both clearer and brighter than I had ever seen, invested somehow with an added depth, as though alive and moving; and in memory too, I could direct a beam of recollection back to the earliest days of my childhood. All this I suppose, this conjuring act of the senses, was the result of a very focused kind of attention, the effects of which seemed quite magical at the time. But it was not a way of focusing I have ever wanted to repeat.

After a few days, and many a fantastically exaggerated tale of enemy casualties, this too passed quietly into the stream of time.

Then one morning, perhaps because I had come up against some natural inner limit, or was prompted by a reminder I have long since forgotten, I experienced a sudden and profound stab of homesickness. Memories of the world I had left behind flooded back with the pain of an unacknowledged wound, and I knew that it was time to make plans. I could not stay; it was not my war, and I knew I did not belong there.

After a ceremonial departure, for which the men at the cave lined up to embrace us in turn, I walked with Pål, Qādeer, the Russian deserter and two other men to the frontier. Pål had plans to join a different mujaheddin group elsewhere in the country, and went on to many further adventures and a succession of close calls. We reached the frontier three days later, and just before we descended into Pakistan, Qādeer knelt down and, with a tender gesture, scooped up a handful of his country's dust from beside the trail, and poured it into the pocket of his shirt. Even now I recall the precise moment that we began descending from the border, and the intense feeling of exile, as troublesome now as it was then, that accompanied it. I was smuggled back to Peshawar without mishap, nursing feelings of both relief and regret; the former short-lived, the latter strangely indelible.

*

I was in London a few days later, appalled by the city's gloomy and unnatural haste, the superabundance and variety of food, and the devastating sight of women in short skirts. At Charing Cross I bumped into an old schoolteacher, who looked me up and down with a disapproving eye.

'And what have you been up to this summer?' he asked.

'I've been to Afghanistan to live with the mujaheddin.'

He paused, then said: 'What a lot of nonsense you talk.'

Four

The *inscrutability* of the East is, indeed, I believe a myth ...
the ordinary inhabitant is incomprehensible merely to people
who never trouble to have anything much to do with him.

Dame Freya Stark, *The Journey's Echo*

TEN YEARS LATER I was to be granted what I had so often longed for on that first brief journey: the freedom to travel through the countryside without risk. Admittedly the risks were relative, but compared to the period of the Soviet occupation, the solitary trouble I had envisaged for myself in Panjshīr was akin to bachelorhood after marriage.

For three days the French team I had agreed to travel with had been delayed, but on the fourth we broke from Kabul and headed north. I felt a deep sense of relief at drawing closer to the simpler pleasures of the countryside. Against my every expectation I had been seduced by the luxury of the city, staying longer than felt proper, and was impatient to move on alone into the mountains.

Under a clear and brilliant morning sky, in a pickup truck loaded with a cargo of stove pipes and medical supplies for Guillaume's clinic, we weaved out of the crowded streets. The road led out of the city from its northwestern corner, over the Khairkhaneh Pass, and onto the single road which heads north like an arrow across the Shomāli plain.

Guillaume, wisely, sat in front with a silent Afghan driver, who mastered the shell-scarred road with nonchalant expertise. In the back we were crammed like bullets in a magazine with our knees nearly against our chests. I would get accustomed to this ritual over the coming weeks. Space does not have the same meaning for Afghans as it does to cosseted Western limbs, and when it comes to wheeled transport the number of seats in a given vehicle is largely irrelevant: the space adapts to the number of passengers. I wondered whether the more complicated *asanas* of Hatha yoga might have originated on

Afghan soil for practical reasons, to which more esoteric motives were only later ascribed.

I was squeezed painfully between Guillaume's Afghan interpreter, a kindly, weary man in his forties, who looked as though he had been asleep for a week before he had joined us in the truck, and the morose French photographer I had met the day before. The interpreter, in his tired suit and incongruous attaché case, held his head between his hands in a woeful gesture for most of the way, looking up only when we hit a particularly bad bump, or to begin a bout of chain-smoking. Then he would cover his face again and sink back into a private and unfathomable grief.

The Frenchman, too, was deeply unhappy. He was afraid we might hit a landmine and had not yet entered into the spirit of things. He wore green moleskin trousers which I coveted, the flat woollen Tajik hat called a *pakoul*, and one of those expensive, brightly coloured synthetic jackets that the adventurous are thought to wear. His back trouble made him hiss like a snake on the bumps and grip my arm in undular spasms of pain. He popped tranquillizers the whole way and took pictures from the window of brightly dressed children walking barefoot along the dusty verges.

It was still a beautiful road. At the edges of the plain, enclosing a fertile band of cultivated land several miles wide, high snow-draped mountains rose to ten thousand feet. In the fields alongside, old men walked barefoot in the furrows of their winter ploughings. Children and women were loading boxes of grapes on trucks bound for Pakistan. On either side there were countless ruined buildings that had once been tiny villages. Even in ruin, made from the same soil out of which they appeared to grow, they retained a certain dignity, more like places abandoned quietly than the victims of modern battles. Only the inverted tank turrets lying in the fields nearby, or the hollow rusting carcasses onto which they had once fitted, betrayed the unnatural origins of the destruction.

Before the war the route was shaded by a high canopy of mulberry trees which Soviet troops cut down in 1980. They lined the verges with anti-personnel mines. Now de-miners were poking among the ruins as we passed. We stopped once to photograph a team of them at work, and their leader greeted us like a proud sergeant and told us about the fifty men working under him. They were making their way at a pitiful pace along the roadside, crawling behind perspex masks through passages three feet wide, planting tiny forests of red flags next to unearthed mines. Whoever had planted them there had done so with a grotesque element of practicality: the area the men were clearing was a tiny cemetery. The Frenchman lay in the dust at the verge of the road and, inches from their faces, photographed the men at work. I could hardly bear to look, feeling sure he would distract one of them, with fatal results.

Villages surrounded by delicate groves of poplar and fruit trees decorated the folds of the mountain bases. In springtime the trees burst into bright splashes of pink and yellow blossom. To our west huddled the village of Istalif, the name a corruption of the Greek word for vines, *stafiloi*. A hundred years before, during their retreat from the plain, the village was razed by British troops.

We continued north through the small town of Charikar, still famous for the manufacture of knives and scissors, though today they are made from the steel of old Russian armour and riveted with the brass of melted-down ammunition cases. Beyond, at Jebel as-Serāj, we turned east at the head of the plain, where the road became a rough track. At midday we stopped, grateful for the unbuckling of limbs, in the village of Gulbahār, which means Spring Flower. In the warmer months, down by the river, it used to be a favourite picnic spot; Bābūr recounts picnicking there in the sixteenth century. Squeezing through the tiny main street we stopped at a *chaikhāna* to eat kebabs from crudely forged iron skewers. A dignified old man wearing a huge turban sat in a corner and watched us eat. He wiped plates with a rag at the speed of a slowed-down film. The noise and chaos of Kabul was already worlds away. We had entered the countryside and, with it, a different time.

The Panjshīr begins here. One of Afghanistan's most important valleys and a conduit of trade and communication for millennia, it snakes nearly a hundred miles to the northeast from Gulbahār towards a tangle of high peaks near the Anjoman Pass in Badakhshān province. Once thickly forested, in the early years of Islam its forests were cut down and burned for the smelting of ores and precious metals. Today, apart from the valley floor which is intensively cultivated, the slopes of the mountains that enclose it are cruelly barren.

It was also the scene of ten major offensives against the mujaheddin, the most extensive and bloody military engagements undertaken by the Soviets since the Second World War. Huge armoured columns crept repeatedly into the valley in attempts to subdue the obdurate resisters and their elusive leader Massoud, whose early victories against the lumbering forces of the invaders had earned him the title 'Lion of the Panjshīr'.

Beyond Gulbahār the track narrowed and led through a high gorge fifty yards wide. I felt the thrill of finally passing into mountain territory. The track hugged the left side of the gorge, the face of which rose vertically above us. Sixty feet below the river swirled furiously, and on the far side, a rocky wall shone golden in the afternoon light as if lit from within.

Here I saw the first of countless ruined armoured vehicles, rusting in the jade-coloured torrent beneath us. It was hard to believe that on this sinuous and narrow track, hundreds of tanks had once rumbled into the valley, and been beaten back along the same route.

*

I had read about the Panjshīr offensives while I was still in school. They had the ring of archetypal guerrilla conflicts and found fertile soil in my fifteen-year-old imagination; heavily armoured columns harassed by highly mobile fighters, who struck with terrifying unpredictability from secret mountain hideouts. Modern versions, in fact, of the engagements fought by British troops in southern Afghanistan, whose red uniforms and white topees were sighted (with incredulous relish, one imagines) down the barrels of tribesmen's *jezails*. Hiding on the steep slopes of the surrounding mountains, tribesmen were reluctant to engage the enemy on level ground where they were vulnerable to his greater firepower and kept their precious height, swooping down, if at all, only at the last minute. They could block their enemy's retreat with boulders in a narrow gorge, and cut the columns into manageable sections, picking off stragglers almost at will.

If your officer's dead and the sargeants look white,
    Remember it's ruin to run from a fight:
So take open order, lie down, and sit tight,
    And wait for supports like a soldier.*

The enemy, for his part, had more sophisticated weaponry as well as greater numbers of men and resources. He could rain fire on a suspected guerrilla position, deploy large flanking brigades to picket the mountain tops, and use heavy force against the inhabitants of the valley floors, destroying the villages that gave the guerrillas food and shelter.†

A hundred years later the Soviets would use the same tactics and have to relearn the same bitter lessons, for the military principles on both sides, dictated by the land itself, were virtually unchanged. Only the scale and means were different. Guerrillas still used rocks to block

---

*   Thus wrote Kipling in 'The Young British Soldier', which ends with the more famous lines: 'When you're wounded and left on Afghanistan's plains,/ And the women come out to cut out what remains,/ Jest roll on your rifle and blow out your brains/ An' go to your Gawd like a soldier.'

†   The predicament of heavily laden and slow-moving columns through narrow valleys is graphically described in British military despatches of the period. Major General Sir Robert Sale writes of an ambush in the Jegdelek gorge not far from Kabul: 'Yesterday the force under my command was again engaged with the insurgents of these mountains, and the affair was the sharpest which we have had ... Holding all the salient points of the hills, and secured by breastworks, they showed a determination to dispute with the utmost obstinacy the progress of our flanking parties, and to endeavour to prevent the debouche of our advance and main column. To enable us to effect this I had to detach companies from every corps in the force to the right and left, which, aided by the artillery, won their way inch by inch up the lofty heights. Much, however, remained to be done, and the fire of the mountaineers from several of the tallest summits was unabated, and success was everywhere doubtful ... as the cumbrous train of baggage filed over the mountains, the insurgents, again appearing from beyond the most distant ridges, renewed the contest with increased numbers, and the most savage fury. Our rearguard made the best dispositions for defence and rescue; but the suddenness of the onset caused some confusion.' (*Papers relating to the War in Afghanistan*, House of Commons, 21 January 1840).

narrow passes, but now had rocket-propelled grenades to destroy vehicles from half a mile away, planted anti-tank mines to burst them like lice in a flame, or tried to score a prize hit on a petrol tanker with an incendiary bullet. A favourite strategy was to destroy the first and last vehicles of a long convoy on a narrow road, then shoot up as many of the trapped tanks and trucks as possible before returning fire forced them to abandon their positions.

The Soviets replaced the picketing teams of old with armoured helicopter gunships, laid down broad fields of fire with grenade launchers, mortars, artillery and tanks (the latter of limited use in mountainous territory), scattered the high passes with countless mines and, most devastating of all, rained bombs over wide areas in mind-boggling abundance.

The first of the Panjshīr offensives was launched in 1980, the year that Brezhniev's head of military intelligence announced the 'final and irrevocable defeat of the counterrevolutionary bandits'. Watched from afar in Moscow by a confident military high command, 'Panjshīr I' was a devastating failure for the Soviets, whose fighting doctrine had yet to emerge from the shadow of Stalinist might, and fifty years on still conceived of overwhelming force as the primary means to wipe out the elusive *basmachi*.*

Soviet and Afghan government bombers pounded the valleys in advance of the armoured dinosaurs. Nineteen-year-old conscripts sweated in the cramped cockpits of tanks designed to sweep at speed across the plains of northern Europe. Ahead of them teams of minesweepers searched the road with metal probes and cumbersome detectors at an excruciating pace, while huge military bulldozers cleared

---

* Meaning bandits, the name given to guerrillas resisting Russian advances into the Caucasus in the nineteenth century. The mujaheddin were also called *dhuki*, ghosts. It would take the Soviets years of experimentation to adapt to the challenges posed by mountain counter-insurgency. As the militaryspeak of one post-war American analysis has it: 'This new battlefield required traditional operational and tactical formation abandonment, redefinition of traditional echelonment concepts and wholesale formation and unit reorganization to emphasize combat flexibility and survivability.' For the conscript, this translated into simpler strategies for survival, such as buying a

the way of boulders toppled from the ragged cliffs. Above the convoy, gunships hovered and swooped like vast dragonflies, raking the mountains with gunfire. But the great army was unprepared for the mountainous terrain and the unfamiliar kind of warfare, and the first offensive ground to an ugly halt after two weeks of heavy losses in men and vehicles.

Ten times during the war these giant convoys crept into the wounded valley, each time penetrating more deeply, each time their advance more deadly. Jets pounded the valley for weeks in advance of the armour; later in the war squadrons of bombers flew specially from the Soviet Union on saturation bombing missions. Villagers sheltered in caves and emerged at night to tend their fields and repair broken irrigation streams. Tens of thousands simply fled, and at times the fertile valley was almost deserted. Retreating troops mined houses and blew up granaries. Guerrillas melted into the mountains, stealing from their hideouts in darkness to re-mine the roads or launch rapid strikes against isolated military posts. French doctors working in secret in the valley reported having their hospitals bombed with pinpoint accuracy; other outsiders who made the difficult trek into Panjshīr from Pakistan told of close shaves with Soviet commandos and the obdurate heroism of the valley's inhabitants.

It was peaceful now. Counting the hulks of ruined armoured vehicles I thought of the Afghan friend I had first met in America, who delivered pizzas for a living in San Francisco. He was the sole able-bodied survivor of Massoud's earliest commando group, whose job had been to divide and harass the strung-out enemy convoys into sections small enough to be attacked. I thought too of the accounts by

---

pair of tennis shoes to replace the standard military boots which had a poor grip on rock, or saving up to trade for a lightweight, Western-made sleeping bag captured from the enemy.

Five years into the war, the Soviets had officially admitted to only twenty deaths in Afghanistan. Exact casualty figures were not published until 1989, when nearly 14,000 fatalities were listed for the ten-year period of the conflict. Scepticism about the official count is widespread on both sides: among Soviet veterans, mujaheddin, and Western studies of the war, the most consistent estimate stands at between 40,000 and 50,000 dead.

Soviet veterans of the Panjshīr campaigns, and as the number of metallic carcasses grew I felt little doubt as to which side, given the choice, I would have opted to fight on.

Green personnel-carriers that had long ago lost their wheels were stranded, rusting, upside down or at forlorn angles on the river's edge. Their sloping ends made me think of eviscerated turtles. Tanks stripped of their innards with barrels as long as our truck lay with their ripped bellies open to the sky. In the river the current roared over other hollow hulks blasted from the road; trout sheltered in the shadows where nineteen-year-old boys had once sat. Other relics rusted by the roadside beneath shady groves of small trees where sheep were grazing. In the fields, furrows of shorn wheat swerved around the inverted turrets of tanks that had burst like pods on mines and landed thirty yards away. I counted two hundred, then gave up as we passed a walled yard filled with further wrecks.

Soon the valley had broadened to half a mile. We crossed the river, now a weaving crystalline band the colour of sapphire, several times on narrow wooden bridges reinforced with lengths of military truck chassis or rusting Russian pontoons. In the villages, the rooftops were supported with spent tank and artillery shells, and the old wheels of tanks or sections of their armoured tread had been incorporated in place of large rocks into the stone walls dividing patchwork cornfields. A hatch from a troop carrier was used to dam an irrigation channel. Everywhere these forgotten splinters of what had been the pride of Soviet armour were being absorbed organically back into the land.

'*Incroyable! Dehors de temps!* Beyond time!' Guillaume would whisper at the beauty of the villages through which we passed, a dozen perhaps, strung along the five-hour route. We seemed gradually to be outstripping time as we moved deeper into the valley, weaving occasionally through a flock of sheep driven along the track in the opposite direction, or returning a hale wave of passage from a turbaned farmer behind a wooden plough.

The road rose steadily and the river narrowed. The few villages grew smaller. In the late afternoon we turned a narrow corner on a rise, and found the track blocked by an eighteen-wheel truck. That it had squeezed this far along was difficult to believe. The driving wheels had lost their grip on the sharp and uneven turn and the container had slipped from the chassis and rolled backwards, crashing through a stone wall like a compound fracture above the curve of a knee. For two hours we waited. Half a dozen vehicles gathered at each end of the disaster. Meanwhile the sun began to dip beneath the lip of the horizon and at the river's edge, beneath a line of slender poplars, some stranded travellers laid out their *pattūs* and prayed together. Gilded by the last breath of the day's sunlight, a dozen heads rose and fell in silence beneath the shade of the whispering leaves. I hadn't seen the sight for years: all of a sudden I was there again, in that locked room where time had stopped.

*

The rumble of an approaching truck brought me back. Seeing his way blocked, the driver produced a length of steel cable and hooked it to the stranded cab of the eighteen-wheeler, and tried to reverse up the hill. With twenty other onlookers I watched things unfold from the slope above the road; it was good country entertainment. The engines roared, wheels spun, rubber burned against rock and the frames of the trucks juddered uselessly.

A boy trotted past on a donkey, a giant clay urn balanced between his knees, and a flock of sheep passed like a dusty wave beneath the chassis of the marooned truck. There was the usual, drawn-out quota of speculation, jest, complaint and some sceptical input from the onlookers.

Half an hour later a third truck appeared, attached itself to the back of the second, and the three engines were gunned into life. The cables jerked taut, wheels moaned smokily against the rock, the frames of the trucks creaked like submarines on an ocean floor, the air was filled with fumes from the straining engines, and with a roar of applause the three lurched up the slope. The road was clear and the crowd dispersed with all-round murmurs of satisfaction.

Now the sun had set and it was growing cold. Villages perched on high crags above the road began to dissolve into the shadows like the young women we had earlier seen by the verges, turning from the gaze of a foreigner. Soon their fading outlines were betrayed by brief glances of light from oil lamps in tiny windows. It was dark when we reached the village of Khenj. Our breath steamed luminously on the air, caught by lanterns swinging from timber balconies that leaned into the narrow street. Guillaume's guide led us to a *chaikhāna* where a five-hundred-pound Russian bomb was set in the earth at its base like a traffic bollard.

We climbed an ancient wooden ladder, stooped awkwardly through a small door into a smoky room, and were greeted by an array of fiercely curious stares. Between them, spaces appeared like little partings in a human sea, and sitting cross-legged on a wooden dais we were served bowls of oily broth with potatoes and a few pieces of gristly meat.

It was a wild and lawless place: the law, at least, was not our own. All eyes were on us. Guillaume exercised a misplaced Gallic charm as if he were in a Parisian restaurant; the guide tucked into his broth; the photographer saw only menace in the others' eyes, and glowered apprehensively from a corner.

The men watching us were a ferocious-looking bunch, ragged and turbaned and intense. Air smoky from the fire and swaying shadows thrown by the lanterns magnified the impression of lawlessness. I tried to imagine the men around us shaven and under fluorescent lights, equipped them mentally with copies of the *Evening Standard*, and found nothing more sinister in them than the characters who sit opposite you on the London Underground. But for the most part the European eye is unaccustomed to such intensity and readily finds something intimidating in it: Eric Newby's adventures in the Panjshīr valley and Nuristan are littered with references to 'villanous-looking', 'murderous-looking' and 'mad-looking' individuals, frequently 'smelly', 'verminous' and 'brute', with 'an air of being able to commit the most atrocious crimes and then sit down to a hearty meal'. Uncharitable descriptions – but the sight of such faces made us all wonder. For the first time I felt my journey had really begun. At last, I felt with enormous satisfaction, I was off the beaten track.

*

In the morning it was time to go on alone. I waited in the freezing shadows outside the clinic, a newly constructed concrete building where we had spent the night after unloading the supplies. Now Guillaume was preparing to drive back to Kabul. I was brooding apprehensively about the route ahead and waiting for the sun to creep down the slopes into the valley. A little crowd of children, shouting and laughing, came running down the road on their way to school, shepherded by their teacher. Then, apart from the faint rushing of the river hidden in the ravine below, all was silent again. Hours had passed and not a single vehicle had come our way.

Guillaume asked me what my plan was. I had only the valley for a guide and the name of a man in a village somewhere to the north. For a few moments I was tempted by his offer to return with him to Kabul, and was struck by the foolhardiness of travelling alone in a country where human life had become so cheap. Even in peacetime it was a dangerous place to travel. Alone, I had been told often enough, it would be suicide.

But how then, I was asking myself with the strange logic one employs to disguise one's fears, did Afghans themselves get about? Were they, too, all mad or suicidal? I felt sure the goodness of ordinary people would prevail. But the temptation to turn back is never so strong as when you are about to leave the company of friends. Just then I heard the laboured growl of a truck creeping up the valley, and knowing it was the signal I had been waiting for, jumped into the road to flag it down.

I clambered up twenty feet over the straining ropes of an overloaded Russian *kamaz* truck, one of those giant-wheeled beasts that seem able to go anywhere their drivers have the will to take them, and perched on a high cargo of sacks among ten other men. Below, the others gathered to see me off, and even the photographer managed a smile as we roared away in a cloud of dust and diesel fumes. They all waved, Guillaume with a tender vigour, doubting (he confessed, when I saw him a month later) that I would ever be seen again.

Leaving him behind and the world he represented for a village no one had heard of somewhere in the Hindu Kush, my heart sank. It was a moment of sharp contradiction, with all the rending of opposing feelings that any reluctant parting brings. You pay for the sweetness of uncertainty with the bitterness of leaving the familiar and your most inarticulate hopes and fears are brought suddenly to life at such castings-off. I had to leave but I was full of doubts about the wisdom of going on alone.

Clinging to the lumbering frame of the truck we wrapped scarves around our faces against the freezing wind. The route led through a string of villages and where trees lined the road we ducked from branches between the sacks that formed our swaying nest. In one village an old man shouted angrily at us for looking into his garden, where his unveiled wife was kneading bread, and we giggled like schoolboy kings of the road. Beyond these thinning settlements, measured against the mountains, we seemed to be steadily shrinking, like Alice in the rabbit burrow. The huge truck was soon no more than a tiny louse, creeping between the ever-deepening folds of the hills.

My earlier fears were soon forgotten as the truck begun to climb steeply and the road narrowed to a ledge with crumbling edges the width of a single vehicle. There was a certain thrill in this – to be riding in the proud air on top of a truck in this wild valley – but pleasant is not the word. No money is exchanged for such journeys: the currency you pay is pure adrenaline. No bollards or barriers diluted the visceral rush of fear as the truck lurched over rogue boulders and the top where we clung began to tip over the edge of the ravine, sending us scrabbling like monkeys to the other side of the sacks as if by doing so our chances of survival would be improved. At the most hair-raising sections we clambered down and followed the road on foot to a point where the surface was more reasonable. Lungs heaved in the thin air, but the views of the valley from high up were spectacular. As we climbed we could see further and further back into the valley. For twenty miles blade-like ridges on either side sliced down into the earth, their steep sides lined with tributary scars as if raked by some primeval claw.

We reached Khawak in the early afternoon, when the golden light that lends the barren slopes such nobility by day, and the absence of which creates such a forbidding sense of vastness, had already begun to peel upwards. The truck creaked across a narrow wooden bridge into the village and juddered to a halt. Here the road appeared to end. Hastily I consulted the list of place-names Amrullah had given me in Kabul, but Khawak was only the first of a long list. I had no idea how to go on. The other men jumped down, unloaded their sacks, and disappeared purposefully beneath their loads.

Khawak has served as a traveller's staging-post for centuries. To the north, a famous pass leads over the Hindu Kush: Alexander's winter route on his outflanking of the Achaemenid satrap Bessus. His troops slogged over it in the winter of 329 BC, snow-blind, frostbitten and forced to eat the raw flesh of their own animals. Tīmūr also took the pass in the opposite direction, on his way south to subdue the unruly Nuristanis.

But it would be misleading to call the place a village and leave it at that. It was a village by local standards, but what I saw was little more than a collection of camels, horses, donkeys, mountains of sacks, a few mud dwellings with smoking chimneys, a rickety bridge of split poplar trunks, and a space big enough for trucks to turn in. Around me was a seething flow of men with clothes and faces belonging to a different century, weaving in every direction over the rock and mud and straw.

I realized I had no idea how far it was to Qoriye, the village where I was to meet a man I didn't know, who might be able to help me, if he was there. It would be dark within an hour and I felt acutely alone. My Persian, in keeping with a strange habit of its own in moments of anxiety, had abandoned me. I sat on my bag and thought. In England they were putting up Christmas lights.

'Come on!' called a voice. It was the man I had sat next to on top of the truck. 'Let's have something to eat.'

We walked to a hovel-like *chaikhāna*, the wildest I had yet seen, and stooped under a stone lintel into a dark, smoky chamber where a Russian samovar bubbled like a miniature steam engine in a corner. We ate a bowl of rice together and when I tried to pay there was a minor uproar. Men I had scarcely noticed stood up in protest as I reached into my pocket for some money.

'You are a guest,' said my host, without show, and pressed his hand in gentle protest against mine. Nods of approval rippled through the assembled men. So much for anonymity, I thought: my every word and gesture had been noticed. We emerged blinking into the light. I asked if he would point me in the right direction for Qoriye, hoping he might walk me to a junction in the road that I hadn't seen, the way you guide a lost American tourist to a bus station.

'There,' he said cheerfully, leading me back to the camel-park. 'That's the way to Qoriye,' and pointed to a cluster of snowy mountains about fifty miles away. Then he was gone, swallowed up in the flow of men and beasts.

A small crowd of the wildest faces I had ever seen began to gather around, scrutinizing the details of my irregular clothes. News of a stranger spread like ripples in a dark pool, and I caught snippets of the exchange amid growing murmurs of speculation.

'What is he?' said one.

'A Tajik.'

'No, he's a foreigner.'

'Foreigners have no business here.'

'What's he got in that sack?'

'By Allah, it is big enough.'

'Where is his guide?'

'He is alone.'

'He shouldn't be, in these parts.'

A representative of these characters stepped forward and asked where I was going and what my duty was, my *wazifeh*. I countered with a weary 'I-come-here-all-the-time' look, and said I was joining friends further up the valley.

'But how are you going to get there?' called a voice in a strong accent I could hardly understand.

'I will wait for a *motor*,' I said confidently.

'Ha! There's no *motor* that goes there! *This is the end of the road.*' There was a ripple of guffaws.

'I'll take you!' croaked a grizzled old man with a broad grin. 'On my horse.' He patted the rump of his skeletal charge.

'For how much?'

He named a price, but since I didn't know how far we were from Qoriye, I had no way of knowing whether it was reasonable.

'But not today!' he added with a sinister chuckle. 'It'll be dark soon. *Amnīyat nīst.* It's not safe.'

An ominous half-hour passed. The crowd around me dispersed but would gather again, a few new faces among them, like vultures returning to a man in his final moments. But then a blessing is all the sweeter by the curse that it dispels. I heard the sound of a vehicle. A Russian jeep was honking its way through the sea of animals towards us. A face broke from among the vultures, flagged down the jeep for me, and waved me forward.

'By Allah, he said a *motor* would come, and a *motor* has come!' I heard a voice from the men around me. I smiled knowingly, disguising my enormous sense of relief, and heaved my bag onto my shoulder.

An irritable driver waved me to the back of the jeep. I lifted a canvas flap, and saw faces, like those of huddling soldiers lit by a sudden flare in a foxhole at night. But there was no room; inside there were ten men and their baggage in a jeep designed for four, and I hesitated in a most un-Afghan way.

'Go on, get in!' yelled the driver.

There was a shout as I stepped on an ankle, a grunt as I pulled myself up on another man's shoulder and forced myself into a niche between the bones and bags and metal. Then, a few moments of silence as the other passengers stared at their unexpected acquisition. I stared back, and felt my hip-joint pop.

The wheels spun and we were off, spraying clouds of dust into the faces of the men who had gathered like children to see me go, and who – even as we disappeared around the first bend of the ever-narrowing valley – were still waving.

And there it was again, that feeling that the journey was becoming more than the sum of its parts, more like a clandestine sculpting at work within me, which in the visible world I was merely acting out, to reveal – what? The shape of a character I knew only dimly from a life whose roots were growing more tenuous by the minute. How precious and remote the world of home now seemed! In ordinary life you know yourself from your surroundings, which become the measure and the mirror of your thoughts and actions. Remove the familiar and you are left with a stranger, the disembodied voice of one's own self which, robbed of its usual habits, seems barely recognizable. It is all the stronger in an alien culture, and more so when the destination is uncertain.

At first this process brings with it a kind of exhilaration, a feeling of liberty at having broken from the enclosures of everyday constraints and conventions: this is the obvious, if unconscious lure of travel. But once it has run its early course a deeper feeling more like anguish begins to surface, until the foreignness of your surroundings becomes too much to bear. I had never felt it so strongly before, and wondered: when does it start, this divorce from oneself, and what is its remedy?

The valley was narrowing now and the driver battled with a lurching steering wheel. At times the track was no more than a broken riverbed, and soon we were in first gear, growling forward as our pace grew even slower. And with it, the world.

Time, motion's mysterious partner, was up to its tricks again. Memories of slowed-down time are more vivid; there is more in them. So I remember that overstuffed jeep, the flapping of its canvas roof, and the awful bumping and crashing, with an extra dimension of clarity. I remember watching the rocks slip away behind us like a river, and the incandescence of the evening sky above the rims of the steepening mountains whose walls were turning from the colour of lavender to coal. I remember the fresh-faced fighter whose knees were jammed against mine and who studied me when he thought I wasn't looking but never spoke, and the powdery dust swirling into his blond eyebrows, and the taste of it in my teeth. And I was reminded of how much on a journey time's fabric is elastic, as capricious, almost, as a magician's silk handkerchief, which changes colour, stretches, shrinks, disappears even, according to the master's whim. In familiar surround-ings, days — months and years, even — seem to fly by unnoticed. But when things are unfamiliar time, or rather your sense of it, stretches, sometimes unbearably, as if to make room for the new experience before it can be properly stored. Time is a river; your measurement of it depends on what you fish out. Routine compresses time and the strange stretches it. It even reaches a kind of limit when things turn suddenly and unexpectedly violent or when you are counting the seconds that follow the sound of artillery fired in your direction, and each moment you seem to live a year. But when your river returns to normal and you are back in the familiar current of your world again, it seems so strange, so unfair almost, that nothing much has changed.

*

We reached Qoriye in darkness. A young boy watched our arrival and after I had clambered out of the jeep and brushed the powdery dust from my face, led me to Haidar's house. A mouse-like, softly spoken man of about thirty-five appeared from behind a wooden gate, led me through a dusty courtyard where chickens roamed and into a mud-walled room. He put a lantern on the carpet and we warmed our hands on the flame. The ceiling was made of young poplar trunks and flattened branches, and a glacial wind beat at the tiny window.

I was alone for a few minutes until Haidar reappeared with a kettle of tea which he poured into a white china mug. Afghans never drink from mugs and I looked more closely at it: it was painted with the tourist sites of London. He had bought it in London two weeks before.

He listened with friendly delight to my plans. As we talked, men began to file inside as if summoned by telepathy, until there were fifteen in the room, lining the walls, speculating vigorously as to the origins and purpose of the stranger in their midst, the length of the route I intended to take, and the weather on the Anjomān Pass. An ample meal appeared. How these minor feasts are conjured into existence without any apparent interruption in the rhythm of affairs – no matter the number of unexpected guests – is one of the perpetual and mysterious delights of travel in Afghanistan.

I was given the seat of honour – in the absence of chairs, this is always the head of the room, furthest from the door – and opposite me sat Haidar's father, a venerable old character wearing a turban and long silk gown. He gazed at me throughout the meal with fascinated affection, praising the distance I had travelled and the boldness of my journey, as though we had fought together in campaigns of old. His eyes were cloudy and shone with kindness, and he stroked his beard thoughtfully all the while, a habit which over the years had compressed it beneath his chin like the waist of a Persian vase.

Tales of former travellers, the most recent ten years ago, were resurrected fondly. There was one, punctuated by much guffawing, about a Frenchman who had taken the name of Mahmoud.

'And he had with him a great map,' recounted one of them, 'which he would look at every few minutes. And he would say: "In half an hour we will reach such-and-such a village." And in half an hour, I swear by Allah, we would reach the place. And then he would look at his great map again, and say, "In one hour, we will reach such-and-such a place," and by God, yes, we reached there in one hour!'

'That was the same *khareji* I went with to the Anjomān Pass,' interjected another. 'When we reached the top he took out a great big brown cigarette, this long—' He held a finger halfway up his forearm. 'And he smoked that great cigarette on top of the pass and even asked me to take his picture!' The men roared with laughter. I concealed a stab of embarrassment: I too had just such a cigar in my pack for the same occasion.

Another remembered Sandy Gall, a *khareji* legend, whose name still echoed through Panjshīr. 'Two horses he gave me! Two! A noble man he was!' I thought warmly of the man who, already in his sixties, had made three daring trips into the valley during the Soviet occupation.*

Haidar asked the men in turn what their price would be for accompanying me to the point where the motorable road began in northern Badakhshān, adding that his reputation – his eyebrow, as the Persian expression has it – depended on it. There were long discussions. Finally one man offered a price of roughly thirty pounds, and the others rounded on him cheerfully.

---

* He was utterly unflappable in his Barbour and red-and-white *keffiyeh*, both unknown in Afghanistan. I had met him several years before in Kabul when the mujaheddin stormed the city at the end of communist control. He brewed tea calmly as rockets exploded into houses a few yards from us and, at the airport, as we cowered on the ground during a bombardment of heavy artillery, mused wistfully over the loss of his fountain pen.

'Ha!' they cried, 'Ali Khan's a poor man – that's why he needs all that money!' I wondered about the man they had decided on, whose cunning smile ignited in me a vague feeling of unease. He was fifty, I guessed, shaven-headed, a tough-looking man whose furrowed face and greying beard gave him the stark grace of his land. His eyes were bright and cleverly watchful. I wondered if I should accept the offer, then felt a little ashamed of my own mistrust. These men – complete strangers – had showed such a spontaneous willingness to help me, I could hardly refuse to accept their guide on the grounds of an obscure misgiving. I would be dragging this kind man from his home and family across a mountain range two-thirds as high as Everest in midwinter for the price of a parking ticket.

*

I shared a room for the night with one of the men. He was a carpenter and had come all the way from Kabul to make a few window frames: times were hard, he said. He laid out my bedding with fastidious care and we slept until dawn. It was barely light when I heard the rustling of his morning prayers from the far corner of the room. Afterwards he apologized for disturbing me and disappeared down the wooden ladder that connected the room to the main house.

There was no sound. From a tiny window I saw a bright half moon, and beneath it, Venus, sown like a lonely sequin in the purple fabric of the dawn. I tottered down from the room to the frozen stream by the house, and as I tried to snap the ice to wash my face a ghostly figure loomed from the darkness with a ewer of warm water. It was the carpenter again, who stood beside me as I washed, pouring water smilingly on my hands.

The air was thin and icy. Of my guide, who had said he would come at six, there was no sign. With Haidar I shared a breakfast of tea with bread and honey and afterwards we watched the carpenter making his frames in an upstairs room, and burned poplar shavings in a corner to warm our hands. I learned the names of the tools he was using and thought of what a Western carpenter needs to make a window frame: here he was turning out frames that would outlive him with a single plane made from a blade in a block of oak, a handsaw, and a hatchet-like instrument with a sharp lateral edge.

Haidar took me on a tour of the village. The mud road was frozen solid and its edges iced with frost. A trio of turbaned old men, one of them the village *mullā*, greeted us at the edge of a field. I kept silent and smiled but heard the whole exchange.

'Is he a Moslem?' one of them asked in a near-whisper.

'No, he is one of the *ahl-i ketāb*, the people of the Book,' replied another, using the term by which Christians and Jews are known to distinguish them from *kafirs*, unbelievers.

'But you can tell he is a believer — he looks like a Moslem.'

'By Allah, as good as one.'

'Yes, you can see from his face he is close to Islam.'

'Amazing.'

We walked to the edge of the village. Haidar patted the heads of curious children who had gathered to glimpse the *khareji* and dismissed them with affectionate scoldings. We looked down to the roaring river and he pointed out the ridges above us where Russian commandos had been dropped during the war. He told me the names of the different trees that grew by the water's edge as the sun, still shielded by a dark cornice of high peaks, spread the luminous ink of morning into the sky. Walking back he called out a name beneath a cluster of buildings. A tiny window creaked open, and I recognized Ali Khan's face: he had just woken up.

Then the sun broke free of the mountains and the slopes burst into life at its touch, and the sky began to lighten from the colour of gentian to lapis. Voluble sparrows began to gather on windowsills. We walked back to the house and I stood for a few minutes with the *mullā* as the morning rays stole towards us across the fields. He had but one tooth in his lower jaw, and his skin was red and lined like a silted estuary enclosed by the white fields of his beard. A man trotted by on a donkey, followed by a second carrying his wife, her shape hidden in the billowing folds of an emerald-coloured *burqā*.

'Peace be to you!' waved the rider.

'And to you. May you never be tired!' croaked the old *mullā*. He was filled with silent curiosity, studying me when my face was turned from his.

'I saw a Bible once,' he mused. 'A great big book, it was!' But he had a burning question, I knew.

'Do you pray, make *namaz*?' he asked, striking to the vital issue.

'Here,' I said, pointing to my heart.

'Oh yes, that's good,' he nodded, reassured. 'Very good.'

I asked him if he had been in the village when the Russians had come. Yes, but there was so much bombing, he said, waving towards some ruined houses beyond where we stood, that he and the other villagers had hidden in caves, for days at a time, without food. And there were still mines on the slopes, he added.

My guide, Ali Khan, appeared shortly with a scraggy horse loaded with woven saddlebags and a plastic sack of fodder. He paid no attention to me and with a weary authority that suggested he had undertaken more important things in life, asked for my bag.

'What, this thing?' He looked despairingly at the awkward lump which contained my pack, bigger and heavier than it should have been. I could hear him muttering under his breath as he shifted it experimentally across the horse's back.

'... and it's all the wrong shape ... how am I supposed to fit such a thing on a horse? ... all I've got is this rope and it'll never be long enough.'

It seemed half the village had gathered to see us off. I hoped the horse would behave and not throw me in front of everyone. But we wound away without event through the narrow village street and the old *mullā* gave me a great wave and a smile, his solitary tooth gleaming like a watchtower on a hilltop, and the chatter of onlookers fell away behind us.

*

The beauty of the route was matched only by the cold. A numbing wind drove down the valley from the northeast, relenting only in the lee of intersecting ridges. After half an hour we passed through a final village where the road narrowed to a track the width of a man. I extracted my wolfskin hat, wound a scarf around my face, dug my hands into the folds of my *pattū*, and froze.

Ali Khan strode solemnly behind me, his bare hands folded behind his back, whacking the horse from time to time with his whip, his only possession for the journey, uttering a *choo! choo!* to encourage the horse along with other chidings I could not understand; otherwise he was silent.

This was the main road from the south to Badakhshān, and we soon ran into the first of many traffic jams. An old man driving a donkey, almost invisible beneath a load of firewood and brush, was blocking the way. The horse under me came to a stubborn halt. Ali Khan ran up and pulled him forward, and his flanks dragged against the oncoming load, unsteadying us both. On the flat track this was merely tiresome, but as the track wound higher above the river it became a terrifying ritual. At each of these encounters I felt certain that all of us would end up in the river and, even if we survived the fall, be swept away by the current. The higher the track wound, the more terrifying the ritual. It was like riding a horse on a fifth-, tenth- or sometimes twentieth-storey balcony with no railing, then trying to share it with another.

Ali Khan's habit was to stop alongside the farmers and merchants coming from the opposite direction and gossip for a few minutes like a taxi driver in a choked city street. Sensing his master's absence, the horse would slacken his pace and creep to a complete stop like an exhausted spring. I called him Clockwork, and never did find the key to wind him up. Once he had stopped, no amount of persuasion, flattery, mane-pulling, threats, heel-digging, promises or profanity in either English or Persian made the slightest difference.

I did not know, as I still do not know, what you are supposed to do to get such a stubborn horse to go. I thought you made a clicking noise in your cheek. I dug my heels in his flanks and slapped the reins against both sides of his neck the way cowboys do. Nothing worked. Time after time I would pretend to be waiting patiently for Ali Khan to catch us up, when really I was at the mercy of Clockwork's laziness. After an hour of this charade I got fed up, and consulted his master.

'Ali Khan! How do I get this horse to go?'

'You just say *choo!*' he replied, with a trace of dismissiveness.

'Yes, but when I say *choo* nothing happens.'

'Try.' He sighed tolerantly.

'*Choo.*' Nothing. I tried again with the sort of jerk in the saddle that in films sends horses into an energetic gallop. '*Choo!*' Clockwork, I felt certain, and possibly Ali Khan, was sniggering under his breath.

'Here,' he said wearily, 'it's like this.' And he walked to the back of the horse. '*CHOOOOOO!*' he roared huskily, and Clockwork bolted forward into a spine-shattering trot.

At midday we passed through the last inhabited place in the valley, a village called Pas Mazar.* Here I suggested we take turns to ride. It was actually warmer walking and I felt uncomfortable letting Ali Khan walk all the way. He objected; I insisted, and from then on we changed every hour. It was so cold I breathed into my *pattū* in a useless effort to stay warm. My fingers and toes were already numb, and I shivered uncontrollably the whole way.

So at one o'clock we changed, and I rode Clockwork and somewhere in that barrenness we crossed the river because it was on our left now. We traced our way, imperceptibly but steadily rising, through a lunar, windswept landscape of shattered rock and boulders. The valley was about a quarter of a mile wide, and the peaks above us

---

* It may not be the last, but it is the last place I saw people living on the Panjshīr side. This may change with the season; it may also change over time as more former refugees move back into the valley. I heard three variants on the place names on the route north. If you are travelling in the region and you memorize them, you will be remembered by your guide for life. They are by no means all villages; I thought Shalzor was a village, but it was basically a sheep-pen. So, from Khawak (the wild place by the pass): Shahnāz, Qā'leh, Deh Pariān, Kafjān, Jeshti, Kulkuhā, Kūrpetāb, Pir Gozār, Shalzor, Sar-e Jangal, Cheshme Garm, Ab-i Garm, Zarqa Bacche – then the Anjomān Pass itself. And twenty others in between, said one man. Between the pass and the mines: Kimorgh, Howz (this is the lake), Anjomān, Wushti, Mianshahr, Qalt, Iskazer, Parwareh, Lajwar Sho, Ma'dān (this is the village of the mines). After the Anjomān Pass you are in the province of Badakhshān. Head east for Nuristan, north for Tajikistan, and northeast for China . . .

roughly seventeen thousand feet, about five thousand feet from the valley floor. The sky was clear and a livid blue and the light of such purity that we might have been enclosed in a rare and highly polished crystal, whose magic power seemed to bring distant objects effortlessly within reach, had we been able to uncurl them, of our numb fingers.

We had walked for more than two hours and, apart from instructing me on Clockwork, Ali Khan had hardly spoken. The cold robbed us of the urge to talk but we were both wondering what each other's company would be like. Then an old man with his son drove a pair of long-haired cattle past us in the opposite direction. Ali Khan caught up alongside me, and seemed to be pondering something. He cleared his throat and, finally, spoke.

'In your nation,' he asked, 'do you have cows like that?'

'Oh yes,' I said, 'they're called Highland cattle. And we have black and white cows too, which give people meat and milk.' He seemed to be considering this, and kept up his pace at Clockwork's side.

'And in your country,' he asked in the same tone as before, 'do you ride horses?'

Yes, I said, England was a horse-loving nation.

'And in your country,' he asked again, looking upwards to me this time, 'how often do you sleep with your wife?'

I asked him to repeat the question, because I thought he said 'beat your wife', the colloquial verb being very similar.* Yes, that is exactly what he meant, he said, and his rugged face broke into a wicked grin.

'Well...' I thought, not very often these days, since our divorce, but let's see, in the good old days – 'as often as she permits!' And he understood this right away and the valley echoed with our laughter. It was an incongruous conversation; I had always thought the Afghans fanatically prudish. Here only the mountains shared our secrets.

'Well, in Afghanistan,' he informed me, as though before all else we should understand this important distinction, 'a man "beats with" his wife at least three times a week. Newlyweds do it every day for a

---

* The verb means: to strike together, to dash against; to shoot, fire off, discharge, beat; to sound, blow, or play an instrument, etc.

whole month. Not like the Pakistanis – ' he went on, savouring a deep breath of the virile air – 'their hot climate makes them weak, and they haven't got the energy for it . . .'

I missed a lot of the details that followed, but it had broken the ice between us and Ali Khan became more talkative, lapsing into curious and thoughtful banter.

*

It was early afternoon when we stopped at what looked like a pile of rocks and Ali Khan began to unload Clockwork: with a sinking feeling I realized this was the local hotel. An old man greeted us. He wore a white turban and corduroy jacket and crouched in the shelter of a rough low wall. Around his neck hung a pair of antique brass binoculars. Yes, we would stay there for the night, said Ali Khan. The place was called Shalzor. Its stone walls were three feet high and enclosed the space of a large closet, and the roof was made from sacks and canvas; inside smoked a primitive stove. It seemed ridiculous to have stopped for the night so early, but it was the last resting-place before the Anjomān Pass, and at three o'clock the sun would disappear behind the high peaks and the temperature would drop like a stone.

From the wind-blasted bothy we watched three horses, specks at first, take shape along the track from below. Ali Khan and the old man speculated over their origin; there was no such thing as travelling anonymously in Afghanistan. As they drew nearer I recognized the men I had ridden with in the jeep, who greeted me like an old friend. Their horses were loaded with heavy sacks. They had guns too, which they carried stripped but reassembled as it grew darker. I wondered if they were expecting trouble: the sacks were full of cash. I wondered, too, how six men would fit in the tiny rock hut, until another four men and horses arrived, and the thought gave way to resignation.

Mountain air is thin and holds heat poorly. A few minutes after the sun slipped behind the peaks in the southwest it grew suddenly colder. I had a pair of thick woollen trousers and put them over my light ones. That made four layers, including two layers of long underwear in silk and cotton. Then I put on two shirts, sweater, jacket and *pattū*, making seven layers. The wolfskin hat covered my head, and a scarf my face; an extra pair of long socks went around my neck, and another over my gloves. I was completely frozen.

I wandered from the hut and studied the face of the far side of the valley through a pair of pocket binoculars. A thousand yards away I could make out a man standing motionless on the far crest. What could he be doing there, alone, in this wilderness? I turned my head and was startled by a boy of about fifteen who had appeared silently by my side and squatted next to me without saying a word, staring at the far side of the valley where I was looking. When I looked back, the solitary man was gone.

The boy nodded across the valley and asked me what I was doing. Just looking, I said — we Westerners did a lot of that, but there was really no way to translate the impulse to seek a moment of privacy. I asked him the names of the villages on the way to the pass; they were quite different from other versions I had heard of the route.

Did he know the way to Mīr Samir, I asked, that great mountain whose tip I fancied I could make out in the southeast? This was the peak Newby and Carless had failed so brilliantly to climb. It could only have been a few miles away. No, he said, that was far beyond his territory.

At five o'clock Venus appeared above us in the southwest, and the interlocking ridges began to recede in deepening shades of violet. My notes trail away in an unsteady hand: '5.10 p.m. Too cold to write.' I searched in vain for some familiar constellations in the sky but the peaks were so high only the stars directly overhead were visible. I went back to the hut where Ali Khan was flustered about my absence.

'I was worried,' he said. 'It's not safe. These mountains ...'

'And he was looking at the far side of the valley with his *dur-bin* [literally, 'distance-seers'] and writing the names of the villages between here and the pass in his little notebook,' added the boy in a matter-of-fact voice.

I made one last foray across the frozen ground to relieve myself of the tea we had been drinking in the hut. This normally uneventful operation became, in the cold, unforgettably frustrating. My fingers, after I had taken off my gloves, went quickly numb in the icy wind. I fumbled through the layers of clothing, searching more desperately at each second as the anticipation grew unbearable, but I had no precise sense of feeling where it mattered. Just before the moment of disaster I succeeded. How Apsley Cherry-Garrard managed such an operation in Antarctica, or whether he ever experienced a similar shock at the final excavation of something so alarmingly diminished by the cold, is never described. Nor the sweetness of success.

We had a few mouthfuls of rice for dinner washed down with unsweetened tea. Afterwards the men sang in turn in a tuneless but rhythmic wailing accompanied by the beating of metal saucepans. When it was time to sleep, the air shook with a cacophony of grunting and clearing of throats, and we lined up head to toe like sardines in a can.

*

We stumbled from the hut in the freezing darkness. It was six o'clock in the morning. My old constellations were back in their proper places: Orion was resurrected, his sword flashing in the south; Ursa Major was riveted with renewed boldness against the sky overhead, and Cassiopeia, tilting at a matching incline, rested on the black rim of a distant ridge.

Ali Khan drew the cold-stiffened ropes taut over Clockwork with his leathery fingers. Mine were numb. Our breaths glowed like trailing clouds as we headed for the pass.

It was bitterly cold. I remembered a balaclava I had seen in a shop in London and thought: it'll never get cold enough for that. Now I understood how it was possible for people to simply give up at such temperatures. I wanted to sit down and stop, to huddle against a rock and think of nothing, to submit utterly to the embrace of the cold. I cursed my own stupidity for not having invested in a proper coat, and held my hands under my armpits and blew into my *pattū*. I counted my steps and then counted backwards, made mental lists to add and subtract from, and tried to avoid the sense of expectation aroused by looking at the route ahead to guess where we might next rest. Ali Khan, who never added or subtracted a layer from his clothes, either by night or day, marched stoically forward.

As it climbed the path grew less distinct and we slipped on icy scree and patches of frozen snow. Two and a half hours later, numb and exhausted, we reached another shelter, barely distinguishable from the snow and boulders from which it was made, clinging to a rise on the far side of a broad and frozen stream. Inside, a stove was burning fiercely in the corner, tended by a lonely keeper who made us tea. Even next to it I felt no heat in my fingers. We huddled silently, our hands wrapped around glasses of tea, waiting for the sunrise, as the wind snapped angrily at the canvas walls.

*

The Anjomān Pass is not truly the head of the Panjshīr valley but lies to the south of the river, which below us had narrowed to a few feet. The source of the Panjshīr, I now realized, emerges from a jostling mass of snowy peaks where no path leads. From the west side where we were, the approach to the pass is slow and steady. But it is quite high – over thirteen thousand feet. If not for this pass there would be no direct route to the north; Panjshīr would lead nowhere, and the route to Badakhshān would pass either through Nuristan or along the northern flank of the Hindu Kush, which the modern road follows. Both are much longer and indirect. But there is a pass; and through it the whole history of the place has been funnelled. Afghans trotted over it without fuss; Westerners like myself took cigars in their bags to celebrate reaching it.

Ali Khan talked about hunting as we thawed. There were bears, wolves, snow leopards and various great mountain goats, he said. He conjured an idyllic summer, when the flanks of the mountains were the colour of emerald and the smell of blossom lingered in the balmy air. If I came back then, he said, he would find a gun and we would go hunting for an animal he called an *ahū*. I thought this meant gazelle;* he must have meant the famous Marco Polo sheep (*Ovis polii*),

---

* I have just looked it up in that indispensable but problematic companion of students of classical Persian, F. J. Steingass's great dictionary of 1930. The entry is: *Ahū*, A vice, fault, defect, stain, spot, villainy; flight, escape; an exclamation, cry for help; an asthma; a deer, roe, gazelle; any object of for which prosperous foreigners before the war paid thousands of dollars to hunt in the area. I unbent my tingling fingers and drew a curly-horned animal in my notebook; no, no, he said, it was like this — and drew a duck-like creature with flattened, spindly ears. He apologized for the quality of the drawing, saying pen and paper were not his thing. What he had drawn was an ibex.

Above us the sunlight hit the high peaks with an explosion of gold against ice, and they roared into life as if hungry for its touch. It was several hours' trek to the pass in the remorseless wind. The sun, although it gave more hope than warmth, was a gift more precious than I can describe. The lower Panjshīr had dropped far below us, and looking back I saw wave after wave of mountains and the icy cap of Mīr Samir just proud of the other ranges.

At the pass, the view was breathtaking. Ahead of us to the east was a great cluster of snowy peaks, vast spires of frozen rock eighteen thousand feet high. They looked close enough to touch. Beyond the pass the land fell steeply, scarred with tight switchbacks that disappeared towards a valley several thousand feet below. In the far distance about a hundred miles away towered a vast, gold-draped pyramidal beacon of ice. There was only one mountain like that, I knew. It was the magnificent Tirich Mīr, the 25,000-foot monster on the Chitral side of the border.*

We were three times the height of Ben Nevis, and I wanted a photograph. I fumbled at the controls of my camera with numb fingers, and took a picture of Ali Khan. At that very moment we were joined by a solitary man who had popped up from the other side of the pass. They posed together. It seemed impossible to believe that one day the film would reach home, let alone render intelligible

---

pursuit or chase; a beautiful eye; a mistress. (A comprehensive Persian–English dictionary including the Arabic words and phrases you will encounter in Persian literature, being Johnson and Richardson's Persian, Arabic, and English dictionary revised, enlarged, and entirely reconstructed by F. J. Steingass, Francis Joseph Steingass, 1825–1903, London, K. Paul, Trench, Trubner & Co., Ltd [1930].)

* At least I hope it was Tirich Mīr: perhaps someone can correct me if it wasn't.

pictures. I had hoped to catch Ali Khan smiling. But Afghans strike such stern and martial bearings at the sight of a camera it is rare to catch a smile on film, and the resulting impression — these days invariably embellished with guns and grenade launchers — is deeply misleading: no other people I know break more readily into smiles.

It was simply too cold to linger, and I was warned not to stray from the path onto the scree-covered slopes, which Ali Khan said were covered with Russian mines. Just as I had found it hard to picture tanks squeezing through the valley below us, I had trouble imagining the pass echoing with the clatter of giant helicopters, gunfire and explosions. But not far from us was a huge crater, and wondering whether it was natural or not I looked for others in line with it. Sure enough there were two other craters from what I guessed were thousand-pound bombs, and I thought of how the valley must have echoed.

✻

It was a steep descent, tortured by a three thousand-foot cascade of hairpin turns. The climb in the opposite direction must have been hellish. I could not help thinking of the mujaheddin, hauling all the paraphernalia of warfare up this very trail for years. An entire jeep had been disassembled and brought over this or a similar pass for the use of Massoud and his commanders. I had seen a picture of it: being the only motorized vehicle in the entire valley, it was a prize target for the Russians, who tried to destroy it with fanatical diligence. It was filled with bullet and shrapnel holes, and looked like a salt-shaker on wheels.

Our toes jammed into the tips of our boots as we twisted downwards, stirring tiny wakes of dust above the trail. Gradually the cold receded, and we talked. Ali Khan asked me what it was I was always writing in my little notebook. I told him if I didn't write a diary I would forget the details of my trip, and be unable to write a book from memory alone. As we talked I could see the expression 'a book about Afghanistan' meant something quite different to him, or perhaps, more likely, nothing at all.

'And then you will give this book to your government?' he asked.

'No. It has nothing to do with my government.'

'Then what is your *wazifeh*?'

Books, to Ali Khan, were something to do with governments; it was no good trying to get into the idea of genre. Rural Afghanistan was populated by unlettered poets, not bookworms, whose cultural history flowed down the generations through verse and stories, not in the classroom.* I could tell from Ali Khan's mute expression that the idea of writing a book was something alien to his world, as mysterious as a wandering Afghan bard in a London suburb. As far as my Persian would allow I persisted with an explanation.

'Well, in my *watan* people have heard little about Afghanistan. Sometimes they have heard bad things about its people.' I thought back to the newspaper editor I had offered my first story about the war: he had asked me how I could have lived among such 'barbarians'.

'And some,' I told him, 'think Afghans are *wakhshi* people, wild men, killers, hashish-smokers, and lovers of war.'

Afghans love being told this: he roared with laughter.

'And they may not have heard anything else about Afghanistan.'

'But they know how we beat the Russians, don't they?' he asked, looking serious again. I wished I could say yes; that the ten years of

---

*   It is said that Afghanistan has a literate culture but a non-literate society, in which poetry is a vital element. Outside the state-run school system (which no longer functions) children were traditionally taught basic literacy in village Qur'ānic schools or *maktab*; small and local *madrassehs* also formed a significant role in traditional education. Religious instruction was guided by a *mowlāwi*, whose subjects, in common with *madrassehs* throughout the Islamic world, would range over theology, Qur'ānic interpretation, classical Arabic, the prophetic Hadith or traditions, and Islamic law. In Afghanistan the subjects of study would extend to classical Persian literature and poetry and Sufism, through which a broad range of historical, moral and social values would be transmitted. A well-known *mowlāwi* from the village of Astana in the Panjshīr supplemented his teaching with instruction from Galen and Euclid; he is said to have constructed an astrolabe, calculated the latitude of his village and written to the government to request a correction to the official maps. His home was destroyed by the Soviet bombing of 1984.

continuous warfare at the cost of a million Afghan dead, which Afghans today look upon as an unrewarded gift to the West, were remembered more vividly.

'Some do. But I would like to write about your country and its people, something about the Afghan character; their hospitality, for example . . .'

'That's right, we treat our guests very seriously.' He nodded. And after some time — we were near the valley floor now — and much mangled Persian on my part, I felt I had succeeded in sharing with him a rough idea of my goals. But by his response I could tell he had no idea what the point of such an endeavour might be.

'So how much does your government pay you to write such a book?' he asked.

The sun was almost overhead now, and the air had grown thicker as we had lost height. Suddenly I realized the wind had stopped completely, and I felt a caress of warmth on my face for the first time since we had left Qoriye together.

'Not a penny, Ali Khan, I swear.'

'So you have come here out of your own pocket?'

'Exactly.'

In my own language this was generally understood to mean I was forking out money on a horribly tight budget. But to Ali Khan the notion of a man paying his own way for a journey suggested almost limitless resources of wealth and leisure. Nobody *short* of money would undertake such a thing. Again I was reminded of what a very Western pursuit is the business of travel — what a strange and improbable liberty it really is to be able to wander about a country halfway across the world from one's own. I tried to remind him that my government had nothing to do with it, and that the outcome was far from certain. I think perhaps he was disappointed by the news, or felt there was something I was not telling him. I tried to convey the notion that the writing of a book was a personal endeavour with an equally uncertain outcome, and this too seemed to disagree with him (it began to sound disagreeable to me too). A farmer, perhaps, was dependent on the seasons, and obliged to put his hands into Fate's — that was a farmer's lot. But a foreign lord?

'So when it's over with, and you have written your book,' he said, with the confident air of having understood all this, '*then* how much will your government pay you?'

*

Mention of the war brought out some old stories. He spoke animatedly about the brutality of the Russians. I missed many of the details. He was vehement about their commandos, whom he had fought against in these very hills. The mujaheddin had no respect for ordinary Soviet soldiers, who fought whenever possible from the protection of their tanks and armoured vehicles. It was their 'black soldiers', he said, who were really dangerous: the mujaheddin's name for Spetznaz units. The 'special designation' troops were highly trained commandos attached to the Soviet Intelligence Directorate. They were better armed than ordinary soldiers, better motivated, and specialized in intelligence-gathering missions, ambush and daring raids into enemy strongholds. They are said to have disguised themselves as mujaheddin and attacked villages with the aim of spreading disunity and suspicion among civilians.

Then there were the relentless bombings; the long journeys to Pakistan and its miserable climate to stock up with arms, and some tales of Massoud's military ingenuity against the incredible odds of the time. Yes, said Ali Khan to my question, it was true that Massoud almost always knew about major Soviet operations in advance. Even at the highest level Afghan army officers passed on intelligence to the mujaheddin. What godless arrogance on the Russians' part, exclaimed Ali Khan, to think they could ever take and hold Afghanistan!

Yet by his tone all that seemed long ago now. Not forgotten, but transcended by the urgency of the newer threat to the government: the Tālebān. It was the Tālebān that grieved him nowadays, those misguided men who had taken the sacred name of Tāleb, masquerading under a holy title; and here, too, I missed many of the details, but they were not flattering. I caught only snippets of their ways, a mention of their hashish-smoking, forbidden by Islam, and some unsavoury references to young boys. It was the standard demonization I had heard in Kabul.

'You're saying they are *fased*, corrupt?' I had suddenly remembered the word.

'Corrupt! That's exactly it!' he beamed.

Ali Khan had fought under Massoud against the Russians for ten years. He was a typical Panjshīri; incredibly hardy, committed to a deeply traditional way of life, and possessed of an uncomplicated ingenuity. I thought: what a strange and typical mixture he was of the worldly and unworldly. I had seen something of these apparently opposing qualities among men like him during the war, and there was nothing like the war to bring out the contrast.

That the decision to kill a Russian prisoner or spare his life might lie in his willingness to convert to Islam by uttering no more than a few sacred syllables seemed perfectly normal; but the same men who would take such a decision knew exactly how much explosive was needed to rip open the belly of a Soviet tank. Ali Khan and mujaheddin like him might have been lolling one minute under mulberry trees, reading the poetry of a tenth-century saint, flicking the fruit into their mouths and joking like young boys, and the next, hauling a multiple rocket-launcher over a frozen pass in tennis shoes. There was no conflict in this – no intellectual impasse. They suffered little of the psychological and spiritual dislocation of modern soldiers returning from conflicts in alien cultures. The war against the Soviets was not something separate from life, a campaign imposed by some great ideological machine and carried out by trained fighters who would one day return home: it was life itself, and they were already home.

Reading newspaper reports at the time about the 'Moslem rebels', 'Holy Warriors of Islam', and 'fighters in the name of Allah' – to name a few of the more woeful translations of 'mujaheddin', which simply means 'those who struggle' – you could be forgiven for thinking of them as a mountain-bound troop of intransigent fanatics resisting a perfectly decent transition to socialist rule. These 'Holy Warriors', many of whom were not so holy, represented the majority of ordinary Afghans throughout the country. Farmers, students, professors, businessmen, the lettered and unlettered, rich and poor – all rose spontaneously against the communists and the army that came to support them. They were divided by language and ethnicity much as Europe was divided in its last great war, but united by a profound love for their country and dedicated to the preservation of their own freedom.

This terminology seems worn out today: perhaps we have heard it too often. I had been deeply sceptical of heroic stories which filtered out of the war in its early years – of villagers attacking tanks with shovels, of old men volunteering to walk across minefields to clear a way for younger fighters, of schoolchildren who paid with their lives to denounce their invaders in the classroom – and which kindled the impulse to see the place for myself.

The very first Afghans I met said they would rather fight to the last man than allow the Russians to control their country. This kind of claim had a ring of ancient bravado about it, and one took it with a pinch of twentieth-century salt. But after I had met the people inside the country who were really doing the fighting I felt I would need an entirely new vocabulary to describe them: it was not bravado at all, and no price was too high for its fulfilment. A wizened old villager once put it to me simply: to lose one's home, he said, was nothing; to lose one's health was something; but to lose one's freedom – ah, that was quite a different matter: the Russians would never get away with that.

*

We reached the valley floor now and began to skirt the banks of the river Monjan. It was shallow here, flanked by auburn trees, and weaved in sparkling braids through diamond-shaped islands of grey sand. The air was noticeably thicker and warmer. We were still high, but at least out of that mad world of altitude where things human are not designed to function. The mountains towered above us. On a high ridge I fancied I could make out the crenellated wall of a pre-Islamic fort or the withered ramparts of a monastery forgotten by time; both were tricks of the light and mind.

A few miles on we stopped to rest at a tiny stone shack. In this lonely spot there was a man inside who passed us a bowl of rice from a stone porthole in a smoke-blackened chamber. I studied my map to try to find a lake I had seen in the distance, but it was not marked. I asked Ali Khan what its name was. 'Lake nothing,' he said, 'just "lake".'

In the distance it looked like a slab of lapis lazuli set in the dusty valley floor. Far beyond it, the royal summit of Tirich Mīr, a sunlit pinnacle of ice, rested in the vee of the valley's sights. Ali Khan refused to believe that the mountain was in Pakistan, as if such a noble peak could not possibly lie within the territory of such a base people. Later he conceded that it might well have not been in today's Afghanistan, but certainly used to be – which was true, because it was the British who had drawn the line of the present border to our south. We reached the lake three hours later, having walked through the most beautiful territory I had ever seen. It was Lake Anjomān.

We threw rocks that skittered across the half-frozen surface. The water was the clearest I have ever seen. Foreigners used to trek here before the war and fish for giant trout. All I could think of was how much I would like to return to the place one day with my best friends and blast the walls of the mountains with Puccini and fish in the lake and chill white wine in the water. It was a pedestrian fantasy and I was disappointed by my own thoughts, because at such a beautiful sight I would have hoped for something more sublime. It is strange what thoughts come to you when you are riding alone in silence through such a wilderness; I have forgotten them all now, but I remember feeling certain that life would never be quite the same.

A solitary eagle with a white breast flew high across our path and Ali Khan began to sing. The dust from Clockwork's hooves rose in swirls behind him like drops of golden ink in water. In the valley beyond an armed man on a proud cream-coloured horse cantered across the yellowed grass towards us, then slowed as we approached and let his horse drink from a pool as we passed. Something about me caught his eye, and he called to Ali Khan.

'Peace be to you! Is he a *kharejī*?'

'No,' said Ali Khan. It was funny to hear him lie. 'He's a *watandar* (countryman) from Tajikistan.' The man looked at me and at Ali Khan and we all smiled at this obvious conspiracy.

I was troubled by having been recognized so easily.

'Why is it,' I asked Ali Khan, 'that people know that I am a *khareji*?'

'Well, that's obvious,' he said. 'They take one look at those boots of yours and they know right away, because no man possesses boots such as yours. And then they see those socks, which we wear differently here. And then they notice your gloves, because people don't have gloves. And then they see that jacket of yours, the like of which you never see in Afghanistan. Then they see your *jampar*, and know you are no Afghan. But if it weren't for those, no one would know you weren't a Panjshīri.'

He asked whether in my country I had a horse of my own. When I told him they were too expensive, he offered me Clockwork, and said he had a better horse, a *buzkashi* horse, in a secret place. He would get a pony for my daughter, he said, and come to England to teach her to ride — why, we could even export horses and start a thriving business. All he had to do was get the horses onto a plane at the airport. Our business plan took flight as we passed mountains split with vast tributary gashes and pierced with ragged intrusions the colour of chocolate, rust and slate.

After horses came women, religion, and the merits of different guns, saddles and cows. How was it that women went to work where I came from? In Afghanistan it was much simpler, said Ali Khan; the men worked outside the home and the women took care of the home and animals. How much was a dowry in England? Who paid for the wedding? What did the rest of my family do in life? He was especially interested in my father and brothers. Yet the variety of careers in the West seemed too incredibly exotic to contemplate explaining. I said my father was a teacher and my brothers were merchants.

I was at a loss for many of these explanations even in English, let alone in my unpolished Persian, and tried to find ways in which our worlds might overlap. I found myself not only translating from one spoken language to another, but across a gulf of meanings and significances, against which the business of words and their equivalents seemed straightforward.

Again and again I felt thrown up against the ideological frontier dividing our universes. You can travel across continents to reach a different civilization but the barrier of ideas that separates one culture from another remains as formidable as ever. Ali Khan's questions reflected a world where the constraints (and satisfactions) of tradition – partly cultural, partly the supra-cultural conventions of Islam – ran deeply through all the stages and rituals of life. All of them led me back to the same thought: what an extraordinary place of liberties the West really is, and how incomprehensible these liberties seem to those bound to harsher and more traditional ways of life. They have become so fundamental to the Western way of life we think of them as 'rights' – the rights to choose one's own livelihood or partner in life, to criticize one's politicians, to travel abroad at will, free of restraints or obligations – unthinkable in so many other countries. But if the West is a place of privilege, people suffer differently there too. Exempt from many of the relentless physical and social obligations necessary in a traditional life for survival, they become spoiled and fragile like overbred dogs; neurotic and prone to a host of emotional crises unknown elsewhere.

In the West a man or woman discovers the first extent of these freedoms in adolescence. In Afghanistan, it began to dawn on me, there was really no such thing: a girl was a girl or a woman; a boy was a boy or a man. There was no convenient proving ground when a young man or woman went about for ten years or more wondering how to make himself or herself useful (or not) to society. A boy of thirteen had already learned to shoot or ride or ply his father's trade; while his sister learned the duties of the household essential for married life.

Yet, as in the mountains around us, so impenetrable from a distance, there were in our conversations passes and natural breaches that linked our different worlds. We joked and laughed and pondered the strange ways of each other's lives. Knowing the distance between we were brought all the closer to each other, and as the miles passed I felt I could have had no better companion.

*

A narrow gorge led from the lake into another serene and barren valley. An hour later, as dusk was falling, I noticed the first fields of cut wheat and rocks cleared from the fields to make walls between them. There was a village ahead where the houses seemed to rise organically from the soil. Beyond it the high peaks were bathed in gold, although below them we were in shadow now and the temperature fell every minute. The village was Anjomān, a cluster of about sixty buildings tucked on the southern flanks of the slopes above the river, and bordered by carefully tended fields of wheat. After the barrenness and silence of our route I felt we were about to rejoin all the pleasures of high civilization. An old man ushered a flock of sheep into a stony pen, and on a path between the fields a woman carried a pot of water on her head as her daughter trotted behind.

Ali Khan unloaded Clockwork and filled his nosebag. He ushered me inside a mud-walled *serai*, and went to pray at the village mosque, towards which men were hurrying from every direction at the wailing call of the village *mullā*. I entered an unlit room and sat against the wall. As my eyes adjusted to the darkness I could make out the shapes of several men. They were all suffering from racking, watery coughs which I hoped were not infectious.

An old man with a laryngitis-stricken voice and a bandaged hand scrutinized me for a few minutes, then asked where I had come from. Panjshīr, I said. Was there snow on the pass? A little, I said. He seemed satisfied, and I was delighted to have succeeded in passing myself off as a native.

But the old man wheezed a question as Ali Khan entered.

'Where in this world is your friend from?'

'Ha! You would never believe where he is from.' He enjoyed this little tease; he too got weary of the inevitable questioning and, I noticed, at each stop, a little more protective of me. I heard two men speak among themselves in the shadows.

'Is he a believer?'

'Not a chance,' said the other, 'he's a foreigner and a *kafir*.'

'By Allah, he is NOT!' Ali Khan shot back, overhearing them. And then, almost coyly, he said: 'Everywhere we go people think he is a Moslem.'

I was touched by his defence, which expressed a wonderful ambiguity. It did not matter that I might not be a Moslem: it was enough that people thought I was. In a country where a man's integrity is judged by his adherence to the multiplicitous regulations of religion, the distinction between believer and unbeliever is bound to be fierce. Yet in Afghanistan, where of all the Islamic nations you might least expect to find such a softening at the edges, the natural sense of moderation of the people has always kept extremes of religious behaviour in check. Only under the cataclysmic influence of the Soviets were religious leaders able to gain exceptional power; traditionally the *mullā*'s rhetoric was kept in check.

The vast majority of Afghans are deeply observant of religious tradition, but are no purists, and many of their traditions pre-date the strictures laid down by Islam. There is consequently a definite spirit and an equally distinct letter to religion. What you hear, when a person's behaviour cannot be measured by the traditional criteria, is whether a thing is 'close to Islam' or 'far from Islam'. And unconsciously this provides an antidote for the at times overbearing influence of religious rules and regulations – which is perhaps why Afghans, who have never enjoyed being told too much how to behave, make frequent use of the expression.

*

A lantern appeared and men, as it always seemed, filed inside from nowhere. The room was eight feet by twenty-five, with two windows a foot square in walls two feet thick. Even inside our breath steamed in the icy air. A young boy brought in three blackened metal bowls of broth and a pile of flat bread, and laid them on a long plastic tablecloth.

Each man broke his portion of bread into pieces, taking turns to push the morsels beneath the surface of the thickening soup, so that even before we had begun to eat at least twenty different hands had been submerged into what was to be our dinner. I hadn't much of an appetite. Half a dozen of the men had raging, liquid coughs, and every few minutes spat whatever they dredged from their watery lungs behind the mattresses on which we sat. Ten days earlier I had eaten from gold-plated china at the Turkish embassy.

I had a raging thirst, and began to look around for a cup. Just then the boy returned with a metal bucket out of which he scooped a glass and handed it to the man at the far end of the room. In turn it was passed down the line, until finally it reached me after a long series of quite possibly tubercular baptisms. I wrestled with my squeamishness, thought how disastrous it would be to fall ill, agonized for a few moments, and drank several cupfuls. It was delicious.

After we had eaten the men talked quietly about how hard times had become. They were in obvious distress – their health reflected this – and bore it with great dignity. Ali Khan had acquired an expertise in diverting questions away from the stranger in their midst, and held forth with flair and authority on trade and horses and the prices of staples and the situation in Kabul. He was obviously respected by the other villagers. I felt deeply thankful to have him for my guide and not the timid character I had first contemplated.

Later I wrote my diary under the gaze of at least ten men, who scrutinized at close range the oddly shaped, backwards-moving script emerging from my pen. I wanted to escape and slipped the flask from my pack and walked down to the river, following the roar of the water in the darkness. The boulders at its edges were glazed with ice. The stars were as bright as I had ever seen and seemed almost within reach. I took a swig of the whisky and just the smell of it swept me into a different world. Suddenly I missed the company of friends like a stab of memory, and seemed in the roar of the torrent to hear conversations going on at home and longed for warmth, lawns, and the softness of the familiar.

*

We loaded Clockwork in the pale light of dawn. As Ali Khan tightened my bag over his stubborn rump, the cropper snapped. I improvised a new one from a climbing sling I had tucked in my bag, feeling it would at some point surely be useful – perhaps to bind a splint or secure a man on a safety line to cross a boiling river – but I had never imagined it stretched under a horse's tail.

I was about to put my foot in the stirrup when a frail old man with a white turban appeared at my side. His striking blue eyes were cloudy with age. He made a silent, hopeless gesture at his clothes, and tugged lovingly at my down-filled waistcoat. The buttons on his jacket caught my eye: it was a wartime uniform from the Royal Canadian Air Force. I knew how cold it would be ahead and said I couldn't give him my own. But as I write this I see the old man's eyes and am reminded, with a regret for that moment more than any other of the whole journey, of my selfishness.

The village *mullā* guided us out of the village. Ali Khan was hoping to sell him Clockwork, describing his finer qualities with all the visible untruth of a second-hand car salesman. The *mullā* was appropriately sceptical and said he would have to think about it.

Once more the golden blessing of the morning light unfurled across the high peaks, descending slowly towards us like a luminous balm dispensed from above by a healing god. We rode in and out of the shadows of high ridges, fording tributaries fringed with icicles and boulders coated with sparkling ice. Clockwork performed his usual heart-stopping stunt of veering to the edge of the track whenever it ran high above the river, which was the colour of sapphire now and writhed around boulders the size of hot air balloons. Each stage possessed a distinct and individual beauty, and our pace seemed designed for its fullest appreciation. In places the mountain walls were ragged like a cat's tongue, as sheer as the sides of a dam, or fractured into vast stairways of angular ledges spilling angrily downwards into fans of splintered scree. All was bathed in the pristine light that lent a sense of trespass to our advance.

When Clockwork spotted an approaching horse his ears would spring up like train signals and Ali Khan would run up from behind, *choo*-ing furiously. Then he would beat Clockwork into a shattering trot, to which I, in turn, would do my best to look indifferent. When it was his turn to ride he would drive him far ahead at a speed faster than I could ever hope for, wheel him fiercely around, and canter back towards me.

Talk turned to horses again. I remembered a story that had surfaced unexpectedly from childhood. I was ten years old when my grandfather had recounted it; all of a sudden I remembered the tears welling up in his eyes as he spoke. It was the Somme in 1917, and the young artillery officer had been thrown from his horse by the blast of a German shell. Dazed, he staggered back to his wounded mount, who lay dying nearby. Realizing there was no hope, he kissed its white forelock (I saw again the tenderness with which he had repeated the gesture, cradling the remembered head between slightly trembling hands) and with the one bullet that remained in his pistol, shot his beloved companion dead.

*

We stopped for an hour in the early afternoon at a stone house perched on a rise at a bend in the track. This was the village of Qalt. I walked down to the river to wash beside a grove of slender silver birch whose leaves had surrendered themselves to the season and lay stranded in pools trapped between pebbles. Here the water and the air were as pure and fragrant as I had ever seen, as though the world in that spot were suspended in crystal and things took on their rightful shapes and shades as they were originally intended by Nature, without distortion.

The valley beyond was broad and filled with thorny bushes and small trees with auburn leaves. Magpies gossiped at the water's edge. On the rocks by the track we saw the first of many hieroglyphics; stylized ibexes like the one Ali Khan had drawn for me. They might have been very ancient or drawn by the men who had passed this way the day before, but I had no way to tell.

Ali Khan would often ask me if I were tired, and whether I wanted to ride. I said we should stick to our agreement, and that I was only sometimes tired, 'like in life', I said, and recited my old couplet from Hafez: 'Though the way is full of perils, and the goal far out of sight...'

'Hah! Bravo!' he chuckled. 'Do people read Hafez in England?'

'A few. And they have heard of Mevlānā Jelāluddīn Rūmī, too.'

'Master Rūmī? In England? Well I never ... You must make a translation, so that everyone in England can read him,' he said, and began to spout couplets, which I endeavoured to match but quickly exhausted my supply. I told him that when I was younger I had visited Turkey and paid my respects at the tomb of the saint himself.

'By Allah!' he beamed. 'There's no difference between your religion and mine after all!'

*

We had entered a region rich in minerals and the mountain walls were coloured now, with reds like the blood of bitter oranges or gifted with the desert shades of the grand canyon: grey, ginger, mahogany. One vast triangular mound was the cuprous shade of unpolished malachite. I saw another white-breasted eagle fly overhead, and smaller, energetic birds with purple throats and white caps by the river.

Squeezing through a gorge at the head of the valley we changed direction to reach a col leading to another valley to our north. Its steep sides were the colour of ochre and the soft rock perforated like a honeycomb or some prehistoric monastic settlement. A steep trail which I doubted Clockwork would manage led down. It twisted sharply between overhanging buttresses and splintered boulders. I went ahead, guiding Clockwork by his bridle, while Ali Khan held his tail as a brake from behind. The poor animal slipped a dozen times on the rocks, falling heavily to his knees; he was exhausted, and it was a miserable descent. Then on the valley floor we padded for an hour through soft dust as the shroud of the evening tightened around us and in the distance there was smoke, a house, a bridge, a corral, and the promise of rest.

We had reached Eskāzer. In the fading light I was subjected to a friendly interrogation by a tall man with long, curly black locks and a deep voice. A few other men gathered round to hear the exchange. Their eyes caught the gleam of an oil lantern and were wide with fascination.

'Where are you from, brother?'

'England. *Inglestān*.'

'Hindustan?' (meaning India, which unlike England he had heard of).

'No, *Inglestān*. That way.' I pointed west.

'Near Hindustan?'

'No, further away. Much further.'

'Well then where is it near?'

'Um ... Turkey.'

'Oh, yes – in Egypt! What is your language?'

'English.'

'Never heard of it. Do you have horses there?'

'Yes, but they're very expensive.'

'What about watermelons?'

'Some, but not as many as here.'

'And who is your king?'

'Well, one day maybe, a man called Charles.'

'Gandhi?'

'No – CHARLES.'

'Is he related to Gandhi?'

'Distantly.'

'Does he go to a mosque to pray?'

'A big English mosque.'

'What is your currency?'

'Pounds.'

'Like rupees?'

'Just like rupees.'

He took my wrist in his hand and looked at the face of my watch, asking if I would give it to him. It had been a gift from my wife. Despite this I was quite fond of it. He offered me his own, pointing out cheerfully that it didn't work.

We ate – I counted twenty-one men – in a tiny room built on stilts by the water's edge, opposite a similar building on the far side, where lanterns like fireflies traced the paths of walking men. It was a wild but peaceful place.

Inside, there were the inescapable questions. Did I perhaps know the foreign men who had tried – the implication being foolishly – to climb the great mountain Mīr Samir? asked the whitebeard who ran the place.

'They did not succeed,' he said, because (there was a rumble of agreement from the other men) Mīr Samir could not be climbed by man.

Speculation as to my origins and purpose was inexhaustible. But by now Ali Khan answered questions on my behalf like a charismatic vizier. Hearing him speak I realized he had not only taken in every word of what I had said during the day but digested it into a wonderful fiction of his own. He held forth with a spellbinding oratory filled with shameless exaggeration.

Seldom were there travellers such as I, he began, who had not only fought at great personal risk in the time of the *jehād* but had now forsaken the comforts of home to write a great book about Afghanistan that would be read throughout the West, promoting trade and discourse between our nations and quite probably have consequences (although unspecified) of incalculable significance for the future of Afghanistan.

Steady on, Ali Khan, I thought. But he was only warming up. Was I not a scholar of profound religious belief myself? Had I not visited the shrines of saints throughout the East, and quoted to him that very day from the works of Master Hafez and Rūmī? My father, he said, was a great philosopher-poet respected throughout the empire of *Inglestān*. And my grandfather had been nothing less than a famous military leader and expert horseman, who with thousands of men under his command had masterminded the defeat of the godless Germans.

'What's he doing?' piped a turbaned pedant, as I looked for words in my pocket dictionary. 'What's that book of his?'

'That,' said Ali Khan coolly, with a complicitous glance in my direction and a measured note of disdain for the question, 'is a *religious* book, given to him by his spiritual teacher.'

*

As we stretched out for the night in the usual fashion of sardines, the ancient proprietor swept a space for me on the floor. He leaned towards me and asked in a whisper what my *bakhsheesh* might be for him. I took out my pen and said it was there; one day I would write about this place and he would be famous.

'What's the good of that?' he scoffed, and sank into the darkness.

Five

Before the catastrophe all visitors to Afghanistan fell in love with the Afghans, as if with their own fabled past, when we were proud, brave, independent, and witty and generous as well.

Doris Lessing, *The Wind Blows Away Our Words*

THIS WAS BADAKHSHĀN, Afghanistan's northernmost province, and one of its wildest. Eskāzer lay at the junction of three valleys. One headed southwest along the route we had followed, back to Panjshīr. Another led east via Kerān o Monjān to Pakistan (via Zeebak and its lung-splitting pass), Tajikistan (via Ishkashem on the river Panj), and China (via the Wakhān corridor). The other led north, following the Monjan river, via the ruby and lapis mines, to Faizābād. This was our route.

Through soft dust we trailed high above the junction of the rivers. The Soviets had one of their most remote bases here, and had pounded the valley in both directions with artillery flown in by helicopter. Here too there were bomb craters and I was warned not to stray from the track in case of mines.

The river had turned to the colour of jade now and looked quite different from the Panjshīr; the sapphire languor had gone out of it, and the water was a writhing cocktail of minerals, licked into its current from the foundations of unnamed mountains. The valley was narrower too, and the peaks on either side soared to nearly twenty thousand feet. The track wound ever higher above the river, which seemed to swirl just beyond the tip of my left boot. With disaster ever in mind I took my feet out of the improvised stirrups on the highest parts so as to be able to jump from Clockwork at the final moment. I do not regret this persistent inclination towards cowardice: at one point I felt sure it was all over. We were more than a hundred feet above the river, and I was riding. The track bent sharply to the right just where there was a slight overhang of rock, which caught my shoulder. I must have been daydreaming, and woke up with horrible suddenness; I laugh now, but at the time it was an ugly feeling.

I lost my balance and toppled so unexpectedly across Clockwork's back that he slipped on the exposed boulders of the path and fell to his knees. I tumbled beside him, and for a few seconds looked into his mute eyes; he was most un-Lippizaner-like with his legs pinned helplessly under him. Ali Khan was at his side like lightning, heaving his horse to his feet. But Clockwork's hind legs, tired, slipped over the edge of the track, scrabbling pitifully, and he began to disappear over the edge like a man sinking into quicksand. Ali Khan heaved at the ropes around the Clockwork's side and I gripped his mane uselessly, wondering whether his hair would come out in my hands. But his legs, finally, found a momentary hold beneath the ledge and with a truly desperate effort on everybody's part he was up again. We brushed the dust off our clothes, I looked at Ali Khan, he looked at me, and neither of us said anything.

*

Two hours later we glimpsed Ma'dān – the place of the mines – several miles ahead of us, betrayed by tiny wisps of smoke from its chimneys. Ali Khan spoke of the cluster of huts clinging to the desolate mountain as though it were Baghdad under Hāroun Al Rashīd, and our arrival a chapter worthy of the *Thousand and One Nights*. We could get kebabs there, he said with relish. And melons, and grapes even – you name it, he said, and we could get it there. I had by now an immodest vision of unlimited single malt and hot baths tended by doe-eyed *houris*, those willing maidens said to tend to a man's every whim in the Islamic version of the afterlife. Just then a sound like a muffled thunderclap rolled down the valley towards us and instantly I felt a familiar sense of alarm. It sounded like heavy artillery.

'Hear that?' Ali Khan turned to me with a conspiratorial grin. 'It's the mines.'

It was dynamite, and the explosions were bellowing out of the guts of the mountains. That inimitably coloured stone, lapis lazuli, has been mined in the Monjan valley for centuries, millennia perhaps; the mines are certainly pre-Islamic and the mountains are peppered with tunnels. During the war the stone was an important source of revenue. Mujaheddin carried it over the high passes to Pakistan to raise money for weapons. Today there is none of the equipment to cut and polish the stone, so it is carried out on horseback in raw lumps. The best stone is a pure and striking cyanic blue; inferior pieces are flecked with calcite, the crystalline matrix in which the stone is found, or iron pyrite that resembles gold.

Halfway up the mountain about a mile away was a black spot like the entrance to a cave. A procession of ant-like shapes was toiling up and down a thousand feet of zigzagging track that spilled from it; men and animals making their way from the mine to the village below, and back. It was a faintly sinister sight, as if we had uncovered some primitive and demonic industry hidden from the eyes of the ordinary population.

A creaking bridge of poplars crossed the river below the village, and a track led upwards towards a corral where a flock of miserable beasts of burden was gathered in forlorn huddles. There we left Clockwork among his own to rest from the day's trials, entrusted my bag to the keeper of the local *serai*, and set off to cruise main street, Ma'dān. The first thing I had noticed about the place was the ground; all around us were lumps of white stone veined with blue streaks of the gem, each one a treasure but worthless in the garden of their original home. I had the feeling a thief must experience on opening a brimming safe and had a sudden twinge of sympathy for the crimes people commit for the sake of precious stones. There was a small and busy market in the narrow street but it fell short of Scheherazade. All eyes followed us. There was a wild feeling that was not my imagination, a conspiratorial tension, perhaps the vestige of an instinctive sense of sacrilege at the violation of something precious from the womb of the hills.

An armed guard took us to the local commander, who read my permissions from Kabul. He kept a rifle by his side, fingered a set of green plastic prayer-beads and asked about our journey with a softly spoken and attentive courtesy. We drank tea in his tiny room and Ali Khan said my book would change the future of Afghanistan. I had hoped to be able to walk up to the mine entrance itself, but the overall commander of the place was not there and he could not give us permission. As if to compensate me for this disappointment he reached behind himself, putting his rifle aside, and fished out a fist-sized lump of the purest lapis. I tried to hand it back.

'Have it made into a necklace, and give it to your daughter,' he said quietly, and closed my fingers gently around it with his own.

In the *serai* I was given a space at the end of the room on a raised dais. Away from the glare of the lantern I was saved from the relentless scrutiny of the men who filled the room at sunset and Ali Khan I think was greatly relieved, because it was the first time he did not have to explain me. Men hauled in their dusty loads and beat them where they would sleep into the shape of pillows. At dusk a man in a fearful temper — I assume he was the local *mullā* — came into the *serai* and harangued the assembled men for not responding more enthusiastically to the evening call to prayer, accusing them of not being worthy of the title of Moslems and sweeping them from the room with the tail of his turban.

After Ali Khan returned (he, too, had been chastened by the *mullā*'s vehemence), we had double helpings of kebabs and melon and felt like kings. I watched as two ragged teenage boys explained to the owner they did not have enough to pay for their dinner. It was a tiny amount of money, but they were destitute.

'Think you can eat for free, do you?' grumbled the owner. And then from the pockets of the men all through the room came a little pile of notes, which mounted in front of the boys, who gave it to the owner with a look of shame.

When it was time to take off my boots and settle into my corner (a simple but precious thing, not to be trapped between two snoring men) a wave of ammoniac smell like the corner of a filthy stable rose up against my nostrils. What a filthy place this was, after all, I thought, and sniffed my way through the shadow towards it, hoping I might be able to cover it up. It was indescribably pungent. Then as I leaned over the edge, unexpectedly my nose hit a wall of the sweet stink, and I knew I had reached the source. It came from my socks.

*

The next day was our last together, although I didn't yet know it. By now it seemed normal that we would keep going through the mountains for ever. The dawn was the colour of slate. I dressed a blister on Ali Khan's toe in the light after he had returned from prayers, and his eyes fell longingly on the miniature knife that held the scissors I had used to cut a piece of gauze.

'Such a thing would be extremely useful to somebody like me,' he said with undisguised envy, listing the many ways, mostly to do with horses I think, that such a knife could be used. I knew I would give it to him.

We loaded Clockwork and set off to find someone who could change some money: I had no Afghan money left. Going from house to house we arrived after lengthy enquiries at a doorway beyond which a man was playing chess with a much older white-bearded man, who at our arrival brought tea and peeled me a delicious pear. Talk about money led to talk of the price of things in general, and our host shook his head and sighed. It was a conversation I heard repeated with only minor variations throughout the country, and always in the same bitter tones.

'Afghanistan is *kherāb*, ruined,' he said, and swept the pieces from the chessboard to illustrate his point.

'Here –' he put the king in the centre of the board – 'is Afghanistan.' Then he took another piece and smacked it onto a nearby square. 'And here is Pakistan.' A bishop jostled nearby. 'Here is Russia.' A queen closed in from the other side, and new pieces advanced at every name. 'America! Dostum! Gulbuddin! Tālebān!' His Afghanistan was soon encircled by the menacing pieces.

I asked him why such a distant player as America figured on his board.

'They abandoned us,' he said bitterly. 'For ten years we fought the Russians. America helped us then, when Russia was the enemy. When we defeated them, the Americans were gone. Look at this country now, which we ourselves destroyed believing they would help us afterwards.'

He waved his hand over the pieces in angry resignation. 'Afghanistan is *kherāb! Kherāb!*' His desperate note swelled to a plea. We stood up to leave.

'Hold on,' he said, and disappeared into another room, emerging moments later with a lump of the blue gem and pressed it into my hand with a warm smile.

'A souvenir.'

I protested, to no avail.

*

Remembering the day that followed I see first the light that I have seen nowhere else and which consumes in a single leap the impurity of distance so completely as to reveal the speck of a man two miles away; I see the profile of a mountain twenty miles away like a third peak between Clockwork's ears and the sharp outline of a tiny crevice high up that resembles a hooded monk, only it is a hundred feet high. I see the boiling jade snake of the river below us and a track clinging to the high cliffs wide enough for two horses only in a few places and propped up on its corners with sticks jammed between fractured rocks. I see three fantastic summits like spears with white tips rearing up to twenty thousand feet behind us, and down by the water's edge where the valley broadens, forests of small trees glowing gold and ginger in the winter sun with delicate pointed leaves and crimson berries the colour of a country girl's lips. I see on a tiny rock a white-throated warbler singing at the top of its lungs. And I see Ali Khan drawing near, short of breath from the climb, watching me as I look upwards at the walls of the mountains that enclose us, and I see him slip off his dusty turban to reveal the stubble that glints across his shaven scalp and wipe his calloused hand over his head and the perspiration on his chestnut brow and I see the furrows and lines of his rugged face flex magically into a broad smile as he too cocks his head at the giant wall of rock and says:

'Now that's what you call a fine big old mountain, eh?'

And with a suddenness that made me sad I saw the track had broadened to the width of a vehicle and I knew our trip was coming to an end. If there was a road it meant there would be a vehicle, and as soon as there was a vehicle Ali Khan would have completed his mission. We stopped to rest and eat a plateful of cold rice at a final lonely *chaikhāna*. Two men walked in as we ate; one was a tall fighter with a thick beard, staring eyes, a frozen half-smile and an unruly energy about him; the other was a forlorn teenage boy. The wild one barks in a loud voice, and slaps down his Kalashnikov with a clatter; his presence is intrusive. The boy picks up the gun and removes the magazine; he is toying with it. But he has difficulty with the magazine. The wild one sees me looking at the boy with a troubled expression, grabs the gun back from him, snaps the magazine back into place, shoulders a round into the breech, turns his gleaming eyes onto me, and stamps the rifle on its butt in front of me.

'You show him, then!' he barks. And smiles.

It is an Egyptian model of Kalashnikov, about ten years old. A little nervous, because I have not handled such a weapon for years, I take off the magazine, clear the chamber of its bullet, make safe and clip the bullet back with its family into the magazine. The owner grins a wild grin.

'It's yours,' he says, 'for seven *lakh!*'*

'I don't need it,' I say, and hand it back.

He chats with Ali Khan as we leave, then walks on ahead of us. As we round a bend I see a black bird on a rock in the middle of the river. Just as I am wondering what kind of bird it is there is the crack of a rifle shot, which echoes madly in an effort to escape from the valley. A tiny fountain erupts a few inches from the bird, sending it squawking. Further on there is a whiff of cordite in the air and I see the wild one slinging his rifle over his back.

We walk for another hour. Then there is a large mud-brick building ahead on the right and Clockwork veers towards it like a guided missile. We turn into it beneath high double gates and see in its compound four jeeps, and a man working under one of them. It is a strange sight because I have not seen a vehicle for what seems like years. Also it means that Ali Khan will leave me here, and I realize my journey with him is at an end.

'Aha!' I say as we enter.

'Aha!' says Ali Khan.

*

---

* A *lakh* is a hundred thousand Afghanis. At the going rate, therefore, a little less than a hundred pounds.

By midday the temperature had already begun to fall, and with it, my spirits. I was privately sad that Ali Khan would be leaving me in this wild place the next morning and found myself irritated by small things. There were fifteen men inside the *serai* and, subjected to the usual round of stares and questions, I quickly felt claustrophobic. To escape I scrambled up a hillside to write my diary alone, and when I came back the men were finishing their lunch. The cook told me there was no more food; Ali Khan looked down at the empty bowl in front of him and with a sheepish look strange to behold in such a tough man, apologized and said he didn't know where I'd gone.

A man on the far side of the room noticed my crestfallen expression and handed me his bowl with a handful of rice in it. Another rummaged for an age under the folds of his clothes and withdrew a dried-up lump of meat. I could only wonder how long it had been maturing in his pocket, but after all the effort he had made to excavate it and the earnest smile with which it was offered, I found it impossible to refuse.

It seemed likely I would be horribly ill as a consequence, and I began to feel even more gloomy. The wild-eyed commander came in and barked intrusive questions at me, and when I was rude to him in return he left the room, muttering, 'Well, I never...'

As darkness fell the room filled to bursting and soon there were forty dust-covered men smelling like the insides of old gloves squeezed up against one another. An aggressively nosy Turcoman with a pock-marked face and breath like a poisoned wind decided to sit next to me.

'What's this then?' he asked, poking my bag. 'What's the matter with you? What language do you speak?'

'English, (bad breath).'

'Then how is it you're speaking Persian?'

'So that I may answer your many questions.'

'Ha! Blgh blgh blgh blgh.' (At least this is what it sounded like in Turcoman dialect.) 'You didn't get that, did you?'

'No, I didn't,' I replied wearily.

'Well that's because you don't speak Turcoman, DO YOU?

HA!' he yelled, inches from my face, collapsing into laughter at the ingenuity of his own humour.

Ali Khan in the meantime made friends with his neighbour and was absorbed in a gripping exchange of horse stories. I began to feel acutely homesick. The surroundings seemed intolerably heavy with strangeness, and my despair vaulted as the night wore on. I looked at Ali Khan and felt angry, and was fed up with the sight and sound of men spitting and coughing and breathing over me.

When it was time to sleep the Turcoman snored violently inches from my right ear, which I managed to block with one finger. But from the other side I was jolted out of even the slimmest chance of sleep by Ali Khan, who had developed an explosive cough. Every few minutes his body would erupt in spasms as loud and sharp as a karate instructor smashing bricks. Then at one o'clock in the morning, half the men began packing their things and cleared noisily out of the room (at what unfathomable signal, and to where?). It was a horrible night.

Yet I marvel now as I marvelled then at what strange things are thrown up on the shore of consciousness by the tide of the night. I dreamed I went to visit my godfather, the news of whose death I'd received in Pakistan the very day before I first left for Afghanistan ten years earlier. He was a French writer and lived in Paris, but I'd never had the chance to know him as an adult. In the dream I was overjoyed to see him because I was grown up now. He was in a study where the sun was shining on walls of books with beautiful leather bindings and gold-leaf titles. The walls fell slowly over us and the books floated down in waves, but we were unhurt. When they had settled he looked up at me and smiled a smile of incredible kindness.

*

In the morning I said goodbye to Ali Khan, after paying him and giving him my penknife, half the *keshmesh,* and a length of nylon rope. We embraced and he trotted away on Clockwork in a little cloud of dust without a backward glance. I struggled with a feeling of complete abandonment, and went back to the *serai* to write up my diary.

The day before my ritual diary-writing had quickly drawn a crowd but now there were only a few conspiratorial glances in my direction, and my presence no longer caused a stir. Yet it was small consolation for being stranded in this wilderness, and I heard the creeping voice of worry begin to infect my thoughts.

Men and donkeys passed the *serai* on their way north. A few traders came in, virile old men who looked as though they had stepped from the Old Testament, rested their sticks against the wall and huddled for an hour against the stove before moving on.

Watching them disappear I wondered how long I would have to wait for a vehicle heading in the same direction. One would come, said a man. One would not come, said another. There were three military jeeps in the compound. No one was able to say if any of them were going north. I found the wild-eyed commander and asked him; he didn't know either, and laughed when I said I wanted to get to Jurm, the town at the head of the valley. I waited.

From the smoke-blackened chamber next door some bowls of rice were passed through the room. I sat next to an old man, who said there were lapis mines in the hills. I wondered if he knew how long they had been mined by man.

'Two thousand, six hundred and fifty-two years,' he said. Then he, too, left.

Appalled at my own smell I followed a track down to the water's edge and washed my upper body behind a boulder. My arms seemed white and very thin. Then I went to ask the commander again, determined this time to extract an answer as to how to get to Jurm.

He had an unruly, masculine energy that made him difficult to approach; he seemed unable to concentrate and I tried to think of something with which to win his attention. I took his picture, and he asked why it had failed to come out of the camera. Then I remembered that in my bag I had a set of three small throwing knives which I had brought along for just such an occasion.

'Come and see something,' I said.

There was a door in the wall, and I threw the knives in succession from about twenty feet away. He was impressed.

'You're a *lūtī*,' he said with a laugh: a bandit. 'I'm staying away from you!'

'No,' I said, 'I'll show you how to do it too.' And to keep his attention I told the best knife story I knew: of a young British officer challenged by a German soldier with a bayonet. With a kick the knife was sent flying. It caught the light as it spun upwards, and down again until it lodged between the bones of the Englishman's wrist, from where it was pulled free and turned swiftly against its owner; a twist of fate if ever there was, it had left a strangely ragged scar, the shape of which I knew well enough.

A line of men quickly formed to have a go. I pulled the knives from the door and handed them to the commander. The result was strange. I had taken for granted that these tough men with their guns and sanguinary history would know instinctively how to throw knives. But it was obvious from their efforts they had never before seen a knife thrown.

The commander hadn't even the vaguest concept. He tossed the knives in turn with a delicate hopping motion as if he was throwing confetti or a hoop over a stuffed animal, or upwards in a gentle arc the way you throw a dart. The other men tried and the knives fell short and wide or slapped sideways against the door. Not one of them succeeded. They had no model, I realized, to imitate. They had never seen knife-throwing gypsies at a circus or cowboy films of men throwing daggers into their enemies' hearts.

I paid special attention to the commander and showed him how to hold and flick the knife at the instant before release, and after ten minutes (and a near miss as a man opened the door from the other side and wondered why people were throwing knives at him) he got the hang of it. The first time a knife stuck satisfyingly into the wood he looked at me, and then his hands, in utter disbelief.

✻

There was the rumble of a motor. A pickup truck pulled into the compound, and unloaded a dusty cargo of weary-looking travellers, who wandered off into the hills.

I asked the driver if he could take me to Jurm.

'For a *lakh*,' he said.

'I could buy a horse for that amount.' The joke rippled down the line of men.

'Yes, we could buy horses at that price!' Then the commander appeared with two cigarettes for me and for the first time seemed calm and coherent; he said I should pay 30,000 Afghanis for the trip to Jurm in a truck and no more. The truck would take me and the others, he said. It sounded like a lot of money. It was three pounds.

There followed hours of discussion and debate. The driver wanted a dozen paying passengers; those who wanted to travel were only six. The would-be passengers dispersed, then gathered again for further debate. Twice we got into the truck and twice we got out again and waited another hour. It was a wearisome ritual, but I would get used to it. Often under such circumstances there are hours of waiting and waiting and nothing whatsoever appears to be happening. No visible process of decision is taking place; there is no change in company or news or weather – and then at some invisible signal a mad rush begins, a stampede of activity, and the truck (car, bus, tank) tears off in a shellburst of dust.

✱

It was three o'clock and the day was almost behind us when the disgruntled driver relented. We had just pulled up the steep road beyond the *serai* when a burst of automatic gunfire brought us to a lurching halt; latecomers hailing us to wait. Four breathless desperados emerged five minutes later from beneath the slope and clambered into the back. The barrel of an automatic rifle stuck into my foot. I noticed that the sick old man Ali Khan had allowed to ride Clockwork the previous day was wedged into a corner at the front, shrouded in his *pattū*. His eyes were half-closed and as we set off again I wondered if he would survive the trip.

I had never seen a truck drive so dangerously fast over such a bad surface, much less been jammed into one with twelve other men. It was a relatively modern pickup, but the Afghan roads had aged it prematurely. The shock absorbers were compressed to their limit and the chassis bumped against the rear axle with such force that time and again we were nearly flung into the road. It was impossible to move at will. One of my feet was completely numb; my knees were against my chest, and I had to grip the side of the truck at an excruciatingly unnatural angle to keep myself from bouncing out.

The driver kept up the pace for four or five hours. I looked over to the old man from time to time and pitied him. Like the others I had wrapped myself in my *pattū* and held it tight with my teeth against the cold and swirling dust. We wound high above the river and at times the road gave up altogether and we ploughed across watery beds of scree and lurched across flood-carved tributary gulleys like an ant straddling the teeth of a comb. As it grew darker we nearly collided with an oncoming truck on a narrow track two hundred feet above the river, and ground to a halt in a long and heart-numbing skid.

Roughly halfway along in a village we dropped off three men and gained five. We were fifteen now. A huge dog barked furiously at us from a rooftop and a crowd of suicidal children chased us through a cloud of dust. On the outskirts of the village a man tried to catch up with us, and ran heroically behind us for about a mile. Several times, as we slowed to negotiate a frozen rut, he came almost within reach of the hands stretching out to him from the back of the truck, but the driver refused to slow down. Eventually the running man was knocked sideways as he tried to clamber in, momentarily crushed between the body of the truck and the verge, and tumbled into the road behind us. It was a horrible sight, but he survived. Soon it was dark. I felt certain the old man had died. Then everything was dust, shadows and the icy wind.

We were steering a rough and ready course on Polaris (which I still couldn't find from Ursa Major because of the height of the surrounding mountains, but from Cassiopeia instead), weaving between the interlocking spurs of a gradually broadening valley. The mountains began to loosen their hold on the landscape, and I could make out pinpricks of light in settlements above broad terraced fields. I shared a cigarette with the man squeezed next to me. He wore a white *pattū* and turban and asked me where I was from.

'England, you say? I am a teacher,' he shouted, over the roar of the wind and crunching rock. 'I teach English.' And I thought what a relief it was to find someone I could talk to in my own language, and what a place to find him! He pointed upwards and asked:

'What is this?'

I felt he was about to announce some proverb of timeless wisdom.

'That's the sky,' I said.

'Yes it is!' Then he pointed upwards again.

'What is this?'

'That's the sky and those are stars. What about them?'

'Yes it is! No it isn't! Yes it is!' And like the ugly Turcoman he began to laugh at his superior command of language.

An hour later we arrived in Jurm, unbuckled our limbs and paid the demonic driver by torchlight. There were the usual protests and counter-protests at the price. A few men disappeared into the blackness, while the others banged on various gates looking for the local *serai*. An old man was roused, led us into a passage with an oil lantern, and we worked ourselves into spaces between rows of sleeping men, covered ourselves in our *pattūs*, and fell lovingly into the arms of sleep.

*

In the morning the room was nearly empty. For a few moments I could make no sense of the new surroundings until, with astonishment, I recognized my fellow passenger the old man sitting nearby. He beckoned me and we drank tea together; he too was going to Faizābād. I was very grateful for his company; I admired his powers of survival, and he had none of the intrusive curiosity of younger men. He said a truck would come to take us to Faizābād. Whether it would come the same day he couldn't say.

It was seven o'clock and the village was beginning to stir. I wandered along the single main street to its end, and along a narrow path of soft dust flanked by a line of whispering willows on one side and a mud wall on the other. Scattered beyond the fields I could see clusters of earthen houses with wisps of smoke rising from their chimneys. Beyond them was a patchwork of freshly ploughed fields over which the vapour of the morning hung in layers, and beyond them the hills, softer now, perhaps only a thousand to two thousand feet high.

I was struck by the beauty of the place, and seeing the neat mud settlements and the glittering streams between them, hearing the flutter of willow leaves, and smelling the dust and freshly turned soil and the smoke of early morning fires was reminded of the timeless matrix of elements from which the natural pattern of settlement originally sprung. Here it seemed uninterrupted and as intimate as ever. The fierce slopes of the mountains were gone, exorcised by our night-time journey, and already an age away.

Three women passed, drawing veils of white, yellow and blue across their faces as I approached. Some children chased a stray cow through the street. The stalls on either side came gradually to life and soon the central thoroughfare was full of men, women, children and animals. The women were veiled and the young girls were all very beautiful. There was a *chaikhāna* with a balcony on the upper floor opposite the *serai*, which I could watch in case someone made off with my bag. I ordered kebabs and basked in the sunshine, luxuriating in the twin pleasures of hot food and solitude.

❋

By one o'clock the sun had thrown a pale yellow light over the bare hills and the day felt already spent. I was worried about the way ahead. Always there is this kind of suspense on a journey where you are both isolated and robbed of your own language. Under such conditions the means by which you make sense of things begins to be transformed; you can no longer rely on familiar signals but a cryptic sequence of tiny events, the pattern of which you sense more keenly as your isolation grows. It leads to a kind of parting of the ways; you either let go of your worries and put your faith in the natural unfolding of events or are plagued with anxieties, which multiply as darkness falls.

I could hear two voices at work. One was an incessant reminder about safety, fear of loneliness and insecurities of every kind. How would I know if a truck came and went? Would my bag be safe in the *serai*? Time and again I had been told it was unsafe to travel alone ...

I had from the beginning of the trip been aware of this first voice; an almost relentless tale of worry about how things would turn out at every stage, like that of a homesick child longing for the familiar.

It had its own legitimacy but as anyone knows who has been touched by the spell of travel there is another voice struggling to be heard, and now for the first time I was able to hear it; a calmer signal on which I was unwilling at first to rely. It was the impulse to put my trust in the natural course of events, and to surrender, not passively but intelligently, to the restraints and opportunities of the moment. Was I not fed and warm and in a place of beauty? Things would work out . . .

Were these the equivalent European in me and the Asian, of the head and of the heart? I am tempted to think so. The Western mind is trained to think its way through life. The trouble with the habit is a tendency to formulate everything in terms of something else, instead of actually experiencing it for what it is; the definitions of success and failure, joy and difficulty, tend to be factory-set at home. There is nothing like an Asian journey — beginning with a catalogue of physical challenges and inconveniences, and all the assaults on conventions regarding time, distance and straight answers from people — to threaten the definitions and the sense of self that builds on them.

Asia is different; it opens an unfamiliar door onto experiencing the world. Yet this shift, should it occur, is only a natural adaptation, a rebalancing of the mind as the cloud of ordinary thoughts gradually begins to still, like mud settling to the bottom of a pool. There, given time, shapes begin to emerge, wonderful shapes if the sight of them would only last . . .

*

I walked once more along the main street towards the other end of the village. Just then I caught sight of a pickup truck disappearing into a side alley. It had a flag of some kind on its antenna and I went to see who it might be. Two men got out; the flag said 'Afghanaid', and I introduced myself. A tall man with a rich black beard answered me in perfect English. He wore a white *shalwar* and skullcap. I explained I was trying to get to Baharak at the head of the valley, then on to Faizābād.

'No problem,' he said cheerfully. 'We can take you along tomorrow. But why not stay tonight with us at our office?' He sent a man with me to carry my bag, and we walked together along a winding path carpeted with fallen leaves, several hundred yards up the slope behind the village. I was given tea and then – bliss! – a bucket of hot water and a private room in which to wash.

*

Mohammed was in charge of the local branch of the English charity, and oversaw an ambitious list of ongoing projects to help restore the region's former prosperity. It had suffered badly during the war, he explained, and traced the trail of misery back to the period of Soviet occupation. Fighting had disrupted everything. Restrictions on the traditional movement of a population dependent on fragile patterns of supply and trade resulted in years of neglect.

'No one was allowed to move freely,' he said. 'The Russians shot at everything that moved – even ordinary buses.' And the single road to the region had been so badly damaged during the war that gradually the region had begun to starve. Soaring prices for basic foodstuffs had forced farmers to live in poverty in the cities. Lack of fuel led to the over-cutting of wood and deforestation, leading to soil depletion, leading to landslides and the choking of the irrigation systems, leading to further neglect ... like all wars it had left a legacy of different battles.

It was a pleasure to talk to such a devoted and experienced man. Having just emerged from the wildest territory I had ever seen, the terminology was as impressive as it was incongruous; suddenly the room was full of talk about crop rotation, erosion management, seed hybridization, community development, income generation and instruction programmes. And would I like to see the model nursery tomorrow?

*

We drove out in the morning to inspect the young trees and vegetables growing on an experimental plot on the outskirts of the village. At last I learned the names and varieties of trees I had seen on the way: the most common were two species of poplar (in Persian called *chenār* and *sepīd-dār*); two of pine (*Pinus helopinsus* and *Taja orientalis*), acacia (*Rubinica*), Russian silex (*Alentus glandalosa*), Sheng (*Fraximus*) and cattal. Acacia and Russian silex were planted in areas of deforestation on account of their long roots, which are more resistant to the effects of erosion.

Then we drove on to Baharak at the head of the valley across a high green plateau of soft beauty. In the fields and on the riverbanks of this remote land, barefoot farmers in turbans guided wooden ploughs around the rusting hulks of Russian tanks and armoured troop-carriers.

In the town we stopped in a busy main street lined with newly built shops. The old bazaars had been destroyed in the war, said Mohammed. I saw truckloads of armed young men, boys mostly, preparing to make their way to the front in Kabul. They were smiling and friendly and my heart lurched at the thought of what awaited them. Then we changed vehicles and piled into an overloaded truck with an Afghan family, who, not wishing to stow a foreign guest in the back, decamped from the comfort of the cab and reinstalled themselves among sacks and bundles behind. I protested to no avail, and we set off on the final leg of the trip to Faizābād.

✻

Here too as in Panjshīr it seemed incredible that tanks had managed to squeeze along the cliff-hemmed route, which twisted sharply high above the river as we left Baharak. It was a three-hour journey but in distance only thirty miles or so. The unsurfaced road was badly damaged by water erosion and at one point a new but badly built bridge had been washed away by the spring floods earlier in the year, leaving only the concrete footings. We waded through a swift current to the far side while the truck lurched across.

Faizābād is the regional capital of the Badakhshān and its largest town. The river Kochka bisects the settlement like a jade serpent set in wild stone, licking at crumbling cliffs. The majority of houses, generously interspersed with groves of poplar, are on the northern side of the river and spread up a gentle slope for a mile until the mountains begin to rear. On the southern side the slopes are steeper and a string of thousand-foot peaks overlook the earth and the jade and the barren, rolling hills beyond. I was told they too were once forested; certainly before the war there were orchards of pistachio and walnut on the lower slopes that have now gone, but for centuries at least it could not have been the dense forest that I heard evoked.

We dropped off the Afghan family at their home and they begged me to be their guest but the luxury of being able to speak English with the others was too much to resist, and I gently refused. Then we were installed at the Afghanaid office and my bag was carried into a room, a kettle of tea soon appeared, and again I had the luxury of hot water, more this time than I could have wished for. I washed my hair and felt like a king, then was introduced to three other staff, all of whom spoke English.

The first was a rotund and jovial character in his fifties, a forestry expert under the former government. I felt vaguely intimidated by his intelligence and inquisitiveness; something about him seemed out of place. I said I was hoping to write among other things about the positive aspects of Afghanistan, and he replied: 'Well, you'l be lucky if you can find any,' and laughed in a rather un-Afghan way. I was still attuned inwardly to the simple ways of rural Afghanistan epitomized by Ali Khan, and these men carried with them a Westernized air to which I adjusted only slowly.

Over dinner I became conscious of an unsettling impulse which at first I couldn't place. Then hearing the others speaking not in Persian but in Pashtu, I realized their sympathies lay less with the government than with the Tālebān. The older man denied it when I asked, but I could tell he was reluctant to express his true allegiance. Having all been trained in Pakistan, it was perhaps inevitable. After the meal a softly spoken young man with big kind eyes and who wore a black leather jacket showed me into the spare room. I asked him if he thought the Tālebān would ever take Kabul.

'They will,' he said confidently, 'there can be no doubt.' He went further and said they were the only chance for peace in the country.

Look at what had happened in the areas under Tālebān control, he added; they had restored order and de-armed corrupt commanders who the government had allowed to prosper. Rumours of Pakistani and American involvement were false.

Perhaps he was right. He certainly believed in what he said. The Tālebān had restored a measure of security in the south, but what of the civilians dying every day under Tālebān artillery and rockets? How had such impoverished and religious men intercepted and forced down a Russian cargo plane bound for Kabul a few months before? Pakistani support for the Tālebān was an open secret, and American officials had closer ties with the Tālebān than with any other faction; perhaps the Tālebān had convinced their sponsors they could control the entire country.*

It was a particularly Afghan trait: there was always one enemy and only one solution to the general woes facing the country. In different places the problem, along with the solution, was perceived differently; what was valid in one region wasn't necessarily applicable in another. You only needed to travel in non-Pushtun areas to realize just how unlikely a Tālebān victory really was. I was tired and we left it there.

The following evening over dinner the older man talked volubly about the war and the desperate need for economic rehabilitation. There were several keys issues, he said.

The first was that the majority of Afghans were weary of the fighting and the country was starving. Secondly the present government was kept in power only by Russian money, not by popular support.

---

* News that an American oil company and its Saudi partner were planning the construction of an oil and gas pipeline across Afghanistan emerged only later in the year. The proposed pipeline would link the rich oilfields of Daulatabad in Turkmenistān with the Pakistani port of Multan, passing through nearly a thousand miles of Afghan territory.

From American commercial interests to American complicity in the Tālebān's rise to power is but a short step in many, especially Afghan, minds.

Citing the continued instability of the region and the Tālebān's failure to secure international recognition, the company's plans for construction were suspended in August 1998.

And thirdly, even if the Tālebān took Kabul, the fighting would go on because the different groups would never agree to share power.

What was the greatest obstacle to peace? Guns, he said. So long as there were so many guns in Afghanistan there wasn't a hope of peace. This was a country where people were so poor they broke up old Russian tanks and hauled the pieces to Pakistan to sell for scrap metal. But with money you could pay a man to fight; and in a country as poor as Afghanistan this was easier than ever before.

The war, in other words, was kept alive by a vicious economic circle; its commanders were living in luxury while ordinary people died. Massoud was a brave man, he said, and respected for his role in the long war against the Russians. But his was only another power-hungry party, not a viable government.

It was no good asking America for help (did he mean the government's appealing to Washington for recognition?) – Afghans felt utterly abandoned by America. Here there were two analogies describing people's feelings towards their former allies in the *jehād*: one of a fire (war) having been put under a pot (Afghanistan) and left to boil long after the water had disappeared (the Russian withdrawal); the other of a man helped to the top of a tall building (the *jehād* won with American aid to the mujaheddin) then having had the stairs removed from under him, leaving him stranded. A crippled victim of the cold war, in other words. Once, America had been perceived as a far-off but benevolent father figure who had the power to influence and resolve conflicts; but how could a father abandon its young? The mujaheddin had ruined their own land in the belief that America would later help them rebuild it, once the common enemy of communism had been dealt with. And in the meantime the best Afghan minds had fled the country and were working for foreign salaries abroad – how many of them could be expected to return to a place where a civil servant earned twenty dollars a month?

Only the United Nations could do the job, he said, but properly this time and on a large scale. The UN Secretary General's Special Envoy on Afghanistan, Mahmoud Misteri, whose name by a cruel pun in Persian meant 'tinkerer', was just that; he came and went, tightening nuts and bolts here and there and preparing the country for more war.

What was needed was a UN peacekeeping presence that would demilitarize Kabul and spread its influence through the country by buying every last gun. Who wouldn't give up their guns for money? (Who would give up their money for guns? I wondered.)

It was gloomy and simplistic talk. I went to bed dwelling on the indifference of the Americans; the bankruptcy of the UN; the greed of the different mujaheddin parties and of their foreign sponsors (he hadn't mentioned these); the misery of a proud people. I schemed wildly at the edge of sleep; what if it were really as simple as buying every gun in the country? I did some mental sums, and calculated I would need roughly a hundred million dollars to break the dreadful momentum of war. There would be collection sites in every town with seed and livestock bonuses for the first comers. Word would quickly get around that money was available and the guns could be gathered up by the truckload; soon even the most corrupt commanders would be robbed of their very armies; Pakistan would be forced to give up its old dream of manipulating the trade routes to central Asia through Afghanistan, and the general population could begin the task of rebuilding their shattered land. All that was needed was to establish the taste of peace. A hundred million dollars would do it: the budget of the latest Hollywood blockbuster . . .

*

After the mountains, Faizābād seemed like a place of high civilization; yet against it, Kabul was a megalopolis. I walked into the town in the morning to explore, along what I imagined would in season be leafy avenues, past a compound where the wrecks of tanks and armoured vehicles had been piled up in rows, through several large and dusty open squares, and along a thoroughfare of windowless stalls.

It was poor here. Shopkeepers perching beside their wares stared as I passed, unaccustomed to the sight of a stranger. Storefronts were piled with ascending rows of the most basic household goods, hardware and second-hand clothes; a few were carpet shops. I stopped at a forge where one man worked a bellows and two others were beating a red-hot axehead with sledgehammers in rhythmic tandem, while a fourth, between blows, turned the glowing lump of metal at the end of a pole.

There was a break fifty feet across where the river trickled in watery fissures down the slope, and I hopped from stone to stone to regain the shops on the far side. After half a mile they became private homes again, and it would have been easy to lose yourself in the maze of diminishing alleys that led away from the main façade.

To the northwest stretched a long grassy field dotted with countless bumps, which closer up I realized was a huge cemetery. Beyond it a flock of goats being led into the hills stirred a cloud of dust, and a caravan of half a dozen heavily loaded camels followed them into a dark and narrow gorge.

I crossed the river again and found a track leading upwards where a team of men were carving terraces into the rocky hillside. This was the water-sheet management project I had been told about. A hale and elderly farmer supervising the men waved me on. Pleased at the pace my lungs and legs were able to manage, I scrambled upwards on a steep grassy slope. I was alone; the view over the town was perfect, and no one would see me gazing at its inhabitants through my binoculars. For a while I sat in the shelter of some boulders and watched the tiny worlds of life in the enclosed courtyards of houses, not without a faint sense of shame at this very un-Afghan violation of privacy.

Further along the track narrowed to a goat trail and I followed it for about a mile, skirting the grassy side of the hill. I wanted to walk along the ridge as you normally would on a hillside above a town, but there was a string of military installations there and the thought of a stray mine held me back. At the head of a promontory beneath me I could see the grass-covered bumps of what looked like ruins, and wondered: the remains of a Kushan fort or Soviet artillery battery? On the far side of the valley I could see what resembled crumbling castles clinging to high cliffs, and felt a pang of longing to stay in this wild place for a year and explore. Never had I been drawn to a landscape more than these sculpted canyons and plutonic precipices or the solemn beauty of the green-gold slopes that guarded them.

To measure the distances between such places against the ordinary scale of miles gave no sense of their isolation. I had met tribesmen who had asked if England were a town near Kabul, itself a remote enough place to the majority. Afghanistan's rural settlements were a hundred times more remote than the villages of European countries; measured on the relative scale of remoteness the country was vaster than the whole of Europe. Briefly the clatter of Soviet helicopters had brought the region within the orbit of the modern world, but their echo had long since faded.

Walking on, my eye was caught by some hollow ammunition casings washed from the hilltop in a narrow gulley, and I wandered closer. There were live rifle bullets and anti-aircraft shells a foot long; further up there were tank shells with Cyrillic markings. I thought of how a shepherd boy would see these and be tempted to put them in his pocket or throw them off the slope, and visualized despairingly how they would be washed gradually down the slope and end up in fields to be struck one day by the point of a plough.

Just then there was a burst of heavy-calibre gunfire so loud the air seemed to shake. I cowered against the slope and wondered if I had been seen; there was no natural cover and I put my hands pathetically in the air. I had lost the track and was now clambering over a gully full of half-buried explosive debris, hoping the slope was unmined. There was another burst of fire and I struggled with the impulse to run, cursing myself for breaking my own rule about leaving well-worn tracks, especially in the vicinity of military sites. I huddled in between some boulders and tried to place the source of fire which the echo made more difficult; there was a third burst and I realized it must have been a gun on the ridge fifty feet above me, where I could make out the wisp of a military antenna, and that my presence was almost certainly a coincidence.

Then there was no sound but the roar of the river from below, and I headed down as a wall of shadow began to topple slowly across the town.

*

Back in the compound Hamid was washing his clothes in a metal basin. He had worked for Afghanaid for several years and was preoccupied with the problems of sustainable agriculture in impoverished areas such as here in the north. He explained that even the most well-intentioned relief organizations had tended in the past to throw money at difficulties and then wonder why things seemed to get worse after an initial improvement. Their mistake was to decide on the perceived problem and then decide how to solve it without first examining the fragile local economic ecosystems. The best relief projects could cause more harm than good if the expertise and resources which enabled them to function disappeared the following year along with their providers.

But things were changing. Now, he explained, it was policy to sit down with the elders of a village and ask them what their greatest problems were, examining local resources through local eyes to come up with solutions. Earlier in the year he had been in the region of Ishkashem near the border with Tajikistan, looking into micro-hydropower technologies to relieve the problems associated with deforestation. They were long and difficult trips and local people were suspicious of their motives.

'We used to come back with lice,' he said, as he wrung out a shirt. 'You can't wash them out; they hide in the seams and the only way to kill them is to iron the clothes.'

He spoke in a quiet voice and I was impressed by his gentle manner and considered answers. Even to his gestures there was a cat-like softness. He emptied the water into a second basin and rinsed off his hands in clean water without spilling a drop. He squeezed the excess from his fingers as if it were gold dust, and I knew then that he had spent time in prison.

Briefly he talked about the old times; he had been at Kabul university when the communists arrested him. I asked him why. 'They didn't need a reason,' he said without bitterness. 'They arrested anybody they wanted.' He had also been a keen musician and studied with a teacher of the *robāb* who was also a Sufi. The master would play from evening to dawn, bringing alternately tears of sadness and joy to the eyes of the listeners, each melody suited to the different hours of the night.

*

By five o'clock it was nearly dark. The light had drained westwards into the mountains and above its incandescent residue dangled a frozen sliver of moon. While the others talked animatedly in the main room I found Hamid quietly studying a thick volume on chemistry.

'Nitrogen depletion in the soil,' he said, tapping the page beneath a line of complicated chemical equations. 'Artificial fertilizers aren't viable. We need to find local substitutes. Look at this.' He rooted out a stick coated in a tar-like mixture. 'Sheep dung ground with mustard seeds, the traditional equivalent of a paraffin lantern.' The dung acted as a binder, and the oil in the seeds burned evenly for hours. 'We can learn from this kind of thing,' he said, smiling gently. Then he showed me pictures of his family, who lived in Pakistan, and presented me with a gift for my daughter. It was a jewellery box made from translucent stone and inlaid with a tiny lapis flower.

Over dinner the head of the place apologized for not being able to be more hospitable. I had no complaints and wondered what he meant. As gently as possible he was requesting me to move on. He talked about the suspicions the staff had to put up with from local people. It was not easy, he said, working in a part of the country where they were considered strangers, dressed differently, and drove about in a shiny pickup truck.

'And as you know,' he added, 'we are not strictly allowed to have foreign guests.' He made a veiled enquiry into my plans, then apologized again at having to request a note from me, confirming I had stayed and passed safely onwards.

'Sadly, this is normal under the conditions,' he said. Yet it had the flavour of an imported ritual, which I'd not encountered elsewhere. I glanced at Hamid and could see he found the line of talk distasteful.

Away from any immediate threat it was easy to forget this was a country profoundly traumatized by nearly two decades of war. I was reminded of the traveller's privilege of immunity from whatever troubles might gather in the wake of his passage. But with it this privilege carried all the exigencies of motion, exacting an equivalent toll on both body and spirit: the bittersweet taste of repeated partings, the burden of receiving hospitality beyond the deserved, the wearying ritual of explaining oneself in a foreign language to strangers, the stress and suspense of repeated warnings about the way ahead, as well as the daily struggle with the shifting scale of time, to whose unstable fabric the journey held a kind of magnifying glass, stretching it out unbearably under the influence of danger and condensing it into rich pools of experience in moments of comfort. I signed the note like the traveller who builds a cairn, a token of his passing, before moving on into the uncertain grasp of the way ahead.

*

The following morning, after a ceremonial departure in which the entire staff lined up for a parting embrace, I was driven into the town. I didn't want to leave at all, and wrestled with the idea of staying on somewhere and finding someone to strike into the mountains with. Somewhere, someone ... In springtime perhaps. It would be beautiful then. We could take the road from Faizābād, and thread northeast towards Lake Shiva near the Tajik border, where Pushtun nomads gathered by the thousand in the hotter months ...

We jolted into town. I asked the driver how the road was to Taloqān, the westernmost town still in government hands, to which the truck would take me.

'Kherāb ast! Ruined!' he said. His hand traced a plunging arc. 'So many trucks are falling off into the river. So many are dying.'

We found a giant kamaz in the town, already loaded and ready to leave. My bag was passed up and I perched on a bulging cargo of goatskins and heavy engine parts. Opposite me sat an elderly turbaned man and three women in blue burqas. At the last minute a sheep was hauled upwards and three more men clambered up the frame of the truck. I waved goodbye and the engine roared into life, sending a cloud of black exhaust like a blast furnace into the street. The horn shrieked, and supplicating hands were raised in unison to the heavens. I raised mine too and uttered the customary prayer, little guessing that the most terrifying portion of the journey was about to begin.

Six

This evening was like some golden age of human happiness, attained sometimes by children, more rarely by grown-ups, and it communicated its magic in some degree to all of us.

Eric Newby, *A Short Walk in the Hindu Kush*

WE HAD NOT YET REACHED the edge of the town before the first floundering. A government fighter flagged down the truck just as we crossed the river, and insisted on inspecting the cargo. Under the conditions of the time it was the nature of such interruptions to be drawn out and resolved not so much by a logical solution, but by a protracted fraying of tempers and an eventual consensus of pointlessness. So it was with our marooning: a wearying ritual obeisance to the gods of war.

The fighter was young and seemed uncertain of his task. He shouldered his rifle and clambered up the back of the truck, studied our faces in turn and began to poke about among the engine parts and goatskins, asking repeated questions of their owner. Then, unsatisfied with the explanations, he ordered us all out of the truck.

First went the women, incongruously balloon-like against the sharp angles of the truck, with all but their bare hands hidden by elaborately embroidered *burqas* of cornflower-blue silk. An elderly turbaned gentleman in a dark corduroy jacket followed them, helped by the fighter; then a ginger-haired man wearing a black fur hat; a patriarchal whitebeard clutching a trembling crook; a stocky, bearded man with mirrored sunglasses and what looked like a tea towel over his head; a pair of Turcoman-looking traders whose goatskins it appeared were the cause of the hold-up, and finally the sheep, a huge creature with mad-looking horizontal pupils and a great wedge-shaped tail like a flipper, which shook in protest as it was manhandled to the ground.

There were long arguments between the soldier and the owner of the skins. Other passengers interjected voluble protests in turn, which drew out into counter-protests and a general raising in temperature of the debate. The driver, and even passers-by, entered the fray. I wandered away. A military jeep with a 'GB' sticker drove past, followed by an old man on a donkey. Then a boy chasing a metal hoop, guiding it with deft blows from a hooked bar. I noticed, too, the familiar sight of a bullet hole in the windscreen of the truck at the exact height of the driver's head.

An hour had passed before the owner of the skins, with a conspicuous show of exasperation, began flinging them one by one down into the road, where they threw up little clouds of dust at the soldier's feet. But after only a dozen or so the scale of the task became apparent to all – there must have been hundreds of skins on board – and a renewed cry of protest rippled through the stranded assembly. Then, as if the whole thing had never mattered to him, the soldier wandered grudgingly away, and with a wail of the horn we were all hastily reinstalled.

The road led west in the shadow of a steep bluff of dark rock, and soon we were in the open, overlooked by soft hills. Homes sprawled around their bases, and directly above them, rocks as big as the houses themselves, anchored to the slopes by no more than slender collars of mud.

Our way was paved with the pure and ochreous light of the season. The houses trailed behind us and we passed the airport, where a truckload of armed teenage boys were filing like cattle up the ramp of a military plane. Even at a distance I could make out their smiles as they prepared to set off for the front lines around Kabul, and the sight fell across my feelings the way a cloud obscures the sun on a spring day.

The runway was made from metal strips laid over the grass and scattered all around were the hollow carcasses of armoured vehicles. There were green metal bunkers dug into the ground, their tops blown off, their watch-slit prisms refracting nothing but the empty sky. I thought of the grim task of having to defend the airport from the mujaheddin during the war. And though the folly of the Soviet period seemed worlds away now, it lived on privately for me at such moments and ignited a curiosity about the fate of Soviet soldiers as much as their resisters. Faizābād had been a key stronghold of the north and fiercely contested for years. Yet as we passed it did seem hard to believe that battles had been fought over these serene acres of mountain fastness, which were as beautiful and remote as one could imagine.

Not far beyond, the surface of the road began to break up like the fraying end of a rope. Soon it was raked with deep and interweaving ruts of frozen mud. Our pace dropped to a crawl, and the frame of the truck began to sway and creak like an old galleon in a rising storm.

I was standing behind the cab and watching the route ahead, gripping the metal crossbars like a charioteer. This was not the Afghan way, which was less ostentatious. The other passengers, long immune to the novelty and risks of open-air travel on ruined roads, huddled stoically against the sides. The exception was the man with the sunglasses. He too stood at the truck's edge and watched the road. With his beard and scarf and his face set against the wind, he looked more suited to the saddle of a Harley Davidson. There was something about him I couldn't place, and for once I was doing the guessing about someone else.

*

It was mid-afternoon. Already the sunlight like a tide had begun to slip back from the hills, and as we entered a wide gorge enclosed by high walls of broken rock its touch was withdrawn from our faces. The temperature began to fall and the road tightened against the cliff. We lurched forward, rising steadily, over braided furrows of mud as the note of strain from the engine began to grow, and before long we were steering between fallen boulders on one side and the deepening gorge on the other.

The road narrowed, too, as it rose. It was high and broken enough for even the steadiest nerves, but now its ruined surface began to curve and bend and fold, fractal-like, hanging from the cliff face in tortured pleats. I looked out over the wheels to see how much space we had to bargain with, and with a sick feeling saw the tyres bulging at the very edge of the cliff. The river coiled a hundred, then two, then three hundred feet below, without so much as a handhold on the intervening slope. On the nearside of the road rose a sheer wall of rock, inches from the body of the truck.

As we climbed, the cry of the engine grew more desperate. There were two sounds now: the first, a kind of wail, bleeding from the heart of the engine as it begged to be allowed into a higher gear; then over this, the heavy growl of the cylinders under enormous strain. It was like riding a mechanized dragon caught at the end of a lasso, its brute determination transmitted to every seam and rivet. A hot breath of black exhaust, as dense as it was noxious, billowed from underneath us. It rolled upwards against the cliff then down again over the body of the truck where we clung, our mouths clenched.

It was getting dark and I began to wonder how long we could possibly continue. But darkness was no obstacle to the iron nerves of the driver, whose accomplice, a teenage boy, would lean from the open door of the cab like a sidecar racer and look out over the rear wheels at the most dangerous points, yelling directions back over the roar of the engine. Soon all but a dusty yellow swathe of road in the headlights was obscured by the darkness. I wasn't sure which was better; not to be able to see ahead and give up all chance of making a last-minute escape, or to forgo this tiny insurance for the relative relief of not knowing at all.

I was on the side nearest the precipice, and worked on a mental plan of escape. At the moment we began to topple over the cliff, I would swing to the far side on the central bar of the canopy and jump free just in time. This would mean using the women opposite me as a kind of stepping-stone, and I abandoned the plan out of shame. But it was a pointless plan; first because if the wheels did slip, there would simply be no time for anything; secondly because I could not keep up the anxiety of thinking about the consequences. You can only be afraid for so long; after a long mental battering you are eventually forced inward to that deeper and stranger place to which fear is only an overdressed guard at the portal.

Often the driver would bring the truck to a complete halt as he decided how to attack the next section of road. In the back we could see nothing of the road now, but sensed these momentary pauses as the preludes to the most dangerous sections, like hairpin bends where the camber sloped horribly towards the cliff, or where the road had been partially washed away and was supported only by loose rocks plugged with broken sticks. Then we would hear the preparatory bursts of throttle, the screeching into first gear, and the old man in the back would croak: 'A prayer, a prayer!' and our palms would turn heavenward through the dust as we banged against the metal frame, too cold now even to grip.

The sheep, traumatized by the terrible ride, became demented. It refused to sit, despite being wrestled time and again to its knees. It staggered and fell repeatedly against us in turn, pissed in straggling arcs of terror over our feet until the canvas was awash, and trailed cascades of droppings as it bounced like an ice-hockey puck from side to side and end to end, its eyes ever madder with distress. At one point I forced it to lie down, and for a long stretch warmed my feet under its stomach. Then at another violent tilting of the truck it would repeat its frantic efforts to stay upright until finally, hours later, it grew too exhausted to care.

In the west a sickle moon hung like a nomad earring over the vee of the valley. Its cold light was reflected from the river like the scales of a writhing mercury snake. Under its silver spell our dusty faces – except those of the women, who stayed hidden like treasure under their *burqas* – took on the ashen hue of corpses. Mantra-like, I heard the words I had been left with in Faizābād: *so many trucks are falling off . . . so many are dying . . .*

I knew I had to find some method to distract myself from the fear.

*

I settled upon an alphabetical series of mental lists. It was impossible at first; I hadn't the concentration. It was too cold to think. I banged against the side of the truck, and the old man was saying his final prayers out loud . . . I had decided to begin with twentieth-century names associated with Afghanistan, but was stuck for a long time at A, trying to rein in the relevant thoughts like wild horses.

Then in a flash they came in a trio: Andropov, Brezhniev and Chernyenko, under whose generals the population of Afghanistan was cruelly reduced by a million souls. A strange coincidence that all of these leaders had died in office . . . For D, I had Daoud, founder of the Republic of Afghanistan in 1973, killed by the communists in the 1978 coup ... I moved on slowly, jumping forwards and backwards through the letters until I had worked my way to Zāher Shāh, Afghanistan's last king. Some names yielded associations for a different slot: the king, for example, I had already put aside as early as Daoud, who was his nephew and usurper.

E quickly yielded Enver Pasha. Enver was a Turkish soldier and, depending on the historical version you preferred, either a visionary or a bandit opportunist. In the wake of the First World War he set out for central Asia to rally resistance against the advancing Bolsheviks, in the hope of wresting a Turkish-speaking state from the confusion. By 1920 the Russians had seized Bokhara and driven its emir into exile in Kabul. The Afghan king Amānullah, wary of the advance towards his northern border, offered support for Enver's movement. And not far away from our lurching truck, into what is now Tajikistan, Afghan sympathizers had smuggled gold and arms to the former Turkish general and his native Tajik ally, Ibrahim Beg. Had the movement crystallized, Afghanistan's fate would have evolved quite differently. But the Russians proved unstoppable, the rebellion fractured into chaos, and Гnver was killed by the Bolsheviks in 1922. Perhaps, I wondered, even today, somewhere to our north across the fissured Amu Darya, one of Enver's youngest fighters was still alive, and knew the spot where he had fallen. Perhaps he could help clear up the verdict over Enver Pasha's character ...

I was stuck for a long time at F, went on and eventually came back. The truck pitched wildly and a fresh wreath of exhaust fumes billowed over us. I remembered the French soldier of fortune and explorer Ferrier, whose account of the Tīmūrid monuments in Herat from 1845 I had read in an old edition of the *Encyclopaedia Britannica*. G was easier: General Boris Gromov was commander of Soviet forces in Afghanistan and the last Russian soldier, officially at least, to cross out of Afghanistan over the 'friendship' bridge in 1989.

It was colder than ever now. At H, I recalled meeting Abdul Haq, the mujaheddin commander famous for his daring raids against Soviet installations and infrastructure around Kabul, a man wounded in action, it was said, twenty times. Then came Inayatullah, easily remembered, the Afghan king who ruled for three days in 1928, and who was flown out of Kabul during the troubles that followed by a British pilot of the fledgling Royal Air Force . . .

The truck yawed suddenly and the old man croaked a hoarse prayer as J drew a blank. The engine wailed its bleeding note. I had a personal connection with K, which surfaced readily; Khalilulah Khalili had been an Afghan diplomat and the country's poet laureate; his son Massoud, himself a diplomat today, had arranged my first journey to Afghanistan. L . . . L was difficult. Eventually I thought of Lawrence – of Arabian fame – who made a little-known appearance on the Afghan border during the brief reign of Bacche Saqqao (this gave me S), and Russian sources site him as one of the experienced imperialist hands behind British strategy in the region.*

In Delhi in 1907, the Afghan king Habibullah was a guest of Lord Minto, Viceroy of India: I could claim him for M, and for a distant relative.

N lifted from memory a well-known name from the mists of the Great Game years: the redoubtable Captain Oskar von Neidermeier, head of a Turco-German mission to Kabul during the First World War. Its ambitious purpose was to persuade the Afghan king to attack British India. The plan was for the Afghan army to conquer all of British India, aided by German-sponsored rebellions throughout the country. But the plot, perhaps not surprisingly, was uncovered by British intelligence; the Afghans lost their plans for a new empire and the Germans went sulking home minus millions in gold. The Amir Habibullah, under whom the plot was hatched, was eventually murdered, and the British were blamed for everything, by everyone.

It was bitterly cold. I couldn't think of anyone for O.

But P reminded me at once of commander Panah, one of Ahmed Shah Massoud's longest-serving fighters, whose reckless bravery in the war against the Soviets had earned him legendary status; he was killed in action against the Tāleban in 1995.

For Q, I cheated, and chose Queen Soraya, wife of the ill-fated

---

* Or more likely, as Louis Dupree puts it, he was 'merely sulking in his garrison as a result of post-World War I British rebuffs to his Arab friends and to his own monumental ego'. *Afghanistan*, Princeton, University Press, 1973.

King Amānullah. Her appearance, unveiled, at European state occasions outraged conservative Afghans back home, prompting rumours that the king had turned against Islam (and was also planning to bring back machines from Europe which would make soap from human corpses). I looked across to the ghost-like shapes of the women huddled opposite. They rocked against the patriarch between them, but made no sound.

I was at R and General Roberts, the soldier remembered by Afghans a century later for his iron rule, and whose forced march of vengeance from Kabul to Qandahar after the British defeat at Maiwand* was one of the great military feats of the period, earning him the title of Lord Roberts of Qandahar in 1911. His statue flanks Admiralty Arch in London.

At S, I thought of Bacche Saqqao and one of the most controversial interludes of modern Afghan history. Bacche was an unlettered Tajik from Kohistan north of Kabul, whose name meant 'son of a water-carrier'. He became king in 1929 and ruled for nine troubled months. Like Enver Pasha he was killed by enemy bullets, having returned under promise of immunity to Kabul to face his successors – and the manner of his death passed into legend as alive today as ever; like Enver he is remembered differently on different sides.

---

* The battle of Maiwand took place on 27 July 1880, when a British force under Brigadier Burrows met the Afghans under Ayyub Khan. Nearly a thousand British and Indian soldiers were killed. One of the lesser known 'survivors' of the battle was Dr Watson (of Baker Street fame), whose admirers even requested a monument in his name to be put up on the battlefield. Another was Bobbie, a small white mongrel and mascot of the 66th Regiment of Foot (later the 2nd Royal Berkshires) on the attempted march from Qandahar to Kabul. Along with 300 of the regiment's dead, Bobbie was abandoned in the withdrawal from Maiwand, having been badly wounded in the back and neck. Despite his injuries he crossed the besieging Afghan lines and arrived several days later at Qandahar, over fifty miles away. In 1881 Bobbie was decorated for his bravery by Queen Victoria. Eighteen months later he was run over by a hansom cab. He was stuffed and kept in the colour sergeants' mess for a few years, then moved to the regimental museum in Reading.

Wilfred Thesiger worked for T. The great explorer used to escape from the heat of the Iraqi summers by taking long rambles in the Hindu Kush, where his meeting with Eric Newby and Hugh Carless produced one of the funniest endings in travel literature.* U was hopeless; but V brought to mind another of the most intriguing and tragic figures of the Great Game, the raw details of whose story I tried to remember between violent lurches, each of which threatened to tip us unceremoniously into the chasm below.

His name was Captain Ivan Victoriovich Vitkyevitch, a Russian agent sent to Kabul for the ostensible purpose of discussing trade with the Afghan leader Dost Mohammed. This would have been some time in the 1830s. But like the British – who had also despatched to Kabul one of their own agents, the better-known Captain Alexander Burnes – the Russians were less interested in trade per se than in securing allegiances and military treaties to advance their control of the volatile region.

From somewhere I had a stubborn vision of Burnes and Vitkyevitch meeting in the desert near Herat, exchanging visiting cards with the utmost courtesy, then hurrying off to write coded reports to their superiors in Moscow and London. Their fates now intertwined, they met again in Kabul, where the Englishman invited his opponent for Christmas dinner. Working in secret, but knowing of each other's efforts, they concocted a variety of guarantees and ultimatums to win over the Amir, who played both sides for the best deal. But Burnes, frustrated by the Afghan leader's counter-demands, stepped down in 1838. This marked the end of a gentlemanly face-off, and from then on the Great Game gathered momentum as Russian and British powers vied for influence in less and less gentlemanly ways. Burnes returned a hero to England and to a knighthood; in St Petersburg, Vitkyevitch was snubbed by Foreign Minister Nesselrode and shot himself a week later. Three years later Burnes was killed by Afghans at the British residence in Kabul, precipitating the most disastrous retreat in British military history.

---

* Described in Eric Newby's *A Short Walk in the Hindu Kush*, Picador, 1981.

Soldiers and spies were not the only foreigners roaming Afghanistan at the time; I had Joseph Wolfe for W! He was the indefatigable English clergyman who, between many other adventures, undertook a mission to plead for the life of Captain Arthur Connolly of Bokharene bug-pit fame.* Wolfe's devout eccentricity is said to have endeared him to the bloodthirsty Amir of Bokhara, who spared his life, regarding him as a sort of curiosity.

For X, I had nothing, and struggled a long time with Y, remembering in the end Major Yate and his 'unsoldierly sigh' (in Robert Byron's words) at the destruction of the Tīmūrid monuments in Herat by the British.

Z proved impossible.

*

It had taken a long time. I have not counted the names which didn't fit properly, the associative diversions, the moments of panic, or time spent huddling and clinging in a state of mental dislocation: this otherwise straightforward act of recollection had lasted nearly two hours.

There was a bang like a gunshot under the truck and a sudden hiss of air — the dying breath of a rear tyre. We were still high above the silvery river, and there was no sign of an end to our ordeal. For a few moments all was still. The moon had sailed gently higher, yawing

---

* Lieutenant (later Captain) Arthur Conolly of the 6th Bengal Native Light Cavalry was one of a select band of bold and ambitious young officers who volunteered for the perilous task of gathering intelligence from the volatile Central Asian territories between British and Russian spheres of influence. Ever confident of the Crown's reputation in Asia and of his own powers of persuasion, Conolly entered Bokhara in October 1841 on a mission to secure the release of a fellow officer, Lt. Col. Charles Stoddard, then a prisoner of the ruling Emir Nasrullah. Suspicious of British motives and slighted by the lack of a personal response to his letter to Queen Victoria, the Emir ordered the Englishmen's public beheading soon afterwards. The grim account of their final and suspense-filled days in a vermin-filled pit, penned in Conolly's own hand, reached his sister in London twenty years later.

heavenward, its light colder now, with Venus still trailing faithfully from the hook of its lower orb.

I went on to ancient names. The tyre was reinflated from the truck's compressor. The engine roared back into life and resumed its mournful growling as we lurched forward. Again there were gaps, but it was an impressive list. Between Alexander and Zoroaster, whose birthplace was Balkh in northern Afghanistan, it included the great miniaturist Behzād of Herat, Chingiz Khan, the Achaemenid king Darius, Eucratides, the poet Ferdosi, the dynasty of the Ghorids, Queen Hutaosa (said to have been Zoroaster's first convert, along with her husband King Vishtasp), the last great classical Persian poet Jāmi, Kanishka the great Kushan monarch, Mahmoud of Ghazni, the Sufi sage Nasruddin, Ptolemy (who oversaw the Egyptian territories after Alexander's death), the founder of the Qaderiyya Sufis, Roxanne (Alexander's Afghan wife), Seleucus, Timur; that left I, L, M, O and ... nothing for U or V. The White Huns would have to do for W, and as for X ...

I went on to modern place-names and their ancient equivalents. The ancient satrapies of the Achaemenid empire had wonderful and mythical-sounding names: Arachosia, Bactriana, Chorasmia, Drangiana ... What were the ancient names? Herat was Herovia, Balkh was Zariaspa, Kabul – perhaps – was Strabo's lost city of Ortospana, and Qunduz was called Drapsaka. The Oxus river was called the Jayhun, and the Jaxartes the Sayhun. The Indus? I couldn't remember the Indus ...

There was another puncture and the truck ground to a halt. I had been wrestling with alphabets now for several hours. We had left the river and were following a loop of road inland. The road was just as bad, but the relief of getting away from the precipice was indescribable.

Around us stretched an unearthly landscape. I shook a thick layer of the spectral dust from my *pattū* and poked my head over the frame of the truck. We were stranded in a crater-like amphitheatre of oddly shaped hills, like an interplanetary ship, becalmed. There was no colour; the land had been reduced by the light of moon and star to a single phosphorescent glaze, the surrounding slopes scarred by shadow-filled ravines, and buttressed by long conical ridges like sleeping rows of Cappadocian fairy chimneys.

For an hour all was still until, like a dragon on a predatory prowl, roaring and wreathed in furious swirls of dust lit eerily by the beams of its headlight eyes, another truck approached from the opposite direction. A borrowed tyre was manoeuvred into place with bangs and yells from underneath us, and we crept on again, back, I realized with a sinking feeling, towards the truth-extracting road.

I grappled again for some mental foothold to counter the fear, huddled with arms around knees and, as battle with the broken road resumed, wishing only I could spread wings. But of course! A bird, a phoenix, the mythical Simorgh! I could follow its flight on a circular tour of the country and have no fear of gravity at all. I could ride on its back between its wings from dawn to dusk and from the Chinese border to Iran...

*

From China, then, the Simorgh's home. We could start there, at one of the loneliest meeting places of frontiers in the world; the sixteen-thousand-foot-high watershed where Tajikistan meets China and Afghanistan in an ill-defined and perennially chilly embrace, just at the eastern reaches of the Pamir knot. It would be a difficult beginning of course, flying between walls of ice – and colder even than it was now – through freezing clouds of air so thin our lungs would burn. But if we could...

If we could, we would make it out of those swirling ice-needles and winds into a forest of snow-draped mountain peaks, carved into leaping ridges and valleys of heart-stopping immensity by glaciers of the mountain ranges that collide here, the Pamir and the Hindu Kush. And on, between them, where a valley stretched west, and along its floor a snaking river, the Pamir, an icy torrent without hope of escape in any other direction, imprisoned between walls reaching on either side to twenty thousand feet.

So unforgivingly remote; a strange place for a frontier, and more strangely shaped; a narrow finger of land only a few miles wide, a wilderness of grey moraine strewn with boulders the size of houses, hemmed in by high cataracts of rock. This was the Wakhān corridor, a stem-like incursion from the leaf-shaped body of the country, so designed as to prevent the borders of two once-proud empires from ever touching.

It was a hard morning's flight; we hugged the valley floor to stay in the marginally thicker air, and never saw Concord peak or Lake Victoria (Ozero Zorkul to the Russians), that loneliest of lakes mapped in the days of the Great Game by men of heroic obscurity.

Numbed with cold we tore west for nearly a hundred miles, until I felt a nudge from the Simorgh's beak, as he nodded beyond a wingtip to the first signs of human life far below us. It was a tiny hamlet, just at the junction of the Pamir and the Wakhān rivers. From here on, I remembered, the northern border was called the Ab-i Panj on the Afghan side and the Pyandzh in Tajikistan. Spires of ice-buttressed rock reared all around: to the north, in Tajikistan, at the convergence of the Ishkashemsky and the Yuzhno alichurskiy mountain ranges, and to the south, in a lofty confederation of the highest peaks of the Hindu Kush, Naoshaq, Tirich Mīr and Saraghrar.

But on the valley floor I could now make out some wisps of smoke, rising from a cluster of mud-brick houses barely distinguishable from the earth. We banked, just to be certain, circled at a thousand feet, and glimpsed a forlorn assembly of animals; half a dozen skeletal Rosinantes, some two-humped Bactrian camels and a yak, its wild coat matted in frozen clumps.

Here the Wakhān was only ten miles wide. On either side the grey mountain flanks arced upwards into the clouds and although it was ten miles wide at the narrowest point we seemed to be squeezing between walls of rock. The first proper villages started to appear at Eskāshim, where the Panj began a long diversion to the north, forming roughly, as I picture it now, a shape like a mammoth's head, with the Wakhān for its trunk.

We banked north towards Badakhshān, a wild and spectacularly sculpted region of rock and winding torrents, following Polo's route to China in reverse (and at one moment glimpsing, I fancied, on the flanks of an inhospitable slope, a specimen of the great mountain goat named after the wayward Italian himself, the majestic *Ovis ammon polii*).

Then along the valley of the Wardūj from Zeebak to Faizābād, we looked down on tiny villages clinging to its corrugated hem, their borders flanked with increasingly broader terraces of meticulously cultivated fields.

Imperceptibly, the mountains were softening. And soon, lines of poplar trees began to enclose these tenaciously maintained settlements, adding a tracery of natural tenderness to the sweeping rocks. Above them there were pistachio and mulberry groves on the higher slopes. A road appeared. It wasn't surfaced, but looked solid enough for wheeled transport by the time it reached the junction of the Warduj and the Kokcha rivers near the village of Baharak, and where the bridges weren't washed out by the floods of the previous spring, it allowed – I guessed, from the sight of an ant-like truck creeping along it – an average speed of about ten miles an hour.

From here a tributary road led north towards Lake Shiveh, where caravans of nomads gathered in the summer months, and I felt a twinge of regret that it was the wrong season to glimpse them. But the Simorgh, sensing my longing, hypnotized me most mischievously, and for a few moments I caught sight of a string of a thousand camels padding along the dusty trail, led by hardy, sunburned men and, swaying above them, swathed in black folds, women of harsh and aristocratic beauty.

Beyond lay more mountains, threaded by jade-coloured torrents seeking release beneath the plutonic precipices of the northernmost border, which looped dramatically southward again after snaking to within fifty miles of Kirgizstan, and descended, splintering into a network of watery fissures, in the more manageable territory above Yangi Qāla.

Here, where the mountains eventually surrendered to the northern plains of Turkestan, a descent brought frozen feathers into warmer air, just above a cluster of strange tumescences that stretched inland where the Ab-i Panj was joined by the greenish torrent of the Kochka.

*

We rested briefly: it was a good place for a rest, and the Simorgh shook his feathers as I slipped from his back to look over the site and dream a little of history. We were in Bactria now, one of the richest historical oases of all Asia. Its past was recorded in greater than usual detail by classical historians on account of the brief but tumultuous incursion into the region by that brilliant, charismatic and bloodthirsty young Macedonian, who tore through in 330 BC at the head of an army of forty thousand, paving a sanguinary way for generations of Greek settlers and the cultural influence that would far outlive them. Yet the hastily constructed empire fractured quickly after Alexander's death between the feuding monarchs of Macedonia, Egypt, Bactria, Persia and India, surviving only another two hundred years among a succession of competing dynasties ruled by Bactrian and Indo-Greek kings. Then, out of the north, rode the nomads...

And today all that remained of the Greeks' easternmost city lay around us in a rambling graveyard of severed busts and toppled Corinthian capitols. Locals knew the place by the enigmatic name of Ay Khanoum, the Moon Woman, and as a favourite hunting-ground of the former king. It hinted only whisperingly at what was once the largest Greek city outside of Greece, and to judge from the scale of its monuments, one of the most opulent. Its two-thousand-year sleep was rudely broken by French archaeologists in the 1960s, after forty years of research.

It was late morning. There was no sound but the faint rushing of the river. I scrambled into one of the excavated pits, where a layer of carbonized roof timbers hinted at the city's final moments. It was tempting to imagine the scene, as the site was overrun by nomadic central Asian hordes roughly a hundred years before the birth of Christ; the terror of its Hellenistic overlords at the vision, across the river, of the narrow-eyed and battle-hardened horsemen advancing beneath a cloud of dust; the cries of alarm ringing through the high fluted colonnades, the frantically invoked prayers at the sacred enclosure of the mysterious Kineus, the dreadful flight from the city gates, the toppling of polished statues and dressed rock shattering in the flames and falling, never to stir for two millennia, into rivulets of molten bronze...

Then over gentler territory we continued west, above the southern bank of the deepening river which, released now from the walls of rock, was bordered with wide alluvial flood plains. They stretched in a broad and sparsely populated swathe all the way to Turkmenistan. Unnamed ruins eroded under us on the thin and stony soil. Near the river there were marshes and salt-flats; further inland I could see a belt of desert flecked with stunted tragacanth and tamarisk bushes, reaching as far as the rounded foothills of the Turkestan range.

Long ago the entire area may have been cultivated – plants bloom luxuriantly in the soil when tended – but the irrigation canals so vital for agriculture were destroyed in successive invasions from the north, and now they were visible only as bumps and tumours in the otherwise abandoned land. Out of the barrenness, the small town of Tashgurgan loomed up late at midday, just north of the high narrow gorge where – it must have been here – Bessus waited in vain to ambush Alexander twenty-three centuries ago. Tashgurgan was famous in Afghanistan for its timeless charm and boasted the oldest covered bazaar in Asia, half-destroyed now, it was said, by Russian commandos in retaliation for the killing of their commanding officer's brother.

Mazar-i Sharīf was soon visible. Out of the sprawl of the city led a straight road busy with trucks. There were some ruins on the outskirts, which we dared not linger over for lack of time; to the northwest in Balkh, Bactria's ancient capital, we could make out the massive eroded ramparts of the city walls. But there was little to suggest its former glory as one of the most influential commercial capitals of the East.

I felt an old pang ignite. Centuries ago, while Christianity was still an outlawed cult, Balkh had been perhaps the greatest trans-continental caravanserai of the ancient world. It was also the fertile cradle of a complicated cultural matrix, where local and imported religions fused with the irresistible monotheism of later religions, spawning exotic pantheons of deities.

Balkh was already an important Zoroastrian centre when Alexander reached it in 329 BC. Fittingly, it was here that Alexander is said to have taken Roxanne, the daughter of a Bactrian leader, as his bride, and to have staged one of the more ostentatious marriages in history, claiming himself to be a god in the process. Five years later Alexander was dead; but the sumptuous settlement he rebuilt was called the 'Mother of Cities' by the Arabs who overran it in 645. Its greatness would endure until the arrival of Chingiz Khan, who crossed the Oxus nearby with a hundred thousand Mongol troops in 1220. The devastation that followed was total, and Balkh and the surrounding region never recovered.

We flew on over unmapped pools of oil bubbling like inkstains into the sands near the northwest border, turned south over the gas fields of Shibergan, and glimpsed the hollow tombs of the Kushan nobles unearthed at nearby Tilya Tepe with a hoard of over 20,000 artefacts, mostly gold, by Soviet archaeologists in 1978. We saw the emerald-coloured northern foothills and, in their poplar-hemmed folds, high-cheeked Uzbek farmers winnowing wheat like the spray of fountains of amber. There was no time to pass over Andokhoy, fifty miles to the northwest (was this the Bactrian city founded by Alexander, destroyed by barbarians, rebuilt eponymously by Antiochus son of Seleucus, and peopled with the colony of Syrians from whom the Sūrī dynasty of Ghor, who forged an empire as far as India in the twelfth century, took their name?). We followed instead the summer route of nomads towards the mountains of the Turkestan range, and left the plains for the rising chaparral country of the northern foothills, through scattered forests of pine and winding vertical canyons of layered rock. Here again the roads faded to rough tracks manageable only by jeep. Gone were the sprawling settlements of the northern lowlands; here there were only villages linked by precipitous trails, clinging like limpets in mountain crevices.

I felt the air cool again as we approached the Safed Kuh range, the White Mountains; a relatively low range for Afghanistan but, even so, impassable by road in winter. The eight-thousand-foot saddle was white with snow and I dug my hands beneath the Simorgh's feathers, and drew them out only after we had swooped down again into the Khorassanian plain. Then we bore towards Herat, passing over the nipple-shaped roofs of the outlying Fārsiwān territories, until we glimpsed the two hundred-foot high turquoise Tīmūrid towers rising from the broad and once-prosperous valley.

Herat too had been a great jewel in the string of Silk Route cities, a settlement born out of the mists of prehistory; a fabled place that had figured conspicuously in every period of Afghan history. As a cultural centre in the Tīmūrid era it had no rival; visiting embassies came and went from China to Rome, exchanging royal trinkets of tigers and horses. In the nineteenth century it was saved from the Persian army by an Irishman; later the British destroyed its most glorious monuments in a Russophobic panic. In 1978 ten thousand Afghans were killed there in an uprising against the communists, sparking the Soviet invasion.

The Simorgh nodded towards the east, as if to ask a question; yes, it was tempting to cut into the central region of the Hazārajat, a region so tantalizing as to deserve exploration, but without a local guide I sensed even the Simorgh was reluctant to try the route. Even from the air it would be a challenge to follow the winding mountain trails: it would have to wait. We followed from our airborne observatory the old circular road instead, and headed south along it to Qandahar, into Pathan territory, towards the deserts where the *bād-i sad o bīst rūz*, the 120-day wind, blows viciously in the summer months over the barren floors of extinct lakes.

It was the route taken by the Mongol armies in 1221; they had brought devastation to the settlements along their way. Cities built under the Ghaznavid Sultan Mahmoud, and likened to Paradise by Arab historians, lay beneath us in ruins; at the junction of the Helmand and Arghandab rivers the royal castles of the Sultan's winter quarters sprawled in desolate splendour. Their founder, the famous slave-king of Turkish descent, was one of the most brilliant generals of the Islamic world. At the turn of the eleventh century he swept out the Buddhist rulers of southern Afghanistan, sacked much of India and invaded Iran; in his spare time he surrounded himself with a thousand scholars and four hundred poets in his capital at Ghazni, where pillaged Hindu statuary was used to build the thresholds of the city's mosques.

Even in winter it was warm there; Afghanistan's climate, as complex as the landscape, finds here its opposite pole from the ice-bound reaches of the northeast. Not far away lay the lifeless Dasht-i Margo, the Desert of Death, an unexplored expanse of volcanic pebbles, polished endlessly by sand and implacable winds. It must have been a truly terrible place for a battle; the British suffered one of their worst defeats here in the summer of 1880: Maiwand.

Tamarisk and camel-thorn are all that grew between the dunes and shale-strewn flats of neighbouring Registan, the Land of Sands, but nearing the southernmost city we looked over seasonal lakes and marshes where the rivers found eventual release from the mountains of the interior. It was late afternoon when we stopped to preen dust from feathers at Qandahar airport, the refuelling point envisaged by American cold-war strategists for nuclear bombers on their way to targets deep inside the Soviet Union.

By now I was impatient to reach Kabul: our mythical day was drawing to a close. So we headed almost exactly northeast over the southern mountains of the Pathan heartland; somewhere down there snaked the ever-contentious Durand Line. In places an unmistakable pungence, I was sure of it now, rose up on subtropical thermals from the poppy fields in Tālebān territory; in forested Paktia (Heroditus's Paktyika of the thirteenth satrapy?) we caught the scent of pine lifted on alpine breezes.

The road was busy with traffic; overstuffed trucks laden with fruits, nuts, animal hides, timber, fuel, guns and drugs plying in both directions. Flanking the ill-fated highway on either side stretched mile after mile of ruins. All the way to the capital, the burned-out, stripped hulks of tanks and armoured vehicles littered the verges. And in countless places I could make out a strange sight hard to notice on the ground but unmissable to the airborne eye: hilltop structures of baked mud, half destroyed in battles that had left their violent signatures impressed into the earth. In every direction around these former military posts and installations stretched ray-like lines of craters, each one the imprint of a fallen shell or mortar round. The effect was curiously evocative; they looked like tiny portions of the surface of the moon, or the corpses of abandoned stars.

The destruction reached a desolate climax in Kabul, where the south and southwest of the city lay almost completely in rubble. Yet even here, where one might least expect, we flew carefully to avoid the strings of children's kites, and continued over the mountain-ringed capital to the Shomāli plain. We followed the straight road north and, as the shadows began to lengthen, headed for the breach in the looming mountains at Gulbahār. Just short of the mountains I requested a final circling, to see if I could spot some trace of the ancient summer quarters of Kanishka; for here, perhaps more than anywhere in the country, the land was impregnated with all the strivings and ambitions, the victories and defeats of the centuries. Incomparably rich archaeological finds testified to its strategic position as the meeting place of the routes north to Bactria and central Asia, west to the empires of Persia and Rome, south to India, and east to China.

No surprise that Kanishka, one of the greatest figures in early Asian history, made his summer quarters here at Kapisa, near the modern Bagram. In the early second century of the Christian era he was the undisputed ruler of the vast Kushan empire; a world-class sovereign who controlled an empire of extraordinary eclecticism, the cities of which pulsed with luxuries exchanged between Rome and the Far East and all points in between.

To judge from the proliferation of deities on the coins from Kanishka's era, it was a period of religious tolerance. Trade and agriculture prospered; palaces and temples multiplied. Under Kanishka and his successors unique cultural fusions occurred, as Graeco-Roman artistic styles imported to the region in Alexander's time blended with the Buddhist stream from the south. Panoplies of existing pagan deities fused creatively between the two, giving birth to mutated artistic styles whose relics – Buddhas with Apollonian features or Hellenic gods atop Bactrian steeds, winged Aphrodites bearing Indian caste-marks, Persian phoenixes ('Not phoenixes!' I heard an indignant voice cry over the wind. '*Griffins!*') drawn by Oriental charioteers – reflect dynastic titles resembling chemical compounds fused at high historical temperatures: Indo-Parthian, Graeco-Bactrian, Sino-Siberian, Kushano-Sassanian.

From here the fusion of East and West in the art of the Gandharan schools of the period spread to the Far East along the ancient caravan routes to China and Japan, where its echo is seen today. Meanwhile the religious tolerance and humanism of the era was exemplified in such cities built under Kanishka as Taxila, where Zoroastrian, Buddhist, Christian, Hindu, Jain and Jewish communities all are known to have co-existed peacefully and productively.

Then, some time in the fifth century AD, yet another nomad wave swept southward, this time comprising a people as mysterious to historians as they were ruthless. These were the Hepthalites, or White Huns, militarily adroit and fiercely destructive, scattering a legacy of ash and corpses. By the following century, Chinese pilgrims visiting the sacred sites of their Buddhist heartland describe only ruins and abandoned monasteries.

*

It was time; the plain closed in, pincered now by the *Koh-i Bābā* range to the west and the ten-thousand-foot crenellations of the Panjshīr valley's southern folds. The route back to Wakhān, our starting point, took us into the valley, whose tiny villages seemed to rise out of the soil itself. Around them, in patchworks of fields, old men guided wooden ploughs through the precious soil, while women and barefoot children were now ushering their animals into stony pens. The valley walls steepened and the river narrowed, rising still, its flow quickening, towards the Anjomān Pass — where even the Simorgh had to catch its breath at the sudden drop on the far side, as the mountain seemed to fall away three thousand feet into the slate-coloured sands of the Monjan.

From here, glancing over a wingtip to the east, it was just possible to see the ice-draped peaks enclosing the steepest and wildest valleys of the entire land in Nuristan, home to insular tribes of legendary recalcitrance and the last of the country's peoples to be converted to Islam. Before the turn of the twentieth century it was called Kafiristan, land of the unbelievers. They made their own wine and worshipped a complicated collection of spirits and deities, claimed to be descended from Alexander's troops, and carved wooden effigies resembling the giant *moai* of Easter Island.

But the light was beginning to fade . . .

The peaks towered steadily higher, and land below seemed to shrink in on itself under the advancing waves of shadow. The sky began to deepen to the colour of lapis lazuli, and the solitudes its measureless dome enclosed seemed more remote then ever until — like pinpricks in the thickening curtain of night – tiny oil lanterns in the windows of houses at Ishkashim betrayed our route leading back into the Wakhān.

And the circle was closed, just as the first stars appeared, like diamonds sown into the cosmic drapery of the Milky Way – the trail of stardust, according to Afghan lore, thrown up by the Prophet's stallion Dardul as he galloped across the skies to heaven...

*

There was a hiss of brakes and for a moment all was still again. We had reached the *serai* in Artin Jelau, halfway to Taloqān. I looked up; the stars seemed close enough to touch. But the winged steed had disappeared.

*

A blaring of horns sent the mummies scuttling back to their trucks. It was still dark and even colder than before. I was swept up in the rush for the door, ran half-asleep out into the street, and clambered up what I hoped was the right truck. After the usual shouts, prayers, hissing of brakes and grinding of gears, we headed southwest now.

Behind us the sky began to lighten, like a picture growing visible in a tray of developer. Soon we were high again above the river, although the quality of the landscape was transformed. On both sides of the valley the cliffs had turned to networks of smooth sculpted caverns, and in the surreal exhaustion of dawn I remember thinking I had been transported to the insides of a sort of cosmic Swiss cheese, only there were Russian tanks upside down in the river below.

The grey deepened to blue as the day was born, its colour growing more intense by the minute, until the world seemed enclosed by a sapphire dome. The dawn was gathering strength. A flock of sheep, driven by a turbaned whitebeard, flowed around the truck like a shoal of fish. In the river and on the verges of the road, which had mercifully begun to widen, were more rusted carcasses of ruined armour; tanks, armoured personnel carriers, winches and military bulldozers, their axles twisted by mine blasts. We came to a gorge cut by a roaring tributary – this was the Teshkān, I think – which we crossed on an

228

unpleasantly high and narrow bridge with only inches to spare on either side. As it joined the Kochka the colour of the water changed abruptly, cloudy with silt. We left it, turning south, and moved into gentler territory with an enormous sense of relief. Yet for all the peril I was sad to leave that wild territory. I had seen tracks leading north from the far side of the river into the ragged hills, and felt a magnetic longing to follow.

It was still early morning when we reached Keshm, spilled gratefully from the truck and celebrated the end of the cliffside portion of the route with kebabs and glasses of tea. A huge Afghan I had never met paid for my meal. The *chaikhāna* was powered by a Russian car dynamo turned by paddles driven in the irrigation stream alongside the pavement. I wandered a little down the tree-lined street towards the crossroads around which the town seemed to have grown, bargained at a stall for a chequered scarf, then heard the blare of the horn from the truck.

A day's drive took us to Taloqān. We had two more punctures on the way, made a protracted stop in a lonely village to buy diesel, and laboured in long slow climbs over golden slopes which from a distance resembled rippling waves of gilded, windblown ice. For hours we drove through the shallow water of a riverbed where the road had been washed away and, on the final and only surfaced stretch of the entire route, ran out of fuel just as the sun began to set. For the first time I talked with the other passengers, and revealed my identity to the traders.

'I knew it,' chuckled one of them to his friend, 'but I couldn't place you.' Then he turned suddenly pensive, apologized for the condition of the road, his lack of learning, and for the state of things in general.

'Things are bad in these times,' he added forlornly. '*Insh'āllah*, it has not caused you too much trouble.'

The other man – the one who looked like a Hell's Angel – turned out to be a Russian Tajik from Dushanbe and had come to Afghanistan – I supposed but didn't ask – to seek out fellow Tajik revolutionaries. But he lacked the Afghan sparkle.

'Islam is the only way,' he said grimly, and the other men exchanged a dubious look. There was some logic to his comment; of all the former Soviet republics the roots of the Islamic resurgence grew deepest in Tajikistan. But the presence of 25,000 Russian soldiers along the border was a good indication of the difference in view from Moscow. We wished him well as he swung a small rucksack over his shoulder and walked alone towards the town.

The sun was low and pale. Farmers were burning winter stubble in fields divided by rows of slender poplars. Turbaned men passed on bicycles and donkeys. A gaggle of half a dozen women walked by wearing *burqās* of light blue and yellow. The smell of the smoke was comforting. There was an hour of delicious stillness and the magic of the dusk settled over us like a spell.

It was dark when we finally reached the town itself and with the usual swiftness and sense of purpose the passengers dispersed into the streets and the warren-like passages that led from them. I hailed a pony trap decorated with bouncing red pom-poms and driven by a teenage boy. Had he ever seen a building or a flag with a red cross on it? I asked. He nodded enthusiastically and cracked his whip over the back of the horse repeatedly until we reached a grid of mud-walled streets on the outskirts of the town. From here we asked our way from others, until I caught sight of a rooftop flag I recognized and banged on the gate of the building below. It was the office of one of the French medical groups. Thinking myself clever I asked the pale and apprehensive face that soon appeared whether he knew of a good hotel in the area, explaining in my best French that I just happened to be passing...

'Sorry, mate,' came the answer in a thick Australian accent. 'I don't know what you're talking about.'

I switched to English, and explained myself as we walked across the yard to the house.

'Chris,' he called down a corridor, 'it's an Englishman.'

We turned a corner, where I met the unexpected sight of a tall, handsome woman with long dark hair, and felt something of the shock and thrill that men in countries stricter about such things must experience when they first see Western women.

'Oh, another one,' she said matter-of-factly, and looked up.

'Do you see many?' I asked.

'There were two a few weeks back. But they had horses. Have you got a horse too?'

So the rumours of the wandering Englishmen were true. Chris looked me up and down with what seemed like friendly disapproval, and I was suddenly aware of how I must have appeared: shrouded in a *pattū* and mujaheddin-style scarf and hat, coated in dust, reeking like a goat and hauling a dirty grey sack behind me. But her words were sweeter than I could have hoped.

'Welcome,' she said, with a heart-melting smile. 'There's hot water in the shower and dinner's at seven if you'd like to join us.'

✻

It was another encounter made sweeter by its brevity; in the morning they left by jeep, and I was alone again. We had stayed up late and talked about Chechnya, where their clinic had been bombed by Russian jets and they were the only non-combatants to be seen heading towards, rather than fleeing, the front lines. I was sad to see this courageous husband-and-wife team, as hospitable as they were unassuming, disappear.

The weather had broken. Where there had been mountains the day before there was now a milky void of low cloud. This was a country where the mountains impress themselves indelibly in the traveller's unconscious sense of orientation; now they had disappeared, it seemed a vital piece of the drama of the landscape had been removed. It began to rain, and the rain turned to snow.

Polo mentions Taloqān in his Travels. It was well known, he wrote, for its abundance of almonds, pistachios and the roughly hewn slabs of rock salt extracted locally from the hills. The vines, lions and horses said to be descended from Alexander's own Bucephalus were gone, but time had not laid its touch too heavily on the place.

There was a single central crossroads which I imagined had hardly changed over the intervening centuries. From there the majority of buildings radiated in a quarter-mile grid. I think only the main street had a hard surface; all others, as the snow began to melt, turned to shallow rivers of mud. Near the centre the market ran in arcades of whitewashed brick but the order fell away quickly in the smaller streets to a chaos of mud and timber overhung by dripping awnings made from canvas or woven reed matting.

As ever the market was busy, noisy and a natural recreation for the eye. It was far more varied and extensive than the market in Faizābād. I wandered, for the most part unnoticed, for a few hours, given away occasionally by my boots, which even a generous coating of mud failed to disguise from the Afghan eye.

A man selling plastic overshoes was doing a thriving trade. Soaps, snuff boxes, combs, string, shampoo, watch straps, socks and 'wonder rabbit' batteries — all were from China. Many of the stalls had jars of local honey for sale, but the thought of a cracked jar in my bag was discouraging. There were dozens of carpet stalls, from which their owners, cross-legged and dressed in turbans and the long striped cotton gowns of the north, peered watchfully into the flow of passers-by. In the metalworkers' street, men were hammering away energetically at sheets of galvanized zinc, producing stoves, buckets, trunks, ewers and pots and pans of every shape. Another was lined with carpenters' stalls turning out cupboards, windows and door frames.

In one incongruous cluster of shops there was a second-hand clothes seller next to a quasi-pharmacy displaying tiers of pills and medicines, tended and dispensed by a nine-year-old boy. Next came a line of severed goat's heads, these also neatly arrayed, and next door to these a stall where, in the way others laid out fruit and vegetables, there was a selection of rockets, ammunition and grenades.

I went back to the crossroads and found a wooden stairway leading to a busy *chaikhāna*. It was warm and crowded inside and the air was thick with the oily vapour of grilling kebabs. The platforms were covered with blood-red 'Bokhara'-style carpets. I shook the snow from my *pattū* and ordered kebabs. A boy brought half a dozen skewers, and just as I was about to eat three men sat cross-legged opposite me. Something, I could tell, had alerted them to the foreigner in their midst.

'Your bread's the wrong way up,' said one of them, gruffly. But I didn't understand at first.

'Your bread,' he said again. 'Turn it over.'

It was only then I noticed for the first time the difference in texture between the two sides. I turned it smooth side down and the three men nodded approvingly, and the atmosphere lightened.

'Are you a Tajik?' asked another.

I told him about Inglestan.

'Hindustan?' His brow contracted into furrows of puzzlement. 'Where?'

'Inglestan!' interjected his companion, with a tut of exasperation at the other's ignorance. 'Not Hindustan!' It was a touching show of one-upmanship, and he shook his head in dismay at the other's dim-wittedness. 'Inglestan, yes, of course. Not *Hindustan*. Inglestan is—' He turned to me. 'Well . . . completely different – isn't that right?'

I lingered there after they had left, reluctant to leave the warmth of the place. It was early afternoon and already the day began to usher in worries about where to stay that night, which grew into general misgivings about the way ahead. Mazar-i Sharīf, the next major town in the north, lay beyond the front. There would be little, if any, civilian traffic. In Kabul I had heard it said that an invitation from either the rival government or some foreign sponsor was required to pass into the opposition's territory. I hadn't taken this seriously at the time, and now regretted it.

I was about to leave when an icy gust of wind swept into the room. Four men appeared at the door. They sat down cross-legged a few feet away on the opposite platform, the fresh snow clinging to their eyebrows and beards. Two of them carried automatic rifles. The third unslung a light machine gun, rested the barrel on its bipod, and eased from his neck a twenty-foot-long ammunition belt which slithered in coils like an anaconda down onto the carpet. The fourth carried nothing, wore a plain white turban and dark *pattū*, and sat down a few feet from me with an air of both dignity and calm.

He was obviously their commander, and his appearance was so striking I caught myself staring. His brow was broad and unlined and his narrow face tapered downwards from high cheekbones towards a rich black beard. A pair of dark oval eyes, as kindly as they were intense, strengthened the dove-like impression of his features.

His face was not only beautiful but seemed to emanate an extraordinary purity, an interior integrity with which I associated profound goodness. It did not seem properly to belong to my own world, which was perhaps its fascination, and the sight of it was like a gem flashing from layers of worthless stone. And I was staring not just because his face was utterly unlike the faces I knew from home but because I felt all of a sudden that if I were to attach myself to him, apprentice-like, and follow him to his home and enter into his life and language and hardships and battles and pleasures, I might learn something substantial about the country and its culture and all that was hidden from the casual onlooker I really felt myself to be, able only to observe what was most superficial. And I felt too with equal certainty, based on nothing but that glance, that had I made the suggestion he would have agreed and honoured the spirit of the impulse without question.

He acknowledged me with the faintest of smiles and an almost imperceptible nod, and our worlds were momentarily bridged. A glimmer of questioning in his eyes told me he was as intrigued about the solitary foreigner as was I about him. And thus passed our moment of exchange, which was not shared by his men, who eyed me with the usual reserve and curiosity. Yet I knew I couldn't stay.

I record this only because it was, in a sense, an incident I was beginning to recognize as typical of the place, as characteristic of encounters with individuals as with the landscape itself. Always there was this flash of beauty out of the backdrop of harshness, like a ray of light thrown across a cave; a drop of sweetness distilled from the sea of indifferent experience, prompting feelings which, if translated into physical terms, were the equivalent of glimpsing a fertile and delicately cultivated valley after hours of walking through barren mountains; feelings of tremendous relief and affirmation which carried with them the scent of a different way of living, to which the usual constraints of life would not really apply. In time, such moments were insubstantial, but in memory proved ineradicable; they awoke different urges which if laid bare would appear as madness to the ordinary world. And this was a large part of the magic of the place and its people; one might follow such promptings and not be considered mad. To be true to such moments, recklessly true perhaps, was the challenge, the parting of the ways, that travel throws into one's path; and I was deeply disappointed with myself for having let it pass.

I wandered back into the town. The sky had cleared in places and through a break in the trees I caught a glimpse of the hills, and realized what had been rain in the morning had been snow higher up. Where they had been golden the day before they were now draped in whiteness.

By four o'clock it was nearly dark. From everywhere came the sound of bolts sliding into latches and the slamming of doors; by half past four the streets were almost deserted. At a quarter to five I heard the cry of a muezzin go up from a nearby mosque, then another, and a third. The calls overlapped irregularly, like the waves of passing boats onto a shore. Seeing the streets so suddenly empty, I felt a pang of exclusion, followed by a momentary longing to heed the call to the mosque myself. But instead I walked back towards the grid of streets where I had started, as the question of where to stay for the night began to loom anew.

*

The office of the Swedish Committee for Afghanistan was in a walled compound in the southern quadrant. I met its director almost by accident, as he happened to be seeing some staff from the gates as I passed. Like a turning key, my plans were suddenly freed from uncertainty. He ushered me indoors, fired a string of gruff questions, and said: 'Right. You can stay here.' So I took him up on the offer, and stayed for two days, after which he said we could travel together to Mazar-i Sharīf.

Dr Salīmi was an Afghan but had spent his adult life in Texas. We talked in snatches during breaks in his busy schedule. His irascible manner disguised a deep concern for the fate of his country. He worked under enormous stress and said his greatest challenge was having to disappoint people who looked to his organization as a source of limitless wealth and influence. People took it personally, he said, when he had to turn down projects beyond the committee's brief, and failed to grasp the notion that he had a plan, as well as a budget, to stick to. The powerful were the worst, he added, the poorest the most helpful and most eager to participate.

I had met staff from the Swedish Committee on my first visit to Peshawar. Some had made daring trips with the mujaheddin to supply local populations with emergency food and medicines. I remember the director at the time, Anders Fange, recounting a long journey on which he had survived on potatoes and wild onions. Since the Soviets had left, the committee had expanded its work into nineteen provinces with a wide variety of projects, from drilling freshwater wells to providing blackboards for schools.

Inevitably perhaps, Dr Salīmi carried the burden of someone who returns to their native country and finds it transformed for the worse. It was bound to be a difficult task to establish peacetime norms and standards in a land where the war had torn apart the integrity of its institutions. Only recently he had fallen out with a local teacher who wanted to hand out annual graduation certificates to every pupil at his school, even to those who had failed the year. Salīmi had refused the teacher permission, explaining it would be a disservice to the pupils, who could not risk building their qualifications on a false foundation. The teacher saw it differently; it was winter and the month of fasting was coming – why not pass them all and get the year over with? Here clashed the momentum of their worlds.

Later, in a more pensive mood, he confided that things had changed since the war more than he wanted to admit. 'When I was a child here,' he said, 'and someone had a problem, people came to help without any expectation of reward. Now it's like the West. When someone's in trouble they either don't care or want something in return. It never used to be like that.'

I had two days of luxurious privacy in which to write up the account of events and tackle for the first time Eric Fromm's *Escape from Freedom*, which I had brought from Kabul. Plain but delicious meals appeared at the hands of a genie-like *chowkidar*. Then on the third morning we left at dawn in a pickup truck with two other Afghan staff. At about sixty miles, it wouldn't be a long journey. But somewhere between the towns of Qunduz and Mazar we would pass out of government territory.

The road through no-man's-land had a particularly bad reputation, and was said to be haunted by unruly Uzbek fighters with a habit of robbing travellers at gunpoint. Robbery was the least of it, said the Afghan doctor squeezed next to me. Everyone was scared of the Uzbek militia. I remembered them from the mujaheddin takeover of Kabul; Massoud had chosen them to spearhead the most difficult attacks, in which their reputations had been confirmed. The Uzbek 'wolves' were fierce fighters, took no prisoners, and were said to be indifferent to their own wounded.

To lower the chances of being singled out we had changed out of the typical dress of the north and hidden our valuables. I spread out my money in various and what I hoped were unlikely places, filling breast pockets with bundles of small-denomination notes to distract from more substantial ones elsewhere, and hoped our assailants wouldn't be too keen.

Soon we were streaking west on a worryingly empty road and across a high plain bordered by bluffs of ferrous rock, which tightened close to the road and then receded as we drew towards Qunduz, the last town in government hands. We ate kebabs in a smoky restaurant in the busy main street. I wondered where the taxi-park was in which Peter Levi had stumbled across a Kushan column-base. Qunduz and the surrounding area was still an archeological Klondike. Somewhere nearby had been discovered the finest collection of ancient Greek coins in the world.

As we ranged southwest I realized the region's greatest wealth was probably still underground. Again and again I caught sight of enough bumps, ridges and tumescences to make a team of archaeologists go weak at the knees. And these were in one of the most accessible parts of the country. What, I wondered, of the roadless uplands of Badakhshān and the deserts of ancient Aryana to our north?

War had devastated the region around Qunduz, and I felt myself reeling inwardly at the sight. In the mountains the crimes of warfare were absorbed more readily by the land, and since Kabul, apart from the occasional carcasses of armoured vehicles, there had been little evidence of the conflict to remind one of its scale. But here the record of years of battles was inscribed on the walls of countless buildings. In every direction we saw the dreadful hieroglyphics of blast-torn brick and shattered plaster, of shards, splinters and fragments scattered by the road, of roof beams exposed like bones from flesh, of lamp posts leaning like wounded men and wires dangling uselessly from twisted pylons.

For mile after mile, even far beyond the town, whole settlements lay in ruin, their amputated walls dissolving slowly into mounds of rubble like the stubs of melted candles. I asked the man next to me when they had been destroyed. The Soviets, he said, had levelled the villages during the war. Everything within shooting distance of the road had been blown up with dynamite, to protect their convoys from ambush. We drove along an avenue of tree stumps which I knew from descriptions had once been tall catalpa trees; this too, he said, was the work of the *shoravi*.

I never grew indifferent to the sight of all this destruction: it was heart-rending. I could accept that it belonged to the past, that the villages would be rebuilt, that the spirit of the people would carry through the process of reconstruction and healing. But the destruction had not truly ended; countless mines and unexploded shells lay buried among the ruins, capable of extending a legacy of mutilation for generations to come.

There was a certain shame in seeing all this. Acute shame, faced with the immediate and visible evidence of such wilful destruction; and deeper and more pervasive shame, at the level of one's own species, in the sense that Donne may have been referring to when he wrote of being involved with mankind, and the part being involved with the whole. The thought sat uneasily with me as we sped by in comfort, until I found myself wrestling unexpectedly with a new notion. I wrote it down soon afterwards; it made perfect sense at the time, but I have the notes with me now and wonder about it, because the keenness of the logic of those moments has now long passed. Yet it seemed just possible that in the chaos and the destruction, the trauma and the devastation, some great natural reckoning was perhaps at work, which on a human scale found expression in the catastrophe of war and which, beyond the narrow grasp of the ordinary explanations for such disasters, was merely pursuing its own organic course. To what logic did ants turn to comprehend the fall of the gardener's spade? What would visitors from a different universe make of the fact that the greatest catastrophes of the human world and its heaviest burdens tended to be borne by the souls of the most innocent? They would know nothing of man's most cherished explanations for these inexplicable iniquities, and be little comforted by notions of predestination, or of the solace of religious faith, or of the sins of former lives — much less the notion of a benevolent and omnipresent divinity. Our picture was like the ants'; as incomplete as ever . . .

I felt a tap on my knee.

'This is the dangerous part,' said my neighbour gently, nodding to the road ahead.

And then, I think, we were in no-man's-land. Unchallenged we had been descending gently into a valley guarded at its entrance by a band of mist. For a few moments a curtain of whiteness obscured the world beyond and the windows were streaked with trailing lines of moisture, like wandering tears. We plunged through the airy pleats of mist and emerged into a landscape of unexpected beauty.

Half a mile away on either side rose rust-coloured cliffs between whose crests the sky arched like a lapis bow. Flanking the road were ripe fields the colour of emerald, undulating under a caress of wind. And ahead in the northeast corner of this unexpected embrace of colour two rounded bluffs of blood-red rock swelled from the earth to enclose a high vertical gash of shadow, as if their huge immobile walls had once been touching but had drawn apart to offer passage to the ranges that stretched beyond them.

All of a sudden I caught sight of a solitary man, walking along a mud embankment that cut obliquely through the fields, half a mile ahead of us. Like a hermit sage in a Chinese painting, he seemed to fit the landscape perfectly. Was it his surroundings that converged with such integrity around him, or the man himself who, by his presence at that moment and in that swift configuration of space and light, lent such nobility to the entire scene? For a few moments they were inseparable, and he might have been the first or last man in the world.

Swiftly, our paths converged. He was carrying a light machine-gun over his shoulder. As he neared the road we drew so close I could even make out the colours of his turban, which was made from a chequered fabric of yellows, blues, greens and black. It seemed drawn from fragments of our surroundings, like a mosaic of tiny portions of the sun, rock, grass and shadows. He was lean and his sunburned skin stretched over high cheekbones, but his features were utterly different from those I was accustomed to. He was clean-shaven; he had the eyes of a Mongol; there was no trace of a smile across his face.

Our glances met as we flashed past, and his look seemed to contain both darkness and light of great intensity. Then on the far side of the valley we climbed out of the mist and were in sunshine again. Suddenly there were battle-ready tanks by the side of the road flying flags I didn't recognize from their antennae, their barrels pointing in the direction we had come.

We had crossed. Like divers surfacing after a deep descent, we exchanged glances of relief, and breathed again.

Seven

This was a land where spirits ran free and high and a fierce exuberance filled the air, blowing away dry logic and dull reason, making almost anything seem possible.

Robert Schultheis, *Night Letters: Inside Wartime Afghanistan*

MAZAR-I SHARĪF LOOMED UP several hours later. The turquoise dome of the central shrine, from which the city takes its name, shimmered above the dusty sprawl of its surroundings like a supernaturally misplaced gem.

It was not until that evening that I realized how the anxiety of the journey there had been diverted, like an underground river, away from the surface of things. I dreamed I was in a battered yellow taxi, vaguely aware of the company of friends; we were driving down a long open road in the countryside when, ahead, a checkpoint loomed. With broad smiles we introduced ourselves as journalists, expecting the usual friendly waving on. But something wasn't right. A fighter ordered us out of the car and our sense of anxiety suddenly grew. The smile on which I relied so heavily in such moments was ignored. Two fighters ordered me gruffly onto a path which ran from the road towards a muddy culvert below. I tried to read their intentions but was baffled by their unfriendliness; worst of all was their silence.

Then it happened: the moment which above all others I privately dreaded; the moment I had flirted with, willingly and unwillingly, but always with an element of calculation and of restraint. One of the fighters, a ragged and wild-looking teenager, cocked his rifle and held it to my forehead. I felt the huge coldness of the muzzle and a terrible moment of panic and helplessness. Here was the end of the ambiguity, the end of the flirtation.

I heard a voice say: 'A prayer, under the circumstances, is cheap.' The voice was my own. Didn't Turgenev write that the prayers of an ordinary man were an idle way of hoping that two and two wouldn't equal four? Yes ... but what was the alternative? Stillness, the voice said. A complete stillness, in which the design of things might unfold most truly and without hindrance: that was the best prayer I could think of.

I felt a tiny bead of sweat creep from the back of my neck. It swelled and, in slow motion, detached itself and began to roll downwards, growing hotter as it gathered momentum. It rolled like molten metal between my shoulder blades, getting ever bigger as it turned, branding a path between the muscles of my back. It grew so large I was sucked into it, along with the surroundings and all sense of time, until I seemed to be standing within it as it rolled, as hot as the sun, inexorably downward – while all around, like debris thrown up on the crest of a tidal wave, whirled the events of my life.

Just then the other fighter ran up next to his companion, grinning broadly, and pushed the rifle away.

'It's all right,' he said, 'we were just kidding,' and handed me the rifle. Then he led me back to the car, and waved us on with a wink and a grin. I woke up; the barrel against my head had gone. But the sweat was real.

*

Mazar was peaceful. Since the Soviet withdrawal it had escaped the destructive struggles for control inflicted on other cities, and experienced nothing comparable to the fighting in Kabul. And against the capital its atmosphere seemed almost disappointingly subdued, its people more withdrawn and circumspect.

Arriving in Mazar I had tried first to find a hotel in the centre of town. At one, my bag was searched, I was turned away for lack of papers, and told there was no provision for foreigners. At another the price was criminally high. Disconsolate, I wandered around the central square, avoiding the gaze of glum-looking, shaven-headed conscript soldiers at the street corners. They lacked the spontaneity and curiosity of the mujaheddin in Kabul, and I began to wonder what could explain the apparent reticence of the place. Then slowly I became aware of the ubiquitous gaze, bearing down from outsized posters and crossroads banners, of the self-styled ruler of the region. Crew-cut, draped in flashing epaulettes, and emanating all the charm of a professional wrestler, General Dostum was everywhere.

I presented myself, refugee-like, and not without a sense of failure, at the gates of the Red Cross. The regional delegate was a Swiss national in his thirties called Jean-Paul, who put me through a friendly but astute interrogation. By evening I was among the trappings of home again, ferried through the city in a cross-emblazoned jeep to the luxury of a guest residence: a walled villa complete with garage, a small lawn and badminton court. There was hot water too, European cooking, satellite television, and the chance, I reflected, to boil the lice out of my clothes.

My new host had taken warmly to the Afghan way of things, and was both impressed and fascinated by the Afghans. Unperturbed by the fate of his predecessor, who had left office with a stray rifle bullet in his neck, he confessed to a private admiration of the deference and helpfulness of Afghans towards the Westerners who lived like kings in their midst.

Given the nature of his task this was all the more surprising. It was politically sensitive work, and he apologized for not being able to speak in detail about it. But it was not a job for the faint-hearted. His main task was to visit the region's prisons and register the names of prisoners of war, the majority of them held under appalling conditions without even the pretence of a judicial process. The idea behind such visits was to prevent prisoners from disappearing without trace, to see they were adequately stocked with blankets for the coming winter, to forward messages to relatives of the detained and, where humanly possible, to assist in the reuniting of families.

All this called for unusual skills; for diplomacy and psychological insight and sufficient steadiness of nerve to negotiate with military commanders accustomed to dispensing authority from the barrel of a gun. On top of this came the stresses of missions through territories ruled by fighters whose allegiances might change from day to day. There was also the importance of being indifferent to traditional inducements from powerful people, both Afghan and foreign, seeking favour: the Red Cross had a rigorous policy of neutrality to uphold.

Modestly, he swept all these challenges aside. 'It's not so difficult,' he would say with an almost coy smile. 'Wherever you go, people are not so different.'

From what kind of background had such a man sprung? I asked him how long he had been involved with the world of humanitarian assistance. Not long at all, he said, it was nothing like that; a matter of months ago he had been a teaching professor at Harvard University.

South Asian politics? I wondered. Post-colonial sustainable development?

'Analytical philosophy.' He grinned his coy grin.

It was easy to understand his affection for the local staff. At the residence, other than a pair of Scandinavian doctors on temporary postings to the city, were a trio of Afghans who looked after us attentively. There was Homayoun, a mild-mannered *chowkidar* with eyes as round and dark as an owl's, whose room was a converted cargo container in the courtyard. In the mornings when the others had left we would sit in the sunshine and trade expressions in English and Persian. I asked his advice on making trips in the area and he shook his head sorrowfully, discouraging me from staying in local guest houses on account of the number of *wakhshi* characters about. It seemed prudent to follow this advice, which I heard confirmed from other Afghans almost daily.

Fauzia came to clean the house on alternate days, and was responsible for the most immaculately folded laundry I had ever seen. She radiated immense kindliness. She had lost her husband and three oldest sons to the war, and her six year-old daughter hovered butterfly-like around her as she worked.

Then there was Abbas, the cook. His bull-like frame would appear from the kitchen door and loom over us at mealtimes, but his big hands laid out plates with cat-like softness. The sight of him wearing a white apron and chef's hat was as sad as that of a beribboned captive bear, and all the sadness of exile seemed to be contained in his small, watery eyes.

I would talk to him in the kitchen while he cooked. Years earlier, he told me, before the war had turned him out of his home and away from his children, he had been to Italy, where his stay had been cut short by the murder of his boss by the Mafia. But even this was hardly as distressing to him as the discovery that in Italian households, unexpected guests were frequently turned away with a polite excuse, and the ill were left alone in private rooms, untended by their relatives. He shook his head in disbelief.

His experience of Iran had been hardly more cheerful. In Tehran, an irreligious city in his opinion, people had laughed at his habit of blessing bread before eating it. No, Kabul was his home, and he had land there. He had run a pastry shop before the fighting forced him to leave, and now look – he was a waiter. He was glad for the work, but the kitchen was small and didn't suit him. He waved a resigned hand over the Formica. He was a big man, he said, with a big heart, and he needed a big kitchen.

*

A day or two after arriving I also met Faheem, a highly intelligent teenage boy who spoke excellent and thoughtful English. His ambition was to work for the Red Cross, but he was too young. After we had met a few times, he invited me to spend the night at his home.

We walked there together the following evening as it grew dark. It was a modern building, prosperous by Afghan standards, on three floors, undamaged and, by its air of normality, oddly remote from other homes I had visited. I was expecting to meet every member of the family and waited for a long round of introductions, but although there were voices from a downstairs room the other adults failed to appear. Faheem belonged to an almost secular middle class that had been all but devastated in Kabul, which that evening might have been a different country.

Proudly he showed me his English homework but he was having trouble over spelling. By comparison Persian spelling was easy; words sounded the way they looked. Could I please explain how it was that 'rough', which looked so similar to 'dough', was pronounced so differently? Why 'cough', which should sound like 'bough', rhymed instead with 'trough'? He was exasperated at the logic by which 'through' became 'thorough', and almost in tears by the time I explained how 'though' was not to be confused with 'thought' ...

We played a game called *mansūr*, and flicked tiny pucks across a board made slippery with powdered chickpeas; he was an expert and I came away with a lowly score. A meal appeared, brought by his younger brother, who walked with a pronounced and permanent limp.

'It was a doctor's fault,' said Faheem matter-of-factly. 'He gave him the wrong injection.' That, apparently, was the end of the matter. I was reminded automatically of the American woman who had sued, successfully and for a vast sum of money, the fast-food chain from whom she had bought a cup of coffee and scalded herself.

There was no doubt about the high point of the evening. After dinner Faheem announced in the manner of a guilty secret that it was time to watch a video: 'with *girls*', he said, and I shuddered to think what we would see.

It was a triple-bill Pakistani musical, of the kind I had glimpsed on television in Peshawar. I had never watched one for its entire length, much less for as long as the hours that followed. These deeply popular films are based on love stories that centre around the mounting passion between a very beautiful, sari-clad young woman and a very unbeautiful, surly, mustachioed man who wants nothing to do with her.

They sing throughout; she in a high-pitched wail and the man in a throaty counterpoint. Her diaphanous veils wave to and fro in a complex semaphore of courtship, but all her efforts are unrequited until the man sees her disappear in a crowd with a coquettish backward glance.

At this crucial signal he is driven wild with desire. Soon he is beating his breast with longing and, in a variety of lonely places, undergoes a transforming period of self-reproach. Then, dressed very much like a matador, he returns in search of his beloved, and before long is having to fight off a string of rival contenders as the lovers are united, by lakesides and on mountaintops, to exchange bursts of enthusiastic gyrating.

So far so good; the theme is traditional and restrained. But then the choreographers go to town: as the passion mounts, so too does the man's habit of throwing his woman about, dragging her feet first down a snow-covered slope, or throwing her fully clothed into a swimming pool. Each time she survives the treatment, returning with the same ecstatic smile to yet another bruising round of ardour.

Our film came to a raucous climax as the final woman was tossed down a line of tight-trousered, overweight men, their hips all jerking and thrusting in unison.

*

I had been allowed to stay as a guest of the Red Cross until the next flight out of the city, which was expected in a week's time. I began to settle in. In the evenings we watched episodes of *Inspector Morse* on satellite television, followed by news from Europe. In England the threat of a strike by water authorities had been disrupting life. A tearful woman recounted how her marriage had been brought to breaking point by the incessant noise of emergency water tankers driving through the street beneath her window. In France a transport strike was making people's lives similarly miserable.

'How lucky we are,' commented one of the doctors whose daily work was to sow up bullet wounds and amputate the legs of mine-stricken children, 'not to be exposed to real disasters, like those back home.'

He had spent time in the south in areas held by the Tālebān. 'Let them have their religious law,' he said. 'What does it matter if a man dies by an electric chair or a bullet? As a doctor, I can tell you it makes very little difference.'

*

I realized it would be too difficult to venture alone outside Mazar-i Sharīf and decided to be content with the sights of the city itself. The shrine was the obvious point of departure. Its fame derives from its being the burial place of 'Ali ibn Ali Tālib, the fourth and final Caliph of Islam, son-in-law and cousin of the Prophet. Ali's central import-ance to Shi'ism makes the site particularly sacred to the Shī'ite population of the country, although an identical claim to the burial place is made for Najāf, in Irāq.

Legend surrounds its origin; one version is that the shrine was built over the spot where the camel carrying the body of the murdered Caliph finally expired; another that the uncorrupted body lay hidden for centuries until it was pointed out to a local ruler in a dream, and the shrine raised over it. Much later, the present city grew up around the shrine, and in the nineteenth century came to eclipse Balkh as the region's capital.

Such tales of the dead surviving in an uncorrupted state are not uncommon; they abound in the hagiographical literature of the Islamic world and extend to the popular level. Even during the Soviet occupation there were rumours of young mujaheddin whose bodies, infused with the purity of an untainted life, had been discovered intact years after their deaths. I had heard a story at the time of a foreign correspondent who was shown the grave of a teenage fighter. Villagers had lifted the heavy stone just far enough aside to allow him a glimpse, beyond the swirling dust at the end of a broadening shaft of sunlight, of the serene face of a young *shaheed*; hardly dead, it seemed, but gently sleeping . . .

Given that the location of shrines is not a random matter, Mazar may well have been a place of veneration long before Islam came to the region in the mid-seventh century, and its sanctity preserved adoptively under a different guise. This is certainly the case for many other shrines throughout the Islamic world, just as churches in England were once raised over pre-Christian temples.

There is a Nasruddin story – not surprisingly, given the centrality in the culture of the veneration of holy places – about shrines which, symbolism apart, has the usual, improbable ring of truth. Nasruddin's father is the keeper of a popular shrine when Nasruddin sets off one day by donkey to seek his fortune in the world. After years of wandering his donkey finally expires. A passer-by sees Nasruddin weeping by the grave of his faithful friend, and throws him a few coins, taking him for a grieving disciple of a holy man. Word spreads of the site until a wealthy and pious merchant bestows upon Nasruddin enough money to build a mosque over the donkey's grave, to which the faithful flock, assuming they will benefit from the blessings of the deceased saint. Years pass; eventually Nasruddin's own father makes a pilgrimage to the site, and is astonished to find his son the keeper of the place. Hearing his son's tale, he confesses: exactly the same thing happened to him, a generation before...

At the shrine in Mazar the faithful gather daily in the square to beg for alms, to touch the standard lowered over its dome on the first day of the Islamic new year, to kiss the threshold and wipe the blessing of the place over their faces, to offer prayers believed to be of special efficacy when uttered from the resting place of the saint himself, and to seek the traditional merit of pilgrimage.

I had circled it a few times during daylight but was put off from venturing inside by the watchfulness of armed guards. It seemed likely that darkness would provide the best protection for a solitary visitor, so at dawn, a few days after I had arrived, I slipped from the house and followed the muddy streets to the gates of the mosque, making for the central courtyard.

It was dark, icily cold and the shadowy figures of men shrouded in *pattūs* were everywhere. They were streaming in silence into a mosque adjacent to the great shrine itself, and I was swept up in the flow of bodies. Close to the door the shapes were filing towards, I broke from the current of movement and headed for the shrine, but was guided back towards the door by a kindly old man who took me for lost.

Inside, I found myself unexpectedly among the ranks of several hundred men preparing for the dawn prayer. I was acutely conscious of the risk of being recognized; even on a busy street an outsider was quickly betrayed by the tiniest irregularities of movement and expression. To leave was impossible; the mosque was filling with men from both ends. At that moment, in front of me, a line parted gently to allow me a space, and I took my place as the guiding voice of the *mullā* began to echo about us, and felt myself falling back, awkwardly at first, into the grasp of the ritual I had learned years before.

*

The canonical prayers are one of the mainstays of Islam, and are performed five times a day at sunrise, midday, afternoon, dusk and at night before sleep. The language is the Arabic of the Qur'ān, which is the sacred rather than liturgical language of Islam, like Hebrew to the reading of the Torah. Collective worship, of course, has a social function, and prayers are offered in the company of others whenever possible. But alone, they may be performed anywhere. Traditionally at least, the act of worship is so finely woven into the fabric of life that the interruption in the day's endeavours, even in the extremity of war, is as unobtrusive as the motion of the sun. The sight is not familiar at first to the modern visitor (and this might mean less devout Moslems as much as non-Moslems), and he is apt to feel awkward as his host lays out a prayer rug a few feet away and begins his whispering genuflections. There is no need; the conversation picks up where it left off, with the frequent addition of an unselfconscious apology towards a guest; the sense of things is not one of interruption but of renewal.

Often in Kabul I have been in a taxi when the driver has politely asked if I wouldn't mind waiting while he attended the midday prayers; I have been on buses, too, when the driver pulls over near a stream or well to let the passengers pray, the way other buses will stop for a meal.

Prayers are preceded by ablutions. Few daydreams survive the salutary effect of cold water at the back of the neck. Every gesture has an accompanying invocation, uttered inwardly. In the absence of water, dry soil may be used (once, while walking through a barren stretch of land with a team of mujaheddin, I had been mystified by the sight of men unslinging their rifles and patting their hands into the dust at their feet). In the countryside one sees people at prayer on their rooftops, in their dusty courtyards, in fields and on mountaintops; the sight of a solitary farmer, who after the day's toil spreads his *pattū* to begin his devotions, is one by which only the most hard-hearted can fail to be moved.

The prayers are highly formalized in both gesture and word, and although there are variations according to the different branches within Islam, they express certain fundamentals of the faith: they are an act of worship and humility; they loosen the noose of the world which tightens around the soul in the course of the day and redirect the thoughts and feeling towards the Divine; they affirm, in the moment when the forehead touches the ground, the equality of all before God.

There is a collective portion to the prayers and a personal, in which the individual chooses verses of the Qur'ān to repeat privately. Being backed up, as it were, by a physical effort, the degeneration of prayer into a merely mental process is discouraged; in this there could be said to lie a certain genius. Needless to say, the practice of putting on one's best clothes for the act of worship is considered extraneous, not to mention impracticable. Needless to say vanity, being a human tendency, knows no exclusivity among different faiths and insinuates itself into the ritual in various ways: in the subtly hierarchical shuffling of lines during communal gatherings, expensive prayer rugs, or extravagant supernumeracy prayers.

At the heart of the prayers stands the opening verse of the Qur'ān, *al-Fatihah*:

> Praise be to God, Lord of the two Worlds
> The most merciful and most forgiving
> Lord of the day of Judgement
> It is You who we adore and in Whom we seek help
> Guide us along the straight path
> The path of those who are righteous
> Not that of those who suffer Your wrath
> Or of those who stray.

*

I sat for a few moments as the lines of men dispersed, listening to the sounds of the mosque and was relieved at the success of my anonymity. It was then I noticed the elderly man who had remained sitting next to me, who now turned, with an expression of intense concern, to study my face.

I had a sudden vision of my unmasking, the outcry at the presence of an impostor, and the spreading of the incendiary news through the enraged faithful. But with a schoolteacherly politeness he informed me I had performed my prayers wrongly, pointed out my mistake and its remedy, and suggested I not be so sloppy in future. I thanked him and he disappeared without a backward glance. And nowhere did my fears seem less justified. From where then, I wondered, had the cliché of the rabid Moslem mob sprung to mind?*

The mosque was filled with echoes like the music of water in a cavern; of men chanting in solitary meditation, and of others gathered in little circles, swaying gently to the rhythm of their recitations.

Outside the dawn was filling the sky with grey, lifting with it the strangeness of the day's beginning. Hundreds of snow-white doves wheeled over the domes. For a tiny sum people were buying handfuls of grain to feed them, like the pigeons in Trafalgar Square. Here the doves have a religious significance: one in seven is said to be a disguised spirit, and to feed it is an act of merit; in such a way even the feeding of birds becomes a rite.

All around the grounds of the shrine the destitute and war wounded, both young and old, began to gather. From some a muttered plea for charity went up to passers-by, and from others, an unutterably weary invocation of the name of God. An old man made his way painfully towards the entrance of the shrine with the help of a forked stick as a crutch, and a blind man, perhaps my age, whose artificial legs rested against the railing behind him, cradled an empty bowl in his lap.

I found myself at the northern entrance. The archway or *ivān*, flanked by sturdy minarets, evokes the prototypical design of the

---

* Is there an icon of the Western media more adored, less edifying, and subject to so little self-scrutiny than images of Moslem people at prayer? Seldom is there a Western news report or film depicting events in a Moslem country that does not begin with the alien cry of the *muezzin*. Yet the collective expression of devotion incumbent on all Moslems is perhaps the least extraordinary aspect of the Islamic life. Stolen, as it so often is, from its cultural context, it conveys at best a sense of the impenetrable or archaic. So far as I know there is no exact equivalent in contemporary Islamic media. But I have sometimes wondered what the Moslem interpretation might be of news reports from the West if they began always with footage of glum faces filing into churches in their Sunday best in order to drink the blood of a human God. 'In no really significant way is there a direct correspondence between the "Islam" in common Western usage and the enormously varied life that goes on within the world of Islam.' (Edward W. Said, *Covering Islam*, Vintage Books, 1997). I recommend this forceful and cogent work to anyone interested in this neglected area of study.

Registan in Samarqand, but is humbler and lacks the ostentation of its Tīmūrid forebears. Smaller shrines cluster beneath the two main domes. The predominant colour is turquoise. Arched panels bearing intricate floral tilework are brought into relief by jade borders and every inch of surface is covered by tessellating mosaic in yellow, blue and green glaze, in places flowing and in others rigid. The tiles themselves did not seem old but followed the old designs and successive restorations of varying quality have given the walls an air of neglect, a feeling amplified by ongoing changes to the balustrades above and walkways below, where the flagstones were being broken up with sledgehammers.

An ancient guardian took my shoes at the gates to the inner courtyard and I walked over the icy stone towards the entrance of the shrine itself. Already a stream of visitors and pilgrims was flowing to and fro, offering prayers at the threshold, planting kisses on the portals, and exiting with reverent caresses of its frame, hinges and handles.

Inside, the line slowly circled the tomb of the saint, its glass enclosure covered by a gilded lattice polished bare in places by infinities of prayer. Beyond it the sarcophagus was draped in a dark green shroud.

Cross-legged and lining the walls of the chamber, white-turbaned guardians read verses from the Qur'ān. Above their steady murmur of devotion rose the occasional gasp or wail from the faces pressed around the tomb, echoing around the dome above like captive birds suddenly released. A woman was clinging to the gilded lattice over the glass, sobbing uncontrollably; a one-legged man pressed his forehead against it as tears streamed silently over his cheeks.

I sat for a while, deeply moved by the sanctity of the place, until the sight of so many grief-stricken souls became too much. I found my way back to the guardian at the entrance, who picked my shoes unhesitatingly from a hundred other pairs as I approached.

*

Beyond the world of the shrine the life of the city was gathering momentum. I was drawn along a tiny street where the steel-blue smoke of fresh kebabs billowed upwards. A man with a Moghul-looking face was waving an axe-shaped fan of woven palms over his coals, and offered me a seat on the wooden platform outside. As I ate I reflected on how quickly things that had not long ago seemed extraordinary had become the norm. It was nothing now to rub shoulders in a restaurant with a man across whose lap rested a loaded automatic rifle, or whose companion balanced a rocket launcher against the table instead of an umbrella. Nor did I flinch inwardly any longer, at least not quite so deeply, at the sight of a one-legged woman or a child who had lost her hands to a mine.

Conversely, the most apparently straightforward of endeavours was fraught with concerns unimaginable at home. To visit a nearby town you could not blunder into the place; you asked first whether there was fighting there, whether the road was mined, or whether the life of your guide would be endangered by helping to fulfil your whim. You heard a far-off thump and began to count the seconds before the explosion, wondering where to dive – then realized it was only the sound of a slamming door. The simple act of taking a photograph drew a crowd, not invariably friendly, as quickly as a car accident. And to allow one's eye to follow the passing face of a beautiful woman was to raise no less than a triple-headed spectre of shame, fear and longing.

'You *ate* in ze bazaar?' asked an incredulous Jean-Paul when I returned.

*

Over the next few days, taking the shrine as my bearing, I got to know the streets in a growing radius. On the east, flanking and behind the hotels, were carpet shops filled with the blood-red Turcoman designs of the region, and some bookshops displaying scientific textbooks in Persian, Russian and English. The shelves of curio shops were forlornly bare and dusty and I found next to nothing crafted locally. I was tempted only once, to buy a set of tiny porcelain teacups marked MADE IN JAPANESE OCCUPIED CHINA. Richer to the eye were the open-air markets to the north, dense with the cries of fruit and spice sellers, and an avenue of butchers' stalls, whose grisly wares dangled like exhibits from a chamber of horrors.

Something about the atmosphere was difficult to identify, and it puzzled me like a forgotten name. It was only after several days that it dawned on me the majority of men were clean-shaven. There was no trace of the *pakoul* that graced every other head in Kabul, but a predominance of chequered green and turquoise turbans.

There were also fewer armed men in the streets than in Kabul; mostly grim-looking soldiers or men with the strongly Moghol features that dominate the populations of northern Afghanistan. They were lean and their build was lighter than those of the south, they smiled less readily, and their hard looks suggested something of the desperado. To judge a people from their faces is guesswork, and more so when their features belong to a unfamiliar frequency in the spectrum of faces to which the eye is accustomed. But I had seen the Uzbek militiamen fighting in Kabul a few years before, where their unforgiving reputation had been confirmed. They were not the kind of people to trifle with, and I wondered what might happen if ever the Tālebān took Kabul and came to try their luck in the north by force.

✣

I was fond of taking a short cut back to the house; a fairly typical street where every space was filled with industry of some kind, however humble. For half its length it was lined with mobile stalls, all decked fastidiously with household bits and pieces: string and shoelaces, batteries, chewing gum and children's rattles, soap, honey and spare parts for bicycles, batons of coloured fabrics, earrings, toothbrushes, combs, make-up sets, mirrors and padlocks. Opposite them stretched a dozen or so shops, all seemingly dedicated to the dissection of radios and clocks, the guts of which were displayed in dusty rows behind the windows. In one hung a partridge in a wicker cage.

Further along, where the pockets of commerce were defined by no more than the shawl on which the owner's goods were arrayed, I passed an array of second-hand socks, a blanket of round glazed loaves of bread, a bowl of hard-boiled eggs dyed in bright red spice, mounds of rice and chickpeas, and a makeshift table of sacks of herbs and jars of roots and medicinal powders. Beside them a small boy was pounding ginger in a brass mortar. Next to him a man was cutting leather for the sole of a client's shoe, and further on a turbaned beggar was shaking the flies from his cracked feet. There was a stall where you could buy fresh orange, banana or pomegranate juice from an electric blender rigged up to an overhead power cable, or sample meat-filled dumplings draped with yoghurt, or even – from a slowly filling blackened wok – freshly popped corn.

There was a corresponding spectacle of sounds. On the pavement it was mostly merchants shouting out the prices of their goods, imitated by cocksure children, balancing trays of snacks or trinkets on their heads with one hand and guiding a path through the oncoming passers-by with the other. I heard too the voices of a trio of women deliberating over rolls of lace; a seven-year-old girl humming to her baby sister, who bounced gently on her back as she walked; a blind man, whose plaintive singing was rewarded by listeners with a few crumpled notes; a wandering dervish who muttered blessings as coins clinked into his bowl; an Indian folk song, played too loudly through the torn diaphragm of a car loudspeaker that dangled in the doorway of a music shop, and various sounds of commerce: the squeaking of locks and hinges, of firewood being loaded into carts, the grunt of man, his face a ghostly white, heaving a sack of flour on his back, and the clatter of weights striking the pan of a primitive scale.

Add to this the ceaseless noise of traffic: the clatter of passing pony traps with their whips and bells; bicycle bells; the buzz of mopeds and the growl of heavy diesel engines accelerating under load, together with all their horns; feeble horns which splutter across bad wiring or rise and fall with the pitch of their engines; car horns, which squeak or wail like air-raid sirens, and the two-toned bellowing of pneumatic truck horns, which deafen and drown all other sounds as they pass.

All along, the way is charted by a repertoire of distinctive smells: the oily pungence of grilling kebabs, the smell of freshly baked *nān*, spices both familiar and (to me) unnameable, the smoke of cheap cigarettes or the untrimmed wick of a paraffin stove, dust, diesel fumes and the unmistakable reek of human effluvia...

*

It was around this time, in the lull of forward motion where unacknowledged fatigue catches a traveller unawares, that I succumbed to a growing feeling of restlessness, a sense of malaise at odds with the good luck and freedom from serious difficulties that had characterized the journey so far. It would swell just when I was most comfortable, and had returned at the end of the day to the house and the safety of a private room, its hot shower, and ample meals. I felt it most acutely in the disembodied world we saw on satellite television: the reruns of *Baywatch* and all its aggressively swaying silicone, the MTV videos, the advertisements for cars, lingerie and bad whisky. I felt newly sensitive to the violence of the world that had spawned them, which now more than ever seemed hideously irrelevant.

This was the urge to go native: to be free of the artificial comforts of the sheltered guest and launch unprotected into the surroundings. It was easier now to understand those Western visitors to Afghanistan who had stopped in this virtually unknown land on their way to India and ended up staying for years.* My old sense of the place was breaking up and recrystallizing around a different centre, the pull of which was irresistible.

Alone again and writing up the day's events by candlelight I was visited by the stream of smiling faces I had encountered during the day – of begging children and shopkeepers and even the miserable-looking soldiers I had thought so sinister at first – and felt ashamed of the comforts by which my experience of the place was softened.

It was not simply the degree and extent of the suffering of ordinary people that roused such feelings, but the strange symmetry with which they were equipped to bear it, without lapsing, despite their intimacy with despair, into cynicism. They still smiled.

I wanted to draw closer to this fountain of spirit, which was not

---

* To finance the solace of semi-permanent intoxication many had sold their VW vans to Afghans, who twenty-five years later were hiring them to the Afghan Red Crescent in Kabul. These lovingly maintained relics replaced vehicles stolen or ruined on the appalling roads. They also had the advantage of being less sought after by bandits who, exercising considerable vocational discrimination, preferred late-model Land Cruisers.

merely stoicism, or the weary acceptance of a people accustomed to hardship — neither of these could explain the smiles. Nor was it enough to sweep away the riddle with talk of 'the Will of Allah', which was in any case a largely foreign cliché and seldom invoked by Afghans themselves. It was very puzzling: I found it impossible to be unaffected by it.

*

Back in Faizābād, I had been recommend by Hamid to ask after *Mīr* Fakhruddin, who was said to be a well-known Afghan musician living in Mazar. Word of my enquiry had got around among the Afghan staff, and a few days after I arrived, Abbas the chef arranged for a young man to take me to the *Mīr* himself. I wasn't sure who or what to expect; not, certainly, the quiet circle of instruction that we interrupted in a room above a busy street, where the *Mīr* was reading to half a dozen men.

He was sitting at a desk, wearing a karakul lambskin hat and long gown, a stocky man in his fifties with a trim grey beard and big, dark eyes that made an immediate and enduring impression.

I explained how I had come across his name as one of the men disappeared and returned with a glass of tea for their guest, to whom they listened, smiling — except, I noticed, the *Mīr* himself.

From the atmosphere I sensed that perhaps these men were the *Mīr*'s pupils. He had been reading to them from a book as we had entered: perhaps they were dervishes, and he their teacher.

The thought was confirmed when the *Mīr* asked if I would like to read a few lines from the book in front of him, putting to a gentle test my claim to have read something of the Persian poets. The book was the *maqālāt* or discourses of Shams of Tabriz, that saintly and enigmatic luminary whose appearance in Konya in the middle of the thirteenth century had led to his encounter with Jelalludin Rūmī, sparking one of the most celebrated spiritual partnerships in the world.

I read a little, and the *Mīr* would pause at certain words to ask what I understood of their meaning. Then he would nod, and bore into me with his eyes. From the others there were some curious and friendly smiles; the *Mīr* seemed satisfied and returned the volume to his table. I apologized for the interruption and expressed the hope we might meet again. If I wanted, he said, we could meet the following day: someone would send for me. The men embraced me in turn as I left, and one of them tapped his heart, and winked.

*

I hadn't caught the details. The next day there was a knock on the gate, and I was summoned by the *chowkidar*. With an expression of bemusement he said some of the *Mīr*'s dervishes were asking for me.

I had not expected two carfuls of them. In the front seat of one of the cars I squeezed into a space and met a tiny sea of handshakes and smiles. Then we were bumping northwest out of the city towards Balkh. It was a day of celebration, I was told; the birthday of the founding saint of the Sufi order, or *tariqat*, to which they all belonged. We would go to Balkh to pay our respects at the shrines there; for my interest in Sufism, said the *Mīr*, the visit would be most beneficial.

I looked at the trio of faces squeezed into the seat behind me. The *Mīr*, dressed in his karakul hat and long gown, was looking ahead with his enormous, intense eyes. Next to him was a man with a pale and kindly face and a greying beard who wore a puffy down jacket, and another man wearing a suit and tie. One of them was an architect and the other a government official; all were dervishes of the Qāderīyya *tariqat* or order, one of the four main Sufi orders represented in Afghanistan.

The land was flat and the horizon grey. Above it the clouds hung in pregnant overlapping folds. We were in Balkh half an hour later. Today the city where Zoroaster is said to have been born, where Alexander married Roxanne, and which the Great Khan's ten thousand Mongol troops reduced to ruin is little more than a village overlooked by the immense, corroded walls of the ancient city. Modern Balkh is an avenue of single-storey shops overhung by tall plane trees. It leads to the central square which is dominated by the Khwaja Abu-Nasr Pārsā mosque. The mosque is half in ruin and has suffered more from restorations than from time itself. But it was still beautiful, I thought, as we circled it before entering to pay our respects to the saint it honours; the tapering ribs of the turquoise dome, the spiralling columns that flank the entrance, and the tilework, both in colour and design — half-ruined as it is — all seemed more exacting and intense than the shrine in Mazar.

We were ten in all. Nearby was another shrine. It looked like little more than a bunker from above. Stooping under a stone lintel we descended into the darkness of a rectangular chamber below to offer prayers beside a stone sarcophagus. To judge from its depths it must have been several hundred years old. Yes, said one of the men as we went inside, it was the tomb of the ninth-century saint, Rabi'a of Balkh. *Rabi'a Balkhi!* I had no idea. She was Afghanistan's earliest Sufi poet.

The *Mīr* began a long recitation, which grew in pitch until he broke into a sonorous and rhythmic mode. Then a second man began a chant, which was taken up by the others like a thickening heartbeat: *Allah! Allah! Allah!* . . .

The chamber reverberated with sound and the *Mīr's* voice rose higher as the pulse of the others grew deeper. The world fell away. For ten minutes the rapturous pitch was sustained until, over the roaring beat of the other voices, the *Mīr* let out a series of long cries of crystalline intensity: *Allah! Allah!* Some of the men were weeping; the pulse began to soften, and the *Mīr* brought the prayers to a close.

We filed outside, and the world gathered into three dimensions again.

*

Led by the *Mīr* we crossed to the western side of the square and followed a winding muddy trail to a cluster of other shrines. At each, fluttering in the breeze, tiny votive strips of fabric had been tied to sticks planted in the ground at the head of the sarcophagi. At another the overhanging branch of a tree was coated in tiny nails. The practice of leaving nails in the branches of these shrine-trees is widespread, rather analogous to the lighting of votive candles before an icon. Popular belief assigns different thaumaturgical powers to different shrines around the country; there are shrines for the insane, the childless, even for those who have been bitten by wild dogs.

Another was almost completely ruined, and fragments of carved marble had been piled up around the sarcophagus. One, I was told, was a non-Moslem shrine. At another an elderly beggar hobbled across the stone platform and the men pressed some small notes into his hand. We walked across a cotton field in the drizzle to another shrine and offered prayers beside a sarcophagus several feet underground, just beyond the huge ramparts of the ancient city's outer walls.

Our final stop was a shrine in the ruins of a mosque. A barn-like roof mounted on steel girders had been put up over it, disguising the antiquity of the site, which lies close to the road. Sheets of loose corrugated iron flapped in the breeze. I quickly recognized it from its description by Peter Levi, who had been taken there by Bruce Chatwin, who in turn had read of it in a little-known report by the Russian archaeologist Pugachenkova: it was the mosque of Hajji Piyāde.

*

I had often wondered about this lonely ruin, the first impression of which Peter Levi had likened to the sight of San Marco in Venice and which he called 'a lost meeting-point between Sassanian and Islamic art'. The Hajji's shrine – I supposed – which was a small, domed mud-brick building with a rectangular base and about ten feet high, lay in the courtyard of the three-sided ruined mosque nearby.

Nothing is known of the community once served by this ruined monument. It lies alone on an open plain near a pond and cluster of trees; whatever other structures once kept it company have disappeared. Yet for all its thousand years, it retains an impressive vigour. Its remaining walls were perhaps sixty feet square; the façade was no more; and four interior columns remained, three of them joined by original arches.

The bases of the columns were rooted fast in solid mud, making it hard to tell how far they descend. Nowhere had I experienced more sympathy with the archaeologist's urge to dig. At first glance they seemed to be woven out of brick. At the tops of the pillars, which were only six feet from the ground, ran bands of vine-like stucco and intensely swirling foliage which, given their age, seemed extraordinarily well-preserved.

Since nothing is known of the site from written sources, its history can only be guessed at based on the style of its ornamentation and decorative motifs. The low arches, the width of the heavy rectangular capitals on which they rested, and the bold rosettes that reminded me of keystones above medieval doorways in Provence all combined to give a powerful impression of antiquity, which put me more in mind of a Norman church than the glazed and spiralling extravagance of the mosque of Khwaja Pārsā we had earlier visited. The geometric patterns had none of the sophistication of later Islamic design; the tendency towards abstraction had not yet taken flight, and the dominant motif of the stuccoes — vines, stalks and curling tendrils — was marked by a realism that would disappear utterly from Islamic ornamentation. Dating from the ninth century, it must be one of the earliest surviving mosques in the country. Most likely the walls were originally united by nine domes, the *Noh Gumbad*, by which the site, I later found out, is also known.

*

It was late afternoon when we drove back to Mazar. The group split up and I joined one of the dervishes called Hashmatullah at his home with half a dozen others. After a generous meal he sang prayers for two hours while the others sat entranced or broke spontaneously into a rhythmic *zikr*. The men I had met, he explained, belonged to a variety of *tariqat*s. Their guide and teacher had died a year ago; now there was a man! he said. If only I had come then; he was the kind of *pir* who could look into a man's heart and see everything there was to see; he would have known my very hopes and sorrows, said Hashmatullah; would have known even how much I missed my daughter. He had the power by his gaze to raise men to an exalted state or put them to sleep on the spot...

Suddenly I realized how late it was, and was afraid the others at the house might worry if I didn't return, and I made my apologies. The others insisted in walking me home. We went a hundred yards through thick mud, until out of shame I implored them to go back. There was a long and friendly protest, and at last we said goodbye. It was already dark. At the last moment one of the boys turned and said:

'What about curfew?'

We looked at our watches; in fifteen minutes, at ten o'clock, no one could risk being caught out of doors.

'Do you know what to say if you're challenged?' asked Hashmatullah.

I had no idea.

'Well, if a soldier points his gun at you and shouts, you just call out: '*Az khod!*'

'*Az khod?*' This meant, roughly, 'one of us'.

'Yes.' There were some incongruously cheerful giggles from the other boys. 'Don't worry. It'll be all right.'

I looked along the deserted street ahead, remembered the fearsome reputation of the Uzbek militias, and felt particularly reluctant to leave the company of these kindly young men.

'Shouldn't you tell him how to answer in Pashtu as well? What if he's challenged in Pashtu?' This from the same boy.

'How's your Pashtu?' asked Hashmatullah.

In Pashtu all I could say was 'I am going to Parachinar,' which was three hundred miles away; a thin excuse for being caught after curfew.

'It's too late for that. Never mind. Go, and God protect you.'

They sent me off with cheerful waves. I threw one end of my *pattū* over my shoulder and strode forward, Afghan style. Soon I was checking down side alleys, slipping quickly across one while a soldier's back was turned, and out towards the central square. The streets, so riotous by day, were completely deserted: there was no sound but the distant barking of wild dogs. The period around curfew was a dilemma. To limit the risk of being seen, you could go skulking in the shadows, which would be harder to explain if you were challenged; or you could march confidently along and be certain of a late night interrogation by bored, armed soldiers. The most sensible answer, to judge from the streets, was neither: *nobody* went out near curfew.

Fear has its own seductive language. How easily the concerns one has dismissed in moments of comfort come back with renewed and irrational vigour when you are alone again! I had a picture of explaining myself to a pair of unsympathetic soldiers after all my excuses had failed to pass muster, and suddenly all the danger, the anarchy, the lawlessness of the country seemed more virulent than ever.

There was a sentry post ahead, and I could make out a trio of soldiers inside behind a small steamed-up window. There was a light outside it, which threw a fan of brightness in a wide arc across the street. I watched the soldiers moving around inside for a few minutes, waited for what seemed like long enough in case a sentry was circling the block, strode across as boldly as my nerves would allow, sank gratefully into the darkness beyond, and hurried on.

There was no response to my banging on the gate at the residence; the wall, which was smooth and ten feet high, would be a challenge to climb. So I collected a handful of small stones, and tossed them over the wall, until I heard the lock turn in the gate and met the astonished face of Homayoun, whose jaw hung in surprise at the sight of me in local disguise.

It was exactly ten o'clock.

*

I met the English-speaking dervish Yusuf the following day. He invited me to visit the hospital he had designed and had built in the north of the city. A team of workmen was putting the finishing touches to the construction as we arrived, and Yusuf conferred with them in turn as we walked along freshly laid concrete pathways.

It was unlike any other structure I had seen in Afghanistan. The main building consisted of a series of interlocking geodesic domes built from panels of pre-stressed concrete. They had been painted white and resembled a cluster of small observatories or a miniature version of the observation tower at the Arizona Biosphere.

When I expressed surprise at the design Yusuf explained that with his architectural team he had wrestled over the problems of its construction for a long time, being reluctant to build the usual concrete boxes, which although less complicated to construct were difficult to heat in winter and grew too hot in the summer. They had taken their inspiration from the traditional domed structures of the villages around Tashgurgan and expressed them in modern materials.

'We wanted to do something that was not only useful but beautiful,' he said. A workman was preparing soil in flowerbeds that curved between the walkways. 'There is a *hadith*: everything should be in balance.'

Inside the rooms were light; the high domed ceilings were a refreshing and unaccustomed shape. Yusuf expressed the hope that the design would provide a better atmosphere for sick people to heal in; it was well understood, he said, that the shape and colour of rooms could influence the healing process. There was an appropriate design for a hospital as much as for an office or a home; the design had to take account of the building's function, as well as the community it served. He was deeply concerned with the problems of community and the potentially integrative role of architecture; all too often the social aspect of buildings was overlooked.

We sat together and drank tea in one of the rooms. I asked him how he had come to be involved with the *Mīr* and Sufism. His father had been a Sufi; but as a young man he had no time for it; only later, when the communists had sent him to prison, had he taken an interest. I asked how long he had been in prison.

'Seven years,' he said, with a faint smile.

After his release he had escaped to Pakistan, been reunited with his wife, and begun his studies as an architect. I wanted to ask him what it was that had drawn him to the *tariqat*, and what form his instruction had taken; it puzzled me to reconcile this industrious and forward-looking man with conventional notions of mysticism. He seemed to anticipate my question.

'You can look at it like this,' he said, opened a notebook, and wrote, with a calligraphic flourish, a couplet of rhyming lines from the Indian Sufi poet, Bedīl:

> Greed for a hundred worldly glories is beggary;
> When you reach contentment, poverty is wealth.

Then he tapped the pen against the first word: *Hars*. It meant greed, or attachment.

'That is the problem,' he said gently. 'That is the problem that Sufism addresses.'

*

It was yet another approach to that extraordinarily rich and variegated territory of Islamic mysticism that has come to be known as Sufism. The roots of Sufism dive into the most primal of human longings, namely the striving towards some quality of existance more substantial than ordinary life appears to offer. The universal impulse towards mysticism has appeared in every era and under the banner of every religion, but seldom has a mystical tradition been expressed in such a creative variety of forms, or found its way so extensively into culture and society, as Sufism in the Islamic world.

An ancient tale recounts the encounter between a number of blind men and an elephant. One found its feet, broad and immovable; another its trunk, long and flexible; and another its ears, seemingly huge and thin, and each described the unfamiliar beast in vivid terms. But being blind, none was able to describe the elephant in its entirety.

Defining Sufism is a similarly confounding task, partly because of the range of mediums in which it has appeared at different times and in different societies, and partly because Sufism is a Way rather than a system or philosophy – just as the elephant is a living animal and not a statue, whose function is to live and not merely to be admired. It is generally agreed that the term Sufi, although seldom heard among Sufis themselves, derives from the traditional garments made of wool (*sūf*) worn by the earliest ascetics of Islam. Another popular derivation has the Arabic word *safa'*, meaning purity, as the origin of the term. But in the literature of Sufism, a variety of names describes the men and women belonging to the spiritual elect on the Path to Reality (*haqiqa'*): the People of the Heart, the People of Truth, the People of Allusion; the Friends; the Near Ones; the Lovers; the Poor Ones; the Dervishes.

The earliest masters of Sufism were for the most part solitary, saint-like figures who travelled extensively, sharing their methods and insights with small numbers of dedicated followers. Early descriptions of methods of prayer and contemplation strongly resemble those found in devotional Christian manuals such as the *Philokalia*. Sufism borrowed freely from existing pre-Islamic tradition in the territories where it evolved, and was correspondingly enriched, but it was still within the distinctive framework of Islamic thought that its fundamental doctrines evolved.

Within a century of the death of the Prophet Mohammed, hospices and places of retreat for wandering teachers and those under their guidance had grown up over a wide area and become an established aspect of Sufi tradition. But the early Sufis, among whom were numerous women, as well as others from non-Moslem backgrounds, did not form schools of mystical instruction after themselves, nor did they formally assign successors.

The Sufi's claim to knowledge of the Real (*al-Haqq*, the Sufi term for God) through means other than those put forward by conventional theology has always caused consternation among the religious orthodoxy, and the overt expression of mystical rapture was frequently perilous. Many Sufis took their beliefs to the gallows. In the famous ecstatic utterance of Mansur al-Hallaj (818–922) 'I am the Truth!', the religious orthodoxy of Baghdad found evidence of the ultimate heresy: that of personal contact with the Divine. Later (but not all) Sufis held the example of Hallaj as proof of advanced spiritual attainment, but the conflict between Sufi and orthodox doctrine, and recognized religious leaders, continued.

It took the genius of such luminaries as the Andalusian saint Ibn al-Arabi (1165–1240) and the Iranian-born al-Ghazzali (d. 1111) to present Sufism in such a manner as to win the (frequently grudging) approval of orthodoxy. The innate human yearning for the Divine, the soul's hunger for Truth – these are no more than manifestations of the Real's longing to return to Itself. The mystic's experience of God is the lifting of all obstacles that separate him from the all-pervasive Unicity of Being, in which his ordinary consciousness, at times of rapture, is said to drown.

Much of subsequent Sufism rests on the notion that when the lesser, egotistically oriented self of a person is displaced, the greater or Universal self is found, enabling the experience of contact with the Divine. The ordinary, sensible world is simply the reflection, at its more attenuated end, of the Divine emanation, and Man its most exquisite mirror. As the dust of egotism is blown from the mirror ...

The foundation of Sufi practice is neither asceticism nor retirement from the world, although there may be periods of both. The austerities of monasticism were disapproved of by the Prophet himself, and Islam never fully lost the company (or the genes) of its most spiritually inclined. It is perhaps the Sufi's willingness to undertake his spiritual training in the rough and tumble of life that accounts for the breadth of Sufism's appeal. In Sufism there is the renunciation of ties, but the most obvious among these — the visible ties of the material world — are the least essential.

'Is there anything more astonishing,' writes a nineteenth-century Sufi master, 'than that a man should put the blame on his professional activity for not being able to perfect himself?'*

This training, far from being a dreamy excursion into peace and love, throws the seeker against nothing less unpleasant than his own self, the unruly *nafs* or ego. Variously termed as an unveiling, a polishing and a purification, it is a process by which the would-be Sufi first undertakes to grapple with the multiplicitous wiles of pride, vanity and attachment. He is not concerned with acquiring powers (although the lore attributing supernatural phenomena of various kinds to Sufis is astonishingly rich) but of uncovering something that already exists.

The struggle is aided by rigorous spiritual exercises, the most essential of the Sufi's disciplines being the practice of remembrance (*dhikr*) of the Real, and the focusing, excluding all else, on the meaning behind it. And the practice itself is brought to life, tested and guided by a teacher who helps the adept, inwardly speaking, to stand on his own feet. As it is essentially invisible, and by nature deeply personal, little description of this intimate process finds its way into written sources. Hence the obvious limitation of a study of Sufism from observation of ritual alone, or from texts addressed to suit the mental apparatus of people at a particular time or place, in which the experiential 'spice' has been robbed of its vital flavour.

The study of Sufism through the intellect is reminiscent of the story of the *mullā* Nasruddin, who searches for a lost key beneath a lamp post where the light is good — aware nevertheless of having dropped the key in the shadows a hundred yards away. The folly of

---

* From the *Resālāt* (letters) of Mulay al-'Araby ad-Darqawi of Morocco (d. 1823).

philosophical proofs in the pursuit of mystical insight is likened by the Persian Sufi Shabestari (d. 1339), in his important work the *Gulshan-i Rāz* (The Garden of Mystery), to a fool wandering the desert with a candle, in search of the sun.

Partly because it was impossible to relate mystical insights directly, and partly to limit the cry of heterodoxy, a highly evolved symbolic language was used to present, and represent, Sufi experience. Nowhere is the result more conspicuous than in the so-called love poetry of the Persian Sufis, who took up the motif of human love as a metaphor of spiritual longing. It was first expressed by the famous woman Sufi, Rabi'a ad-Dauwliyya of Basra (d. 801). Later Sufis developed it to an unparalleled creative level. (The Bacchanalian evocations of the mathematician and minor poet Omar Khayyam, whose frequent allusions to wine and dusky-eyed maidens have been taken as hallmarks of the heterodoxy, if not of the downright licentiousness of Iranian mystics, became well known to Western audiences through the florid translations of the Victorian era.) Less well-known symbolic vehicles of mystical thought were incorporated in cryptic numerologies influencing the design of religious buildings, gardens and even fabrics, as well as a profusion of stories and fables which at first glance seem to contain little more than moral teachings.

The twelfth and thirteenth centuries saw Sufism transformed from loosely knit bodies, formerly united more in spirit than in any institutional sense, into organized and hierarchical structures. Through the various and eponymously named *tariqats*, the message and discipline of Sufism were distributed ever more widely through the Islamic world. Sufism spread through territories newly fallen under the banner of Islam. The influence of the *tariqat* was undoubtedly instrumental in bringing about the conversion of local rulers to Islam (as in the Balkans and Anatolia) and in restoring vital social structures disrupted by warfare, particularly in those regions devastated by the Mongol irruptions of the thirteenth century. In central Asia, Sufi centres of study and the shrines of saints, which became centres of pilgrimage and worship, were endowed by Sultans themselves, and the esteem in which they were held by conquerors such as Tamerlaine and Bābūr is well known.

Centres of Sufi teaching were linked with chivalric and artisanal organizations, and frequently with the royal court of the rulers of the era, notably the Tīmūrid, Ottoman and Moghul courts. And while committed to performing socially productive or charitable roles, the *tariqats* became vast repositories of mystical knowledge, presented in a multiplicity of forms. Many became known for their specialized techniques, informed by mystical insight, of music, healing, dance or the interpretation of dreams. Their enormous variety led to *tariqats* claiming descent from the same order frequently adopting variant doctrines and rituals when implanted in different territories. At the same time, *tariqats* formulated complex lines of ascription linking them to their founders and ultimately to the Prophet Mohammed. Sufism became institutionalized, and much of the simplicity and intensity of its early days was lost.*

The contrasts between formal religion and Sufism are instructive. If Islam could be at times an authoritarian (and dogmatic) father to its people, Sufism became a benevolent (and eclectic) uncle, able to bestow gifts which a strict but well-meaning parent could not.

Islam and Sufism evolved hand in hand, but were propelled by different forces. While religious authority sought to establish the welfare of society through the body of laws known as *Shari'a*, Sufism offered an inner Way, and a form of devotion that took into account the spiritual freedom of the individual. Sufis took prophetic traditions, religious ritual and verses from the Qur'ān, and enriched them with inner significance.

Whereas the traditional meaning of Islam is understood as 'submission' to divine law as laid down by prophetic revelation, and shaped by the forceful dichotomies of good and evil, the lawful and the unlawful, and the cultivation of virtue over vice, the Sufi is engaged in a process of 'surrender' that transcends conventional dualism: everything goes, as it were, into the fire, until only the Real remains. Where religion speaks of sin, Sufism speaks of 'heedlessness'. Where the *mullā* emphasizes preparation for the afterlife, the dervish exhorts a spiritual

---

* Yet this is not the place to explore the apparently paradoxical notion that Sufis have existed, and do exist, in every age and culture.

death in this very lifetime. And where theology formulates the limits of Heaven and Hell, mysticism alludes to multiple and interpenetrating worlds emanating from the Divine, accessible in accordance with the seeker's spiritual capacity.

It is difficult not to feel, glancing even briefly at its influence, that Sufism has created some of the world's most 'worldly' mystics. It cannot be said to be a mysticism of quietists. Its members advised kings, held positions of high civil authority, formed the core of armies and resistance movements,* wrote the leading scientific treatises of their day, and composed the most widely read mystical literature of all time – the rousing echo of which, embodied poetically in the Andalucian *zajal*, spread through Medieval Europe on the lips and strings of the Troubadours, impelling the genesis of courtly lyrical poetry and the epochal transformation of relations between the sexes in the West.

*

I wished I had been able to talk for longer with the kindly man opposite me, whose practicality and diligence were difficult to reconcile with coal-swallowing dervishes or the snake-charming *faqirs* associated with Indian mysticism. But we did not have much time and our discussion remained incomplete.

I left Mazar the following day. A teenage boy was riding in the back seat of the taxi I had hired; he saw me writing in my notebook, and asked if I would give him my pen. I refused, having earlier decided not to give to anyone who asked; but it was a worthless biro, and the more he asked, the more I regretted my hard-heartedness. As we drove along, he persisted with the same question, over and over again.

'Why not?' he would ask, fawning. 'Why won't you give it to me?'

'Because.' I resolved to look straight ahead and ignore him.

---

* The elite Janissary corps of the Ottoman armies, closely allied to the Bektashi *tariqat*, come immediately to mind; also the century-and-a-quarter resistance to Russian advances in the Caucasus, directed by Naqshbandi leaders; the dervish movements of Libya and Sudan, which formed the sharp end of anti-imperialist revolts; and in more recent times, Sufi-organized activity against occupiers in Afghanistan and Chechnya.

'Why not?'

'Because it's my pen and I need it.'

'Oh, *why* won't you?'

'Because——' and I was stuck for excuses now, until the thought suddenly came to me, '*I am attached to it.*' And at the very same moment I remembered the line from Bidīl, and saw the tapping of Yusuf's pen against the crucial word: attachment.

And that, it occurred to me at the time, was the best practical demonstration of Sufism I could have wished for.

Eight

But that will not bring back the things we loved: the high, clear days and the blue icecaps on the mountains; the lines of white poplars fluttering in the wind, and the long white prayer-flags; the fields of asphodels that followed the tulips ... Never.

Bruce Chatwin, *A Lament for Afghanistan*

It was mid-December now. A dusting of snow had fallen on the mountains around Kabul. By day they glimmered icily, and in the evenings the final few minutes of sunlight would spread along the frosted peaks in a rose-pink wave, and the city seemed to be enclosed by a high rim of gently glowing petals.

I was happy to be back. Tim, good-natured and laconic as ever, became my landlord again. Amān, the Hazāra chef, welcomed me like a long-lost brother, squeezed me in a bear-hug until my vertebrae cracked, looked fondly into my eyes, went through an interminable repertoire of greetings and tugged my beard affectionately, saying I now looked like a *mowlāwi*, a religious sage, and even — with a mischievious chuckle — a bit like a *Tāleb*.

There were other unexpectedly warm welcomes. Shopkeepers near the house enquired about my trip, and men whose faces I had to struggle to remember would cross the street to exchange a customary hug, and say how glad they were that I had returned safely to Kabul. My beard, which was beginning to take on a respectable air, was the object of high praise. Feeling as though I had come home, I stopped at a nearby barber to get the wild look out of my hair.

A long and careful cutting ended with a scalp-rejuvenating massage and a musky-scented lotion being rubbed into every hair. As the last severed tufts were brushed from the back of my neck, an admiring face stood back above me in the mirror. With no idea of the going rate for such luxurious treatment, I asked how much I should pay.

'Whatever you like,' came the reply, with a deprecatory shrug of the shoulders. I realized my mistake; now he would be too polite to impose a price. It was no good, at this point, trying to elicit a direct response; such directness was a deep breach of etiquette.

This reluctance to put a figure on things is by no means uniquely Afghan, but there can be few other places where the visitor so often encounters, at the end of some service rendered, this show of wistful indifference to payment. Pendulum-like, the equilibrium between politeness and opportunism swings from genuine displays of magnanimity to the shamelessly exploitative. I thought, at one end, of shopkeepers vehemently reluctant to accept more than the usual price for things from a foreigner, and at the other, of certain carpet sellers in Chicken Street, who smilingly passed off moth-eaten scraps of wool to the unwitting as if they were national treasures. The barber, I suspected, was somewhere in between.

There is always this unwillingness to reduce the event of a purchase to something entirely quantifiable, and various rituals are enacted to ensure that what takes place is more than a simple exchange of goods. The more substantial the transaction, the more it becomes a social event; not only because the customer may one day return, or bring with him some news of unforeseen import, but also — this at least is my own interpretation — to dilute the suggestion that the aim of what is taking place is merely the satisfying of a material longing. Tea is brought, news is exchanged, and no effort is spared to make the visitor comfortable.

'Well...' begins your host, and there is silence for a few moments as you feel yourself being weighed, studied with the wordless intensity of eyes that have taken in every detail of your dress, posture and physical manner.

'*Chetūr hasti?* How are you?'

'Fine,' you answer, and the eyes weigh you more subtly now, as if some inner measure is being taken.

'*Jour hasti?* Are you happy? Not too cold? Here, get closer to the stove...'

You hear the crackle of wood from within, and through the steam rising from your glass of tea you meet again that silently forceful gaze of enquiry.

'*Khub!* Well! What do you think of Afghanistan?' This catches you off guard.

'Afghanistan is ... a beautiful country,' you reply.

'Ah, yes ... a beautiful country,' comes the echo, with a suddenly far-off look. 'Yes, it is ...' And such are the times that your innocent response evokes all too often a look of inconsolable sadness.

Occasionally of course, and particularly among carpet sellers, the contact between buyer and seller is reduced to one of showmanship (in a flash you are surrounded by a sea of unrolled carpets, each '*finest quality!*'). At others, when means are more modest, the customer is treated with humbling concern, as when an old man rises stiffly to give a token dusting to the cushion where you are about to sit, gives up his perch nearest to the stove, and despatches a fleet-footed grandson to fetch a cupful of sugar for your tea. Should you buy something, then almost invariably, when reassurances that the transaction has been satisfactorily completed are being exchanged all round, something of little material value is added to the package being bound in bales of newspaper and string in a corner of the room: a set of plastic prayer beads, a pair of embroidered children's slippers or a woollen hat. This *bakhsheesh* seals the spirit of reciprocity over the whole event, ensuring that it becomes more than the sum of its parts.

The cry of *bakhsheesh!* in its charitable sense is usually heard only from the lips of wily children. Even in the impoverished capital there are not many of them – begging is frowned upon except as a very last resort – and those who make a business of handouts roam in little teams on corners and near shops where foreigners are most likely to be intercepted.

With supernaturally keen eyes they are able to detect from a thousand yards the sight of a pale hand reaching into a pocket, and gather round a promising donor at bewildering speed, enveloping him with a chorus of pitiful pleas. These expert elicitors of compassion, all of Dickensian raggedness, gauge their target's resolve by the minutest changes in facial expressions; a single stray particle of indecision is enough to get these walking geiger counters clicking with anticipation. They follow you with heartbreaking tenacity; the further you walk, the harder it is not to give in. Should your resolve eventually crumble, ten streets later, there is from all around a clamouring of tiny and prematurely aged hands. Then in an instant they are gone, like scrap metal dropping from an electromagnet. But should you hold your ground, the look of disappointment on their faces haunts you with unbearable vividness well after you have returned home, and for not having been able to part with a few pennies for a hungry child you feel the remorse of a murderer.

I fished out a few notes and pressed them folded into the barber's hand. He made no effort to verify the amount but thanked me warmly and we said goodbye. For nearly an hour of his attentions, and the best haircut I had had in years, I handed over the equivalent of nearly two pounds; on my part it seemed a mean exchange. As I left the shop I glanced backwards through the window to see if I could catch his expression as he counted the money. Through the dusty glass I glimpsed him fanning out the notes in front of everyone in the shop, their jaws dropped in unanimous astonishment. He looked like the winner, had there been such a thing, of the national lottery.

*

Some thank-you visits and catching up on news of friends was in order. I went first to the office of Amrullah, our liaison with the government, to thank him for his advice and help in getting to Panjshīr. This yielded a spontaneous invitation to lunch.

'We don't think of you as a foreigner or a journalist any more,' he said, after we had helped ourselves to a delicious *qabli pilau*, 'but as a friend.' This was typically Afghan courtesy, but it touched the intended nerve. He asked me about my plans and I expressed curiosity about the chances of crossing the country via the central route. He looked doubtful, saying the passes on the way were probably snowbound by now; besides, there was a front line between Kabul and the centre, and there was nothing the government could do to help if I ran into trouble trying to cross it. But if I wanted, he suggested, there was always the possibility of taking a military flight to the outpost of Chaqcheran, right in the heart of the country, which was under government control. This seemed like more than courtesy.

'We want you to see the country,' he added, expressing sadness that the times made travel so difficult. The worst aspect was the ethnic tension between different regions, which never used to be a limiting factor in moving from place to place. Now, he said, it was a matter of life and death.

I wondered for a moment whether his concern over my plans might not all be for show; kind words to flatter a sympathetic guest. But the following day a letter was delivered to me at the house, printed on the stationery of the Ministry of Defence and signed by two different hands in impressive-looking calligraphic swirls. Provided I remembered not to show it to the wrong people, it looked both authoritative and indispensable: a *laissez-passer*, introducing the bearer with a respectful request for assistance from the allied mujaheddin of Ghorband, Bamiyan and the province of Ghor.

*

I went to find Rafiq. He was Iranian, lived in Switzerland, and had ended up in Kabul by accident. He had told me his story when we had first met and made friends a month earlier. Having left his former job he had wanted to settle down to a state-sponsored career change; providing he showed some evidence of actively looking for work he was paid almost his entire former salary by the social security system. There was no hurry; he enjoyed the leisure, saw much more of his children, and applied diligently to organizations where he would have as little chance of employment as possible. One of them had been a foreign relief agency which seemed unlikely to be interested in someone with no relevant qualifications. Never did he guess that they might be in immediate need of a Persian-speaking interpreter in Kabul...

He lived comfortably with two other quadrilingual Iranians in the new town; between them they formed a little enclave of urbane aloofness, ever so faintly superior to both Afghans and Westerners alike.

From afar, the Moslem countries of the region – Afghanistan, Iran and Pakistan – are, culturally speaking, frequently lumped together. At closer range the differences sharpen dramatically, and are reflected in the national prejudices of each. Iranians generally think of Afghans as coarse and dangerous, but also as belonging to the untamed protospecies which, under the influence of Iranian sophistication, has been given its most civilized expression in Iran. Iran's southern neighbour, Pakistan, regards Afghans as at best quaint and incomprehensibly patriotic, a nation of impoverished reprobates; at worst they are considered mindlessly violent. The Afghans for their part look upon Iranians as hysterical, effeminate and pseudo-religious. And both Afghans and Iranians look down their Aryan noses at Pakistan as a hybrid non-country peopled by irreligious sycophants of the West. That between them these countries represent some two hundred million souls, several thousand ethnic and tribal groupings, and more than a hundred different languages gives an indication of the hollowness of these prejudices.

I found Rafiq's house and banged on the gate. An elderly *chowkidar* wearing a corduroy jacket emerged and embraced me with such warmth I felt like a son returning from years of absence.

'Well, it's Mr Rafiq you'll be wanting, is it? He's inside. Come on, you'll catch your death out here ...'

He led me inside, chuckling to himself, until we reached Rafiq's bedroom door. Just then he hesitated.

'You had better go first.'

'Is he sleeping?' I asked.

'No, not sleeping,' he replied, slightly vexed.

'Is he ill?'

'He's not ill,' he said, shrugging his shoulders mischievously, 'but sometimes he is – *strange*. Listen.' He moved aside.

I put my ear to the door. Every few seconds I heard a demented, dog-like wailing. He sounded drugged. It was certainly strange. My impulse was to let him be, but I knocked gently, and when there was no reply I put my head around the door.

He was sitting on his bed by the window, listening to his Walkman.

'Oh my *God!*' he cried, with extravagant delight.

'We thought you might be unwell.'

'I was singing. It's so beautiful, I can't help it. Listen to this.' He held up the headphones. This explained the wailing: it was Pavarotti singing *Nessun dorma*.

'Oh, *merde*, Jason,' he said as he ushered me into the main room. 'I

282

was singing to cheer myself up. I am so depressed.' He sat down, lit his pipe, and looked thoughtfully at the sticking plaster in the crook of his elbow. In the morning he had donated blood at the children's hospital to save the life of a little girl. It had left him depressed and at the same time strangely uplifted.

'Seven years old – my daughter's age,' he said. 'You should have seen her. She was incredibly brave.' He turned towards the window and looked out over the sandbags.

'What can we do?' he puffed. 'I don't know. *Enfin*, life is an experience.'

I liked Rafiq. Among the other foreigners in Kabul he was something of an anomaly. His Western air was only skin deep, an expedience betrayed by a glint in his eye that went unchastened even in his most professional moments. The Swiss, he confessed, were a bit too methodical for his liking, but he had adapted to their ways, lived up with chameleon-like skill to the role of his disguise, and slipped as flawlessly between Eastern and Western personas as a palmed ace to a magician's deck.

His English was interwoven with French expressions, and the combination draped in a delicate and deeply charming Persian lilt. In conversation there was a suggestion of melodrama, mirrored in expansive sweeps of his hands, to everything he said. He did not laugh but his engaging smile broke easily into eye-watering giggles, which had the effect of disarming others where his consummate politeness had not already done the job.

We caught up on news. He confided that his European colleagues, especially those much younger than him, took themselves far too seriously.

'But you can see they're not committed,' he groused. 'I don't think Westerners really understand commitment. Look at these Afghans! You know how it is – some of them would die for you. But what happens in the West? *Merde!* As soon as there's a problem – *Allez oop! Je m'en vais!* Right then, I'm off!'

He was having trouble too, he admitted, with the opposite sex. For some reason they seemed sceptical of him, and all his approaches seemed to be having the wrong effect.

'Perhaps you're too romantic,' I suggested. 'You will just have to be more direct.'

'But I *am!*' he protested theatrically, blowing an exasperated plume of smoke above us. 'Yesterday I told one of the Swiss nurses she had *very* spiritual eyes.'

'And what did she say?'

'She said: FUCK OFF.'

'You should have introduced yourself first.'

'They always want it both ways! *Enfin*...' He puffed ruminatively. 'I don't understand European women. They're so cold. Man and woman are destined to be united, to complement one another. *L'amour! L'amour!*'

I asked when he would next be seeing his wife and children.

'*My God!* If my wife could hear me talking like this! *Merde*, I miss them more than you can imagine.' Then, looking suddenly serious, he said: 'You know, of course, I would *never*—'

'Of course not.'

'But still...'

We laughed.

*

Back at the house, Tim was not well. He had caught amoebic dysentery and was looking thin and pale. At mealtimes the table was strewn with pills supplied by an English nurse from the Red Cross.

Amān confided that the meals he prepared for Tim were specially made for their healing qualities. He had learned the recipes from a book on medicinal foods, and used the word 'Younani' to describe the cures.

'A big book,' he whispered conspiratorially, 'it's back in Bamiyan. I'll show it to you when you come. We'll slaughter a sheep and have a great feast...' He scurried into Tim's room with a tray.

Younani! It meant Greek — a reference to the medical knowledge derived from the Greek settlers: two thousand years later Amān was surreptitiously treating his patient according to the principles of the Four Humours.

*

The house was still a contradiction; it lacked most of the comforts which, back home, it seemed scarcely possible to live without. But it had been luxurious once, when it was the residence of the Bulgarian ambassador. The double-glazed windows were all cracked or blown out, and the chandelier above the spiral staircase had no bulbs in it. There was a huge fitted kitchen with Formica cupboards, all of them empty; a modern gas stove, for which there was no gas, and a double sink where water hadn't flowed for years. Occasionally the telephone spluttered into life, but so unreliable was the exchange that it was always a wrong number. This mattered little to Jān, who would engage the other party in a long conversation, gaining news of some distant relative in the process. There was, I think, no system of billing.

We made do amply with a portable paraffin burner for cooking and heating water. In the upstairs bathroom there was a shower with a smoked glass door, but we crouched on the floor instead. The marble tiles were so cold that the act of washing demanded unaccustomed bravery and skill; things to avoid were slipping, scalding, running out of water too soon, and covering oneself with soot from the sides of the metal bucket.

A generator in the garden gave us a few hours of electricity during the day. Tim kept a single room warm with a locally made stove fuelled by diesel; the entire house smelled faintly of the fumes. The evenings were long. Often after dark we would sit for long periods saying nothing. Tim and I would read; Jān sat broodily within stoking distance of the stove, smoking. Our ears were still tuned like hair-triggers to the telltale thump of salvoes, and several times, with the swiftness of a mongoose, Jān would leap up; in an instant we would all dive away from the window and shelter against the wall. But there was no impact; he had heard an errant rumble of artillery.

Between these gloomy interludes I got to know him better. His home was the Panjshīr valley. Life had been peaceful until the Soviet occupation when, through no greater fault than having been born there, he became, in the eyes of the authorities, a counter-revolutionary bandit.

After that he had been a fighter, had travelled to America, England and Pakistan, and he had not seen his own parents for eleven years.

When the communists fled Kabul in 1992, he had returned to the city hoping like countless others for an end to the conflict, beginning instead a life of renewed suspense and hardship. The present disruption meant he could no longer send his children to school or rebuild his home, ruined by bombing, in Panjshīr. Even the extra money I had given him for food, he admitted he had given to the housekeeper for her daughter, who had fallen ill.

'What if a rocket fell on my house?' he asked, after we had got talking. 'That would really be a problem,' he said, 'a huge problem!' We chuckled and shook our heads at the madness of the times, and I wondered whether I would be able to smile so readily in the same situation.

'It'll be years before this is all sorted out,' he went on, surprising me with his frankness. 'Even if the Tālebān take Kabul it won't end there. Others will fight to take their place. It'll go on. Five, maybe ten years, I'd say . . .'

No wonder he looked gloomy. Yet perhaps this was the bitter cure that Fate was forcing on the country, driving it towards nothing less than a sort of bedrock of disillusion, beneath which no hope could sink; perhaps only this would eventually lead, among all groups, to an abdication of belief in a military solution.

*

Rashīd visited during the day. Apart from employing him as his driver, Tim worked hard with him to improve his skills as a reporter.

'A lot of other people said they would help me,' he said. 'Nobody did.'

Unlike Jān, who was fastidious both in physical appearance and manner, Rashīd had a faintly degenerate air. He had seen too much, I supposed, in his life as a conscripted soldier under the communists, and some embittered portion of his self had taken refuge in cynicism and irreverence.

I asked him about the scar on his forehead. He had three good ones in all, he said fondly, as his fingers traced the telltale marks over his scalp. One was from when he had been riding a donkey with his brother and fallen off; another when he had sneaked into a stable and been discovered by a farmer who hit him over the head with a shovel; and another from his teenage years, when an old man had given him a pinch of chewing tobacco so strong it had knocked him out. In turn I told him about the time I had dropped a flaming stick into a disused underground petrol tank when I was nine years old. It had exploded generously, but other than the grit embedded in my forehead for a month afterwards I had escaped without injury.

He liked that story; it led to the subject of accidents in general. The most spectacular one he had ever seen had been a mid-air collision at Jalallabad airport. The Russian pilots of a pair of helicopter gunships had been showing off near the control tower when their rotor blades had fatally intertwined.

'Yes,' he mused with relish, 'that was a really good one.'

I asked him why the communists had sent him to prison, and he let out a lavish snort of disgust. 'Why did they kill a million and a half Afghans? No good reason.'

*

At the offices of the International Committee of the Red Cross, I was thrilled to find several messages which had arrived via the satellite telephone link. There was something miraculous about receiving news from the other side of the world that had bounced through space and down again into my very hands, and I scrolled through the lines with a sense of awe and anticipation. Yet reading them I was inexplicably disappointed, as if they had somehow failed to convey the news I really wanted. I was aware of how much and how unconsciously I attached to them an obscure sense of faith in the distant world of home. To send a message to that world was no small matter; into it went a private distillation of all the isolation and daily fears of the journey. And surely, went this reasoning, a response from that far-off place, that home of wealth and of peace and privileges unthinkable in our own surroundings, would somehow return the reaching-out with a corresponding munificence that, descending into such different surroundings, would both redeem and inspire. A tall order . . .

The messages ended with expressions of hope that Kabul was not too harrowing for me, because my family had seen photographs now of the city's ruined streets and miserable-looking children and had a notion I was trudging through the smoking rubble and having to endure terrible hardships.

Outside I joked with a trio of boys who worked as helpers and drivers. They were giggling about the foreign women who were toing and froing around the courtyard. One was a particular favourite of them all; to them she was as mysterious and as unapproachable as the Afghan women I had met seemed to me. Someone put forward the question on their minds: would a foreign woman ever 'go' with a Afghan man?

Well, what did they think? I asked. Would an Afghan woman go with an foreign man? They laughed out loud and shook their heads in unison: not unless he wanted to die.

*

In the evening there was a party at one of the foreign agencies; a typically noisy and progressively less restrained event where the stresses and fears of living in the city found an easy avenue of dilution among friends.

I always felt ambivalent at such events, where the company, music, food and wine made one feel at home. Yet this was anything but home, and the comforts seemed at times like a charade that deceived by its familiarity and by which I felt weakened in a way that was difficult to define. Nor was I ever entirely free of the thought that beyond these chambers of pleasure was a city full of people both cold and hungry. To stay too long kindled an obscure feeling of dishonesty.

The music was loud; people were dancing; the habitués clamoured around the bar. I met a young English photographer who was on his second trip to Afghanistan, and developed a fondness for him because he was about the same age I had been on my own first trip. I encouraged him, in the usual way that you wish for others what really you want for yourself, to have complete confidence in himself and never be afraid to be alone, to further his travels and always question the meaning of things.

There was a little cluster of French nurses who huddled together in a corner and reminded me of caged partridges, a drunk American woman from whom I fled when she said she wanted to get to know me better, and an Afghan chef who peered every so often from the kitchen door to glimpse the wild gyrations of a red-headed nurse, who was dancing with solitary abandon in the centre of the room.

I drank wine for the first time since leaving Kabul a month before, and shared with Tim the cigar that had miraculously survived the journey north. The effect was almost overpowering, and my diary for the evening deteriorates into a less than coherent ramble about being caught between two worlds, and the longing I felt in both directions. I was also deeply homesick.

In this pernicious state I fell into a long and wearying conversation with a Dutch accountant. He worked for one of the relief agencies, he said, and was in Kabul for a few days. He was also aggressively curious about my plans to write a book about Afghanistan, and asked me to explain myself.

Even sober I found it hard enough to articulate my motives for writing about the country; motives which had taken shape over years with a complex restlessness of their own and been further transformed by the experience of the previous month. I confessed that my usual explanations sounded hollow even to myself, but that perhaps if he stayed longer in Afghanistan he might understand better what I meant.

'If you do not have a plan,' he said sternly, 'you will find *nothink* to write about!'

This put me in a cynical mood.

What, after all, was a travel book? That young Italian had started it all in the thirteenth century, and had given the telling of tall tales from foreign parts its subsequent respectability. On the whole it had not changed much since Polo's time: a man or a woman sets off for foreign parts ignorant of both the language and geography of the place, with an out-of-date map and borrowed phrase book, preys shamelessly for as long as the family trust fund will allow on the hospitality of the native people, and returns home to hastily record his or her first impressions in a semi-fictional collection of descriptions that affirm the prejudices of the day. Then, reminded of the mediocrity of the experiences described and to ease the risk of any intellectual burden on the microscopic attention span of the reader, he or she retrospectively invents a fashionable 'quest' around which the narrative can be twisted in every direction except towards the truth, fits it tidily with invented dialogues, speculative history, sweeping inaccuracies, mistranslations, verbose accounts of having braved hazards endured daily by ordinary local people without complaint, portrays as revelation long lists of trivial facts known to every local schoolchild, and bludgeons the original spirit of the endeavour in an attempt to appear erudite with the academic verbiage of out-of-print encyclopaedias, disguising all the while the discomfort of being at sea in an alien culture by resorting to the quirky, condescending humour that its couch-bound audience will think of as funny. The result? Only a confirmation of what everybody already knows: better to stay at home.

The Dutchman was glowering. How, he asked, could I undertake to write a book about a journey if I did not know where the journey would *lead*? And how, he asked, quite crossly now, could I make a journey if I did not know what I would write about it?

Those, I said, were exactly the risks one took, but he shook his head pityingly, like a missionary before the unrepentant. He persisted, and inwardly I gave up hope, turning defensively cryptic. I suggested that a journey was a kind of story in itself, providing one had the will to read it, just as a story too could be a journey, providing one had the experience to bring to it, and that both found their mark differently in different people.

'You are talkink nonsense!' he said finally in a tone of disgust. Then I was aware of a bulky human presence next to me at the bar, who had been there for some time, listening all the while. He turned to the Dutchman and said in a thick New Zealand accent:

'Why don't you just shut up?'

Then he turned to me and I saw the handsome, bearded face of a man of about fifty. His nose looked as though it had been broken a couple of times and he had the indestructible look of a seasoned mountaineer. Our eyes met and he said:

'What you just said is the first bloody intelligent thing I've heard all evening.'

This was how I met Bob McKerrow, Ropate to certain of his friends, head of the Afghan Red Crescent. From that moment we became fast friends, although I would not see him again for another month.

✻

The next morning was clear, cold and brilliantly sunny. I had agreed to meet Rafiq for lunch and walked to his house just as an explosion of artillery in a street not far away shook the ground. When I arrived I found Rafiq sitting gloomily on the couch, poking at something in the ashtray with the tip of his pipe. It was a piece of shrapnel, still hot, that had ricocheted around the garden before landing at his feet; the shell I had heard earlier had landed in a nearby patch of open ground, killing, we later found out, a small boy.

'*Merde!*' said Rafiq.

For lunch we were served roast beef with mashed potatoes and gravy. This was so unexpected I complimented the cook when he appeared, and he broke into a broad smile when I mentioned I was from England. He used to be the cook at the British embassy, he said, and asked if I knew a Mr Pirs. He must have meant Piers Carter, the former ambassador. That was over twenty years ago.

'They were good people,' he said, 'such good people.'

Rafiq talked about his escape from Iran. After the revolution he and his wife had fallen under investigation by the secret police. They were held briefly in prison and decided to flee the country. Rafiq led the way; an uncle in the south gave him refuge and helped to arrange his escape. After various further adventures a Baluch tribesmen had smuggled his through the hills by camel and across the border into Pakistan; it had been the most gruelling trip of his life.

'He was incredible,' he said, recalling the toughness of his guide with obvious fondness, and making me think of Blackbeard, my own first guide into Afghanistan. 'He never said anything. He just looked back at me from time to time. *Mon dieu*, even when I was completely exhausted he just looked at me. And then when I was at death's door — *sur le point de mourir* — he would give me a drink of water. *Quel homme!*'

Afterwards while we sipped on our tea some others came into the room, among them an English nurse and a rather unfriendly Englishman. He was a *Times* correspondent from London. There was so little

291

qualified reporting from Afghanistan we expressed delight at having a reporter from the outside world in our midst.

'I didn't want to come,' he said grumpily. 'I'm only here because of her.'

'Her' was the English nurse, a friend who had persuaded him to visit Kabul to report on the plight of the city. He did not look at all happy with the assignment.

'I hope,' I said warily, 'that you won't just mention negative things. Reports from this place tend to be unnecessarily gloomy.'

'News is news,' he said defensively. 'That's what we get paid for.'

'But it doesn't have to be bad news, does it?'

'Look — it's no good whining about it,' he snapped. 'I've got a job to do.'

I had yet to read a foreign account of positive developments in the country. The creative efforts of Afghans seeking remedies for the complex challenges of the conflict were seldom mentioned in news reports; instead, one heard only of the anarchy and destruction and, hanging over everything, a suggestion of irremediable darkness and despair. Perhaps there is a deep and unacknowledged need for news of disasters which, when not available from home, must be brought back captive from afar. Visiting film crews asked to be taken to the Jāde-ye Maiwand, the ruined street I had wandered down on my very first day in Kabul, and went to hospitals to film limbless children. Even the journalists living in Kabul took a dim view of correspondents who flew for a weekend into the city, grumbled about the difficulties, and reported authoritatively on the 'situation'.

Apart from the seldom explicitly reckoned-with notion that good news was unworthy news, the religious dimension to the conflict only complicated matters, and the hastily exported versions of events tended to be almost comically apocalyptic. Reports leaving the country were couched in a language strangely at odds with our experience, as if they were written about a different and arid place, where there was nothing but 'warring tribes', the threat of 'Islamic Law', and something called 'fundamentalism': emotive and disturbing terms which so few people seem able satisfactorily to define.

Those who stayed longer got to form a more complex and fluid picture of the forces at work and were exposed to arguments, each with their own proofs, from different sides. These complexities tended to be concrete rather than religious or ideological.

For those getting to know the country at first hand, the conflict could not be analysed in abstractions, much less in the hazy terminology of the 'Islamic'. Understanding the place was inseparable from the land itself, its peoples, and an entire spectrum of encounters with them. Between us we had made friends or shared the hospitality of Afghans in every corner of the country and on every side. And in the resulting mosaic of experience there were both unambiguous geometry and vaulting arabesques.

The intellectual desert from which the current denigration in popular media of all things Islamic has grown encroached less on Afghanistan than elsewhere; the poverty of the Afghans, I think, and their friendliness towards outsiders had a mollifying effect on the usual demonizations. Yet it had its consequences. I will mention only one, in a historical sense; a single worm from the can.

During the Soviet period, the remoteness of the war and the dangers of entering the country illegally made it especially difficult to gather balanced and reliable news of the conflict at first hand. These factors also provided unusual opportunities for news-gatherers to further their careers without the scrutiny that existed elsewhere. One well-known American television reporter, frustrated by the difficulties of getting into Afghanistan, even passed off mocked-up battles filmed near the border as rare combat footage from inside the country. Another documentary portrayed the mujaheddin as little more than sadistic, hashish-smoking renegades, who decapitated their prisoners and threw themselves into battle in a state of drug-heightened relish.*

---

* By chance I had met the director in Peshawar on my first trip. We talked about our favourite books, and he was kind enough to write a list of recommendations. I have it still: Marquis de Sade, *Justine*; the autobiography of Rudolf Hoess, commandant of Auschwitz; *The Devil's Brigade* about an SS unit of the French Foreign Legion in Indochina; Niccolo Machiavelli, the *Discourses*; Solzhenitsyn, *The Gulag Archipelago*; Nietzsche, *Ecce Homo*.

Throughout the ten-year occupation of Afghanistan by the Soviets, only a tiny proportion of Western reports of the war ever referred to the men, women and children opposing their invaders as a legitimate force of 'resistance'. Almost without exception, Afghans fighting Soviet troops or the communist regime they protected were described in such all-encompassing terms as 'Islamic guerrillas', 'Moslem rebels' or – most unenlightening of all – 'Holy Warriors'.

None of these labels could evoke the extent of a genuinely popular resistance; of such defiant acts as a housewife, unhinged by grief at the murder of her husband under torture, stabbing a Russian officer in a crowded bazaar; of the Afghan army officer passing advance intelligence of Soviet offensives to his relatives in the countryside; or a child delivering poisoned grapes to a Soviet garrison. Nor did they hint at the high level of discipline and organization of mujaheddin groups elsewhere in the country. The prevailing image of the resistance was generally that of a band of desperadoes holed up in the mountains; an image already reinforced by century-old stereotypes of the Afghans' intransigence and genetic affection for war.

The broad insistence in Western media on Islamic qualifiers, as if these were in themselves somehow informative, served only further to obscure the efforts of millions who defied the Soviets during the period; it was a terminology which prevented Afghans from acquiring in the West a genuinely human face, as if, being Moslems, perhaps they did not respond to the bombing of their homes or grieve over their dead in the same way as did people of other religions. The validity of the very ordinary reaction – resisting an invader – was thereby undermined, almost as if one had to be a Moslem, or for that matter a 'rebel', to oppose foreign domination. So far as I am aware Vietcong soldiers fighting the Americans were never referred to as 'Buddhist rebels', any more than French resistance to German occupation was termed the reaction of 'Christian insurgents'. But the labels remained, and do remain, largely unquestioned, along with all sorts of events in Islamic countries which are imputed with an obscuring religious dimension that in other contexts would go unmentioned.

During this same period, Western classifications of the different resistance groups involved in the conflict were conspicuously divided along 'moderate' and 'extremist' lines, as if their ideological orientation to the West was the criterion that defined their existence, rather than highly complex local factors of ethnic, cultural and political import.

Today it is partly the powerful influence of this kind of simplification which makes the present civil war so apparently impenetrable; because the conflict refuses to reduce to black and white it appears, however subtly, to be the product of less rational beings than those of the peace-loving nations of the West.

From all such talk our daily endeavours were mercifully free. Against the scale and immediacy of the suffering, serious discourse on the conflict lost much of its appeal. Events spoke for themselves in a world which had become deliciously concrete. Our cares condensed to simple but personally meaningful achievements, like being alive at the end of the day. We shied naturally away from talk of politics, unless it was necessary for some aspect of work; of religious discussion there was even less.

As to 'Islam', we had, after all, only one substantial objection: its lack of decent wine.

*

At some point during these few days after returning to Kabul I had met up again with the English soldiers who ran the headquarters of the HALO trust, the British charity and de-mining outfit. From time to time they gave informal briefings to visitors on the dangers of mines and unexploded bombs, and it seemed prudent, in one of the countries worst afflicted by mines in the world, to go along.

Mines have been called the perfect terrorists; they wait for their victim in silence, never give up, and require nothing to maintain them. Mines laid during the First World War still surface in northern Europe and occasionally explode beneath a tractor's plough. Until fairly recently they were cumbersome things and took a certain skill and effort to place; the practice of scattering mines indiscriminately in large numbers was pioneered by American forces in Indochina. Only a very small proportion of mines contain self-destruct mechanisms; once primed, a mine stays ready to explode until it is destroyed. Today hundreds of different kinds are produced cheaply and in vast quantities, notably in countries where they are not used.

Large but uncertain numbers of mines — estimates range from one to ten million — remain buried in Afghan soil. The majority were laid during the Soviet occupation, and left behind. In theory an army makes maps of its minefields, which for obvious reasons must be precise. In the case of the Soviets in Afghanistan, only some of these minefields, mostly around military installations, were ever mapped. The belts of thousands of mines that were sown in defensive rings around cities such as Herat and Kabul, or scattered on mountain passes from the air, were not.

Following the Soviet withdrawal, huge numbers were laid by opposing mujaheddin groups without even an attempt to record their positions. And in southern Kabul, where the front lines had ranged back and forth across the city, the problem was most acute. Mines had been laid by retreating fighters in streets, abandoned homes and their gardens, and there they remained. The de-miners had set up their field office at the epicentre of the problem, in southwest Kabul near the university. There I joined a handful of other foreigners for an hour of sobering instruction.

Mines fell into two categories, explained the burly ex-sapper with a Midlands accent as he guided us over the array of odd shapes. There were anti-vehicular mines and anti-personnel mines: designed, in other words, to blow up either tanks or people. Anti-tank mines accounted for less than 10 per cent of all unexploded mines in Afghanistan and were relatively easy to find. We were shown heavy, metal mines of Second World War stock from England and Russia, and modern plastic bars filled with liquid explosive. The most common in Afghanistan, an old favourite of the mujaheddin I recognized at once, was the Italian-made TC-6. It had a shell of bright yellow plastic that looked a little like a salad shaker. Inside was a fifteen-pound charge of TNT powerful enough to flip a tank the way a seagull flips a baby turtle. The Soviets hated these particular mines because of their low metal content, which made them difficult to detect. But the worst culprits were further on, and we moved to a table strewn with a bewildering variety of smaller mines.

These, we were told, were designed to do their work in three ways: by direct blast, in the case of the smallest mines; by fragmentation of their metal casings, in a manner similar to hand grenades; and directionally, by means of concave blocks of explosive lined with a dense layer of metal pellets which, when detonated, tore at supersonic velocity into anything across a wide arc up to two hundred yards away. In this last category fell the famous American Claymore mine and its Russian equivalent, the MON series. There was even a French version, we were told, which used plastic instead of metal pellets.

'Why plastic?' somebody asked. 'To make them spread further?'

'To make them harder to find by X-ray,' came the grim reply, 'once they're inside the victim's body.'

Some of them were alarmingly simple in design: there was a Russian mine in the form of an innocent-looking wooden box the size of a bar of soap, with a mousetrap-like detonator inside that triggered a few ounces of explosive. Others were the result of insidious genius: triggered by seismic sensors, the 'bounding' mine, when detonated, jumped into the air to the height of a man's groin before exploding, increasing thereby the radius of its hail of metal fragments.

Laying mines was easy; clearing them up was a different matter. The dangers, in all their obscenely calculated permutations, were truly nightmarish. There was seldom such a thing as a typical minefield. And it was not enough simply to find a mine in order to remove it: another mine might have been placed underneath it, and be triggered by the removal of the first. Mines could be booby-trapped in the shadows of passageways, connected by tripwires to doors or windows, and hidden in ceilings. Mines planted above ground which looked easy to disarm might be surrounded by other mines buried underground. Mines could also be attached to an object of value or curiosity, detonated by the hand of a curious passer-by. Disconnecting the wires between apparently small mines might set off a much larger mine, buried in the very spot that those observing the act had chosen for protection.

As if this were not enough, mines also got dislodged by rain or floods and became reburied, infecting areas previously cleared. During battles or in damaged buildings they moved about and ended up at odd angles and uneven depths. The POM-type mine, which looked like a hand grenade mounted on a little wooden stake, was notorious for falling over and becoming highly unstable, ready to be triggered at the slightest touch. Other mines, like the tiny Chinese type 72 – no bigger than a Jaffa cake – were, because they contained only a minute amount of metal, virtually impossible to detect.

Two types of anti-personnel mine were particularly widespread in Afghanistan: the Russian-made PMN and the PFM. The PMN was round, the size of a small ashtray, and an early version in use during the first years of the war was so powerful it tended to tear the leg, or legs, off its victim. In the later model the amount of explosive was judiciously reduced – we could see it, orange, set like a mousse in its little plastic mould – in order not to kill but to maim; the grim rationale being that a dead body was easily buried, but a wounded man, woman or child, who might live for several days, slowed up able-bodied bearers, and had a particularly demoralizing effect on others.

The PFM 'butterfly' mine was specifically designed for use in Afghanistan, and dropped in huge quantities on the trails and passes of the mountainous borderlands in the south. This mine could be remotely dispersed by artillery or helicopter, was small and difficult to see, and had the added expedient of containing, again, just enough liquid explosive to maim. Several million are thought to remain where they fluttered to earth during the war.

We were ushered, subdued, into an adjoining room.

On a long table was spread what was described as a typical selection of the unexploded ordnance, or UXOs, found around the city. UXOs posed a different problem. They were easier to detect, not having been designed to be concealed, but huge numbers never exploded. Finding them in their living rooms or back yards, villagers impatient to rebuild their homes assumed these odd-looking bits of metal were no longer dangerous and threw them aside – with disastrous results.

We were shown tank shells and artillery shells; some filled with phosphorus, high explosive, or thousands of tiny steel flechettes – a design outlawed, in theory, on account of the horrendous wounds it caused. The most common type of UXO in Kabul was the 82-millimetre mortar, a favourite of short-range battles in built-up areas. Their detatched tail fins were used by merchants as weights for their scales.

We moved on.

In another room were a dozen of what looked like ten-foot lengths of grey drainpipe. These were the 122-millimetre rockets that made life in the city so nerve-racking. They were called Katyushka. A pretty name . . .

Outside we were invited to see a team of de-miners at work. Cautioned to stay on the prescribed paths, we crossed the road and entered a broad square divided into sections by flags and fluttering tape. This was the university campus. Twenty local men wearing visors and protective aprons were inching their way forward in lanes a yard wide. From all around we could hear the squeaking of their metal detectors. In the countryside the detecting process went more quickly, we were told, but in the city it could take up to five hours to clear a path a few feet long. There were no short cuts; every single tiny scrap of metal had to be carefully probed and removed; old bullets and their casings, nuts, bolts, nails, coins, razor blades, batteries, bottletops and even the metallic foil of cigarette packets all slowed down the process.*

After our tour I accepted a lift back into the centre of town with

---

* Statistics, which are not the same as facts, should be interpreted cautiously. UN estimates that roughly a thousand years and billions of dollars will be needed to clear the mines in Afghanistan suggest the problem is intractable, and may discourage useful funding on the ground. US State Department figures on mines remaining in Afghanistan are now being questioned on account of the haste in which they were gathered. Extrapolation based on the cost of removing a single mine can be correspondingly misleading: it does not necessarily cost twice as much money to remove two mines as it does one. Vast sums are currently spent on technologies for detecting mines which, however ingenious, have tended to remain unavailable or impractical in many of the regions worst afflicted by mines.

the friendly sapper. We drove through half a mile of devastated buildings, and passed a damaged courtyard where a turbaned man was hauling out rubble and flinging it into the street.

'Look at him,' he said. 'See? That's the kind of silly bugger that gets blown up.'

*

Kabul was still under siege. Every day and night the opposing armies writhed snake-like in combat along the southern front, winning and losing pockets of territory in the fight for the capital. It was a crucial time. Rocket and artillery fire fell in the streets with the same terrifying unpredictability, and the level of hardship grew. The nights were steadily colder. Disruption of the usual trade routes to the north and south meant firewood was in short supply, and the cost of alternative fuel was increasingly beyond the reach of ordinary families.

One morning, as we were sitting in the house reading and writing, we heard five thumps in succession from the hills to the south. Tim began to count and we moved away from the window. There was a crashing rumble somewhere off to the east, then a trio of explosions much nearer.

At the instant the sounds reached our ears I had the distinct feeling, almost as tangibly as a light extinguished in the next room, that someone had died.

'That's down by the river,' said Tim, and we grabbed our things. We were directed to the Pul-i Khishti mosque, where a shell had landed in the courtyard during the midday prayers. Already the crowd which had gathered around the dead and injured had begun to disperse.

There was a shallow crater on a bloodstained flagstone, and all along the ground floor of the mosque the windows were shattered and spread in pools of shards and splinters on the carpets inside.

*

Ever since arriving in Kabul I had been disturbed by the apparent indifference of Afghans walking the streets to the sound of rockets fired in their direction. Often, hearing the ominous thumps from the south, I had tried to match their lack of reaction by forcing myself not to alter my pace, not to move closer to the protection of a wall, and not to count inwardly the seconds that remained before impact: all without success. It was a threshold I wanted to but had been unable to go beyond.

The opportunity came unexpectedly one afternoon. In the street were several young fighters who guarded a nearby house. They often saw me leave with my camera tucked under an arm, and would make clicking gestures and raise their hands questioningly. One day the light was perfect; I photographed them in turn. There was the usual problem; as soon as I put my eye behind the lens their expressions froze into stern intensity; as soon as the shutter had clicked they were all smiles again.

We made a group picture, a rifle was thrust into my hand, and one of them began focusing the camera at a crazy angle.

As we were arguing about who should stand where, there was a roaring sound that seemed to come from every direction at once, growing to a scream that made the ground tremble. A jet tore overhead, afterburners roaring, at attack speed. We scattered and crouched; the volume of sound was terrifying. By the time we had come to our senses we heard a deep, rolling explosion to the south, and knew a government jet had struck at an enemy position.

The sky seemed to stretch open with the noise of the engines. The jet pulled up steeply after the strike and looped back over the city, and as it roared upwards in an almost vertical climb we saw the wings flash in the sunlight as the pilot threw his craft into a trio of victory rolls. This was a provocative act of showmanship, and gave to the whole proceedings a quality not unlike a very violent game of tag. Sure enough, within a few seconds we heard the thump of retaliatory rockets fired towards the city from the hills.

'Get on with the pictures,' said one of the soldiers, seeing me back quietly towards a wall, counting to myself.

'But the rockets . . .'

'What's that to us?' he asked, with a deeply scornful grin.

'*Hīch gapi nīst*,' said another of them, waving a dismissive hand. 'Nothing to worry about.'

We had only a few seconds.

'Come on – take the pictures,' said one of the pair, their shoulders linked in readiness for the camera. They were all grinning broadly as the shock wave of the first exploding rocket, about a hundred and fifty yards away, rippled through our bodies. I flinched deeply. We were standing in the middle of the road, without the slightest protection.

'*Come ON – take the picture!*'

I forced the camera upwards and looked through a shaky viewfinder. There was a second detonation, like the fall of a heavy oak tree in a nearby street. And a third, as I drove myself to keep photographing. There were a few more thumps, further off now, and the danger passed. The boys patted me on the back in turn.

'See?' said one of them.

I felt the full exhilaration of having resisted the impulse to hide and give in to the fear. The reward was an immense feeling of freedom and lightness. From that day on I shared a special bond with the boys on that stretch of street and whenever we met, we greeted one another like old friends.

*

There were others who were more modest about their experiences, who bore it all much better, and whose commitment was greater.

Tom and Libby had lived in Kabul for years, part of an international team dedicated to treating ophthalmic disease all over the country. They were also deeply religious, and their dedication was nourished by their faith.

We had been invited one evening to their daughter's eighteenth birthday party. It was open house. We shed coats, hats and gloves on a voluminous pile, passed a candlelit Nativity scene that prompted a stab of homesickness, and went into a room full of people of every age. A young mother cradled a baby and one elderly American doctor reminded me of George Burns.

Here too we seemed to have slipped into another world, a kind of *Little House on the Prairie* transposed into a war-stricken setting without so much as a fraying at the edges. I found it very moving. Loved ones gathered around a piano and sang a birthday song, flanked by ladies holding oil lanterns and singing in tremulous voices: *'I shall climb every mountain ... ford every stream ... something something something ... follow my dream.'*

It sounded just like the trip to Panjshīr.

Tom and Libby were no crossroads preachers but hospitable and practical people, and in their conversation there was no trace of proselytizing. War or peace, Tom took his children on picnics to the interesting sites around Kabul, picking their way on occasion through unexploded bombs and mines to find the best spot in the shade of a Buddhist *stupa* or shrine. As we heaped our plates with pancakes and lashings of maple syrup, Tom recounted, with unassuming evenness, an incident from the week before that had our jaws dropping in both horror and mirth.

He had been driving through what we knew was a notoriously dangerous stretch of no-man's land south of the city, making deliveries of food and medicines to the needy. Politics not being the deciding factor, he weaved through the territory assessing the needs of both soldiers and civilians, and on both sides of the lines. On this particular day he came across a dead body blocking the road. Thinking he would deliver it to a nearby military post, he hoisted the corpse onto the roof of the jeep and drove on. On the way down a hill, his brakes failed, and he crashed into a bunker full of soldiers. As he was struggling to retrieve the corpse that had flown off the roof, a hilltop sniper shot through the windscreen of his vehicle. He ran inside the bunker for protection, but the soldiers, nervous at the attention drawn to their position by the jeep, insisted he remove the vehicle.

'I can't go out there,' he protested.

'Move your jeep,' replied the soldiers.

But the jeep refused to start; he ran inside again and, at gunpoint this time, was told to move his car. He had made it somehow – corpse and all – and nursed the jeep back to the city in low gear.

We knew how terrifying no-man's-land was. To go there voluntarily and regularly suggested an extraordinary confidence in the efficacy of prayer. His wife sighed affectionately at the tale, as if Tom were recounting the trials of his day at the office. Which, I suppose, he was.

After several more rounds of pancakes, we watched an episode of *Mr Bean*, and walked home through the powdery moonlight.

*

With Tim, the Agence France-Presse correspondent Mark Levine, and the English photographer Sam Faulkner, I went to a final party at the headquarters of the United Nations. At the door, an informative notice read: MINES AND BOMBS THREATEN YOUR SAFETY.

Here I fell into conversation with a softly spoken and articulate Englishman, one of only a handful of UN staff who had remained in Kabul during the fighting of the previous few years. We quickly discovered a mutual fascination for various little-known ancient sites in Afghanistan, as well as a reference we had both read to a village rumoured to lie near a pair of monumental stone reliefs in a remote part of the interior (this was Peter Levi's conjecture about Malminjak). That this was nothing more than a line in a specialist's book, and a speculation at that, gave our meeting a satisfying complicity. We agreed to meet the next day.

In the course of the usual merriment someone's chair broke underneath them, and they fell off. There followed a round of ironic jokes about the next day's news, describing the wounding of a UN staff member in Kabul. 'Peace talks collapse in Kabul' went one; 'UN calls for new Chair in Afghan negotiations' was another.

We were subscribed to a fraternity of fear, upon which all humour drew.

It was snowing heavily as we left. The wipers on the Land Rover struggled to clear the windscreen of thick, swooping flakes. We peered outwards, shivering, waiting for the shapes of soldiers to spring into the snow-streaked beam of the lights with their scream of challenge. When it came, Sam ducked onto the back seat, cursing volubly, while Tim and I feigned indifference to the rifles levelled at our heads. We passed clutches of cigarettes into the sentry's bare hands and were waved on. All I could think about at the time was the weather: if it was snowing in Kabul, it would be worse on the passes higher up.

*

I woke next morning to the sound of children's laughter beneath my window, and walked back to the UN. From the corner of the street the strings of a dozen kites were bowed in long arcs over the rooftops.

Jolyon Leslie had worked on and off in Afghanistan for nearly seven years and by his own account had loved every minute of it. He spoke fluent Persian and quietly eschewed the gatherings hosted by his colleagues, maintaining instead an active social life among Afghan friends. His reputation as a hermit had been undone when a fellow staff member knocked on his door one day ('Probably looking for beer,' he joked) and found the house full of Afghans and their children.

Among his official duties he monitored the protection of treasures from the Kabul museum. The story of the museum is one of the sadder in the history of the nation's heritage. Until a few years ago it was still one of the world's richest repositories of central Asian art and artefacts. The diversity of cultures nurtured on Afghan soil made its archaeology correspondingly unique, and since the museum's inauguration in 1924 its contents had been enriched yearly with incomparable finds.

By the time of the Soviet invasion the museum's treasures spanned forty thousands years of human endeavour; the oldest were Palaeolithic flint tools excavated in Badakhshān in the 1960s. The museum later became home to such matchless collections as the 2,000-piece hoard uncovered at Bagram, ancient Kapisa, the Kushan summer capital. Both in range and artistic level these artefacts told of an intensive and sustained period of exchange between East and West during the early centuries of the Christian era. The Bagram treasure included lacquered ornaments from China, Alexandrian glassware, Roman bronzes, and a series of exquisitely carved ivory panels from India. The museum also held one of the most extensive coin collections in the world: forty thousand specimens dating from the eighth century BC. Its shelves were lined with Graeco-Roman statuary in marble, Buddhist reliefs in schist and limestone, and hundreds of the very first representations of the Buddha in human form; evidence of that first and fertile fusion of Oriental and European artistic disciplines that flourished in the area for roughly the first six centuries AD. Later periods were represented by several thousand bronzes and ceramics from the Islamic dynasty of the Ghaznavids, carved wooden effigies from pre-Islamic Nuristan and, in the museum's library, more than two thousand rare volumes.

On a spring day of 1993, as fighting raged in the southwest of the capital, a rocket pierced the roof of the museum building and exploded, spreading a fire through the upper floors and engulfing countless artefacts in flame. A heroic effort to rescue the remaining treasures was organized by dedicated Afghans working under extremely dangerous conditions, and cases and crates of statues and coins were transferred to the vaults of the building. Over the following year, with the help of the United Nations, the rescued pieces were catalogued and sealed in metal storage cases, and the building's broken doors bricked up and padlocked. But subsequent visits revealed widespread looting; steel doors had been blown open with explosives and padlocks shot away, and by 1994 more than three-quarters of the museum's finest items had disappeared. The entire coin collection had been taken; the Bagram ivories were gone, and even a bas-relief depicting the Dipankara Buddha, one of the museum's heaviest pieces, had been mysteriously hauled away.

The disappearance of so many priceless artefacts was generally blamed on the mujaheddin, but the thefts suggested a degree of discrimination improbable among unlettered fighters. The treasures were undoubtedly seized on behalf of well-informed art dealers both in Pakistan and further afield: ten Bagram ivories are known to have been offered for sale in Islamabad for a quarter of a million pounds; Buddhist statues are rumoured to have found their way to Japan, and Islamic coins to Middle Eastern collectors. A third-century Gandaran sculpture was claimed, by the Afghan archaeologist who later recognized it as one of his own excavations, to be sitting behind a glass case at the Metropolitan Museum in New York.

'We spent a fortune de-mining the area,' said Jolyon, as we talked about the museum's fate. 'But now I wish we'd left the mines in the ground. *That* would have discouraged the dealers.' He regretted that we couldn't visit the museum; for the moment it was simply too dangerous.

I shared with him my hopes for travelling west, and he gave me the name of an Afghan friend in a village along the way, together with a letter of introduction. One of his staff drew a rough map of the village, wrote the name of the headman, and underneath, lest I lose my way, penned the words: 'ASK FROM ANY ONE.'

It was one more of many unexpected kindnesses.

*

I went to Amrullah to ask about the military flight to Chaqcheran. He was in his office with another Afghan, and broke off his conversation to tell me the news wasn't good: the weather had not improved, there were no lights on the runway, and no radar. On top of this, there was now a risk of interception by fighters from Dostum's air force in the north.

It had been a nice offer, and I thanked him. I would have to try the overland route.

'I have been to Ghor,' said the other man, oracle-like, and in English. 'It is very high.' His eyes rolled upwards towards cloud-wreathed summits, then descended with a faint smile. 'And I think you cannot go there.'

'Why not?'

'There is ... no *oxygen*.'

*

Tim bore his dysentery stoically. He was coming to the end of his assignment in Kabul and news of his transfer had just been confirmed by his bureau chief. He was heartbroken to be leaving and the prospect of abandoning his staff after nearly two years, at such an unhappy juncture in the city's fate, weighed heavily on him.

He had bought a bottle of whisky, rumour of which had spread at incredible speed, and with the other correspondents and two visiting journalists we gathered one evening for a ritual imbibing. We swapped stories with the usual irreverence, while in a corner of the room, Jān stoked the stove with cupfuls of diesel and watched us silently.

On the couch lay one of Tim's favourite souvenirs: a Russian tank-driver's flak jacket, lined with bullet-proof ceramic pads. He made a show of putting it on — it weighed a good thirty pounds — and wondered if he should wear it for the flight back home.

'It'll look a bit odd at those posh dinner parties back in London,' I suggested.

'And they'll think you're pretty strange when you take your shoes off outside the door!' somebody added, with a guffaw. This, after all, was the custom. But transposed into the world of home nothing could have seemed more comic.

The whisky was broached and trickled into a wide clamour of glasses. Tim confessed to the fantasy of having a dinner jacket made from camouflage material, immaculately cut, by one of the tailors in Chicken Street.

'Lined with fat-tailed sheepskin,' he mused. 'They'd do it too, for fifty thousand Afs . . .' He shifted the metal plates of armour across his chest as he poured another round.

'Might be useful when you're checking for mines in the garden!'

'Pity your girlfriend!' quipped someone else. Then in a squeaky voice: 'Don't worry darling, there *are* no mines on Clapham Common!'

He poured a third round into our eager glasses. We would be sad to see him leave. His longing to return to a familiar world, and his dread of it, were ours too. We could see ourselves, in time, getting to grips with the same fate. But there are few greater pleasures than mocking the affliction of a friend, and on empty stomachs our lust for the incongruous took immodest flight.

We tried to picture him back in England, the celebrity guest at genteel dinners, and worked ourselves into fits of laughter at the image of this brave man, fresh from the anarchy of the front lines around Kabul, surrounded now by dreary *objets d'art* under fastidiously adjusted lighting, sitting in his flak jacket before the ranks of silverware and cut glass, and trying to follow the inanities of polite conversation: the latest gallery openings, the fickle fundraisings, film premieres, and restaurant reservations proudly made months in advance; the hollow compliments, the fifth-hand speculations, the intimate details of celebrities nobody had met or ever would, the timid platitudes that passed for the philosophical . . . and saw him, tucking his shoeless feet under him on his chair, thrusting his bare hand into the steaming serving dishes, wiping his face on a pressed damask napkin and passing it, Afghan fashion, to his horrified neighbour. Then, amid the speculative, hushed asides, he would reach into a pocket and draw out a half-pound block of cannabis, quietly softening a corner in the flame of a candle ...

'He's been in — *Afghanistan.*'

'You know — went a bit native.'

And then he would have to answer the daring enquiry from some ultra-knowledgeable soul:

'So how is Ka-*bull*? Did you meet lots of tribesmen? Weren't you afraid of a ritual castration? Did you have to eat a sheep's eye? And why *are* the *muja-heja-hajji-din* always fighting?'

We imagined, through eyes now watering with laughter, some well-intentioned friend approaching his house along a quiet English drive-way, and Tim springing from the bushes with a shotgun — he leaped up from the couch in imitation of a soldier at a checkpoint, with a scream of challenge that had us rolling on the floor — and thrusting the barrel into the terrified driver's face: 'THE PASSWORD! WHAT'S THE FUCKING PASSWORD?'

Back amid the tranquillity of English life he would hear a door slam and roll at lightning speed from his bed away from the window, counting the seconds ... ('It's just the postman, darling ...') and would stop in garages to ask if the price of diesel was up or down, if the road to London was safe, whether it was clear of mines, and how many checkpoints there were between Golders Green and Hampstead; whether the basement was adequately supplied in case of heavy attack; whether the bathtub was full of clean water — and we pictured the expressions at the supermarket checkout as he tried to bargain over the final price of his shopping.

'That's my very last offer,' Tim called out in mockery of himself, 'I'll give you ten quid for the lot. And no *bakhsheesh*!'

By now our ribs were aching.

'And don't forget,' said someone amid the guffaws, 'if you see a foreigner on the street—' we were quite raucous by now, 'to ask him to COME HOME FOR A MEAL AND MEET YOUR FAMILY!'

There was another parliamentary explosion of laughter.

'You'd get punched in the face.'

'They'd lock you up,' I said.

I reached out instinctively, hearing the ring of bottle against glass, and looked up to see Jān, who had been sitting silently all the while in the far corner of the room. His smile had followed, uncomprehendingly, the rise and fall of our mirth; several times I had caught the image of his face in the window, and wondered what he must be making privately of our laughter. But as I looked over to him I saw the face of an unhappy man.

✳

Later I told Tim about my travel plans.

'Leave a trail of some kind,' he said. 'In case.'

At night I wrote by the light of a single candle, fully clothed inside my sleeping bag, listening to the thumps from the mountains and the rustle of the plastic over the window frames, which like an eardrum ballooned inwards under the shock wave of each explosion. It was strange to hear death making its rounds over the sleeping city; stranger still, it seemed, that the sound of it had become normal. Years before, when from fifty miles away I had sat at the mouth of our cave and watched the artillery cascading into the mountains around Kabul, I had so often wondered who was firing at whom, what their thoughts were, when they slept and where their homes were. Now I wondered the same things, only without the same sense of awe. It was a different conflict since I had first encountered it. It was no longer a guerrilla war against a single occupying force, no longer a struggle of reckless enthusiasm against an unequivocally cruel invader; Afghans were now fighting Afghans for their own ruined capital, cowering in trenches against the obliterating thump of shells.

I had one final wish before I left: to meet the man who, ten years earlier, had arranged my first trip to Afghanistan. Khalili, it was said, had recently returned to Kabul, and I went on foot to find his father's house in a district called Taimāneh. On occasion such foolhardy forays were accomplished, with the help of enthusiastic locals, in record time. But I walked for hours, asking directions in shops and from passers-by, without success.

At a crossroads I caught sight of a pair of men directing traffic, and approached them hopefully. They wore traffic police caps, trench-coats of heavy felt, and from their shoulders dangled Second World War machine guns. They greeted me warmly but looked me up and down as though I had arrived from a different planet. Their tone was kindly but their manner was what Americans call intellectually chal-lenged. I asked for directions to Taimāneh.

'Aren't you a foreigner?'

'I am.'

'Then where is your car?'

'I haven't got a car,' I said.

'You're a foreigner, so you must have a car.'

'Not all foreigners have cars.'

'By Allah, yes they do.'

'By Allah, they do not.'

'Then how did you get here?'

'I walked.'

'You cannot have walked. You are a foreigner. You must have driven.'

I gave up. Cold and tired, I trudged back to the house. But on the way, seeing men at prayer on dusty patches of verge and in their shabby courtyards, my sense of despair was gently lifted. It was dusk. As the day drew its final breath the air seemed suddenly pregnant with a peculiar animation. I felt a surge of that sense of well-being which had crept its way so improbably into the heart of things, a light where I had expected darkness, against which all the troubles and chaos of the place, which weighed so heavily at times, seemed no more than a thin disguise beyond which a great spring of life continued to flow unrestrained. More than ever I felt tremendously privileged by being alive and healthy, and walked home with the thrill of having received an unexpected gift.

The darkness came down like a curtain; the dusk was drawn into the night, and the men at prayer disappeared like extinguished candles.

*

I found Khalili the next day, having got better directions in advance. He was looking older, and slightly stooped. He was nearly fifty by now, I guessed. Yet I would probably always remember him as the debonair Afghan whom I had first met on a sweltering afternoon in Peshawar more than ten years before. He had offered me a Dunhill as I sat down, and listened to the hopes of a nineteen-year-old boy with a sympathetic enthusiasm that I had never forgotten.

Bowing gently, he showed me indoors. We went upstairs and were brought tea in a room with tall windows that looked out to the north. I commented on the view; he joked that in New York he had stayed in a hotel where they had wanted to charge him an extra two hundred dollars for a view of Central Park.

'Here we have the view for free,' he mused.

I reminded him of the details of our first meeting. The encounter had remained as vivid to me as the events of yesterday. To enter Afghanistan with the mujaheddin had seemed something beyond the reach of my dreams; I had been utterly thrilled when he had turned to me and said with a smile: 'Don't worry, I'll arrange your trip as soon as possible. Everything will be all right.'

'I remember now,' he said, nodding slowly. 'I thought you were very young. But what could I say to a nineteen-year-old boy? I couldn't say no.'

It would have been easy for a man of his privileges to turn his back on the war and begin a more comfortable life elsewhere. He remained political officer for the resistance and had been a favourite link for foreigners trying to enter Afghanistan with the mujaheddin.

After the war he had followed in his father's footsteps as a diplomat. Recent troubles had found him expelled from Pakistan and obliged to return, gratefully I sensed, to his family home in the beleaguered capital.

I asked him about some of the difficult moments since that time. Two came immediately to mind. The first was in 1992 when the communists, abandoned by a crumbling Soviet Union, had finally relinquished power in Kabul. In the north they handed over their garrisons and airfields to Massoud and his commanders, and thousands of men who had lived for years as fugitives in their own country prepared to enter the capital. A struggle for the final prize began to loom, polarized around the forces of Massoud on one side and those of Hekmatyar on the other.

'It needn't have happened,' said Khalili. 'Massoud begged him not to turn Kabul into a battlefield.' They had talked for half an hour by radio, he said, and the conversation had been recorded. But Hekmatyar had refused to share power with his old rival and prepared to advance into the city, where Massoud decided to meet him for the fight.

For the few days leading up to the battle an air of suspense hung over the city. The government had collapsed, the mujaheddin were closing in, and the outcome was far from certain. At the time, having long ago promised myself to return to Afghanistan for the fall of Kabul, I had thrown up everything and headed back, managing at the last minute to hitch a ride on a flight into the city from the north. I joined a convoy of helicopter gunships crammed with men, guns and rockets, which swooped into Kabul at nightfall as the opposing armies locked into battle, sending fountains of tracer bullets cascading into the sky in every direction.

There were several days of intense conflict in and around the city until Hekmatyar's troops, out-gunned and out-manoeuvred, were pushed further and further south. After the battle had subsided it did just seem possible that a new era had begun. Correspondents flying out of the city from the still-smoking airport terminal wrote of the takeover as a virtually closed case. The city was calm and it was spring, and for the first time mujaheddin and government soldiers walked side by side in the streets, and families were reunited with long-exiled relatives. There was astonishingly little vengeance towards those who had worked under the communists. Senior officials who had most to fear from the mujaheddin had slipped away in preceding weeks, to be given asylum later in European countries where nothing was known of their criminal pasts. The notable exception was the President, Dr Najibullah, who was also the former head of the deeply hated secret police. He was intercepted and held at the airport, and later detained in a UN building in the city; rumour had it he was working on his memoirs.

I remembered sharing, as much as an outsider could, the enormous feeling of both promise and suspense on the city's streets. For the first time it looked as though the country had been granted a chance to heal from years of war. No one could have predicted that the most savage chapter in Kabul's history was about to begin; it was then that rockets began to pour into the city from the south, levelling entire suburbs. Uncounted numbers of civilians died and Kabul, having survived ten years of war relatively unscathed, began to be devoured alive.

'That was when things started to go wrong,' said Khalili with a bitter look, 'when Pakistan felt it was losing control. We became very isolated. In the cold war if you were against Russia you could count on American support. But look what happened afterwards!'

This was the second time, he said, when everything seemed to hang in the balance. It was 1994. Kabul had become the meeting point of three savage and roving front lines. The Shī'ite forces under Mazāri controlled the west, Hekmatyar's the south, and Dostum's the north and east.

No doubt there were other versions, but it was a dramatic story: with their enemies closing in from all sides and running perilously short of ammunition, the government hung by a thread. Their positions raked with gunfire, Massoud's commanders were radioing their leader with increasingly desperate reports.

'He was incredible,' said Khalili. 'It looked completely hopeless. But this was Massoud –' he leaned towards me now – 'when everyone else saw only their own position, he saw the whole picture. He gave orders to each of the commanders in turn, told us not to worry and that the outcome was in God's hands. We said our prayers and he went to sleep. He just closed his eyes and slept. And the next morning we were in control, just as he predicted.'

But there was a bitter note to the tale.

'My God! We had the Americans against us in Pakistan, Uzbekistan against us in the north, and Iran against us from the west. Was a country ever so isolated? It was a unique situation. But we have come out of it.'

Now once again the city's fate seemed to hang in the balance. With so much talk of outside influence, or at least approval, behind recent events, I asked if he thought it was really American policy to support the Tālebān.

'To be optimistic, I would call it *lack* of policy,' he said, 'but I suspect it is policy. On the other hand I think America recognizes the Tālebān can never rule Afghanistan. Afghanistan cannot be ruled from outside the country.' Then he added, half to himself: 'It is *completely* impossible.' The thump of an exploding shell rattled the windows, and he sighed heavily.

We moved gratefully away from politics, and talked a little about poetry. His father, in a very Afghan combination of talents, had been both a diplomat and the country's poet laureate.

'Afghans love poetry,' he said, adding that during the war he and Massoud had in their spare time often read poetry together, and that Massoud himself had expressed a longing to leave the war behind, to head into the mountains and simply devote his time to reading the works of the nation's great poets.

Now, if things allowed, he had a dream of building a house to the north of Kabul and settling down, and of getting back to the education the war had denied him. He reached over and put his hand on a heavy book which lay on a small table next to his chair.

'For fifteen years I have hardly had a moment to read,' he said, and picked up the volume. It was the *Tāj-e Tawārīkh* of the Amir Abdur Rahman, the first of Afghanistan's rulers to forge a nation out of the patchwork of kingdoms that made up his territories.

'Now the same task faces us.'

Was there anything he could do for me? he asked. I told him about my plans, and he reminded me of the weather and the hazards in general of heading into the centre of the country.

'It will be dangerous,' he said, 'but I can see you have made up your mind.' He smiled. It was the same smile I had seen more than a decade before. I felt a profound sense of completion, as if the loose end of a decade-long circle of experience had finally been drawn into place.

'Well,' he added, 'risk is risk. I wish you luck.'

I went home and spread out my maps.

Nine

I remember thinking we were as remote from the world then as we should ever be in our lives.

Peter Levi, *The Light Garden of the Angel King*

CIRCUMSTANCE HAD MADE the choice of road relatively easy. The roads to the south and east were blocked by fighting; the famous Salang Pass, which was the main route to the north, closed.

With a finger I traced the main route leading west on the map. It led north from Kabul for about thirty-five miles, then turned west through a breach in the Grandfather range and followed the winding course of the Ghorband river. Beyond the village of Ghorband, it thinned to a track and began to fissure and wave like a thread suspended in a breeze. Seventy miles or so from the first westward fork it came to Bamiyan, home of the largest carved Buddhas in the world. I couldn't follow it much further on the maps; it carved its way through what appeared to be narrow gorges and wound over passes more than ten thousand feet high.

What a road! It was sometimes called the central route, and was said to be passable in a sturdy vehicle, but only under ideal conditions.*

---

* A pre-war edition of Fodor's guide to Afghanistan counsels those tempted by *la route du centre*: '*Si vous êtes plein d'ardeur et d'audace, si vous avez surtout de temps, et si vous êtes en possession d'une véhicule rompu à toute épreuve, si vous êtes équippé pour faire face à de nombreuses crevaisons, si vouz êtes frugal, si votre sommeil peut se satisfaire d'un confort très relatif, bref, si vous êtes prêt à tout…* (Providing you are full of both enthusiasm and daring, if above all you have plenty of time, if you possess a vehicle capable of standing up to the ultimate challenge, if you are ready to deal with numerous flat tyres, if you are frugal, if you don't mind sleeping under very relative conditions of comfort, basically, if you are ready for anything …)' Even the habitually stoical Nancy Hatch Dupree waxes poetic in her description of some of the more treacherous stages: 'Chances are that once you are in the canyon you will meet no living soul to

It led past the famous megalithic Buddhas, beside the unearthly-coloured lakes of Band-e Amīr, wound through the remote provincial centre of Chaqcherān, continued west past the solitary minaret of Jām, and on towards the hot springs of Obeh and the shrines of Chisht-i Sharīf, before emerging finally on the plain east of Herat.

Nobody I had asked had the slightest idea whether it was passable. It was not much further than a hundred miles from Kabul to Bamiyan but asking about the conditions on the way was like asking a Londoner the state of affairs in the Hebrides. Somewhere too, at a point I was unable to discover, a front line divided the territory under direct government control from that of the Hazārajat, the central region occupied by Hazāra fighters. There was word of a truce, but not much more.

The Soviets had maintained a small garrison there during the war but the region had known little military action. They kept their soldiers out of the mountains and seldom engaged its defenders, who had a reputation for fierceness. Yet the story of the Hazāra populations of Afghanistan is, of all its peoples, perhaps the least known.* Only now are accounts of their history, written not by the official Afghan historians of the past but by Hazāras themselves, beginning to appear.

Two factors explain much of their relative obscurity: their physical appearance and their religion. There is a variety of theories about their origins. One is the commonly accepted notion that the Hazāras are the bloodthirsty descendants of Chingiz Khan himself. Another puts forward the notion of autochthonicity; that as a people they have lived in the region at least since the time of Alexander, are descended from Turkic central Asian stock, and are in fact one of the nation's earliest original groups, the influence of Moghul blood being a

---

offer succour ... Proceed, therefore, knowing that you have been warned ... I am reluctant to recommend this route without grave reservations.' *An Historical Guide to Afghanistan*, rev., ed. published 1977 by the Afghan Tourist Board.

* A Christian Evangelical database lists the Hazāras as among the 'Top 100 Most Unreached' ethnic groups of the world, and invites prayers on their behalf.

relatively recent implantation. But all the country's ethnic groups made this assertion: I couldn't think of one that did not claim for itself the status of Afghanistan's true, oldest and one-and-only indigenous population.

Another theory, based mainly on linguistics, puts forward the Hazāras as a mixed race of Turkic, Moghul and Persian origin. Each argument has its own logic and its own proofs. What is more certain is that the Hazārajat, the knotted central mass of the country bordered very approximately by Bamiyan in the east, Sar-e Pol in the north, Chesht-i Sharīf in the west and Oruzgan in the south, remained a virtually autonomous state until the end of the nineteenth century.

Allied to an almost impregnable natural setting, the region's independence remained unbroken by successive efforts of Pashtun monarchs in Kabul. Then came the Amir Abdur Rahman: an accomplished soldier, dedicated autocrat, and committed to a grandiose vision of unifying the territories under his arc of control. All the force of the Amir's ambition, frustrated in the north by Russia and in the south by the British, was focused mercilessly on everything in between. The continuing independence of the Hazārajat was considered an intolerable threat to central government, and lenience was not Abdur Rahman's guiding principle. The memory of his purges still evokes bitter memories among virtually every ethnic group in Afghanistan.

The subjugation of the Hazārajat became the most extensive campaign of his rule. Disunity among the various Hazāra tribes was at first exploited peacefully, with special allowances for sympathetic tribal leaders and tributes paid to the capital in exchange for continuing independence. But a series of rebellions broke the Amir's patience. He declared the Hazāras infidels and introduced crippling punitive taxes throughout Hazāra territories. The traditional systems of rule and property ownership were gradually dismantled, and large areas of land were confiscated and given to Pashtun nomads with government support. Hazāra leaders, both religious and tribal, were imprisoned or stripped of their powers and replaced with Pashtun governors loyal to the king.

This was a violent and drawn-out process. There were widespread and bloody uprisings, and in the final decade of the nineteenth century the Amir's army was fighting its bitterest campaign. A hundred thousand government soldiers, the largest force ever gathered in the Amir's reign, were employed to crush resistance in the Hazārajat; feeding such numbers along hazardous supply lines disrupted the economy of the entire nation.

Against superiority in firepower and organization the resisters could not hold out, and by the turn of the century the domination of the Hazārajat was virtually attained. Subsequent unrest was dealt with heavily by means of executions, deportations and imprisonments. The Hazāras became the pariahs of the nation; thousands were sold as slaves to ruling families, and the story of their subjugation was swept into a corner of history.

During the final period of British intervention in Afghanistan, Hazāra leaders looked upon the British as potential allies in the ongoing reshuffling of power. The British, for their part, looked favourably on the Hazāras for their own reasons, and in preparation for a third assault on Afghanistan the 106th Hazāra Pioneers, a battalion of eight companies, was raised at the request of Lord Kitchener. The alliance ended when a war-weary Britain cut its losses in the region and agreed to permanent borders in the north and south of the country, and the social and economic deprivation of the Hazārajat continued. Members of the Pioneers are said to have fought with distinction in France after the breakout of the First World War, as well as in Kurdistan, Baghdad and North Africa.

There was a new twist to the plot under communist rule. The Hazāras were held up as model underdogs of Afghanistan's ancient regime, and granted privileges previously unthinkable. Pashtun nomads were expelled from the Hazārajat. Several ambitious Hazāras rose to positions of influence in the government, while large numbers of Hazāra families took sanctuary in Kabul, where their population grew to a greater concentration than ever before, predominantly in the western suburbs.

During the Soviet occupation, although there is ample evidence of a high level of organization, discipline and determination in their fight against their occupiers, they were poorly represented in the so-called alliance of mujaheddin parties in Pakistan, and regarded as heretics by such unforgiving leaders as Hekmatyar.

Yet after a century of repression, by 1994 they were one of the three main contenders for the capital. The leader of the Hazāra resistance even joined forces with the Tālebān against the government, but in a bitter turn of fortune was taken prisoner, tortured and killed along with his senior commanders. Their forces retired to Bamiyan under a new leader, and made their peace with the government.

Today the Hazāras have emerged from all the upheavals of the century as one of the key forces in the jigsaw of power.

'*Shisha ke maida shod, tiztar misha,*' runs a Hazāra proverb: broken glass becomes sharper.

*

Today the central highlands of Afghanistan remain, along with the wilder regions of Nuristan, the least explored portion of the country. Beyond Bamiyan the twisting route is guarded by more than thirty passes with an average height of ten thousand feet and whose names still retain an ancient ring of caution for would-be transgressors: Shotorkhūn, Camel's blood; Ghazzaq, Swollen Wound; Dandān Shekān, Toothbreaker; Kirmū, Worm-eaten; Talkhao, Bitter water.

Bābur himself describes crossing through the centre of Ghor on the route from Chaqcherān to Yakaulang in the winter of 1506. Their guide lost the road, the snow was up to their waists, and men and animals perished. On reaching safety he describes the 'passing from distress to ease and from suffering to enjoyment' as one of the most intense experiences of his enormously eventful life, one 'that can be conceived only by such as have suffered similar hardships or endured such heavy distresses'.

Today's historical knowledge of the almost roadless mountain-world falters like a lost flock in one of its own unmapped ravines. It was sparked off in earnest as late as 1957, when a pilot flying east from Herat noticed what looked like a smokestack in the valley of the Hari Rud. Unknowingly he had glimpsed the second highest ancient tower in the world, a twelfth-century marvel dedicated commemoratively to the enigmatic Ghorid king Ghiyathuddin, the 'minaret of Jām' was, as Western archaeologists would have it, 'discovered'.*

The minaret rises to a dizzy 213 feet from the perilously eroded south bank of the Hari Rud, just where it is joined by the river Jām. Its giant structure resembles a collapsible telescope, fallen to Earth from the lap of a careless god. From its fifty-foot octagonal base to the arcade of arches that make the summit, it is intensively decorated with panels of baked brick. Early visits to the site by knowledgeable types at once prompted contentious speculation (normal for archaeologists, perhaps; almost inevitable for archaeologists in Afghanistan) as to its significance and choice of location.

If the structure was truly a minaret, then where was the mosque to which it had once been attached? What, for example, explained the choice of the 19th *sura* of the Qur'ān, *Maryam*, dedicated to Mary and the Virgin Birth, to be wound around its corbelled balconies a hundred feet from the ground in turquoise enamelled glaze? What forgotten community buried their dead in the twelfth-century Jewish cemetery discovered nearby? Nothing has yet explained the tower's isolation from any known centre of population. If, as its bold inscriptions set a hundred feet from the ground assert, the prayer of Islam was proclaimed in the name of the king of Ghor from northern India to Babylonia and from the Oxus to the straits of Hormuz, where was his kingdom?

How, out of the awesome fastnesses of tottering rock and cliff-

---

* Only the Qutb Minar in Delhi, inspired by its lonely Afghan predecessor, is higher, by twenty feet. There are different versions of the 'discovery'; the flight mentioned in Freya Stark's book on Afghanistan (*The Minaret of Djam: an excursion in Afghanistan*, London: John Murray, 1970) was more likely to have confirmed what was already known. News of the minaret was first officially announced by the governor of Herat in 1943. That it took fifteen years to organize a trip to the site is the best indication of its accessibility. Peter Levi calls it 'that mountain unicorn among Islamic monuments'. There were once even more grandiose precedents in the region. The stupa of King Kanishka (third century AD) was a pagoda-like structure of thirteen floors atop a five-storey stone tower; it is estimated to have topped six hundred feet. Its foundations were excavated in 1908 in Peshawar.

shadowed torrents, was the empire that conquered India sustained? Was it yet to be found or did some unimaginable cataclysm remove all trace of its capital, Firuzkoh, the Turquoise Mountain? How Robert Byron, with his passion for towers, would have loved the place.

A few ruined clifftop forts have been examined in the vicinity of the great minaret, but nothing has been found on a scale to suggest the lost city where, according to Juzjani, the inlaid pinnacles of the palace protected golden statues of *humae* birds as large as camels, and where the mosque held a pair of golden kettledrums transported from the pillaged Indian capital. Years from now this site too will be 'discovered' and locals will scratch their heads at the attention given to the ruins they played among in childhood.

*

I left Kabul in an old taxi, to the sound of rockets falling into the city a quarter of a mile away. It crept towards the *sarāye shomāli*, the northern jumping-off point of the city, above which the road began to rise towards the Khairkhaneh pass. The driver pointed me to a gap between some shopfronts; beyond it was a broad open square hemmed in by stalls, *chaikhānas*, and cargo containers converted into workshops and garages. It was filled with the noise of shouts, engines and blaring horns. Cars and trucks seemed to be coming and going in every direction. I had found the bus station.

Afghan buses are full of character, and are fastidiously maintained by the men who risk their lives daily by driving them. They run until they disintegrate, after which they are frequently reborn in mutated incarnations, their various parts salvaged from scrapyards and lovingly reassembled. Loose bodywork is reinforced with riveted sheet metal. There was one bus with its engine housing built entirely from timber, and the frame of was another patched with strips of Russian field runway. I once saw a bus in a Kabul street that had been run over by a tank. 'We'll have it back on the road in a few days,' joked the undaunted owner.

Floral ironwork, with more whorls than a Provençale bell-tower, decorates rear windows, or is welded to roofs to serve as an anchor for mountains of luggage. Sometimes chains and metal pendants, which jangle musically with a rocking chassis – the modern vestiges, perhaps, of the caravan's camel bells – are draped on their sides in the manner of a necklace. Fertility symbols – a pair of fishes is the most common motif – are stitched into the leather of radiator-grille covers. Buses as well as trucks are often lovingly painted. I saw several idyllic alpine scenes, complete with Swiss chalets and cotton-wool clouds; others bore images of budgerigars, leaping lions and moonlit water-gardens, and above their windscreens in big multicoloured letters: 'Hero Bus', 'Welcome to Bus', 'Modern Bus', 'King of the Road', 'Good Your Journey', or 'We Trust In God'. Always the driver's cockpit is festooned with tassels, tinsel, extra mirrors and plastic flowers, stickers of eyes, the slender hand of a woman, cars and animals. Each has a talismanic and protective significance, as does the traditional religious paraphernalia of dangling pendants carved in the name of God, the Prophet, and his Caliphs, and stick-on verses of the Qur'ān or pictures of the Ka'bah at Mecca.

Sometimes the destinations are painted on the sides of the buses; more often you listen for the voice of a driver shouting out the name of the place you are going. There is no schedule; the bus leaves when the driver decides it is full enough. Even as it pulls away the driver's teenage accomplice hangs from the wing mirror yelling the destination in the hope of sweeping up a few extra passengers.

I found a minibus heading to Jebel as-Serāj, about fifty miles to the north. It was a slower journey than I had expected and I dozed off. By the time we arrived it was already quite dark. The passengers dispersed with the usual speed and I found myself alone in a dusty square overlooked by run-down wooden buildings. It was cold and completely silent. Already Kabul felt worlds away. I caught sight of a boy walking between the houses, and asked for the road to Gulbahār.

'It's that way,' he replied, pointing towards a break in the buildings where a fork led east. 'But it's dark,' he added, with the phrase I had so often heard: 'Amniyat nist, it's not safe.' Then he disappeared into the shadows.

In the darkness it would be impossible to find the address I had been given in Kabul. I climbed a flight of wooden steps into a chaikhāna, where inside a single man was tending to a stove, and in the corner of the room on a raised dais two teenage boys were drinking tea. We sat in silence for a while until, as some plates of food arrived, the boys invited me to join them.

Seeing how poor they were I refused as gently as possible, but we sat together and got talking. They didn't see many foreigners, they said; foreigners didn't come to Afghanistan any more. Conversation led to the old sentiment that the *Amerikha* had said they would help rebuild Afghanistan after the war, but never did. I replied, only half-believing myself, that they and others wanted genuinely to help, but only once there was peace; yes, they said, that was understandable.

The communist leaders Taraki, Amin and Najibullah – and even the King, they said – had been no more than profiteers. Afghanistan was rich in natural resources, with its own supplies of oil, gas and minerals, but what had their so-called leaders done to allow ordinary Afghans to benefit from them? Anyway – what was I doing here, and so far from home?

I explained I was hoping to get to Gulbahār. They looked at each other and grinned: 'Not at this hour you're not.'

I took their advice to stay, and one of them got up without my asking, went across the street, and returned with a helping of hot rice for me. They were gentle and softly spoken young men; one of them had no work, and was heading to the north to try his luck; the other sold diesel at a garage in Kabul. Times were hard; the owner of the *chaikhāna*, they said, earned the equivalent of a dollar a day.

When I made known my intention to travel west towards Bamiyan, they looked genuinely worried and told the most fearful tales about the Hazāras.

'They cut people's throats,' said one of them, 'and rob them as they bleed to death.'

'They take the skin off their enemies,' said the other, 'and eat their flesh.'

The owner of the place, hearing this, looked up and said solemnly: 'The Hazāras are not Moslems.'

I laughed this off cheerfully, but their faces were serious.

*

In the morning the owner refused all payment, and the boys walked me a mile to the address I had been given by Jolyon. The morning sparkled with coldness in the winter sun. We came to a cluster of homes, and saw a turbaned patriarch tethering a horse outside a stable.

'There he is,' said one of them, 'that's Hajji.'

The old man turned and I introduced myself. The moment I mentioned Jolyon's name he broke into a radiant smile and hugged me with the usual spine-crushing force. I said goodbye to the boys, and Hajji swept me towards the inner courtyard of his home, barking commands to baffled family members like a general to his couriers. I felt my pack lifted from my shoulders and was ushered into a room. We swapped the usual courtesies and news and Hajji folded my letter on United Nations stationery reverently into a pocket.

Feigning outrage at hearing I had spent the previous night in a common resthouse, he fired a volley of orders to a grandson. A thermos of tea and a bucket of hot water soon appeared, and I had the luxury of an hour's privacy in the visitors' quarters, a spacious building at the far end of his compound. Hajji returned and we sat in the sun together on the porch. He produced one of those viewers like a pair of binoculars and inserted a disk of miniature transparencies. They were a souvenir of his pilgrimage to Mecca.

'Ah, the Nimrah mosque at Arafat,' I observed, 'the Hajar ul Aswad, the Ka'bah...'

He was visibly moved by my familiarity with the holy sites. Realizing he could not read the English names printed in tiny letters beneath the images, I felt a twinge of shame at the subterfuge.*

At midday I followed him to his home, and was shown into a long room at the opposite end of a large courtyard. Twenty other men, to whom I was introduced in turn, filed inside and sat down to lunch. Was this the normal state of affairs? I wondered. Did Hajji eat with these men every day? Had they been summoned specially? I hoped not. Platter after platter of food arrived; we began with a selection of

---

* Hajji, I now hear, has left his home, which was destroyed when Gulbahār became a new front line between the former government and the Tāleban. Now the account of my stay there seems unavoidably frivolous.

pickles, followed by pumpkin and sour cream, then a variety of *pilau*; my plate was kept continually piled by an attentive neighbour.

Over tea and sugardusted pastries there was long and leisurely talk, into which I was politely drawn by Hajji himself.

We began with the usual generalities; were the UN going to mediate in the current crisis? Many thought that would be a good thing. What was my view of the situation? The laughter was unrestrained when, gesturing to the surroundings and the level of hospitality, I mentioned that I had been assured that in Afghanistan I would meet only *wakhshi* men – desperadoes and warriors. Gradually the conversation narrowed, like a wedge driving into the practical heart of things. How many wives was I allowed to keep in England? What was the cost of wheat? How far did the shot of a twelve-bore spread at twenty yards? When I next came to Afghanistan, would I be able to bring back a shotgun from England?

Hajji's son, a sad-looking man of about forty, took me under his wing. We went for a walk around the village with his seven-year-old daughter, who skipped along the dusty lanes ahead of us.

It was very beautiful. I should have come in the spring, he said, when the fruit trees were in blossom. He greeted other villagers as they passed. Then we sat for a while and watched some boys playing volleyball as the sun began to slip from the gilded mountains. We put our heads into the village mill, a tiny building above a stream where two old men were feeding corn and wheat into huge millstones. Then on the outskirts of the village he pointed out a solidly built structure with high walls. This was the military post where he had served during the war. I had guessed since first seeing him that he had been a soldier; he had that unmistakable look of trauma in his eyes.

'There was a lot of fighting,' he said as I looked up to the watchtowers, and he mentioned that the Russians had treated Afghan soldiers like prisoners and hardly fed them. He looked so miserable at the recollection it felt wrong to ask more.

*

I was looking forward to resting. A strange pain in my joints had worsened and was draining me of energy. My knees and hips ached painfully and I longed more than anything to lie down. When we returned to the house, Hajji's son watched over me with intimidating thoroughness, which had a counterproductive result. Then we were joined by two other young men; one of them had brought a portable radio and began exploring every signal he could find, at full volume, repeating the process on different bands.

A new round of questioning began; less formal and inhibited now, and more relentless. I found it an enormous mental effort to keep up with them. There was hardly a single question I could adequately answer: what was my wife doing at that very moment? How much was a kilowatt of electricity in England? Would I be able to sell Afghan jewellery back in London?

They had a tendency to raise their voices in proportion to my difficulty in understanding. Before long there were two of them shouting at me from either side. The radio was turned up to full volume and was blaring strange music on a wavering signal, and I had a splitting headache.

'YOU DON'T WANT US TO GO AWAY SO YOU CAN RELAX, DO YOU?' yelled one of them.

The whole thing was so transparently good-natured I was too ashamed to say yes. When I felt myself about to collapse I mentioned finally that, after all, it had been a long day, and within minutes they dispersed.

*

Blissfully alone, I smoked a cigarette on the porch, and stared upwards at the inverted carpet of stars. Sirius, beacon-like in the southeast, seemed bright and close enough to touch. I mulled over all the warnings I had heard about the route west, which had begun to sap at my conviction. Now all the difficulties and dangers seemed overwhelming, and I felt as though I had misplaced myself in an alien world for which some earlier and frivolous affection had long since passed, and that the attempt to cross the country alone was something far beyond my means. Yet it was too soon to turn back. A journey had its own languages and at times the way could seem blocked by some vocabulary of experience hard to understand. It would pass. I was determined to continue beyond government territory, ignore the grim counsel of the boys in the teahouse and, if necessary, risk being eaten.

It seemed unlikely the Hazāras were really cannibals. Arab and Persian historians had started it all when they first recorded that the godless Mongol invaders of the Islamic world had the habit of eating the flesh of their victims.* And since the Hazāras were popularly but mistakenly believed to be descended from the Mongols, the two terrible untruths were married in an enduring curse. This was doubly unfair to their people, who came to Afghanistan as peaceful settlers. But as with the most enduring of rumours the truth had little to do with it.

The more I tried to put my fears out of mind the more perversely vivid they became. I pictured a trio of Mongol-faced fighters around a fire at dusk, my clothes distributed among them, my body charring over an improvised spit.

'Not bad, by Allah,' says one, with his mouth full.

'Nothing like a tasty bit of infidel,' says another, wiping the fat from his cheeks on a bloody sleeve.

'That's right,' guffaws a third, 'who says we don't *like* foreigners!' and they all fall about the place in fits of laughter, choking on the tender but curious-smelling flesh.

---

* Among other unpleasantnesses. Ibn Khusrau, for example, records: 'They were terrible to look at and indescribable, with large heads like a buffalo's, narrow eyes like a fledgling's, a snub nose like a cat's, projecting snouts like a dog's, narrow loins like an ant's, short legs like a hog's and by nature no beards at all ... they give birth to children like snakes and eat like wolves. Death does not appear among them, for they survive three hundred years.' Recalling the sack of Delhi, he wrote: 'Their stink was more horrible than their colour. Their faces had no necks. Their cheeks resembled leather bottles full of wrinkles. Their noses extended from cheek to cheek.' The tone of horror in such accounts is matched only by earlier descriptions of Christian invaders of the Holy Land, whose behaviour, being that of a religious people, was even more perplexing to Moslems. There are reports, in both Moslem and Christian chronicles of the time, of cannibalism among the Crusaders. See 'The Cannibals of Ma'arra', in Amin Maalouf's *The Crusades through Arab Eyes*, 1984, for the grim confessions of Albert of Aix and Radulph of Caen.

My hands were trembling slightly from the fever. Brittle leaves somersaulted in a breeze over the icy mud of the yard. Suddenly I remembered it was Christmas Eve. I was not sure if I felt very happy, or very sad.

*

In the morning the entire male population of the family gathered outside to see me off. They watched me through the windows as I packed. My sense of foreboding about the way ahead had not lifted and their presence felt more like a crowd that gathers to watch a condemned man's last actions.

My shoes, which I had left at the threshold of the room with their toes facing the door, had in a tiny act of courtesy been turned around and their laces slightly loosened. Seeing that the pair next to them had been left untouched, I leaned down to return the gesture. In a flash I felt my wrist in an almost fierce grip, and looked up into the son's inconsolable gaze.

There was a round of photographs and countless solemn embraces, and we left in a clatter with Hajji and his son in a cart pulled by his favourite dappled mare. Hajji smiled like a proud charioteer and his long whip whistled and snapped above his horse's back. I wondered then, feeling unworthy of the trouble he had taken over me, whether it would have been more honest to have appeared on his doorstep without the hint of an official guise.

The square in which I had first arrived was unrecognizably busy, and dense with people and animals and vehicles. In the seething market I bought *keshmesh* for the journey ahead, walnuts and dried mulberries, and a bag of *noql* – sugar-coated almond seed – for Hajji. There were the usual scenes of protest from his son as I tried to pay. As with his father there was, even to this detail of hospitality, an almost fierce determination.

For an hour we waited as he went from driver to driver in search of a vehicle heading in the direction of Ghorband. In vain. I said I was happy to go on alone, which would have suited my dismal mood, but they insisted on taking me to Pūl-i Matak, several miles towards Charikar where the road forks west to Bamiyan. I was secretly glad because I was dreading being alone again. We tightened our *pattūs* and at a fast trot headed south over the bullet-ridden bridge, out of the village and onto the ancient plain, and Hajji's eyes wept in the freezing air.

A military truck roared past us. In the open bed behind the cab, men huddled against the sides, and in their midst a lone man with a mad smile was whirling like a dervish with outstretched arms, shouting incoherently above the icy wind.

*

At Pūl-i Matak, where the Ghorband valley stretched west through a narrow breach in the snow-dusted hills, Hajji left us. It was a barren place but for a small cluster of buildings. Our hands were numb and we sheltered in a tiny *chaikhāna* at the fork of the road, where an armed teenage fighter was checking the contents of trucks emerging from the valley.

Geography shapes history; men only add a little colour to its surface. I fancied the pulse of the country beat more strongly in this very spot where the armies of so many empire-builders had wheeled out of the mountains onto the plain, and glimpsed at last a horizon instead of a high crag overhead.

Here the rock and water of which the junction was configured had channelled the flow of the fates of civilizations. I wondered what tales a pebble from one of the valley's cracked bastions might tell of all the languages uttered in its shadow. It would have been familiar with the Persian of native villagers counting their dead in the latest war or plotting ambushes from their camouflaged *sangars* against the creeping columns below. It might even have heard the transistor-pinched voice of a Russian tank commander barking the order, through the head-phones of a teenage conscript driver (and above the rumble and squeak of heavy armour and the clatter of ammunition belts), to prepare for attack against the ghostly *basmachi*.

A century before, it would have heard the echo of clipped imperatives from a cavalry officer of the Bengal Light Horse, venting his frustration on sepoys struggling to extract a cannon wheel from a rut. Or Bābūr on his way to picnic at Gulbahār. Or, a thousand years ago, it might just have puzzled over the grumbled agglutinatives of Shansabanid Turkish horsemen bemoaning the likely trials of the route ahead, on their way to subdue an unruly fiefdom; or strained to decipher mantras whispered by a Korean monk heading west to the Buddhist kingdom of Fan-Yin; or learned the conjugations of a Roman merchant reminding clumsy bearers to be careful with his bundles of Venetian glass, bound for the markets of Taxilla; or pondered the vowel system of a Chinese caravan-driver boasting of his silks; or sympathized with a Kushan princess lamenting a lost earring (what language did the Kushans speak?); or heard Ashoka's Aramaic-speaking scouts looking for a likely spot to carve their master's edicts. Or even – in the early summer of 327 BC to be exact – caught the unfamiliar lilt of another tongue long since vanished from the region, rising out of the flow of a vast hoard of forty thousand fighting men and as many camp-followers: the voice of Alexander himself, discussing some point of strategy with his favourite general Hephaestion. And long before them, before Zoroaster himself was a divine twinkle in Ahura Mazda's eye, there had been other wandering languages for a patient pebble to hear and ponder, from tenuously understood dialects of Prakrit, Brahmi and Kharoshti at their northern limits, to the now-extinct syllables of Soghdian, Parthian and Bactrian, creeping south.

*

There was very little traffic, but Hajji's son refused to leave me until he had put me safely on a vehicle travelling in the direction of Bamiyan. I sensed his frustration but there was no persuading him to abandon his guest. Nursing private thoughts, robbed by the cold of the urge to talk, we warmed our hands against the stove until nearly an hour later a battered bus lumbered into sight from the main road.

For all his trials on my behalf I had no way of repaying Hajji's son but to look into his grief-stricken eyes and thank him in inadequate Persian and with a little cash. He felt the notes as I took his hand, and pulled away as though he had been electrocuted.

'For your father, then – please, buy him some small gift from me.'

Only as the driver of the bus was threatening to leave did he finally relent. We embraced. I studied his face for a clue to his real feelings, discovering nothing, then clambered between sacks into the bus. I wondered: had I insulted him by obliging him to accept money, or should I have given him more? It was impossible to tell. Aboard the bus I caught a final glimpse of him watching me from the side of the road with the same obscuring look of sadness, and felt as though I had inherited a portion of his grief.

*

It was small bus, filled to bursting with passengers and their various cargoes of sacks, bags, bundles and boxes. We snaked west along the ancient road, hugging the mountain walls above the river where the occasional Russian troop carrier rusted in the torrent fifty or a hundred feet below. The valley was a softer, tamer version of Panjshīr, at times no wider than a ravine hemmed by leathery cliffs, at others broadening to half a mile, where the road was flanked with orchards and fields. They were bare now and frozen. The valley floor was at six thousand feet and the ridges between three and four thousand feet above us. I imagined in spring it would have been beautiful. I was sitting on a sack of walnuts between the driver and an old man who settled onto my rucksack like an owl on a perch and studied me from time to time as I peered from the cracked windscreen. Despite the rocking, it was possible to doze.

In peacetime it was not a particularly adventurous route, but it was nearly twenty years since outsiders had taken the road in any number. Before the war foreigners would have boarded creaking buses heading westwards to explore one of Afghanistan's most famous sites, the valley of the giant Buddhas of Bamiyan. Halfway between Balkh and Taxilla on this important tributary of the silk route, Bamiyan had once been a natural resting place for caravans as well as an important centre of pilgrimage known to early Korean and Chinese Buddhists since at least the third century, when Buddhism is thought to have established itself on the mountain-ringed plateau. While other Buddhist centres that grew up under the Kushans were wiped out by the Hephthalite invasions of the fifth century, Bamiyan escaped, presumably on account of its remoteness. The Chinese pilgrim Fa-Hsien passed through in 400 AD and speaks of over a thousand monks in attendance; Hsien-

335

Tsang described a thriving Buddhist community in 632 AD. Soon afterwards the Arab armies controlled Balkh in the north and Qandahar in the south, but left the Buddhist mountain-cradle alone. Buddhism is thought to have survived until the twelfth century under Ghorid rule.

The scale of the old kingdom's monuments is unique. Two colossal statues of the Buddha are carved from sandstone cliffs overlooking a broad and fertile valley. Above it looms the snowy backdrop of the Koh-i Bābā, the Grandfather range. A third-century Buddha is 120 feet tall. The later statue, which probably dates from the fifth century, bores upwards through its rocky shroud to 175 feet. The cliff-bases, as well as those of the surrounding hills, are drilled with hundreds of devotees' cells, many of them decorated with elaborate frescoes that betray the exceptional fusion of artistic elements characteristic of the site: Roman, Hellenistic, Iranian, Indian and central Asian, comparable in range only with such unique artefacts as the winged gold Aphrodite from the Tilya Tepe hoard.

The concentric folds of the Buddha's robes were made from mortar shaped over ropes attached to the stone with wooden pegs and eventually painted. Traces of gold leaf from the hands and heads of the statues hint at the splendour of the original spectacle. 'Its golden hues sparkle on every side,' wrote Hsien-Tsang, 'and its precious ornaments dazzle the eyes by their brightness.' It is thought that the arms of the larger statue may have been movable.

Yet they were not beautiful. The technical difficulties of working in stone on such a scale outweighed the aesthetic achievement, and modern archaeologists are almost scornful of the main statue's overly large head and sturdy-looking legs.* Their faces are unknown. They

---

* As a French expert has it: 'The niche is very simply carved out, the body is heavy, the head is too big, the trunk swells exaggeratedly, the legs are thick.' Byron is outspoken: 'it is their negation of sense, the lack of any pride in their monstrous flaccid bulk, that sickens.' But were the statues ever intended to be entirely naturalistic? The Mahayana Buddhism in which the Prince Siddhartha was represented in human form was, in the second century, still in its infancy.

were hacked methodically away when the last of the Buddhist kings fell to Islamic rule towards the end of the tenth century under Sebuktegin, or perhaps later, when the Mongols swept unstoppably through the region in 1222. Chingiz Khan's favourite grandson Mutugen was killed by Bamiyan's defenders and in punishment the Great Khan himself is recorded as having led the slaughter of its every inhabitant.

The last king of Bamiyan, Jelaluddin, escaped alone from his attackers after a lengthy pursuit by swimming the Indus with his horse. The physical scars inflicted on his former kingdom have never healed. Even the triple-fortified clifftop castle of Shahr-i Zohak was overrun by the pitiless Mongol troops and the conical hill-city nearby the Mongols called Maobalegh, meaning cursed, was renamed Shahr-i Golgolhā in memory of the population that fell to the swiftly wheeling, shallow-faced horsemen. Golgolhā could mean wailing or whispering; the sound of the dying or their ghosts. These places were never rebuilt, and for seven hundred years the valley's irrigation channels remained choked with silt. In the late nineteenth century a partial restoration of the canals brought cultivation back to the valley, but its monuments today evoke not so much the region's former prosperity as the relentless destructiveness of the Mongols.

During the first Anglo-Afghan war Bamiyan was one of the remotest British outposts. In 1840 it took an occupying force a month to reach it from Kabul. Later it gained notoriety as one of the hiding places for British hostages kidnapped by Afghans. The prisoners were eventually released unharmed on promises never honoured, but only the heroism of the captives is remembered in British accounts. In retaliation for this and other anti-British uprisings, the towns of Istalif and Charikar were set ablaze and the great covered bazaar in Kabul was dynamited by sappers. The British retreated as the burning capital fell to mass looting.

How Bamiyan had fared in the latest war I had little idea, except that the Russians had only a sporadic presence there, and more recently, that the Hazāra mujaheddin had been using the Buddhas as target practice for their tank crews. This rumour too had a spurious ring to it, an old story hung on the necks of new characters. It was

Aurangzeb, the last Great Moghul emperor and conqueror of most of India, who was said to have tested his cannon on the Buddhas, which would be unlikely to withstand modern tank fire. But the rumours made me all the more curious to set eyes on the vast recalcitrants myself.

To the west, beyond them, beyond the Valley of the Dragon where the petrified corpse of a fire-breathing beast slayed by the noble hand of Ali himself still sheds mineral-encrusted tears, beyond the Markhor horns that venerate the shrine of Mīr Yakhsuz the ice-burning saint, beyond the unearthly-coloured lakes of Band-i Amir, lay the region of peculiar allure I hoped to reach, the virtual *terra incognita* of the vanished Ghorid kingdom.

*

My slumber was broken by the lurching of the bus. We were rising perceptibly now and in the far distance there were deepening galleries of mountains whose peaks melted into a milky sky. Nearer, tendrils of cloud brushed the high ridges. Behind us the road trailed like a severed lifeline.

I wished I had a companion, and thought of Tim and our final evening together. It had been a long night; under the influence, all his Englishness had dropped away as he spoke about the difficulties of working in Kabul: the constant fear, the lack of a proper break, the difficulty of getting out of the city even for a day. But he loved the Afghans: their smiles, their entrepreunerial spirit, and their sheer love of life that made up for it all. If I wanted to see their spirit, I should visit the children's hospital, he suggested, not far from the house. I could see the grief of staying and the grief of leaving were taking their toll on him. He never normally talked like that. He was quite drunk by the time he told me about the occasion he had pulled up at a hospital just as a fleet of vehicles had arrived with an intake of badly wounded. An ambulance had arrived with a dying man. He had died just as he was being pulled out, his head cradled in the arms of his young daughter. Above the noise of the cars and confusion, a piercing wail had gone up as the child's father was hauled away: he would never forget it, said Tim: the sound had etched itself into his being.

My thoughts had turned irremediably gloomy. I found myself trying to remember Lawrence's terse comment from *The Seven Pillars of Wisdom* as he faced death in the Turkish garrison at Aqaba. I had forgotten the exact words; they were improbably dry and had a ring of truth. It was something like: *At first I thought he would kill me, which was a pity...*

On this cheerless theme I thought too of the well-known Eastern story of Death's visit to Baghdad. The disciple of a certain Sufi happens to overhear Death chatting in a teahouse about the calls he must pay in the city and, terrified, heads immediately to far-off Samarqand to be sure of escaping a possible visit. Later, Death visits the Sufi to enquire after the whereabouts of the very same disciple.

'I expect he is somewhere in the bazaar,' says the Sufi.

'Strange,' muses Death, looking at his list of names. 'It says here I'm to collect him next week, in Samarqand, of all places.'

And again I found myself at that poorly lit shrine where what ordinarily seems most substantial appears suddenly and unreasonably fragile. Even in a country at war, you forget war because the momentum of living is too great – until like a sullen beast it bares its face as if on a vicious whim, and you are reminded of the ease with which life can be extinguished. I felt a sick sense of panic, like a dream of falling off a high building, and realized I was deeply scared about the way ahead. Fear has its own devious logic. Its voice grew bolder by the minute, suggesting ever more persuasive arguments for turning back. *I thought he was going to kill me, which seemed a shame.* No, that wasn't it, either.

It was all coming back now: whenever I had mentioned my plans to travel west, people's faces would drop in horror, like a fortune teller's on finding something terrible in a client's tea leaves. There were the boys in the teahouse who had told me I would be eaten; Amrullah's tale of the two foreigners held by *Wahdat* fighters for years, and the Italian's description of being robbed and beaten. Then came the counter-arguments: the boys were simply recounting an old ethnic prejudice, Amrullah had been indulging in government scaremongering and Franco's wrists, I had noticed at the time, were unbruised.

I wished I knew nothing about the place. I was dwelling not on the obvious inconvenience of being killed but on how unbearable it would be to be kidnapped and for my family to have no certain news, only that I had disappeared. I thought of my daughter, and my resolve began to crumble. Then I had it: *I thought he was going kill me, and was sad.*

*

There is nothing like being far from home in a country at war to reveal the fragility of your original plans, and with a deep sense of disappointment I knew my nerve was faltering. I had earlier hatched a private longing to go beyond the usual risks, to force myself over a kind of threshold of calculation, to jump into a situation where to assess the risks ahead was impossible. I wanted to be free, if only for a day, of the tyranny of knowing what to expect in advance; to ride, in effect, a high wave of uncertainty until I could no longer feel its motion. I wanted to prove that it was possible to travel in those very places that others shunned, and the central route was the perfect place to put all this to the test. I would be beyond everything; in an untried space, without friends or contacts, no foreknowledge, a place at war, freezing, inhabited by teenage cannibals. In Kabul it had seemed a reasonable enough idea. There was just one problem: I was now terrified of my own plan.

*

The bus came to a lurching halt. We were in a wild-looking village – I guessed it must be Ghorband, halfway to Bamiyan – and the passengers began hauling their loads onto their shoulders. It was the last stop and as I stepped into the muddy street, alone again, I felt suddenly abandoned. The passengers melted into the flow of passers-by.

'Where are you staying, brother?'

I turned; it was the young man who had been sitting behind me on the bus. Briefly I wondered at the question's intent, and looked back into a pair of luminously dark eyes set in mouse-like features.

'Is there a *mehmān khana* in the village?' I asked, weakly.

'A *mehmān khana*! Here?' He gave a cynical chuckle. 'Come on. You can stay with me.' He tossed the end of his *pattū* over the shoulder of

his black clothes and began walking in the opposite direction. This
was my invitation.

In the narrow main street two crippled Russian tanks, stripped to
their hulks, sat at the muddy verge in front of ragged stalls. I hobbled
behind my new host, slipping on icy patches under the weight of my
rucksack as he trotted nimbly ahead. We followed the snaking road at
the base of steep cliffs for a mile or so until another village appeared.
Here a man coming the other way greeted us and, eyeing me, lowered
his voice and asked:

'So who's your friend, Sayeed?'

'Him? He's my cousin from ... Kabul.'

'Sayeed,' says the man, 'you haven't got a cousin in Kabul.'

'I have now,' muttered Sayeed, and led me forward into the
labyrinth of mud-walled alleys before I could attract too much more
attention. We climbed a ladder into a long room above a stable, and
drank tea with mulberries and walnuts. The village was called Baham.
It was freezing and overcast. Sayeed disappeared for half an hour and
returned looking disappointed, apologizing for not having found a
chicken for our dinner.

'The Shibar Pass will be closed,' he said gloomily.

At dusk we moved to a different house within a walled yard where
he lit a stove in a tiny room. I stood on the doorstep and watched
plumes of smoke rising from tiny houses set among leafless trees on
the far side of the valley and heard the howls of wolves echoing from
beyond them. It was Christmas Day.

Word spread quickly of a foreign visitor and we were soon joined
by half a dozen other men whose curiosity overtook their natural good
manners like water from a leaking dam. They huddled opposite,
exchanging the unanswerable questions they dared not yet ask, while I
braced myself inwardly for the inevitable eruption of enquiry. In good
spirits I enjoyed these interrogation sessions, which were a small price
to pay for the hospitality. Yet now I felt inexplicably weary, weary at
my own ingratitude, but most of all weary at having to disguise my
weariness.

The room was bare but for the carpets on the floor and a single
peacock feather pinned to one wall beside a photograph of Sayeed as

a young soldier. Gradually the grey light dimmed as if we were retreating steadily into a deep cave. Men came and went according to a logic of their own and only Sayeed's face, like a buoy flashing at the gates of a port, remained a constant in my vision. There was some doleful speculation over my chances for crossing the Shibar pass. We talked until our faces faded into shadow. Sayeed lit a paraffin lamp and we shared tea as the night tightened like a cold noose around us.

'So what about the future,' asked one of the men, inevitably. 'What do you think will happen to Afghanistan?'

'Even God doesn't know the future of Afghanistan,' I said, and they all laughed heartily at hearing this from a foreigner. But even in the shadows I could see the curls of their smiles turn downwards as they faded, as if they had tasted the bitterness of this perhaps ironic truth.

I added: 'From what I have seen, ordinary people all over the country are tired of war,' and the line of heads nodded in solemn assent.

'Ordinary people, yes,' said the village teacher. His manner was didactic, his tone resigned. 'But other countries aren't. Pakistan isn't tired of it. America isn't tired of it. Russia and Iran aren't tired of it. What do they suffer from this war?'

I had no reply.

'Nobody's tired of it except us!' he went on. 'So long as they have the money to give commanders who can pay others to fight, there's no way to stop the fighting.'

There was little reason to contest this; I had not met a single Afghan who hadn't expressed a longing for the war to end, nor encountered a single life unscarred by its cruel momentum. The misery was fuelled from beyond, by players untouched themselves by the catastrophe.

'That's right,' said a voice in grave concord, 'this war is about money. In other countries people make money through business and trade, but here — war is the best business.'

Then out of the silence, a mournful, aged voice from the darkness made us turn. It came from an old man wrapped in his *pattū*, huddling in the shadows behind the stove.

'*Afghanistan, Afghanistan.*'

*

Sayeed brought dinner and our fingers plunged into trays of steaming rice. The men apologized meekly for the lack of meat, as if it were their fault. The monotony of the rice was broken by a small bowl of cauliflower fried in oil. I thought of the orgy of consumption being unleashed in the West at that very moment, of steaming white flesh slapping in hot heaps beneath polished forks, of entire nations agonizing over leg or breast or extra skin, of pursed lips prevaricating above weighty platters, of serving spoons wavering before hands raised defensively over bloated abdomens.

'They'll kill you just for those socks of yours,' said one of the men in a ruminative tone, as we washed down the rice with weak green tea. If I had a friend with me, or a vehicle, someone else agreed, I might be able to pass the front, but alone it would be either impossible or suicidal. My resolve, like a wounded animal harassed by hyenas, fell under attack at each comment:

'The Hazāras are a wild people.'

'Boys who've known nothing but the life of the gun.'

'It's different there from government territory.'

Concealing a burgeoning sense of doom, I said I would find out in the morning.

'Afghanistan is a strange country,' mused Sayeed, when we were alone again, laying out bedding on the floor.

'I know.'

'No — *really* strange,' he said, reaching for a crumpled newspaper that one of the others had left behind. A mysterious wild man, he read, had been captured on the outskirts of the city of Jelallabad and was being held in chains at the airport. According to the report he was five metres tall, covered in thick fur, and 'appeared not to understand Persian'. Sayeed beamed, as if it were a matter of national pride. I told him I had heard that in the Hazārajat a female yeti was believed to visit men at night and press her chest against their faces until they suffocated. His face fell in mock terror and he giggled like a child.

There was another report: the Tāleban had confirmed Massoud's death. It was the third time Massoud had been killed since my arrival in Afghanistan.

I went outside to make use of the mud cabin at the side of the house, having forgotten the troubles imposed in the countryside on such a simple ritual. The ceiling was low and in the darkness I banged my head. Bent double I found my purpose defeated, but crouching in trousers prevented the entire operation, so like any Afghan I had to squat. To do so meant emptying my trouser pockets because squatting provided the exact angle at which everything fell out, and whatever rolled down the surrounding slopes and into the black hole at the centre of the hut would be irretrievable. Then whatever had been taken out would have to be transferred to my jacket pockets and the jacket taken off.

Outside again, a sky made luminous by a canopy of moon-filled cloud shed enough light to empty my pockets. Just then there was the strangest sound. I realized I had heard it several times during the day whenever I had been outside but had assumed it was something else, some unaccustomed mimicry of sound. Faintly, but unmistakably, I heard it again – the gobbling of a turkey. I scrambled up a mound and put my head over the wall. Thirty feet away, its ungainly shape defined by the spectral glow of white feathers, was the biggest turkey I had ever seen in my life. I wondered if I might be hallucinating. At that moment nothing seemed too strange. If not a turkey on the way to Bamiyan on Christmas Day, why not a yeti in Jelallabad?

*

A dusting of snow had fallen in the night. It was bitterly cold. We drank unsweetened tea and chewed stiff strips of bread for breakfast. For more than an hour nothing passed in the onward direction as we waited beneath a bullet-pocked arch at the edge of the village. Once our hopes were raised by the sight of an approaching jeep, but it was stuffed with armed men and roared past us at speed. For another hour

I chatted with some small boys who gathered and dispersed like sparrows, and wiggled toes I could hardly feel.

A ginger-haired man with strongly Moghol features offered to walk with me and, frustrated with waiting, I said goodbye to Sayeed and continued with the stranger. We walked for several miles in silence broken eventually by the grumble of an approaching truck. I clambered into the open bed, where twenty men were huddling among sacks in their *pattūs*, and with a wave was on my way again.

Under the scrutiny of a dozen stern gazes I felt an old pang ignite defensively: to travel with an Afghan friend. With the right company, the inevitable burden of enquiry would be shared more evenly between visitor and host, and polished exchanges would replace my own cracked idioms. There would be no need to reach that point of mental debility where expression in another language seems an impossible exertion. Only an Afghan friend could help decode literal truths from cultural prejudice or, conversely, explain satisfactorily to others the strange Western habits that risked giving offence; the wish to slope off and write, to be alone from time to time, to know the names of things, to visit places for no obvious reason.

In an unfamiliar language you make up a lot of what you lack in the spoken word by interpreting tensions of voice, gesture and ritual that betray another's meaning. In a strange or dangerous place you are forever reading these signals, consciously or not, through an alliance of the analytical and intuitive, and the more hazardous or unfamiliar the circumstances, the greater the meaning you come to extract from ever smaller events. Sometimes a lack of language seems to lighten things, and your contact with others is unburdened by definitions. But at others there comes a point of exhaustion when you simply want to talk about ordinary things, and not have to think about every word. A journey magnifies both extremes; I was feeling the weight of the latter and, meeting the stares of twenty silent men, felt mute and helpless.

*

The truck shuddered to a halt at Sheikh Ali: 147 kilometres from Kabul, 74 kilometres from Pūl-i Matak. Beyond the village, the government's control dissolved like a river into a desert. Here the valley had broadened to a rocky wasteland a mile wide and on the far side I could make out a second road, deserted, leading into snowy knots of mountains to the south. I studied it hopefully for a hint of life but nothing moved along the weaving hillside scar. Instead, a muffled salvo of explosions rolled out of the interlocking spurs in ominous answer and I knew the fighting was not far away.

A villager pointed me towards the top of a nearby rise and the headquarters of the local commander. At its crest a walled cluster of mud-brick buildings was guarded by armed men. A flag bearing the insignia of a mujaheddin party I didn't recognize fluttered from an antenna on the roof. I was led inside, along a dark corridor, at the end of which was a door. I undid my boots, tossed my *pattū* over my shoulder, and was shown inside.

*

I had interrupted a council of war. Lining the walls, their rifles cradled in their laps, were thirty turbaned commanders with weary and battle-hardened faces. With a few exceptions they had strongly Moghol features. They wore grenades and webbing filled with extra magazines, and their clothes were worn and dusty.

A shuffling of men and the metallic rustle of guns yielded a space next to their leader, towards whom, in momentary bewilderment, I was guided in a flurry of outstretched hands. He was addressing the others with a quiet intensity I found unsettling and in an accent that was hard to understand. I looked at their faces and felt I read nothing in them. They looked like mountain lynxes. Next to them the tough Panjshīri fighters I had met seemed like beribboned Angoras. The atmosphere was not sinister, but it was indescribably solemn.

*

Over tea, the commander turned to me. We spoke generally about the war, the situation in Kabul, my journey. He asked why, if there were journalists in Kabul, they never came here? Because, I felt like saying, as I looked around at all the guns and unsmiling Moghol faces, this

346

place is *way* too scary. I explained it was difficult for journalists to go from place to place, and broached the subject of my plans.

'And with your permission, *commandon sāhib*,' I said, 'I am hoping to reach Bamiyan.'

Everything hung on his answer. He sighed, and a solemn smile came over his face.

'I personally cannot prevent you from continuing your journey,' he replied, 'but you should understand this. In the pass you intend to cross and which it is my responsibility to defend, there are two thousand enemy troops, not one of whom would hesitate to kill you,' he plucked at his chest, 'for your jacket. Not a *chicken* could cross that pass without being fired on.' He paused for the words to find their mark. 'But if you want to try,' he added, lifting his hands skyward in deference to the caprices of fate, 'brother, the choice is yours.' He smiled again.

I did not believe the part about the chicken but my sense of failure was outweighed by enormous relief.

*

Nine armed men escorted me back to the village of Baham in a Russian jeep. The solemn restraint they had shown in front of their commander came undone in the unnatural intimacy of the back seat, as volleys of excited questioning were unleashed on their captive *khareji*. The man next to me would repeat them, then render my responses (elaborating with shameless authority) into smoother language for the benefit of the others. A few moments of fast and furious debate would follow before the next question, and that is how it went, all the way back.

There were the usual openers concerning my duty and how much my government was paying me to fulfil it; the usual furrowings of puzzlement at my claim to have nothing to do with governments. Yet their questions revealed more of their world than my answers did of mine. Were there Moslems in England, they asked, and were they free to practise openly? And did I really mean to say they were not persecuted?

Was there alcohol, and did I drink it? Sometimes, I said, with sudden longing. Did we make our own cars in England? What did we make best there? What crops did we grow? What did the letters USA stand for? Which was stronger militarily, America or Russia? Would an English doctor be able to cure the blind boy we had seen in the village? In my religion, what was the place of pilgrimage? Was there circumcision? Was I circumcised? (Fits of laughter all round.) Did we have idols, or worship fire, and were there different sects in my religion?

The muzzles of two rifles poked into my legs as the driver wrestled the jeep over potholes. Was it true that if you were being robbed, you could simply call the police and they would actually come? Was Salman Rushdie English and was the *fatwa* a good thing or not? Was Ayatollah Khomeini a good or bad man?

Could a man and a woman sleep together before marriage? What if — the questions grew more controversial as the men grew more confident — what if another man looked at my wife? I didn't dare say it made no difference and confirm the old Moslem prejudice that the West was a place devoid of a moral code between the sexes. I said that generally, it wasn't necessary for a man to intervene: if a man behaved badly towards a woman, she could tell him herself. Some dubious looks were exchanged. But if a man persisted, they asked, was I then allowed to kill him? No, I said, but I could punch him, if necessary — and they thought this an excellent compromise. It was right that the killing should be illegal, they agreed. I thought how good and how remarkable it was that such men, brutalized by years of fighting, had not lost the power to step back from the violence of their own world.

And was it true, they asked finally, that Western women wore very few clothes in summer? I thought of a bathing suit contest I had once seen on a California beach, and lapsed momentarily into a cruelly vivid reverie. That depended, I sighed, on the kind of family she came from, and they nodded knowingly, muttering, 'The tribe, yes, of course, it would depend on her tribe.'

*

Sayeed showed no obvious sign of surprise at seeing me again so soon and ushered me into his home. I was weary of enclosed spaces and endless questions, another round of which I knew would begin again if I stayed inside. Hoping to nurse a fugitive stab of homesickness alone I asked if it would be possible to go for a walk.

'Walk where?'

'On the hills, above the village.'

'What for?'

'To look, at the mountains, the view . . .'

'Why?'

I had never, before or since, been able satisfactorily to explain to any Afghan the meaning of the impulse. But Sayeed was too polite to refuse a *khareji* his errant habits and summoned three friends to accompany us. Two teenage boys ran up and down the slopes like mountain goats as I struggled breathlessly to the top of the hill, deeply fearful of mines as we passed an abandoned military post. I picked idly at some coloured stones, and noticed the others watching me intently.

'There's minerals in those rocks,' said Sayeed quietly, as if to expose some conspiratorial knowledge. His suspicion was confirmed when I told him the red colour came from iron.

'And what about those hills?' he asked, pointing towards a distant trio of huge, oddly coloured mounds resembling quarried slag, as if our combined knowledge might lead to some hidden wealth.

'Gold!' we both exclaimed, at the same moment.

It was the kind of sight that made me long to explore, to take a friend and a pair of horses and simply head into the nameless mountains and wander, drawing from the richness of their magnificent solitude and learning whatever lessons from the spirit of such places as they might offer. It struck me then that perhaps this longing, which I had never much questioned, barely belonged to Sayeed's universe. Under ordinary conditions it seemed like a natural impulse; but to judge from the look of curiosity on Sayeed's face as I gazed out towards the mountains, it was a strange indulgence. Did wandering about deserted places for pleasure seem odd to Afghans only because they never had time for it themselves? Or was the urge itself an instinctive striving to redress the severing from the natural world that the modern way of life implies, and which among peoples daily close to nature did not arise?

Across the valley the shadows were deepening in the ochreous folds of the hills and the skyline had begun to resemble the crenellated walls of a hilltop castle punctuated by ruined watchtowers and lost to time. Dusk was falling and grey plumes had begun to rise from the tiny houses below us. We could hear the faint shouts of boys playing football in a square behind the village and then, with a mournful timelessness, the cry of the *muezzin*. Suddenly I remembered Wordsworth:

> that blessed moment
> In which the burden of the mystery
> In which the heavy and the weary weight
> Of all this unintelligible world
> Is lightened

And when I turned the others were looking at me, as if expecting some pronouncement.

We walked down again past the ruins of homes destroyed by bombs and returned to Sayeed's house where I wrote up my diary. I had learned to excuse myself expertly for this ritual and although a courteous hush spread through the room for the duration of my scrawling, the more curious men would draw in at close range, kneeling, their faces locked in perplexed delight at the odd shapes flowing from my pen.

'And he reads and writes Persian too,' said Sayeed, with a touch of pride. At this I was handed a children's schoolbook and invited to read; it was the story of Joseph.

'And what about your Prophet?' asked one of the men after I had read.

'That would be Jesus,' muttered another.

'Yes, Jesus — is he alive or dead?' asked a third, and the room fell unexpectedly silent at the crucial question.

*

It is hard to imagine unlettered European villagers enquiring of a Moslem visitor as to the significance of the Prophet Mohammed's mission. Yet here in a tiny and remote Afghan village was evidence of a sincere concern for a guest's interpretation of what to Moslem minds is a vital event.

Few non-Moslems are aware of the profound reverence throughout the Islamic world for Jesus, or of the high esteem in which Maryām, Mary, is held by practising Moslems. There is no historical equivalent, in the reverse sense, to the centuries of derogation in the West of Islam as a system of faith, or the calumny heaped upon its Prophet. And whereas Christianity has distanced itself from Islam, there remains in the Islamic world a deep consciousness of the intertwining roots of both religions, which once flourished on the same soils.

Moslem admiration for Christianity founders on two crucial objections. These are doctrinal, rather than historical: both are considered inimical to the vigorous monotheism of orthodox Islam. One is the putative confusion between Jesus and God, which is seen as confusion between the Messenger for its Source. The other is the symbolism of the Trinity, which smacks heavily of polytheism — to the Moslem mind perhaps the greatest of metaphysical heresies.

Inevitably the trouble trickles down to such problematic events as the Crucifixion. As any sensible Moslem knows, Jesus did not die on the cross: someone else must have, or else He did not die. The belief that a man could die and return to life strikes Moslems as bafflingly misguided.

They have a point. If removing the cornerstone of the resurrection from the Christian edifice is troublesome for Christianity, Islam does not find itself obliged to square metaphysical circles when a simple answer suffices. There is no humanization of the Absolute in Islam. No danger, either, of having the baby of religion itself thrown out with the bathwater of anthropomorphic symbolism. Consequently it suffers from none of the insecurities that arise from the headier mysteries built into Christianity; of the terrible dichotomies between God and Man, earthly and heavenly worlds, flesh and spirit.

In Islam there is no confusion as to which is really which and who is who; no sane reason why dead men should live and three should equal one and vice versa; no conflict between spiritual and worldly endeavour; no need, therefore, for an entire class of men (and now even women) to pretend at interceding between the Divine and his servants – confusions that smack of polytheism, mystification, of a religion gone astray; metaphysical mouthfuls indeed, to Moslems weaned on a powerfully single-flavoured religion, but which Christians are conditioned to swallow whole without flinching.

Even the most modern and sophisticated of Moslems finds the Christian version of things unnecessarily complicated and, whether he admits it or not, misguided. At the heart of Islam, conversely, lies something which, to the Christian or at least Western mind, appears disturbingly – disappointingly, almost – straightforward: something altogether too uncompromisingly, if not oppressively, inflexible. This is the *shahada*, or profession of faith, the proclamation of belief so potent as to be contained within a few syllables; the adamantine nexus around which orbits the religion of a billion souls:

Lā īllāha īll 'allāh

(There is no God but God himself)

The room was silent, and the shadows from the lantern rippled over the men's faces as they leaned forward to hear my reply. But the prospect of venturing into such problematic territory, equipped only with my crippled Persian, seemed overly ambitious.

I said: 'Just as a man's spirit lives on in his children, so too is Jesus alive in his followers.' For a few minutes they discussed the answer among themselves and seemed content. I was off the hook.

'And where's God then?' came a voice.

It was the same man who had begun this troublesome .line of enquiry.

'Here,' I said, and put my hand over my heart. He looked suddenly serious, fell silent, and a moment later later left the room.

*

HOTEL GHORBAND, my diary reads. BOXING DAY MENU: *Hors d'oeuvres*: broth with grit, stale bread, sliced radish. *Entrée*: Unidentifiable parts of sheep's head, leftover rice. *Dessert*: warm green tea. Then below this: AFTER DINNER ENTERTAINMENT: trying to keep the lamp going, trying to understand what others are saying, fielding endless questions, *viz.*: those which I don't understand; those which I do understand but can't answer; those which I can answer, the answers to which would not be understood; those which nobody anywhere can answer.

*

Next morning Sayeed escorted me to the village where we had first met, and found a jeep heading for Kabul. It was designed for four passengers; I squeezed in with fifteen others. Four latecomers clung to the back, forming a human shield against the cold and dust and giving me a good view of their belts. I wondered at their histories and what their buckles would recall if they could speak; they had once all belonged to Soviet soldiers.

Three hours later we joined the surfaced road to Charikar, where I had lunch for thirty pence at the Pangsher restaurant. The owner remembered me from nearly five years before. Next to me sat an elderly and distinguished-looking man with a spotless, hundred-year-old double-barrelled shotgun. Things seemed friendly and familiar again. I ate a delicious portion of kebabs, deeply disturbed at the thought of having even contemplated crossing the country alone.

Persuaded by a wily driver, I indulged in the luxury of hiring a taxi all to myself for the ride to Kabul. It was a prehistoric Volga and crept along the plain at ten miles an hour, but I was happy and felt like a king in his chariot returning from a long campaign. The feeling didn't last; by the end of the journey it was full of other people who had flagged us down for a lift, and whom I didn't have the heart to pass. But finally we rounded a bend of the Khairkhana pass where the skyline fell open to the Kabul valley below, and coasted downwards towards the ragged city. After the bleakness of the mountains, it seemed to possess all the allure of a vast and glittering metropolis.

*

Only a few seconds after I had paid the driver, a man nearly fell off his bicycle in his haste to embrace me. I realized with a twinge of shame I had no clue where I had first met him. Feeling as though I had come home, I headed for the Red Cross nearby, hoping to find Rafiq, and bumped into a stream of familiar and smiling faces. Again the world had changed with alien suddenness, and there were clean-shaven men in suits with walkie-talkies, fleets of undented cars, the flickering screens of computers, and unveiled women with unfaltering gazes.

With no chance of crossing the country by land, I put in a request for a flight to Herat.

Upstairs, an Afghan secretary I had earlier made friends with received me with demure grace in her office, brought me tea and watched me from the edge of her seat as I drank. Now, at rest, like a sailor who feels the ground swaying after days at sea, I suddenly felt the momentum of passage. My world was still in motion, crashing into potholes, jerking into axle-shearing ruts, blown by an icy wind; everywhere there was grey cloud, boulders, scree, gravel, cliff, barren-ness, guns. My hands and clothes were filthy and covered in a layer of fine dust.

'I thought you were an Afghan,' she giggled.

We looked at each other and smiled; she seemed impossibly beautiful.

I walked back to the house, pondering all the while the madness that had propelled me on my abortive foray west. Tim opened the gate and, looking me up and down, said: 'You're back a bit soon, aren't you?'

'I was taken hostage and ravaged by a hundred Persian virgins.'

'Take me there,' he said wearily.

I had been away four days. It felt like years.

Ten

Here at last is Asia without an inferiority complex.

Robert Byron, *The Road to Oxiana*

IT WAS NEW YEAR'S EVE. A fancy-dress party was hosted at the French medical outfit Médecins Sans Frontières. Tim wore his Russian tank driver's flak jacket, and I tore up an old sheet and wrapped myself up as a mummy. There was a huge spread of food and drink. Someone had taped to the walls a series of dolorous quotations from the works of French philosophers. But there was one which I felt an Afghan, had there been any present, would have approved: the fox's words, I think, to St Exupéry's Little Prince:

> On ne voit bien qu'avec le coeur
> L'essentiel est invisible par les yeux

> (One sees truly only with the heart
> The essential is hidden from the eye)

It was a mixed event. In the middle of the room, having a similar effect on the assembled males as honeysuckle on wild bees, was a recently arrived female journalist from Holland. A succession of admirers was virtually lining up to engage her in conversation and, wearied by the endless speculation, innuendo and ill-conceived propositions, she was visibly on the point of losing her temper. At this moment Tim, whose habitual reserve was by now pleasantly unhinged, walked by just in time to catch the wave as it broke. He tweaked the elasticated front of her dress as he passed her, and there was a sound like small-arms fire as her palm met his face, first from one side, then the other, in rapid succession. His glasses sailed across the room into a corner. Whether out of a natural sense of restraint or because he was too surprised to react, he made no effort to resist. As the slaps rained on, accompanied by a high-pitched stream of Dutch profanity, he looked like a cartoon character in a brawl.

There was one of those hushed pauses, then everything was back to normal. The Dutchwoman fled the room, and I fished out Tim's glasses from under a cupboard.

'God,' he mused, as he straightened out his lenses, 'I *hate* people who take themselves so seriously.'

We drove back at two in the morning. The streets seemed suspended in an icy mist made luminescent by the moon. To our astonishment there were no checkpoints; only much later did we find out they had been cancelled for the evening on our behalf.

*

By day our endeavours were more sober. I joined Tim on several more hair-raising trips around the city to verify the casualties from rocket attacks. The capriciousness and anonymity of these events were always deeply disturbing. Once in the fabric market a rocket fell in almost the very spot where ten minutes earlier I had been bargaining for a scarf. In another attack near the presidential palace, two men decided to escape the incoming rockets by driving away; a rocket landed on their car and they were killed instantly; those who stayed behind survived. Another rocket flew through the window of a film production company, killing half a dozen actors and their director.

A high proportion of the medical staff in the city's hospitals were women. There was said to be one female surgeon who had been awarded the civilian rank of general; so expert was her skill in trauma surgery that specialists had visited her from all over the world.

One day, in the west of the city, we pulled up a few minutes after a rocket had fallen in a narrow unpaved street. There was a destroyed shopfront; someone was sweeping up the broken glass; my eye fell on a patch of blood seeping through the dust that had been sprinkled on it.

At the local hospital, a female Afghan doctor, beautiful and weary-looking, gave us the figures: six dead, of whom two were small children, and two seriously wounded. Our total for the day was twenty-four killed. We drove home through

358

a shattered landscape
cratered with hollow woe

At least those were the words that came to me – the only lines I knew of a poem by Wilfred Owen – as we passed the ripped and crumpled homes of Deh Mazang. I had seen scenes like it before but I was still reeling inwardly at the extent of the destruction. In Wazir we lived a royal and frivolous existence by comparison; it was a desperate feeling.

In the east of the city, earlier roving front lines had left every building raked with bullet holes. The area around the old stadium and under the shadow of Tap-e Maranjān were particularly badly hit. In the Soviet-built apartment blocks of Microrayon we saw brightly coloured lines of washing hanging on balconies scarred by grenade blasts.

Tim filed a grim story about a woman called Mah Gul, who lived there. Her baby granddaughter had been killed by a rocket. Before the war her husband had been a relatively prosperous shopkeeper. She had lost him and her eldest son to the Russians, a second son had been left crippled in later fighting, and her daughter had fled to Iran. Now she was supported by her two youngest sons aged twelve and fifteen, who worked as apprentice mechanics and between them earned about ten pounds a month.

The old notion that people get what they deserve had never seemed more meaningless.

*

My flight request came through a few days later. A Red Cross minibus took us to the airport at Bagram. I sat next to a French nurse *d'un certain âge*, Madeleine, whose medieval and rustic-features face reminded me of a mad-looking character from Brueghel's *Flemish Proverbs*. She proudly wore a full-length wolf-pelt coat she'd bought in Chicken Street, saying she felt it made her look more Afghan. It was the equivalent of an Afghan woman, in London, wearing an antique version of Highland dress and thinking it helped her to look like a local. I thought: it was not really surprising that Afghans found foreigners strange. What was more strange was the equanimity with which they generally treated them.

I told her about the pain in my bones, which she cheerfully diagnosed as a case of meningitis, and said I had better have it seen to. She had a fixed smile and a slightly manic, staring look in her eye which made it difficult to know if she were serious.

We boarded the little plane. The pilots caressed their Ray-Bans into place and throttled up the engines to a shuddering roar. Then we were streaking past the wreckage of MiG fighters rusting on the runway's grassy flanks, and at 115 knots we were airborne, climbing in a steep circle to twenty thousand feet before breaking northwest towards Herat. The flat ground fell away like a lost satellite and we were skimming above a glittering sea of mountains. To the east they vaulted in icy crenellations towards the Himalayas. To the west they swelled in gentler waves along the central spine of the Paropamisus range, which expired three hundred miles away near Herat.

I put my nose against a trembling window and felt the thrill of peering into a different world, stripped of its horizontal secrets by our altitude. A high shroud of snow lay over the uppermost peaks and spilled into their serrated flanks in long beads like icing dripping over the rim of a cake. Lower down we could see tiny villages in roadless valleys and the buried bumps and rills of forgotten settlements and rivers branching like wandering nerves.

Nearing Herat we dropped into thick cloud, and the plane began to skip and lurch. The co-pilot got out of his seat, braced himself in the gangway, and addressed the passengers in the best tradition of a disaster movie. We were to prepare for a rough descent. The weather had turned unexpectedly bad, he said, and the navigational equipment was not working properly, but they would give it their best shot.

Soon we were lurching downward through the cloud. I strained at the window for a hint of land, but beyond the wingtips there was nothing but a soupy whiteness in which the aircraft was tossed like a paper boat. Conversations faded. The pilots took off their sunglasses and readied themselves for the approach. My stomach turned somersaults, and the wolf-clad nurse, the mad glint banished from her eyes, hugged the back of the empty seat in front of her and leaned into the aisle from time to time as though she might be sick.

Suddenly there was a flash of brown through the white and we were banking steeply out of the cloud at five hundred feet as the earth leaped upwards like a great tilting plate over the crazy angle of the wings. Through the tear-streaked windows I saw a plain flanked by sullen mountains brooding in the monochrome distance. Then we were down with a bump and a spontaneous but weary round of applause from the passengers.

In the grip of the earth again we taxied to the control tower, past a dozen aircraft disintegrating beside the runway like skeletons in excavated graves. Nearby was an ageing MiG fighter, its nose and canopy muzzled like a dog's.

It was cold and drizzling. We huddled near the plane as a Russian military tanker lumbered across the tarmac, and a man wearing a jump suit and cowboy boots clattered onto a wing looking for the petrol cap. A Red Cross jeep arrived. I sat between the nurse's wet fur and a reticent Frenchman whom I tried hopefully to engage in conversation. He was unaccustomedly unfriendly and I took an instinctive dislike to him which, given that he tried to have me shot about a week later, seems fairly justified.

*

The road from the airport headed north straight into the city, and was scarred with shattering ruts every fifteen feet. Its Russian concrete slabs made even rougher going than the fields alongside so we drove through the mud instead, past the dismal outskirts of the airport; a suburb of wrecked military paraphernalia and abandoned bunkers. We passed buildings that had once been factories, a graveyard of Russian tanks, and on beneath a canopy of tall pines that lined the road.

For years I had dreamed of visiting Herat and never quite believed I would reach the place. During the Soviet occupation the city was for foreigners one of the most inaccessible on earth. News trickled to the outside world like a broken stream; there were no foreign missions to forward details of the conflict, and even the Red Cross were allowed only rare visits to its prisons, which were temporarily emptied for the occasions. For those familiar with the perils of travel inside the country at the time, the very mention of Herat was invested with an allure matched by nothing but the danger of getting there. Only a few very intrepid outsiders ever made the trip.

I am not sure what the others saw. An impoverished city under occupation by fanatics, perhaps. One's impressions of a place are governed by the times. Bruce Chatwin likened arriving in Herat from Iran to 'coming up for air'. And reaching Afghanistan for the first time in 1933, Robert Byron wrote in that periodically rediscovered classic, *The Road to Oxiana*: 'Here at last is Asia without an inferiority complex.' Byron was impressed by the Afghans' self-confidence and 'devil-may-care' bearing; he fell in love with Herat, feeling he had uncovered the forgotten capital of the 'Oriental Medicis', whose history had been obscured in the West by the more accessible Samarqand. Afghanistan, as much in 1933 as now, was a less comfortable destination, and attracted fewer visitors.

I was only vaguely aware that the history of the place formed a tapestry whose strands reached from Oxford to Peking; a fabled site whose religions, languages and coinage had mirrored the pulse of Asia for millennia.

Herat's name looms early on from the mists of written chron-ologies. When the idea of monotheism was still a novelty to the world, the area now called Herat was already known as the oasis of Hera, inhabited by Iranian tribes who had been pushed eastwards by the expanding Assyrian Empire.

It was already an important centre in the fourth century BC. This much is known from the chroniclers of Alexander the Great. In 330 BC the young Macedonian, unsated by the drunken sacking of Persepolis, made his way eastwards to seize the region from the Persian satrap Satibarzanes, and the city was renamed, and probably rebuilt, as 'Alexandria of the Arians'. (The region was Aria to the Greeks; Peter Levi has Artokoana for Herat.) The Greek army moved south not, as might be supposed, with the support of existing colonists in the region, but to encounter the stiffest resistance of its entire eastern campaign. Freed from the yoke of Persian rule, both Greek and local tribal kingdoms were hungry for independence, and fought fiercely for it.

Herat is built on an ancient crossroads of trade and invasion and has paid a correspondingly heavy price. Its natural setting – a broad open plain, nourished by the waters of the Hari Rud, which flows west to lose itself in the sands of the Kara Kum desert – makes it virtually indefensible. To its east rise the steepening walls of the Paropamisus range, which tower over what were once the mountain kingdoms of Ghor and the Hazārajat, and climax in the lofty tangle of the Hindu Kush. To the north leads the route to Balkh and the steppes beyond the Amu Darya. To the south leads the route taken by Alexander across the dusty lowlands skirting the Dasht-i Margo or Desert of Death, where it turns east towards India, or continues south into Baluchistan towards the Indian Ocean.

The dynasties that ruled this portion of Khorassan in Alexander's bloody wake rose and fell in succeeding waves of glory and carnage. Their names make the study of modern history seem pale: Seleucid, Parthian, Scythian, Kushan, Ephthalite, Sassanian, Samānid, Saffarid, Ghaznavid, Ghūrid, Samānid, Mongol, Tīmūrid, Uzbek, Safāvid, Durrāni, Barakzai. And briefly, Russian.

Between the attendant upheavals Herat must have prospered. Classical and Islamic writers called Herat the 'pearl', the 'breadbasket', the 'oasis' of Khorassan, and marvelled at the complexity of its irrigation systems. Under the Kushans, roughly throughout the first Christian century, when trade thrived between East and West from China to Rome and countless intermediate points, the caravanserais of Herat, which lay on the southern tributary of the great silk route, gave sanctuary to men and beasts travelling in both directions.

It must have been a good period to be a highway bandit. Silk, much in demand in the West (the secrets of its production guarded jealously by the Chinese), was the primary commodity. But the East was a treasury of other precious goods: ivory, exotic woods, animal furs and skins, gums, resins and perfumes, spices, medicines, fruits, coral, pearls, amber and metals flowed from India and southeast Asia towards European capitals, particularly imperial Rome and the Hellenized countries. China also provided hemp, paper, saddles, jewellery and the highly-prized musk of Chinese and Tibetan deer. Live trinkets – human as well as animal – were sent to the courts of Western rulers; parrots, monkeys, snakes and elephants were the most sought after, and slaves were traded in both directions. Silver and bronze plate, glassware, pottery, wine and oils travelled eastwards.

For as long as history records, the flow of Herat's precious water has been skilfully diverted by its inhabitants into elaborate systems of irrigation canals, nourishing countless gardens, vineyards and fields of corn and rice. As we drove into the city I suddenly remembered the opening lines of the fable which recounts the visit to the region by an eleventh-century Samanid prince from Bokhara. So captivated was he by its beauty, its gentle climate and seventy varieties of grape, that he stayed for two full years; meanwhile his courtiers and soldiers pined for their own land, and approached the poet laureate Rūdākī with a plea to induce their master, with a poem, to return home. The blind old man took up his lute and began to pluck at its strings, evoking the memory of the beloved Amu Darya river then called the Mūlīyān:

> *Bū-ye jū-ye mūlīyān āyad hamī*
> *bū-ye yār-e mehrebān āyad hamī...*

> (The sound of the Amu brings to mind
> The thoughts of loved ones left behind...)*

The effect on the prince was dramatic; he grabbed the nearest horse and, without putting on his boots, rode straight for Bokhara.

Under the Tīmūrids, with whose name the city is most strongly associated, Herat reached a zenith of cultural fortune in the fifteenth century. The Tīmūrids took their name from Tīmūr, the West's Tamerlaine. Like Chingiz Khan before him, his ambition was world conquest. Using Khorassan as his base he wrested an empire from Turkey to China and from Moscow to the Persian Gulf, levelling cities and leaving a wake of uncountable dead. The great capitals of the east reeled in horror at his swift and merciless horsemen and, one by one, were snuffed out. In glorious Baghdad his generals built pyramids of skulls; at Ankara, the vanquished Ottoman Sultan Beyazit

---

* From the discourse on poetry in the *Chahār Maqāle* of Nizāmi-i-Arau-i Samarqandi, a tiresome compulsory text behind the pages of which I managed to perfect the technique of sleeping in class.

was said to have been forced to kneel as Tīmūr's personal footstool; at the ravaged Delhi, not a bird stirred over the rubble and corpses for three months. Tīmūr's imperial headquarters were at Samarqand, where between the oceanic blood-letting he commissioned awesome monuments and palace-studded parks to be decorated by the hands of captive craftsmen, kidnapped along with their families from the far corners of his empire. In 1405 the enigmatic 'World-Shaker' died, on his way to conquer China, and the empire began to shrink like a dying sea.

Two great kingdoms retained power under his two most capable sons. Western Persia and Iraq were given to Jelalluddin Mīranshah, and Khorassan, with Herat as its capital, to Shah Rukh. The wound to the East was judiciously healed by Shah Rukh's release of the Chinese ambassador, whom his father had detained, and gifts and embassies were exchanged.

It seems that Shah Rukh inherited none of his father's lust for conquest, and the restlessness in his Mongol blood was diverted into more creative efforts. Herat inherited, under a more humane regime, the craftsmen, artists and poets that had once embellished Tīmūr's Samarqand, and their genius fused creatively with the Persian stream from the west.

This was the beginning of the fifteenth century, and Herat blossomed. In architecture, poetry, painting, literature, music, fabric production and jewellery, the city had no rival in Asia, and became the political and cultural metropolis of the continent. Missions and embassies came and went from Cairo to Peking, trading in royal keepsakes: thoroughbred horses, lions and tigers. Herat nurtured wise and holy men as abundantly as melons.

Shah Rukh had an extraordinary wife, Queen Gohar Shād, meaning Joyful Jewel, also called the Bilkis — Queen of Sheba — of her time. The Queen was one of Asia's greatest female patrons of the arts. Four hundred years later she was written of as the most incomparable woman in the world. Her influence in public affairs suggests a leniency towards women characteristic of the dynasty. She commissioned, among many other public buildings, the fabled *musalla* as well as an outstanding mosque in Mashad. The enigmatic queen played an active role in the politics of the dynasty, for which she paid with her life when she was over eighty.

Her son Ulugh Beg became viceroy to Samarqand and, exercising a bent for secular learning (later his own grim undoing), built the famous observatory there. He plotted the movement of a thousand stars and calculated the length of the solar year to within seconds. A hundred and fifty years later, his astronomical tables were published in Oxford.

Under Husein Baikara, who resolved a twenty-year domestic squabble after Shah Rukh's death to become Sultan in 1468, Herat brought forth its final and most pungent blossom. In the words of the Sultan's younger nephew – this was Bābūr – the city was 'filled with learned and matchless men'. The minister Ali Shīr Navā'i, not only guide and confidant to the Sultan, was the era's champion of literary Chagatay Turkish, a famous poet as well as an avid builder and restorer credited with the construction of several hundred mosques, colleges, hospitals, libraries and caravanserais.

Herat's most celebrated artist, Kamaluddin, known to the West as Bihzad, set the world's standard in 'Persian' miniatures. His exquisite depictions of hunting parties, royal picnics, ceremonies of the court, battles, dervishes in solitary caves and scenes from chivalric romances evoke the balmy spirit of the age. The court historian Mīrkhwand wrote a 'History of the World' which influenced the Moslem view of history for centuries afterwards, and his grandson Khwandamir wrote another that would have a corresponding influence on the Western vision of Islamic history. The city was also home to Abdurrahman Jāmi, the greatest Persian poet of the fifteenth century, a mystic luminary whose wisdom was sought out from Sufis and scholars throughout central Asia. The Sultan is said to have wept for hours beside Jāmi's grave.

The flame of culture burned brightly for a hundred years, but began to gutter in a fateful wind from the north. At the turn of the century Samarqand was captured by raiding Uzbeks, and the empire's frontiers grew ever more porous. From within too, the family was afflicted by the curse of high living and a weakness, by Bābūr's account, for all-night drinking parties. Gout-ridden and softened by luxury, the

Sultan had lost all stomach for a fight, and the city went on the defensive. In 1506 the old man died, and his sons, lacking military experience, allowed Herat to fall to the unlettered Uzbeks the following year; three years later it was recaptured by the Persian Shah Ismael Safavi, who drank wine from the Uzbek leader's skull.

The horrified Bābūr, who witnessed the light of his uncle's empire extinguished, was no slouch; kept from his beloved central Asia, he invaded India and became the first of the Moghul emperors. But from the middle of the fifteenth century Herat was a pawn between the empire of the Persian Safavids to the west and that of Bābūr's descendants. Khorassan and, gradually, the whole of central Asia began to turn in on itself and dissolve into the shadows of history.

The authors of its decline were three. One was the superior tactics and firearms of the empires that had begun to enclose it. Another was the distant splash of an anchor into the harbour of Calicut from the deck of a Portuguese trading ship captained by Vasco de Gama, and the opening of the first sea routes to the east. The third was the rise of an insignificant province far away to the north, called Russia.

*

We jolted into the city past a deserted park, a boarded-up cinema, a dry fountain in an overgrown circle and the dilapidated Park Hotel, where Byron had read up on the city's history smoking cigars and drinking arak. Hotels were now off limits to foreigners or full of Tālebān fighters. All along the streets, walls had been daubed hastily with the slogans of the city's latest occupiers.

Herat had fallen to the Tālebān a few months earlier, and the former amir, the veteran guerrilla leader Ismael Khān, had fled to Iran with his closest supporters. There were a dozen versions of how and why it had happened, but it was not by a fight. Its fall was a surprise not only to Herat, but to the government in Kabul and to the Tālebān themselves. Rather bewildered by their own unexpected trophy, they had left much of the running of the city to existing officials. But what they had begun to impose was hardly endearing to a population recovering from more than a decade of strife.

The university had been closed down; female students were being ejected from schools, and male doctors were forbidden to treat female patients. Sport had been forbidden in public. It had become illegal to possess a musical instrument. Men were urged to shave their heads. Each day new and impossible restrictions were issued to the city. There was even a new Tāleban radio station, which daily celebrated the city's 'liberation' and exhorted the population to embrace the new moral order, broadcasting ever harsher decrees to its embittered listeners.

All this smacked of an alien and uncommonly zealous mentality. The Tāleban were strangers here, unlike in the south. Their appearance, dress, tribal origins, language, customs and interpretation of religion were different. Given all this and the deeply independent and self-consciously liberal spirit of Herat's population, I was not alone in wondering how long their control could possibly last. Some recent graffiti had appeared on the walls of the Friday mosque: 'We girls want to go back to school,' said one. Another read: 'Tāleban go back to America.' I felt it would be interesting to be in a city where such issues were in everybody's mind, like being inside a pressure cooker. Sooner or later things would start to cook.

*

In a side street awash with mud, Madeleine and I were dropped at her headquarters. It belonged to one of the French medical outfits; in Kabul their head of operations had recommended I stay there. But even as we arrived I had a sense of foreboding. It was based on only a few moments of observation, but of the kind I'd come to trust. The Afghan staff were offhand and uncharacteristically withdrawn, and I was taken completely by surprise; they had an almost European air. This could only mean that either Afghans in Herat were generally less friendly, or that based on their contact with foreigners their usual friendliness had somehow been eroded.

Madeleine was received by friends in a side room amid a fervid exchange of kisses, but the door closed behind her and I was left in the hall struggling with my muddy bootlaces. The conversation stopped abruptly as I entered. Five staff looked me up and down and all of a sudden I felt the full weight of my intrusion, which there was no attempt to soften. I realized then how spoiled I had grown by the warmth of Afghan receptions.

I explained my situation to the head of the mission, saying that I had been recommended by his Kabul office to visit. But as I spoke, the corners of his mouth turned visibly downwards as though I were a waiter who had brought him a corked wine, and in the silence, his look seemed to say: 'Well, that may be how they do things in Kabul, but you're in Herat now.' Making no effort to disguise the weight imposed by my request, he said he would *consulter* with the others.

I was astonished by his response, as much as by the strength of my own distaste for it. In Kabul each day the war and its terrifying unpredictability bleached the self-importance out of people, but here the sudden reek of it was overpowering. It was unmistakable – that curious arrogance of those outsiders who hovered on the periphery of the war.

There was not a trace of this affliction in Kabul, where the rockets fell daily and the threat of being overrun crouched in the shadows of everybody's thoughts. Kabul had become the heart of the conflict; it was the friendliest place in the country. Herat lay on the edge of it, and although I did not yet know it, my host's reaction was only the first in a series of encounters with that strange meanness of spirit that sometimes creeps into outsiders living in an alien culture. I was reminded too of all the foreigners I had met in Pakistan, who were more knowledgeable and more opinionated about the situation in Afghanistan than anyone – many having never once entered the country itself. The war was like a gunshot, which inflicted on its observers a different type of wound at different ranges: with a graze, an inexplicable selfishness, like the petty cruelty of people who know they've been left out of something; with an open laceration, generosity and humility.

I wanted only a corner to rest and nurse my raging toothache.

'Well, if it's not too inconvenient...' I said, but it fell across his bows. The *problème*, he explained, was that there would be more members of their team arriving within a few days; and *en plus* there was the question of *sécurité* – whatever that meant – *mais enfin*, he relented, if it was just for a night, *bof*...

Bof to you too, I thought. But it did not occur to me at the time that the coolness of the reception might have been influenced by my appearance and the sheer improbability of my story. Nobody travelled alone in Afghanistan; nobody just came to Herat to visit. Furthermore I was wearing the two things that 99 per cent of the foreign population shunned: military-looking clothes, and a beard. This was because I wanted to blend in; most foreigners wanted to stand out. Thinking back, I was lucky to have been allowed to stay: I looked, it occurred to me later, like a wandering mercenary.

We sat around a table with Swiss chocolate and whisky and the others chain-smoked between rapid-fire conversation from which I was excluded. For the first time on the entire trip I felt like an unwelcome intruder. My toothache was excruciatingly painful and I fell asleep in my chair.

*

In keeping with its volatile history, Herat's role in the Soviet invasion had been pivotal. By the beginning of 1979, anti-communist feeling had swelled throughout the country. In Herat as elsewhere the communists mistook the Afghans' resilience for meekness, and moved at a pace unthinkable to the native population. Soviet advisers began to appear in Herat to direct and supervise the infiltration of the administration and the army by party members. High-ranking military officers were demoted and replaced with communist officers of lower rank. Russian engineers also began work to extend the runway at the city's airport and improve the road from Turkmenistan. The radio station and newspapers rang with the arrogant vocabulary of the new ideology, flaunting contempt for the old ways. Merchants were ordered to paint their shops red and display photographs of Taraki or his Prime Minister, Amin.

Afghans being Afghans, there was, to nobody's surprise but the Russians', a very violent uprising.

On 14 March a crowd raged through the city, attacking government buildings and party headquarters, and was fired on by government troops directed by Soviet advisers. Afghan officers refused to lay down artillery on civilians, and mutinied. Communists and sympathizers were dragged from their homes and killed, as well as several Soviet advisers and their families. The new government, backed by Soviet forces, took ten days to restore order, during which time several thousand civilians were killed. The uprising was a key event in the Soviets' decision to invade. It was also the first time Soviet troops – not yet officially in the country – as well as aircraft, flying sorties from inside the Soviet Union, were used to put down an internal disturbance in Afghanistan. The bodies of the killed were bulldozed into mass graves on a bluff overlooking the shrine of the saint Ansāri. The site became a kind of memorial for the mujaheddin and Herat as a whole. Later I saw it from a distance, but I hadn't the heart to visit.

Among the Afghan soldiers who fled the burning city was Major Ismael Khan, who escaped to the mountains with sixty loyal men to set about organizing the resistance to the new regime, and soon became the foremost commander of the region. This extraordinary man, whose name means nothing in the West, supervised for ten years a resistance campaign against the most brutal occupiers of modern times. Those who spent time with him describe Ismael Khan in terms of unanimous respect, as a softly spoken man, deeply religious, scornful of outward show, a born orator, and revered by his men.

When the Russians came in force the following year, Herat suffered particularly heavily for its resistance. Early in the war the western suburbs of the city were carpet-bombed from high altitude, leaving uncounted civilian losses. Under Russian direction the region around the city was divided into free-fire zones designed to isolate pockets of resistance and deny them support and shelter. The ruthlessness and futility of this campaign, in Herat as in most of the country, is attested to by the ruins that today surround the city, as well as by its failure at the time to secure for the government any significant territorial gains.

It was a bloody stalemate from the start. By night the Soviets remained within the heavily mined perimeters of their bases while the mujaheddin emerged to lay mines, prepare ambushes and forage among their ruined homes for salvageable weaponry. By day, anything lying beyond the city's security belts – mujaheddin or civilians, their crops, livestock and ancient irrigation systems – became legitimate targets for Soviet tanks, helicopter gunships, artillery and bombers. Neither side could dislodge the other except momentarily. In the meantime, more than a million Afghans sought refuge in neighbouring Iran. This conflict, which endured for ten years, went virtually unreported.

A handful of independent journalists and volunteer doctors managed the long and hazardous trek in disguise from Pakistan, sheltering in mujaheddin bases in the mountains beyond the plain or among impoverished villagers living on tea and rice and the occasional luxury of meat. The English writer Nick Danziger likened the ruins of eastern Herat to the aftermath of Hiroshima. A Polish journalist witnessed daily bombings of civilian villages. But few of their extraordinary tales attracted much attention.

Over the forgotten plain, its widening ruins, and from secret mountain bases, the resistance confounded Soviet strategy in a deadly game of cat-and-mouse. The Soviet General Andrushkin in Herat wrote to Ismael Khan saying he had dealt with 'bandits' before, and that Ismael Khan's fate would be no different from that of the Uzbek *basmach* Ibrahim Beg, who had resisted the Russians at the turn of the century but eventually had been defeated. A reply was sent back with the general's messenger: 'You Russians still remember Ibrahim Beg after seventy years. I want you to remember me for two hundred.' One can imagine an equivalent ultimatum being delivered on the very same soil to a wily mountain chieftain by one of Alexander's messengers, twenty-three hundred years before. And, no doubt, an equivalent response.

*

In the afternoon I set off down a muddy street towards the *musalla*. Of all the monuments that remain from the city's golden age under the Tīmūrids, the *musalla* complex is the best known. Byron called it 'the most beautiful example in colour in architecture ever devised by man to the glory of his God and himself', which was high praise from such a critical eye. The *musalla* itself was a combination of a vast college and mosque commissioned by Queen Gohar Shād and built by the famous Persian architect Qavamuddin in 1417. Half a century later under Sultan Husain Baiqara a *madrasseh* with four huge minarets was built nearby, along with a covered bazaar and a hospital.

European accounts of the site come from the early and mid-nineteenth century, almost all of them from players, in various guises, of the Great Game: Lieutenant Alexander Burnes of the 1st Bombay Light Infantry, the German (spy) Oskar von Neidermeier, Vambéry, the Hungarian explorer of central Asia, the Russian scholar Khanikov, the French general and soldier of fortune Ferrier, and the Great Game player par excellence, Lieutenant Arthur Conolly, whose cruel fate at the hands of the fanatical emir of Bokhara passed into Victorian legend. All concur in their descriptions of the extraordinary beauty and radiance of the *musalla* buildings, their colours, mosaics and inscriptions.

I had already read an account of the site by Ferrier, who visited Herat in the middle of the nineteenth century after trying unsuccessfully to penetrate Kabul in disguise. In what is a rare description he writes: 'The mosque is completely covered with a mosaic of glazed bricks in varied and beautiful patterns, and the cupola is of amazing dimensions. Several arcades supported by pillars in brick equal the proportions of the Arch of Ctesiphon, and the seven magnificent minarets that surround it may be said to be intact.' This would be unremarkable were it not one of the last accounts of the *musalla* complex ever penned by a European.

An article on Herat in the *Encyclopaedia Britannica* of the time almost predicts its fate. Against a possible renewed attack by Persia, the writer says, the city could 'by a skilful adaptation of the resources of modern science' be made completely secure. Then you read: 'but of course, if an attack by a well-appointed European army were anticipated, more extensive preparations for defence would be required.'

It was not the Persians the English feared would move on Herat. The 'well-appointed European army' – there was only one in central Asia – was Russian. Czarist expansion in central Asia had brought their troops ever closer to the northern frontier of Afghanistan, and the British were nervous about the seemingly unstoppable advance. Russia had absorbed the Kazakh steppes in 1864, Tashkent in 1865, Khiva in 1873, Bokhara and Kokhand in 1876, Transcaspia in 1881 and Merv (hence the joke at the time about 'mervousness') in 1884.

The Czar's frontier generals had a ruthless reputation. The slaughter of 20,000 Turcomans at Geok Tepe northwest of Herat under General 'Bloody Eyes' Skobeliev had not been forgotten by the British public.* Then in March 1885 Russian troops fought the Afghans at Pyandjeh on their northern frontier, and installed an occupying force. The Great Game was in full swing and a Russian assault on Herat, its most obvious prize and considered the key to an advance on India, was expected to follow. England informed Russia that an attack on Herat would be considered a direct declaration of war. Troop reserves were called up in both countries; in their capitals there was constant talk of the inevitable conflict.

Herat was ordered to a state of defence and under British direction the 'extensive preparations' were indeed carried out. All buildings offering potential cover to a Russian force advancing from the north were destroyed. These included the *musalla*, the *madrasseh* of Sultan Husain, an unknown number of minarets as well as the buildings that surrounded them. In Byron's words, 'the most glorious productions of Mohammadan architecture in the fifteenth century, having survived the barbarism of four centuries, were now rased to the ground.'

Nine minarets were left standing, two of which fell in an earthquake in 1931, and another in 1951. Judging from the remaining structures Byron wrote 'there was never such a mosque before or since.' I was excited to be approaching such hallowed soil, hopping and slipping along ridges of mud on the street which, from a rough mental bearing, I guessed would take me there. At the end of it, I literally stumbled onto one of Asia's most famed architectural sites. It was a shock.

In front of me stretched a treeless patch of muddy ground the size of two football pitches, framed by the ruins of mud buildings, mounds of mud-coloured rubble and broken mud-brick walls. Fifty yards away was what looked like a stubby concrete box topped by a dome the shape of an observatory. Near the road stood a solitary minaret leaning like the Tower of Pisa, its base piled with rubble. Halfway up a bite had been taken out of it by a rocket blast. Beyond

---

* It was described in graphic despatches by the intrepid Edmund O'Donovan, special correspondent of the *Daily News*, who managed to witness Skobeliev's massacre as it occurred.

it was another building, with a shallower dome than the other but equally bare of colour or ornament, equally deprived of a setting in that field of mud.

These were, I realized with a sinking feeling, the mausoleum of Queen Gohar Shad, the sole surviving minaret of her college, and the tomb of Sultan Husein's Prime Minister, Mīr Ali Shīr Navā'i.

*

Stunned, I made first for the minaret. It was in sad shape, which seemed worse for the drizzle and the mud and the danger of mines, but retained enough of its former self for me to see what the fuss had been about. All around its base were fragments of glazed tilework the colour of jade, turquoise, lapis and occasionally mustard. Close up the minaret is huge. Yet every inch of its surface forms part of the overall design; not a fragment is superfluous.

The main body of the shaft is, or was, covered with repeating diamonds of mosaic separated, like scales or folds of chain mail, by lines of horizontally set brick. Each of the diamonds is a mosaic, about two feet high, of a stylized flower with a black heart and petals the colour of mustard. The flower itself, its tendrils even, is made of tinier tiles.

There are two balconies, the first about eighty feet up supported by tiered 'scalloped' niches covered by more elaborate tilework and enclosed by horizontal bands of brightly coloured calligraphy. The upper balcony now forms the top of the minaret, so at least twenty feet of tower have disappeared since Byron photographed it in 1933. The whole structure leans at about five degrees off vertical.

This minaret, I now realize, was the one considered least worthy of attention. Until 1885 it was attached to the main gate of the *madrasseh*, and its twin must have been demolished. But the really beautiful minarets that once marked the corners of the *musalla* and about which Byron among others raved as examples of the most delicate tilework ever devised by man, are gone.

We know one fell in 1951, leaving a final example. But this one too has been destroyed now, some time during the Russian occupation. All that remains of its 'glittering net' of white marble faience, 'azure bloom', 'deep and luminous' colours and 'vast multiplication of design', is an amputated stump across the muddy field, standing barely proud of a slowly dissolving mound of rubble.

When? I wondered, as I looked out towards it. How? Who had seen it topple? I had never known the experience of grief over a destroyed monument: I knew it now.

*

Four other minarets pierced the sky to the northeast. These once formed the corners of Sultan Husain Baikara's famous *madrasseh*. I walked to them across a mound that bridges a dry canal, where two tiny fruit stalls and a few bedraggled customers gave life to the desolate scene. There was a burst of automatic gunfire nearby, and I ducked by reflex, but the men at the stalls had not even looked up.

My fantasy of being able to photograph the city from the top of one of the minarets was quickly dashed. Here too the bases were splashed with red paint to indicate the presence of mines. The entrances are in any case forty feet up, the height at which the minarets were once joined by the walls and arches of the original building. Their size is impressive. The bases are twenty feet across and they tower upwards to a hundred and thirty feet. They all lean slightly at various angles, and two seem almost bent as if they have adjusted to the movement in their ancient foundations with the organic intelligence of a living structure. But the network of marble white faience and rich colour of their surfaces seemed irretrievably lost; what remains is a ravaged shadow. The surfaces are lacerated by gunfire and punctured by rocket holes that have smashed through the thick layers of brick to expose their inner cores. Yet they stand.

The sky was heavily overcast and a drizzle added to my sense of grief at the sight of these once proud monuments. I walked back through the mud towards the mausoleum of Queen Gohar Shād. Not a trace of decoration remained on its sides; the ribbed dome had been repaired but the turquoise tiles that covered it had not been replaced. The band of once ornate calligraphy at its base was three-quarters destroyed. The door itself was padlocked.

A pickup truck filled with armed Tālebs lurched past along the road, followed by an old man driving a skeletal donkey which tottered under a load of firewood.

Across the open space where I had hoped to find a shady garden were pits like shell-holes where tall pines had once swayed. A muddy track snaked to the far side and the stump of the last *musalla* minaret. Not a tree remained. What the Russians had not deliberately cleared for the business of war had fallen first to exploding shells and then to the axes of peasants desperate for fuel.

Three phantom-like women passed by, drawing their veils across their faces as they approached. I lost the urge to linger because the sight of all this made me too sad. I found my feelings towards the place were as complex and deep as if, after years of rumour and suspense, I had met some long-lost relative who did not measure up to my childhood expectations.

I turned for a final look, and just then, somewhere far away to the west, the clouds broke and released a burst of afternoon sunlight that fell in a luminous swathe across the valley. Quite suddenly the minarets were transformed and danced unexpectedly to life, no longer the forlorn colour of mud but a regal shade of turquoise, shimmering with golden highlights against the curtain of dark cloud behind them. It lasted only a moment but my sense of grief was suddenly lifted, as if a whisper, husky with the intimacy of the past, had stolen furtively across the centuries as a reminder that, despite everything, time's respect for beauty was not entirely undone.

*

I headed south towards the citadel, which has figured so prominently in Herat's destiny. It is a massive structure which, after the ragged shops and stalls that you wind through to get there, looms with added strength. It is built on an ancient mound in the northwest of the city near the edge of what once formed Herat's outer defences. The present walls rise from the ruins of an earlier castle built by the Kart maliks in the fourteenth century and destroyed in the Mongol onslaught under Tīmūr. In Shah Rukh's day seven thousand men are recorded to have laboured over its reconstruction, and it has survived all subsequent assaults more or less intact.

More or less. There was a big fight for Herat in 1837, when under Russian guidance a Persian army surrounded the city. Help came to the Afghans in the unlikely form of a twenty-six-year-old Irish lieutenant called Eldred Pottinger who, disguised as a holy man, had slipped into the city on a reconnaissance mission. Hearing of the Persian advance, Pottinger offered his services to the vizier, and took charge of Herat's defences and the troops in the citadel.

A ten-month siege followed. The starving city ate horsemeat and dodged mortar bombs from Persian cannons. The citadel's crenellations were lined with the severed heads of the ever more desperate attackers, who by a thread failed to overrun its walls.

In June the following year the siege was called off; the Persians skulked back to Teheran, and their Russian adviser Count Simonich was officially disgraced by the Czar. But the British were flustered, especially by news of the extent of Russian influence in the Persian camp, and devised a plan to place a British puppet on the throne in Kabul. Soon afterwards they began their catastrophic occupation of Afghanistan, catalysing in the process the Czarist advance into central Asia proper, and the stakes in the *bolshaya igra*, Great Game, grew ever higher. Historical accounts of this blunder read rather like those beginning to appear today of the Soviet invasion of Afghanistan: catalogues of greed, arrogance and bad judgement.

*

'Peace be to you! May I ask, brother, where you're from?'

I had stopped in the shadow of the citadel near a stall, and the owner caught my eye. My boots, and my hesitancy in responding, had betrayed me.

'I knew it!' he said. 'We don't see many foreigners here. Alone, you say? You had better be careful; things have changed since these Tālebs arrived.'

I sat with him for a while. He was not much older than me, and had been a policeman in Ismael Khan's time, but when the Tālebān arrived he had been forced, for a reason I didn't catch, to leave his job. He was burning to talk: what did I think of his chances of getting to America? He had a brother who had gone to New York eighteen years ago but who had died of a brain tumour before he could help his family. But at least he had some kind of education, he said, not like these Tālebs who were ruining the place, and what with the price of things going up at the rate they were, and his old job taken from him, well – this was no way to make a living, although God was kind enough to provide this little shop ... but what was I doing there after all, and what did I think of Afghanistan?

At such moments you feel the weight of an outsider's greatest privilege: to be able to leave. He asked me questions about visas and exchange rates that I couldn't answer. He was visibly let down by the news that I had no official powers. We would chat for a few moments about lesser things until, like a wave, the need to talk about his worries would surge back into him.

When his feelings subsided, I asked about the citadel. Under Ismael Khan, he said, it had been a museum. That much I already knew. But since the Tālebs arrived not a soul was allowed there. They had looted the place, and carried off to their bases in Pakistan such treasures as I could not imagine! The citadel had been full of old and wonderful things, and now they would never get them back. His story was a characteristic mix of fact and symbolism. There was even a statue of a golden bird—

'What kind of bird?' I asked.

'Oh, big, with wings outstretched like a phoenix, a simurgh – too big for a single man to carry.'

'Gold, you say?'

'Solid!'

'It must have been priceless.'

'By God yes, there was no other like it in the world.'

'And old, too.'

'For centuries, yes, it was hidden in the citadel. God alone knows how long it had been there. At least from the era of the fire-worshippers.' The phoenix crown, perhaps, bestowed by Ahura Mazda himself on Rustam of the Divine Lustre, king of the first city of the Arians ...

'And the Tālebs have taken it?'

'Oh yes, it's gone, gone for good!'

I was surprised to see the lines and surfaces of the walls and towers were clean and smooth. This made the citadel the only building I saw in Afghanistan to be in better shape in reality than in photographs I had earlier seen. As you walk at its base from the southeast corner alongside a filthy trench there is an arcade of forty arches lining the ramparts, which you follow to the main entrance.

There was a tank with a Tāleb flag fluttering from its antenna, and three armed men milled in and around the doorway. Walking through the mud twenty feet from them I saw a sign in English giving the hours of opening of the museum. For a moment I was tempted to suggest to its captors that to leave the sign there, now that they had turned the citadel into a military base, would be grievously misleading to tourists.

I wandered past as slowly as was possible without attracting attention, vaguely hoping I might glimpse a nuclear missile being secretly unloaded in the courtyard beyond. My message would confirm the shocking HUMINT reports from Islamabad received six months earlier about the rogue missile smuggled from Kazakhstan, and be verified later that day by high-altitude reconnaissance; soon the encrypted phone lines were buzzing madly at Langley and Vauxhall Cross, and a world war would be narrowly avoided ...

Byron glimpsed the gun-park in the same spirit, and it was difficult, in the atmosphere of the time, not to be infected by the same silliness.

Catching sight of a track that led around the base of the walls I splashed and slipped through the mud along it as far as the huge northwest tower. I had assumed that the citadel, like all citadels, had always been the colour of mud, in the way one forgets that the bare stone inside a cathedral gives no real taste of the decoration that once adorned it. Yet if the traces of decoration that remained on the tower were an indication of the original surface, the whole structure was once an even more spectacular sight – a psychedelic oasis, rising luminously from the dusty plain.

The tower itself seems to have escaped the most recent renovations and is in poor shape, though not by Afghan standards. It is blasted in several places by rocket-grenade fire and its very top looks as though it has been bitten off. The original surface remains only in places (yet even this may be what is left of an earlier renovation). At its base clings the last of a band of a calligraphic inscription in Kufic style whose flowing white letters are twice the height of a man and enclosed by azure-coloured borders. Above it in poorer condition are the last tessellating lozenges, thirty feet high, of brightly glazed tiles in lapis and coral.

How much blood must have flowed over them! The track wound on beside the trench to the deserted north side and, unexpectedly alone for a few seconds, I slipped out my camera and took a picture of the massive walls.

It was drizzling and cold, the sound of the streets had fallen away and the citadel felt suddenly ominous. Spooked, I hurried on with a terrible thought: who knows how long the brain within a severed head can think and feel? And how many of the severed heads ranged along those very walls had, in their last few moments, their consciousness ebbing reluctantly from its physical home, stared down through darkening eyes from the battlements to the spot where I stood — seeing the mounting piles of mutilated corpses and hearing their comrades' cries and the pounding of rifle and cannon fire and the unmistakable liquid thump of lead as it meets flesh — before the life finally trickled from them?

*

Three people passed me in the opposite direction: a man struggling cheerfully to steer a bicycle with a big truck battery on its saddle, and two women in billowing blue fishgills and plastic shoes. Peeking from beneath their hems was the faintly troubling sight of slender white ankles splashed with mud.

At the end of the path was a row of dilapidated stalls. An old man sat in one of them at the foot of a pile of charcoal which reached nearly to the ceiling. Our eyes met, his teeth flashed a smile from his blackened face, and we exchanged a nod of recognition. Then a few paces on I emerged from the near-silence onto the madness of a busy street. Pony traps festooned with bouncing pom-poms were weaving in and out of the path of trucks and jeeps. At a corner I bought a glass of hot milk and a pastry from a seven-year-old boy, and seeing me curl my freezing hands around the glass, a man nearby threw me an orange from his barrow with a cry.

'*Mandeh nabāshi!* May you never be tired!'

'*Zindeh bāshi!* May you live long!' I replied.

I stopped at a pastry shop, its windows filled with cakes and biscuits, and made a selection. When I came to pay, the owner said: 'You are a guest here, pay whatever you wish,' at which I gave him 5,000 Afghanis – about thirty pence – and told him to keep the change. I thought to myself: these Asian shopkeepers know very well that Westerners will overpay them. But just then a ripple of disapproval spread through the shop because I had given far too much – about ten pence too much – and the owner refused the note. I insisted, until the hand of another customer fell in gentle protest upon mine, and I found the note forced back into my pocket. In the end I allowed the shopkeeper to add a few extra biscuits to the packet, and there were nods of satisfaction from all round.

I went back to the French mission to rest and write and left the biscuits as an offering on the table. At dinner an unsmiling Afghan cook, to whom nobody spoke, brought us our food. With peculiar insularity no one expressed a trace of interest or curiosity towards the stranger in their midst. I was glad for the lack of attention because I was still exhausted by the toothache. But the atmosphere was arctically cold, and I began to long, like the homesick courtiers of the Samanid prince in Nizami's tale, to return to more familiar company.

*

Lacking a map of Herat I decided to make my own, and headed the next morning for the central mosque. From it ran a grid of paved roads whose condition quickly deteriorated; in each direction they petered out within half a mile into rivers of mud. To the southwest of the mosque was the central crossroads of the bazaar, whose narrow streets are crammed with life and industry; the bazaar, not the mosque or the fort, is the city's heart.

The exteriors of the buildings that line the main streets of the bazaar are modern, that is, built since 1900, but you see only traces of their original form in a lonely tiled border, carved balustrade or the chipped calligraphy above a once-proud archway. Apart from some newly built shops everywhere else is peeled, cracked, worn and shabby or pock-marked with bullet holes. The burned-out Russian tanks and armoured vehicles have been towed to various lonely spots outside the main city. Although weary, the buildings stand and function, and their interiors are scrupulously clean and ordered where the nature of business allows.

Going west from the mosque you follow the street of the second-hand clothes traders, where bales of Western cast-offs are spread at the edges of the road itself, or heaped in piles through which passers-by rummage and then bargain fiercely for a find. Boots and shoes are subjected to particular scrutiny. The worn-out ones lie in small mountains in the road or hang like withering fruits from string between the trees, but the best have been sorted and bought by more prosperous traders who restore them to a wearable state. Many have hardly been worn at all and look brand new. One shop was filled with cowboy boots, another with Italian loafers, and in another I bargained for half an hour for a pair of excellent walking shoes, leaving the shop three times in mock disgust at the price, until we struck a deal. Later I saw a formidable-looking Pathan gentleman, seven feet tall, turbaned and wrapped in an embroidered *pattū*, striding proudly out of the same shop. On his feet were a pair of green suede Birkenstock sandals.

There are countless jackets too and half the shops on the northern side are lined with layers of them. Here you can find an army conscript's coat in coarse wool, a golfing jacket in chequered silk of garish colours from a Jewish tailor in New York, or an unworn Harris tweed. I bought a wool coat — which hangs today over the back of the chair at which I write this — hand-tailored in Udine by Chiussi & Figlio and, according to the tag that is still attached, inspected and passed by a certain Dino B. two years before I was born.

From the street it is hard to tell what lies inside the shadowy rooms that border it and further along I wandered into a shop full of dresses and caused a ripple of giggles among the women.

There was a well at the end of the street where a boy was drawing water in a bucket made from a truck tyre. Head north here and you enter a street of spice sellers whose shops are filled with multicoloured powders in Russian ammunition tins or layered and sliced to resemble a Navajo sand-painting. There are sacks and piles of grains and pulses, chickpeas, peanuts, lentils, raisins, sunflower seeds and all manner of roots and husks that I had never seen, and a smell of roasting nuts and popcorn in the air. South and you pass fabric shops and jewellers, where small flocks of women, their heads inclined conspiratorially together, are gesturing at trinkets behind the windows.

Fresh bread is laid out on a platform by bakers' shops, where within, half a dozen boys form a production line in the smoky chamber. One operates the bellows for the fire beneath the circular, vertical oven, another kneads and shapes the dough into elongated ovals, another slaps them onto the oven walls and another scoops them off, steaming, with a long wooden paddle.

Here, 'where the great diversity of race and costume imparts much liveliness to the scene', according to the *Britannica*, you move through a swarm of life on the pavements, and in the relentless motion you may not be recognized unless your eye, which is hungry at all the sights, lingers for more than a moment on another's face. A cloud of blue smoke billows into the air from a man cooking kebabs over an improvised grill, another brews tea, and nearby a boy pounds garlic in a brass mortar. An old man creeps by beneath the weight of a huge sack, but manages a smile. A strikingly beautiful young girl wearing a turquoise velvet dress with gold embroidery at its hem is led past by her mother.

In the heart of the bazaar you pass two of the city's old vaulted reservoirs, 'of bold and excellent proportions' – the *Britannica* again – in use at least until the Russians came but empty now, their dry floors strewn with rubble. They are about thirty feet deep. Light filters across the precise brickwork through octagonal skylights. I lost myself in trying to calculate their volumes.

Near them are the few remaining covered sections of the bazaar; enclosures on two stories with domed wooden ceilings. I entered one by a pair of tall green doors, and found myself in a high chamber flanked by whitewashed vaulted rooms like monks' cells, where men were weaving strands of hemp and rope. Their feet were tucked under *sandalis* for warmth and a dozen pairs of eyes followed me with intense but friendly curiosity as I made a circuit to the open courtyard at the back. Two other similar buildings were miniature carpet bazaars; the most beautiful carpets are made with the deep reds and blues of Afghanistan but are strongly Persian in design.

If you leave this riot of sound and head off into a tiny side street the noise falls away like a dream on the tide of morning. Hearing the reflection of your own footsteps magnifies a sense of trespass and you hurry through. There are few men; you see instead young girls in bright dresses carrying water in plastic watering cans on their heads, or women whose faces suddenly disappear beneath their veils at your approach. Between the walls is just enough room for two people to pass each other, and when it happens there is none of the chaos on the main streets to dilute the encounter. Deprived of your anonymity, if your eyes should meet, like armies drawn up across a foreign plain and vying for some as yet unknown advantage, you are exposed to the full depth of the questioning in the other's eyes and remember, however much you may be disguised, that you are a stranger.

A trickle of noise, that swells to a clamouring tide as you approach, guides you out again, and you are relieved, because it was too quiet in those alleys. You are in the street of the metalworkers. Here men are bending and twisting and hammering at sheets of zinc and aluminium amid an orchestra of clanging and tapping, turning out stoves and bicycle mudguards and buckets and spades and trunks. The latter are painted in a crude hand with an improbable scene: a tropical shore beside a gently ruffled ocean, above which a flock of birds fly between cotton-wool clouds.

The sound of metal on metal gives way to the clatter of looms in a street of dim rooms where silk turbans are being made. Lingering at the door, a face may appear from behind the curtain of dense tight wefts, studying you intently. The turbans, mostly a speckled white, are twenty feet long, tightly woven and incredibly robust.

I found myself at the southern end of the bazaar looking onto an open square that teemed with fruit sellers hawking their wares with the same raucous enthusiasm as they do in Berwick Street. Between their mud-caked barrows a Tāleb was struggling to manoeuvre his motorcycle through the liquid road while his rifle slipped repeatedly from his shoulder. To the southwest about a mile away I caught sight of the huge dome of what looked like a newly built mosque, and its shape reminded me of the Taj Mahal. Architecturally it was the other way around; the Taj Mahal, which is thought of as archetypically Indian, is a Moghul adaptation of the Afghan prototype. But I did not visit it, falling prey to the traveller's curse of believing that later there would surely be time.

I ate a kebab and yoghurt for twenty pence and wandered back towards the mosque, near a trio of shops which, long ago – a blink of twenty years – when Herat was a caravan*serai* on the hippie trail, catered to travellers in search of exotic souvenirs. But who shopped there now? I wondered, and stepped inside one, prompted by the beckoning hand of an old man.

The shop was crammed with antiquities stained with age and coated with a layer of the inescapable dust. The owner rose to greet me, barefoot, and waved a rag over his relic-strewn shelves. Then he piled some kindling on the embers of a fire in a metal dish, fussed over a kettle, and bid me warm my hands.

It was like an alchemist's den; everywhere there was glassware in a variety of gentle colours: vases, pitchers, plates, glasses and candlesticks in turquoise, blue, green and yellow. The owner made them next door, he said, and showed me a second room piled with long-necked vases with spiralling filaments like vines around their necks. He also had a visitors' book full of the business cards of foreigners who had come to buy the famous Herati glassware from him; he was one of the last glassmakers in the city.

Just then some men came into the shop, but their heads were hidden from view by the paraphernalia hanging from the ceiling. I glimpsed an incongruous pair of polished black shoes, the spotless hem of a cashmere overcoat, pressed cuffs and a silk tie, and thought, *that is a Frenchman.* Two faces appeared: it was Peter Stocker, head of the Red Cross in Afghanistan, pipe, scarf, hat and all, with a French colleague. He had arrived earlier in the day along with the Dutch reporter Antoinette De Jung, whom I'd met in Kabul. Ducking beneath silks, we shook hands.

'Where are you staying?' he asked.

I told him I had spent a chilly night among the French.

'Go and see Beat at the Red Cross,' he said with characteristic helpfulness. 'He'll look after you.' This boded well and it seemed for a while that the problem of accommodation had been solved. They looked briefly around the shop, then roared away in their blazing white jeep. I promised the shopkeeper I would return, and headed eagerly for the Red Cross compound, slipping along the muddy streets.

*

The sign read:

INTERNATIONAL COMMITTEE OF THE RED CROSS (ICRC)

SUB-DELEGATION IN AFGHANISTAN

BLOOD BANK STREET

HERAT — AFGHANISTAN

Beyond the gates a well-tended rose garden was framed by long buildings on three sides. There was no one about, so I took off my muddy shoes and wandered inside, past a mock-Tahitian bar with palm-frilled awning, a weight-training room, and into the main room. Antoinette was stretched out like a sultan's captive bride on piles of purple velvet cushions, surrounded by her tape-recording paraphernalia.

'Comfortable, are you?'

'It's not bad,' she quipped, and took a sip from a turquoise glass.

I felt sure I would enjoy being a guest there.

*

Beat, head of the delegation, was a cheerful Swiss national in his early thirties. We had a friendly lunch together with Antoinette and swapped travellers' tales. No, he had never been to England. Yes, I had been to Switzerland, even hitch-hiked through the country one summer holiday, when I was in school.

'You *hitch-hiked*,' he repeated. 'Fascinating.' He was smiling, but only with his mouth; his eyes, I suddenly felt, betrayed disdain. 'You're a *traveller*, then,' he said; but the way he said it suggested he was thinking not of Ulysses but of a tramp, or of a venereal disease.

After lunch I asked him if I could stay — I had, after all, been

387

recommended to do so. I was floored when he said no. It was the first outright refusal of the entire trip. On it he hung a lengthy explanation, invoking 'problems with travellers' in the past, which he had not been there to witness. I had not seen this coming, and felt horribly jilted. The compound was full of empty rooms. But it felt too late to tell him that it was his own boss who had invited me.

In the hallway he stood over me as I did up my shoes, nodding as he searched for ways to soften the blow, apologizing all the while with nauseating cheerfulness.

'Jah, I am jealous of you — a *traveller!*' That word again. 'A *hitch-hiker!* Jah, I am sorry. Jah, it's nothing personal,' he said, which it was.

'I'll get over it,' I said, which I did not.

*

Later I went with Antoinette on a walk through the bazaars.

'I'm sorry about that business with Beat,' she said.

'So am I.' I was not sorry; I was wondering where I could find a severed horse's head to put in his bed.

'I'm embarrassed he's letting me stay because I'm a woman.'

'If you're so embarrassed you could refuse to stay.'

'Oh, stop whining. I told you not to wear too much green. And that beard — don't be so surprised.'

I wondered whether I should have worn a dress instead.

Bickering, we walked into the city. Stares of curiosity and delight followed us everywhere. For once the attention was diverted from me to the unveiled woman at my side, providing the opportunity to take some photographs. At an antique stall near the mosque we stopped to peer in a window at some dust-laden curios, and an ancient man in a white turban called us inside. It was hard to imagine he had had a customer in twenty years.

He brushed off a chair, found an extra stool for us to sit on, and made a fire for a tiny kettle on an iron dish in the window. His sad old eyes watched us from a corner to see where our curiosity would fall. Mine was caught at once by some crude stone carvings of weird figurines. The faces on these carvings were strange and devil-like, neither animal nor human, and I had seen nothing like them in Kabul.

What ancient prototype had they sprung from? The closest thing they resembled were demons from Persian miniatures. I could not date them; they might have been a thousand years old or turned out by a nine-year-old child the week before. The old man said they were carved by a tribe of women two hundred years ago and, of course, that they were very rare and couldn't be found elsewhere. We explored deeper into the gloom of the shop and then sat down.

Over tea he dug out a roll of pre-revolutionary 500-rouble notes in mint condition.

'You don't find these any more,' he said. They were beautiful but I was taken by the statues. I bargained for a devil-like face and a strange-looking beast the shape of a lion with a broad grimace, and on its back a reptilian baby like a crocodile. When we had settled on a price he disappeared into the back and emerged with a thick document. It was a Ph.D. thesis on Herati music from the University of Chicago, dated 1974, and inside the cover was a picture of the author and the shopkeeper, holding the long neck of a beautifully inlaid tambour. He was looking younger, and much happier.

We bought piping hot bread where a flock of children gathered at the sight of my camera, then wandered to the west, where the ruins grew more frequent and the mud thicker at every step. A man supervising the rebuilding of his house offered us tea. It had been destroyed by the Russians, 'just like all the houses here', he said with unexpected cheerfulness, and pointed to the waves of ruins stretching westwards. He explained that the road we were on had been a security perimeter and heavily mined during the war, and beyond it a free-fire zone, bombed daily by Russian jets.

'So happy to have met you,' he said as we moved on. 'When my house is rebuilt I should like to have the honour of inviting you to be my guests.'

I escorted Antoinette back to the gates of the Red Cross which, still smarting from the morning's rejection, I refused to go beyond. I went to look for more sympathetic accommodation elsewhere in the city but the options were not encouraging. I was unwilling to return to the French. The hotels were filled with armed Tālebs. The United Nations guest house I had heard of was fifty dollars a night, and far beyond my means. I knew almost any Afghan family would take me in but it felt wrong to expect that.

It was all such an effort for such simple things. I wanted to go somewhere I could rest and read and be alone, without having to explain myself to anybody. Beat's flippancy had left me thoroughly disenchanted. His action was not so much a personal affront as a violation of the spirit of things, in a country where he himself was a guest.

Even so I had spent the day mentally assassinating his character. I relived our conversation, and all his transparently insincere cheerfulness. I thought of writing him a letter to drive home his immoral lack of hospitality. I wondered if I could get a message through to the head of the ICRC, and have his own boss chastise him. How could someone so ignorant rise to such a position of responsibility? He knew nothing about Afghanistan; he had not even known that Afghanistan's holiest shrine was at nearby Gazargah. He had never hitch-hiked. His fleece jacket had a stupid pattern on it. He had an idiotic smile. He had laughed at me. I shrunk him mentally until he withered.

✲

From the intoxication of self-pity I was rescued by a brilliant idea: the Christian Freaks! That's what Rafiq had called them. They had an office in Herat and I had passed it on my walk the day before.

By the end of the afternoon I was installed in the house of a friendly Dutch couple who were among the most welcoming foreigners I had met; modern-day missionaries who by their hospitality and charm defied the uncharitable epithet I had heard coined in Kabul. They had restored a modern house with their own money in the centre of town and, for a modest sum, I was to be their first guest.

I was impressed by these people, as I had been by their colleagues in Kabul. They eschewed the noisy generators which kept neighbours awake, and cooked their food themselves. Among their fellow staff of about twenty were some of the fortunate foreigners whom the enraged citizens of the 1979 uprising had not slaughtered. Later their loyal *chowkidar* told me the story: when the rampaging mob arrived at the door of the mission, he had barred their way and said, 'If you want them, you will have to kill me first.' Impressed by such conviction in one of their own, they went on, presumably to find some godless Russians.

My new hosts were warm people, genuinely interested to share a traveller's tale or two, a far cry from the missionaries Byron had encountered in Iran, whose behinds, as he put it, 'stuck out as if their spines were too righteous to bend'. They knew the region better than the local aid organizations, spoke fluent Persian, and were there for the long haul; some of them had even brought their children, and others planned to. Afghanistan was a difficult place to live and work and it was impossible not to be impressed by their dedication.

But something held me back from enquiring as to the source of their zeal, perhaps because I feared an answer that would leave me disturbed, and cast a shadow over my honest delight, for the moment, at not being treated like a leper.

So I still wonder, because I was too timid to ask, to what extent their work went beyond the hospitals and clinics they built and maintained around the country. The hospital they ran in Herat was the best equipped and best managed in the region. I wondered though: here in one of the most strictly Moslem populations of the world, how ripe could the crop of souls possibly be?

Presumably they had more success than the archdeacon whom Byron had met in Iran, who made a single convert in thirty years.* The question came to me over dinner that evening, when my new host prayed during grace for the 'hidden Christians' in Herat. Did he mean hidden in the sense of latent, or was he suggesting an existing population of believers? If so, were they recent converts or descendants of earlier Christian communities known to have existed in Khorassan before the Mongol onslaught? In the case of the latter, how would the Christianity practised – or not practised – in such remote outposts of faith resemble, in either letter or spirit, the twentieth-century, European-export-to-Asia version?

Years ago I had heard mention of a village near Ghazni in the

---

* An old woman. On her deathbed, by the archdeacon's own account, her last request was: 'Please summon a *mullā*.'

south that was said to be Christian and whose members held that Christ settled down anonymously in India after the controversies of his youth, and lived to a ripe old age in the foothills of the Himalayas. Did their numbers extend to Herat?

I kept these questions to myself. The tale of the village, like so many others, was just too unlikely to be probable, just too believable to be impossible and, at least in the prevailing climate, defied proving. Not because the East is mystic or inscrutable, but because it reveals its secrets at a pace which the Western visitor is so seldom prepared to embrace: you need *time*.

✻

My hosts apologized for the lack of a heater in my room, which was the temperature of an igloo, but no matter, I felt, against the happy prospect over the next few days of being able to come and go without having to explain myself to anyone. I left the bathroom window unlocked to allow the *chowkidar* to climb into the house next morning with bread for my breakfast, and installed myself in the spotless room. A few hours ago I had been wandering the streets feeling irremediably sorry for myself. Now I felt like a king. There was a small bookcase of approved reading material. What, no Schweitzer, Goethe, Nietzsche or Blake on Christianity? I found a copy of *The Diary of a Country Priest*, and was soon fast asleep.

✻

Horribly early the next morning I was woken by the shrieks of children playing outside the window and an industrious clattering in the kitchen. I emerged from the bedroom and saw, from behind, a tall and slender woman in a flowered dress with a scarf draped loosely around her neck. She was working at the sink and had not heard me, and gave a start as she caught sight of a stranger. She was Afghan, and her gaze, which yielded quickly from fierce surprise to a softer yet penetrating questioning, rooted me to the spot. Her long arms and neck were bare, and she had a tired, exquisite beauty about her. On her forehead was the turquoise trace of a tribal tattoo.

For a few wordless moments our eyes met, until suddenly we

remembered our greetings, stumbling over the words in an effort to remedy the unexpected silence. I could not take my eyes off her. Apologizing for her appearance she wrung the water from her hands and drew a wisp of hair away from her face with a graceful movement of her wrist, and explained how she came every day to do the washing and cleaning and how glad she was for the work among such good people. Her voice had a softly imploring music to it that was irresistible to me and on shifting feet I asked her questions just to hear her speak, barely listening to the answers. Within a few moments she had asked me whether I was married; yes, I said. But you didn't bring your wife with you, did you? she replied. I was shocked and delighted by her boldness.

Here in the house we could talk with a freedom unthinkable in public, but even in the sanctuary of a foreigner's home a mutual sense of impropriety hung low over our conversation like a dark and highly charged storm cloud, and the space between us hummed with illicit tension. We hovered about each another like bees messaging the nearness of honey, never daring for more than a moment to reduce the electric distance between us, speaking of trivial things in inverse measure to the quickening we felt in each other's presence, and jumped guiltily at the sound of a slamming door from the hallway.

I wanted, out of a sudden and excruciating sense of curiosity for her reaction, to tell her I thought she was beautiful. But here there was no such thing as innocent contact between the sexes. Even in its most liberal expression Afghan society disapproved fiercely of foreigners having any contact with their women, and the walls seemed too thin to contain our fugitive exchanges.

The city's new occupiers made these already strict standards seem mild: it was impossible to forget that if they had their way, women would not even be allowed out of their homes, much less consort with foreign men. On top of this we were in a missionary household. But cage a cat and you get a tiger. Had the thoughts that kept me awake that night been known to my hosts as well as the city's rulers, I would have been certain to languish in both Christian and Moslem hells (the latter drawing heavily on the former for its nastiness). It was not yet time for breakfast and I had already fallen in love. No wonder the

Afghans wanted to keep their women under wraps, such was the effect they had on the unwary.

*

Some people arrived, my new love pretended to fuss over the dishes, and I left the house shattered, knowing that any expression of my feelings for her was about as likely as a breakthrough in the peace process. It was not that I seriously imagined anything might happen; it was the sheer impossibility that gave such fantasies their force. But it must have been much harder on the young men of the city. For most of them, those very pleasures, which in the Western world have become little more than recreations would have to wait — only in paradise would they be tended by the nubile and doe-eyed damsels promised to the faithful. A cruel eschatological twist, it seemed to me at the time, if ever there was one.

The visitors were an American couple, friends of my hosts. Herb was a tall, lean, silvery-haired man who spoke in a quiet, clipped Midwestern drawl, a doctor from Kansas and, as I later heard him described, 'a hard-core missionary'. His softly spoken wife Dorothy, never far from his side or lacking a beatific smile, came from three generations of missionaries. I pictured them, rightly as it turned out, swaying smilingly and clapping (but not too loudly) to inspirational songs. They were very cheerful and friendly and I avoided them strenuously.

*

In Herat all the talk was about the Tāleban. New rules were being issued. The most shocking of these forbade women to leave their homes during the month of Ramadan, lest men be distracted from their sacred tasks by the sight of them. Televisions, I heard, were to be banned. But instead of rounding them up individually and hanging them from lamp posts as they had done in Jelallabad, it was ordered that their antennae be removed from the city's rooftops. And now there was talk of closing down the jewellery bazaars, where women were most often seen to gather. Traditional society restricts the freedom of women and it restricts the freedom of men. But even the most conservative Afghans I met in Herat felt oppressed by the latest round of rules.

A Tāleb jeep had run over a small child in the bazaar and driven on. The Tālebān were robbing people at night and making no effort to punish the offenders in their ranks. Tālebān stories had the same flavour. Each day I heard a few more, from Afghans as well as foreigners working with the handful of NGOs that operated in the city. The head of one organization was under pressure to fire his female staff, who were daily more scared to come to work. Another, run by a European woman, had been ordered to close down, and was beginning to receive threats. The Tālebān refused to speak to her directly.

Then there was the story of the old master painter and calligrapher, one of the few remaining great artists in the country trained in the Bihzad style. Soon after the Tālebān took Herat, the old man was summoned to the governor's building, where he had laboured for seven years painting intricate scenes that recreated the classical glory of Herat on its walls. His art, he was told by the Tāleb leader, was 'un-Islamic', and before his eyes the walls were painted over. The old man was bedridden with grief.

'It is a big sorrow,' said the man who recounted the story. '*Hīch namishe fe'llān*, nothing's allowed any more,' he muttered to himself. As we spoke his attention was caught by an announcement crackling from his little radio.

'The Tālebān,' he nodded.

'What are they saying?'

'Always the same thing: that everything is OK now, and the cruel people have gone away.'

*

The most outspoken tellers of tales were women. With Antoinette I visited several families for her radio pieces; alone, I would never have had the opportunity. The women would appear from nowhere: first a mother, then a daughter, a sister, her aunt, three nieces, the mother's best friend, their toothless old grandmother. At first they were deeply cautious and said little. Gently coaxed, one of them would break the silence and tell a story that revealed, after all, that life was a little hard. Another, emboldened, would follow with fewer inhibitions, and between pleas never to reveal their identities the torch of grief would be passed among them, burning more brightly at each turn.

A dreadful picture of their fate would begin to emerge. How could they be expected to remain indoors when half – sometimes all – the weight of the household duties fell on them? Did I know the story of so-and-so, whom the Tālebān had refused medical treatment? One of the women was a teacher at the university and had been told not to return to her job. How was she supposed to provide for the children? Tirades swelled and subsided and rose again like waves. Emotions ran high and ended in tears.

*

Later, I wrote up my diary at the mission as the light faded.

I was interrupted by a gentle knocking from the next room. It sounded like a woman's hand – perhaps it was *her*? The door opened and alas, Herb's face came peering round.

'Not disturbin' you am I?' He circled, a little predatorily I thought, near the table.

'Not at all, Herb,' I replied, with the first of several untruths.

'Warm enough in here?'

'Oh yes, thank you.'

'Just wanted to be sure you had everything you need.'

'Well, that's very kind, Herb, and I'm very happy. Thank you.'

'Well, fine. We'll see you at breakfast.'

'Yes, good.'

'Dorothy cooks a fine breakfast.'

'I look forward to that.'

'I'll let you get on, then.'

He hovered a little near the door. Then, as though the idea had just occurred to him, he asked:

'Mind if I pray for you, Jason?'

I was expecting something like this.

'I'd be delighted Herb,' I said, and put down my pen.

He put his hand on my shoulder and his eyes lifted heavenward, somewhere high above Kansas.

'Lord,' he began, 'we ask you to bless our brother ... and protect him ... and guide him on the many miles ahead of him ...' directing in his reverent twang far more of the Lord's attention on me than I felt comfortable with.

'... and Lord, Prince of Peace, we ask you ...' I baulked inwardly: Prince of Peace? Try telling that to the Afghans, I thought, after twenty years of war! I thanked Herb when he had finished and he went to the door, but turned at the last moment.

'I assume you're a ... a Christian, Jason.'

It would have been fun to tell him I was a Yezidi devil worshipper, looking for traces of my ancestral religion in Afghanistan. But I was not sure if our definitions of the word had much in common.

'I think it would be a fine thing to be a Christian, but I also think you have to work at it.'

He took a dim view of that, shook his head a little and let out an admonishing sigh.

'The Way is open to all men, Jason.'

'And surely, every man has his own way to find,' I said. He had not exactly given me the benefit of the doubt; but then if giving the benefit of the doubt to others in matters religious were the missionary's brief, Herb would have been out of a job. Then it came:

'Have you thought about entering into a personal relationship with Christ?'

Herb, I sensed, wanted nothing less than a full-blown repentance. I smiled and said nothing.

'You know,' he added with a note of caution, 'we don't preach hellfire any more these days, but the Bible is pretty clear on all this.'

He let the words hang, then said, 'Let me know if you want to talk about it,' and left.

I had more serious matters in mind; I had been invited to a party.

*

Back at the headquarters of the French, where my offering of biscuits had remained untouched on the table, the 'party' was in progress; an ignominious gathering of about thirty lonely exiles from the city's foreign agencies.

Ever hopeful for the chance of a conversation without feeling like an escaped convict, I made a beeline for an attractive, dark-haired woman in her mid-twenties. Single, intelligent and lonely, she would be weary of the usual company on these long winter nights, and find herself drawn irresistibly to the stranger who had appeared so unexpectedly in their midst . . .*

She was Swiss, single, and to eyes accustomed to women the shape of billowing ghosts, divinely well proportioned.

'So,' said I, after we had introduced ourselves, 'why Afghanistan?'

I watched as her gaze turned inward and her breath grew uneven, as though she were uncovering some tremendous inner wound.

'Because,' she replied, 'I am a Christian.'

And down sank my heathen heart.

*

I was given a lift back to the mission by one of the other staff, acutely aware in the confines of the car of the smell on my breath of the fugitive beer I had earlier seized on. I felt ridiculously guilty and tried not to breathe in his direction as I spoke, pondering all the while the double absurdity of my likely consignment to hell not by some puritanical *mullā*, but by my co-religionists.

I slunk back to my room and waited for the house to fall silent. Wanting to throw off a deep feeling of claustrophobia, I took the oil lantern from the bedroom and sat brooding on the steps of the courtyard outside.

I felt the cold stone through my clothes. It was well below freezing but I felt an almost physical loathing at returning indoors. A full moon stared down into the garden through broken clouds and draped the lawn with its silvery gilt. Beyond the walls some tall cypress trees

---

* I am reliably informed, by a doctor friend who visited Afghanistan, that there is even a medical term for such lapses of judgement: they are part of what is called 'testosterone-induced hallucination', and are swiftly relieved by the sufferer's return to more familiar surroundings.

swayed and whispered. The moonshadows deepened and lightened as the clouds sailed through the sky, filling and emptying themselves of the light and trailing orphaned wisps of whiteness like stragglers in a long celestial caravan winding into the darkness.

Between trembling fingers I smoked my cigar, dwelling on the rich contradictions of the day and the ever more distant planet that was home. I was still deeply disenchanted by the lack of hospitality I had encountered at the Red Cross and among the French; the Swiss girl's unfriendly zealousness troubled me, and I was fed up with the Christian business, unapproachable women, and the ever crueller edicts of the Tāleban. All this under the grotesque banner of belief. People of 'belief' had destroyed and were continuing to destroy everything of beauty in Herat. Was there not somewhere a belief more substantial and more forgiving than an angry grafting of old flesh onto the brittle bones of religion? Was there anyone who did not derive their identity and sense of purpose from a cause? Were there any normal Westerners in Herat, who had nothing to prove, or would admit to an honest desire?

I felt hemmed in on all sides by people so convinced by their own righteousness that if a trace of self-doubt were to breach the lofty walls of their conviction, they would vanish in puffs of smoke. I blew a defiant puff of smoke at the moon. Then another, at the Swiss girl, and another at the Tāleb soldier I had seen bullying a man in the street. Soon the country was dotted with spiralling vortices of extinguished righteousness, and when the billowing smoke had cleared, only those people were left who wanted nothing more than to get on with their lives and work quietly on their own salvation according to their own means.

If it were spring I would take the beautiful housekeeper (and the Swiss girl too, if her so-called religion would allow it), some foie gras and a decent bottle of Sauternes to a pavilion in a jasmine-scented park, where we would watch the moon through the clouds and translate poetry to one another. She would tell me the story of her tattoo, and I in turn would tell her how I got the tiny scar on my own head, and we would draw closer as we spoke, until—

A loud burst of automatic gunfire in a nearby street broke the spell.

I was shivering violently and the cigar was spent. It was all too hopelessly distant to contemplate. The most innocent association between the sexes, not to mention the Sauternes, would be unthinkable in public; after curfew we would in any case be shot, and the city's parks, ravaged by warfare and the hungry axes of peasants in search of firewood, were gone.

I blew out the lantern and headed indoors.

Eleven

Afghanistan is one of the least reached lands in the world, with 48,000 mosques but not a single church building, nor a viable fellowship of believers in any but a few of the indigenous peoples of the country.

Evangelical Christian Resource on Afghanistan

THE NEXT DAY I FOUND TREASURE, in the form of Raheem, a taxi driver. He had an old Ford Granada with smoked windows and a top speed of about five miles an hour. We drove around for fun, at least as close as we could get to it, while he pointed out the sights.

He was twenty-seven, unmarried, a former soldier of the government and later with Ismael Khan's mujaheddin. I liked his gentle and unhurried manner and the straightforward way he answered questions; if he didn't know the answer, instead of speculating wildly he would shrug his shoulders. He told me Ismael Khan had let Herat fall to the Tāleban to avoid bloodshed, that the government would simply let their occupiers freeze for a winter or two and then Ismael Khan would come back. I hoped, but doubted, that it would all work out quite so smoothly.

I asked why there seemed to be so few Tāleban on the streets. In other cities there had been armed men at every corner.

'They are afraid,' he said. 'They only come out at night.' Then he went a little further and added: 'Like dogs – in the daytime they sleep.' It was less safe these days for everybody, he said. People were reluctant to go out after dark. A pregnant woman had been ordered out of his taxi on the way to hospital. He had been told by a Tāleb soldier to get his hair cut – he rubbed the generous curls about his collar affectionately – and the football team had been forbidden to wear shorts. That was really stupid, he said, and laughed softly. But his real passion had been martial arts, and so saying he pulled out a photograph from the glove compartment. It was a colour photograph of a man with a bare chest lying on the ground. A car had been lowered onto his torso. In the background were the blurred heads of a large crowd.

I studied the grimacing face of the man on the ground: it was Raheem. Such a spectacle would be unthinkable now.

'I had a Chinese instructor,' he said, 'and used to train quite hard. Here,' he guided my fingers to his sternum, where I felt muscles as hard as stone, 'not even a sword can get through.'

I asked, to see his reaction, whether he could teach me his technique.

'If you promise not to speak of it,' he replied.

We drove to the northern outskirts of the city to visit the most famous shrines. Between the ruins there was new construction. We came to a checkpoint where a chain was hung across the road between two pillars and a Tāleb guard sat nearby with a rifle in his lap. I looked at Raheem nervously.

'No problem,' he said, grinning, but even so put up the collar of his jacket to disguise the length of his hair. The Tāleb put his head and the barrel of his rifle through the window and asked where we were going.

'Just to the shrine,' said Raheem.

When we had driven on, he glanced in the mirror.

'Did you see that?' He pulled his collar down again. 'That Tāleb didn't even say hello. You know how we are here: we always say hello, how are you, are you well, and so on. But those Tālebs have no manners.' (Literally, they were *bi-farhang*, without culture.)

We first paid our respects at the tomb of Abdurahman Jāmi, the last of the great classical Persian poets. As a young man Jāmi was said to be a brilliant scholar, but abandoned his formal studies to follow his inclination towards Sufism. His teacher was Sa'aduddin Kashgāri. 'For the first time in five hundred years,' lamented one of Jāmi's professors, 'a real scholar has emerged on the soil of Khorassan, only to run off after Kashgāri!' Jāmi corresponded with the Emperor of India; the Ottoman Sultan courted his wisdom; he introduced Sultan Husain's Prime Minister Ali Shīr Navā'i to the Sufism of the Naqshbandiyya. In his youth he travelled widely but settled in Herat and became a prodigious and reclusive writer. A number of his forty or so works, which include the well-known hagiographic *Nafahāt al-Uns*, poetry, commentaries on the lives and works of Sufis, and treatises on literature, music and theology, are studied by Sufis today; through his written works his influence on Sufism in Persia, Turkey and India was enormous. Jāmi died in 1492 and his bier was carried by the notables of the city, surrounded by vast crowds of weeping onlookers, Sultan Hussein, and his entire retinue in mourning garb.

The area around the shrine had been mined during the war, and the adjacent mosque partially destroyed by bombing. A new mosque was being built in its place, paid for not with government money, said Raheem, but by the poet's Sufi followers. The UN had de-mined the site; we took off our shoes at the gate and walked around the tombstone.

An ancient pistachio tree still sways over the domed marble slab, and its roots seem to dive into the heart of the dead poet himself. The elaborately carved lattice that once surrounded it has gone. The iron railings that enclose the platform of the tomb had been twisted by the force of an explosion. Two old men laboured silently over the damaged brickwork and flagstones, moving between piles of shattered headstones from the adjoining cemetery. On a damaged wall someone had balanced a solitary carved headpiece, severed from the tomb of a Naqshbandi sheikh, which I felt an immediate and tainted longing to rescue.

In a courtyard by the mosque was a deserted building which Raheem said had been a library. On the surrounding wall were the words: 'This area clear of mines', daubed in Persian script. Scattered all around were fragments of a ceramic frieze of bright calligraphy and flower mosaics. An owl flew up from an arched window as we went inside. Beneath its vaulted dome the floor was bare brick, and a stray cat nursed a litter in one corner.

We drove along the hillside and visited a dozen shrines, offering customary prayers by the tombs and, where these lonely sanctuaries were tended by living souls, gave their attendants a small contribution. The furthest from the city lay halfway up a hillside to the north and from a distance the high vaulted entrance and surrounding ruins had the allure of an ancient, abandoned city. On its lonely plateau was a collection of fantastically carved tombstones in white and black marble, sinking slowly into the hillside. In the ruins behind them we peered into a dozen tiny cells for dervishes in solitary retreat, their ceilings blackened by generations of smoke.

At the shrine of Khwaja Gholtān, two men sat by a tomb reading from a book of verse, swaying gently to the rhythm of the words.

'Come, brother, and sit awhile with us,' said a man with a piercing gaze.

Later we drove back into the city.

'They are kindly men, those dervishes who tend the shrines,' I said.

'Those were no dervishes,' he replied. 'Those were Ismael Khan's men.'

'How do you tell?' Perhaps, I thought, there was some secret sign.

'I asked them.'

'Oh. So what are they doing there?'

'Just watching. And waiting.' He winked.

*

There was a final shrine I wanted to see, perhaps the most revered of all, at Gazargāh. Here one of Afghanistan's great saints was buried nearly a thousand years ago. The Pir-i Herat, Khwaja Abdullah Ansāri, was a philosopher, poet and mystic, and a Sufi *tariqat* takes its name from him. He is said to have known a hundred thousand verses by heart, and his written poetry in both Persian and Arabic runs to twenty thousand couplets. His many works range over hagiographies of the major Sufis, commentaries on the Qur'ān and the mysteries of Sufism. His lucid prose is still read today. In 1428 Shah Rukh commissioned the rebuilding of the shrine that honours him, and today it stands on a low hill a few miles from the city, beneath the shadows of the northern mountains. Traditionally at least, it had the right of sanctuary.

The light was fading and I was afraid it might be too late to visit since our safety would disappear with the daylight. Raheem shrugged. The car bounced along a straight but ruined road to the northeast, once flanked with stately pines of which only a few remain. An old man was hacking at the base of one of them as we passed.

We pulled up beneath a dusty grove of trees. The crashing of shock absorbers fell from our senses like a tide, the trees sighed in the breeze of the dusk, and we were looking across the valley beneath us.

Between the darkening girdle of low cloud and the ragged horizon of the southern peaks stretched a band of golden light.

Something caught Raheem's attention and he hopped over a stone wall at the edge of the slope and beckoned me. Around us were a dozen graves, one freshly dug. He peered into it and gazed at the stones that lined its hollow sides.

'A strange thought, isn't it?' he said quietly. 'That one day – you and I – that's where we'll end up, I mean.' We were alone and we looked about us and over the great plain again and heard the flutter of rags tied to gravestones lapping like mute souls in the wind.

We headed for the shrine, and the awesome silence of the place began to work on me. There were three steps leading up, and at each, time seemed to slow, and as I entered, to lighten its hold completely. In its place came a strange animating whisper, silencing the ordinary clatter of thoughts. There is not much sense in trying to describe such a moment. I felt I had slipped beyond some enchanted threshold which time itself was barely able to penetrate.

Some turbaned old men wandered barefoot among the trees and a cluster of buildings. We crossed chequered marble flagstones and removed our shoes under the keen unmoving gaze of two guardians with Old Testament beards who sat beneath the niches that flank the central entrance.* These niches are about ten feet high, and covered with zigzagging lines of black and turquoise that mount towards their apices, the design of which is mirrored on the five sides of the greater vault of the main ceiling. Two panels next to them are geometric mosaics in turquoise and yellow, strikingly reminiscent of the patterns of atoms in molecules revealed by x-ray crystallography. We walked through.

Inside was a courtyard filled with the intricately chiselled headstones of Tīmūrid notables, leaning with age at every angle. At the far end soared the hundred-foot-high *ivān* and its two turrets the shape of

---

* In front of which crouches a marble statue so worn with age that you might pass by without noticing that it is in fact an animal. The story is that the architect of the shrine so revered the saint that he asked to be buried facing it, his tombstone in the shape of a kneeling dog.

lanterns. High up between them ran an arched gallery. The saint's tomb was underneath, draped in green, and protected by a wooden canopy and railings painted turquoise. From the head of the tomb sprang a wild and flowing tree, its main branch almost solid with tiny nails left by the faithful. The headstone is a solid fifteen-foot pillar of creamy marble and exquisitely carved.

The most elaborate decoration in the shrine lies behind the tomb itself at the very end of the courtyard. In its prime every inch of surface was draped with tile mosaic in brilliant colours. It was too much to drink in at one time, intoxicatingly rich in design and detail. Every wall had its own music, but one struck me in particular.

The section, about twenty foot square, was made of tessellating panels in the form of squares and rectangles, the centres of which alternated in dark and light tile against a middle shade in each different panel, like positive and negative photographic images. What appeared from a distance to be the shading within these shapes was in fact a mosaic of angularly stylized Arabic characters, with each character itself composed of tinier tiles. The contrasts in colour lent the panels a three-dimensional effect. I found my eye drawn outwards, and realized that the interlocking borders of each panel were formed by the extended lines of swirling black lettering that enclosed the entire design. The angular and the cursive had thus become inseparable, without having sacrificed their own strong identities which, alone, would have overpowered the overall sense of the design. That the mosaics themselves depicted verses from the Qur'ān added another dimension of significance to the whole, and as if to mirror the paradox suggested in the shapes, allowed a changing meaning, in words this time, to express itself within an unchanging form.

Above this section ran a wide band of bright, densely overlapping calligraphy in white against royal blue. And above this came another panel as extraordinary as the first. Here, interlocking squares and triangles – each, again, displaying an individual design – had been ingeniously skewed to give a strong impression of three dimensions. The pattern of tiles here must have been conceived of in three planes before it was expressed in one. The resulting shapes seemed to tease the eye like a puzzle, and the squares looked like the sides of unfolding cubes, which shifted in and out of one plane and into another before I could quite decide to which they really belonged. I felt stunned; they seemed to detach themselves from the wall and began to open and close, flashing the central pattern – a calligraphic motif of the name of God – like the wings of a butterfly basking in sunshine.

Yet all this genius of design had a lucidity and a sobriety that held me back. For all its intricacy there was no trace of ostentation. Why then, I wondered, this feeling of hypnosis?

Like most newcomers to the medium I had always found the patterns of Islamic art strangely appealing but never dwelled on it much more than that. It is true that its designs have a powerful allure for the Western eye, which is accustomed to such a different style in its own artistic forms. It is often pointed out that the emphasis on the geometrical in Islamic art derives from a prohibition, implicated in its sacred texts, on naturalistic – that is, graven – imagery. Whereas in the West the highest forms of art have manifested in painting and sculpture, the creative dam of genius behind Islamic art was from its outset diverted into complex geometrical expressions – so-called abstract designs, calligraphy, flowing arabesques and, especially in Persia, stylized motifs from the natural world such as trees and flowers – as well as the different media in which they are articulated. This is all no doubt true, but fails to answer the question of meaning behind it.

Something was getting under my skin as my eyes roamed the walls. I had a feeling this was different from any art I had ever seen. And in that cold, lowering dusk, in that shabby courtyard, where the tilework is a third destroyed, a ray of meaning seemed to leap from the walls. It was as if they had suddenly become articulate and, shedding for a moment their almost formal precision, began to dance and weave with meaning. It was the mathematics of it, just like the geometrical precision of atoms in a crystal, that lent them such force. From every panel, every frieze, burst an expression of the same creative breath, each an encrypted fragment of the Divine. This was not the art of decoration but of sacred ciphers, in which the onlooker is invited to participate, not merely stand in awe, and decode the patterns according to his means.

They had, in other words, the sublime intimacy of the impersonal; not only in their scale and generosity, but in the unutterable that they strived to make intelligible through the untainted intercessor of geometry.

*

Raheem watched me with a kindly curiosity, bemused that a heathen should have been so absorbed by the sight of some old tiles, and we walked on. I could tell he wanted to leave but was too polite to say so. It was getting dark, but I was overtaken by the place.

'You go back,' I told him. 'I want to spend the night here.'

'Here?'

'Yes. Introduce me to the keeper.'

We knocked on the tiny green door beneath an arch in the wall of the courtyard. A tall, turbaned old man with a noble and weary face emerged.

'Welcome, brothers, and enter. It's cold outside,' he said in a croaky voice.

Inside a vaulted chamber was a rectangular sarcophagus draped in green cloth. Two other men sat cross-legged in a corner and watched us as Raheem explained my request. The old man, who radiated an immense kindliness, seemed unsurprised.

'Welcome, yes, you are welcome. Stay with us, brother, and be our guest as long as you wish.'

Raheem agreed to return in the morning, with a trace of reluctance at leaving me in such a lonely place. I turned to the old man.

'You show me great kindness.'

'On the contrary. It is you who do us the honour of being our guest. Sit, sit, and we will have some tea.' There was a flurry of protesting arms from the other men as I went to sit on the floor near them. 'No, no, not there — here,' and the old man guided me to the space between the sarcophagus and the wall where a mattress, clearly his own, lay on the floor. It was no use protesting.

'Bismillah! Fetch water, we have a guest!'

A young man with fair skin and blond hair scurried from the chamber, while the old Hajji took a blackened kettle hanging from a stick in the mortar between the bare bricks. With great precision and economy of movement, he began to prime a paraffin stove.

'Oh, yes,' he mused, 'we had a Frenchman here once, who stayed three months. And another, if I remember rightly, some time ago, from Colombia.'

Bismillah returned with water in a can.

'Forty-six years I've been the keeper of this holy place – there we are.' He steadied the kettle on the stove. 'I've seen all manner of people come and go. By the grace of God we even have electricity here,' and he turned on a bare bulb that hung from the ceiling.

An hour or so passed, in which I expected the usual barrage of questions, but none came. Hajji sat near the door and fussed with the stove, musing from time to time into his beard, but never idle. It was the first time, among Afghans, I was simply left to sit in peace.

Others came, sat, talked, left, returned. Between greetings, I sat alone in my corner. A man who had lost both legs to a mine clambered over the doorway and sat with two others opposite me. Another entered and sat in silence against the wall with a desolate expression, staring at the floor. Each time the door opened an icy draught swept through the chamber.

Later Hajji spread a plastic tablecloth across the floor and we gathered around, eight of us now. The desolate-looking man remained rooted to his spot, but the old man entreated him with kindly words to join us until he gave in, and ate like a wolf.

We ate, as always, with our hands from shared dishes piled with mountains of rice concealing lumps of mutton. My neighbour, the man who had lost his legs, pulled the best pieces from the steaming rice and, when he was sure I wasn't looking, piled them on my side of the dish. I knew this stratagem and duplicated it, so at the end of the meal we were almost fighting for non-possession of every morsel. The men spoke little. Hajji croaked a prayer of thanks over the bones and scattered rice, and a ewer of warm water was brought for our hands.

Much later I asked to excuse myself and Bismillah led me outside, lighting my way with great care as we walked barefoot over the freezing marble and out of the main enclosure. Shadows of men loomed up and passed by in silence like ghosts. We passed a huge *ivān* where the light was reflected for a moment on a pool inside. This was the reservoir.

We reached a mud enclosure where Bismillah left me. When I emerged he had a jug of warm water which he poured over my hands. We walked back across a dusty square without a word. All around the complex, lanterns flickered like stars in niches or from behind carved lattices, and from every direction the night was pierced by the cries of men in the ecstasy of solitary prayer. Time had a poor hold on this place; the scene had not changed much for centuries.

Inside the courtyard again Bismillah turned to me and asked: 'Have you seen the Stone of the Seven Pens?' I had read of it somewhere. He led me into one of the chambers adjacent to the courtyard, and brought his lantern close to a solitary rectangular sarcophagus. It was black marble carved exquisitely in three planes. Its corners were miniature spiralling columns with tiny scalloped niches at their tops, and the entire surface was covered with flowing calligraphic verses and floral patterns. In recent stonework, the flowing letters are carved out of the stone. But the masons of old carved around the form of the letters, so that the finished shapes stand proud of the surrounding stone, in a technique far more daring and exacting than the modern.

'The Russians tried to take this one,' said Bismillah mischievously, 'but they couldn't move it. Come on.'

We walked through three high adjoining chambers and he raised the lantern over a dozen other tombstones, sending crazy shadows like the flapping wings of giant bats reeling over the bare walls, which danced in and out of the blackness, sometimes to reveal the corpse-like body of a sleeping man, shrouded from head to toe in a long *pattū*.

Outside we offered prayers at the saint's tomb. I noticed how much more delicately he performed this ritual than had Raheem, caressing the wooden lattice of the shelter, the sides of the tomb, the headstone and the padlocks of the tiny gate with great reverence, then transferring the substance of their blessing over his face and ending with a prayer, his hands cupped skyward, beneath the canopy of the night.

Bismillah prayed stilly and silently beside me, but I had none of his devotion and shifted my weight from foot to foot as they seemed to burn on the icy stone, wishing with more hope than shame that he would only get on with his prayers. Yet even this was forgotten as a sound, utterly bewitching, reached our ears from beyond the shrine and we turned together, our senses magnetized, towards it.

It was human, although barely, and resembled nothing I had ever heard. It came from the entrance, where there was a strange flurry of shadow like moths around a candle. A turbaned man emerged, carrying a lantern in one hand and a stick that glinted in its light, and moved along the path towards us at the pace of a funeral bearer. The sound followed him, and reached us in faltering waves; a deranged yet rhythmic chanting from a deranged shape that had paused beneath the vault of the entrance. Slowly the man drew nearer. I could see he was a Tāleb fighter, and the shiny stick was the chrome barrel of a Kalashnikov with a second magazine taped to the first. Behind him crept a dark huddle, its shadow flailing now on the walls behind, and the sound it made growing louder at every moment.

Bismillah turned his head to me with a stern look as if perhaps the sight were not for my eyes.

'Shall we go inside?'

'No,' I whispered, noticing that he too was transfixed.

The shape was a bundle of men, two of them shaven-headed, lurching forward in a convulsive trance, their bodies jerking like crazed puppets. Between them was a third man, guiding them forward like a sorcerer with his presence at each step. From the throats – no, the bellies – of these two came the freakish sound that had mesmerized us; a rhythmic tandem of rasping inhalations followed by a deep exhalation like the growl of a bear, only stranger for being human. Then over this sound, every few minutes, broke a chant from their guide, a high polyphonous wailing that seemed to nourish the others' trance.

As they reached the shrine the Tāleb put his rifle and lantern on the ground by my feet and sat nearby without a glance at us. The two circled wildly around their master, their chests heaving violently at each breath, their arms sometimes scraping the ground as their bodies waved like rags in a storm. For ten minutes we stood there, until the still one who sang turned away, preceded by his guard, and led the wild men back along the path with the magnet of his preternatural melody, out of the shrine into the black. We hurried back to our chamber.

'What was going on out there?' croaked Hajji, as we thawed our feet over the naked flame of the stove. 'I heard some cries.'

'Just some Tālebs,' said Bismillah, 'making their *zikr*.' There was a sullen note in his voice, I felt, as he mentioned the men who had brought their guns and strange form of prayer to the shrine.

It was a night for such things. Hajji and Bismillah and the other men in the room were dervishes of the Qādiriyya *tariqat*, like those I had met in Mazar, and they had a *zikr* of their own. The men sat in a circle and Hajji began the prayers, kindling a gentle swaying in the others with his lilting invocations. Then suddenly the *zikr* took flight as Hajji signalled with a deep intake of breath for the chant to began. From his chest came sounds my ears could not believe. Suddenly the room was filled with rasping and roaring. It grew in pitch and rhythm and without it faltering the men stood up and began to sway more vigorously, so that the circle tightened and dilated like the valve of a beating heart. I felt certain heads would collide as the swaying grew wilder but like the entranced men we had seen earlier, another instinct was at work that never failed them. The walls seemed to tremble at the force of the sound, which reached the intensity of furious sawing, cutting deeper each minute – but into what, I could not say.

A flicker of movement at the tiny window above the door caught my eye. It was a dark face peering in at us. The door crept open and a Tāleb rather timidly came inside as the sound flooded over him. Hajji spotted him immediately and welcomed him in as the *zikr* continued at full force, coaxed his machine gun from him gently and propped it against the wall. The Tāleb sat down and was joined a few minutes later by another. They were handsome men in black turbans, their skin the colour of chestnut.

Another entered, and another, and the pile of rifles grew as Hajji greeted them one by one, and over the tide of sound I heard him say to one, 'Come, sit, and be comfortable. Leave your gun here, brother, you'll have no need for it, and war is a tiresome business.'

An imposing fighter, his jet black eyes rimmed with turquoise kohl, sat next to me. From under his waistcoat he unbuckled a holster, automatic pistol, and two hand grenades, tossing them onto the tombstone next to me as if they were a hat and gloves. The room filled to bursting; soon there were twenty-five Tālebs crammed inside. Hajji rejoined the circle, restoring the force of the *zikr* with the authority of his breath, but his eyes were alert and shifted expertly every few moments to his guests, whose every movement he took in and measured.

Some of the Tālebs joined the circle, falling back dizzily to rejoin their ranks when they could no longer stand. Their headgear toppled or unwound like streamers. One of them sang for a few minutes in Pashtu and Hajji thanked him with the utmost courtesy. Others stared at the spectacle which was clearly foreign to them, and some smoked and giggled with a shockingly incongruous disrespect. At one point Bismillah left the circle and sat, sweating and dishevelled, against a wall. He watched the Tālebs sternly, and shot me a glance heavy with meaning, before dissolving back into the cauldron of swaying. Never had I seen the contrast between Pashtun and Tajik more clearly.

I wondered, was his look any different from that of dervishes who had made their *zikr* here at the eclipse of Tīmūrid rule, and met the gaze of uncouth Uzbek soldiers who had come – perhaps into this very chamber – to watch their unfamiliar ritual, five hundred years before?

✻

Soon after dawn Raheem appeared as promised, bringing with him the scent of a world where time flowed again, and I was sad to leave. Bismillah embraced me solemnly at the steps of the shrine, extracting a promise to return.

We bumped downwards towards the city at a camel's pace. To the west I glimpsed a turquoise dome and what looked like the pillared courtyards of fortified villas peeking from the pines on the flanks of the hills. An old pang, made more acute by the sense of passage, was ignited. In one of those houses, for all I knew, Bihzad himself had laboured over a tiny parchment, applying the profile of an eyelash with the tip of a single hair.

'What are those places?' I asked Raheem.

'Oh, houses.'

Back at the mission, I explained I had been to visit the shrine at Gazārgāh. To my delight, my host had visited the site himself.

'Yes, it's beautiful up there,' he agreed with a sigh of longing. 'I've often thought what a wonderful place it would be to build a church.'

*

I wanted to leave Herat and travel east into the old mountain kingdom of Ghor. I had heard of some hot springs, ruins, Sufis. Nobody I spoke to seemed to know how to get there. Raheem directed me to the part of town where buses left for the east. A shopkeeper with whom I shared my plans shrugged his shoulders.

'Alone? It may not be such a good idea.' And then, as if he were a little ashamed to mention it, '*Amniyat nist* – it's not safe. People are not used to seeing foreigners. I can see you are a good man, but – others may not know.' He gave a sigh of regret at having to break the news to a visitor that I would be little more than easy pickings if things went wrong.

There was a blank area in my mind east of Herat. I wanted to see it for myself; to penetrate it, to prove it was accessible, to see how this crazy war really fitted together. The centre of the country was under government control; Herat was Tāleban country now. But where did they meet? Was there a front line? Was it quiet or was there fighting? Was it moving or stable? Were there lines of tanks or just a few teenage soldiers lolling about with antique guns?

I followed the impulse for a while and tried to find a vehicle heading east, then began to reflect on the shopkeeper's doleful counsel, and saw myself descending from a bus near nightfall in a strange village in the middle of nowhere. Then all of a sudden I knew I didn't have the courage, or the time, to follow through.

*

In the end I decided to make a lightning trip to the north, to glimpse the countryside beyond the city. Vehicles left at first light from a little street near the citadel. So in the morning I scurried from the house in the darkness, carrying nothing but my notebook and camera under my *pattū*. There was a luminous icy halo around the full moon. I found the street and began a long wait. The shapes of men, faceless and bundled and bent against the cold like dwellers in a troglodyte world, filed in silence into a nearby mosque for the dawn prayers.

Gradually the sky turned to grey in the east. Several jeeps came and went, their coming and going accompanied by the usual debate, negotiations and instant changes in decision. There was some uncertainty about the route I failed to understand; it wasn't passable, it was passable, a jeep would come, a jeep wouldn't come...

I huddled inside a stall with a dozen other hopeful souls and we warmed our hands over a paraffin lantern, waiting.

It was nearly midday when we eventually squeezed into a Russian jeep heading for Qālā-i Nau, I sat in the front with two men on either side; one man was happily compressed between the driver and his door. We were ten in all.

The road led east under a canopy of magnificent oriental pines; the mountains to the north seemed almost within arm's reach but were still hours away. After the monster peaks of the northeast, they looked almost soft and innocent from a distance, their slopes rising in gentle folds towards a smooth glazed dome of brilliant white. Yet this was a deception of scale, which the eye measures only relatively. I didn't give much thought to the route until we grew nearer, as the road began to rise after the village of Karrokh. Soon the mountains began to lose their benign look. Their folds grew deeper, their peaks higher and more tangled.

Qālā-i Nau lay beyond the pass called Band-e Sabzak, which cuts through the peaks at a height of about ten thousand feet. The plain narrowed gradually and the road began to weave, deteriorating steadily, between two fingers of the Safed Kuh range, the White Mountains. Tiny settlements nestled at their bases; we stopped at one for a brief lunch of rice and tea, where the roadside was lined with sparkling silver birch. After it the road began to climb more steeply, and the surroundings whitened under a thickening layer of fresh snow. Soon we had penetrated a desert of whiteness; the road became white, and the crunch of tyres against gravel turned to the crunch of snow; the slopes on either side of the road narrowed and turned to white; and the horizon was white, as if we were driving into a frozen cloud.

The temperature began to drop. Above us the canvas roof flapped angrily in a growing wind. The driver, Khalifa, switched to four-wheel drive as our pace slowed and the pitch of the engine grew more erratic. I looked up ahead through the windscreen, through which the view was beginning to shrink. A layer of ice was creeping across the glass from the edges; not on the outside, which the wipers swept away, but from within. The walls of compacted snow deepened on either side until we were driving uphill along a sort of bobsled course filled with freshly blown dunes of snow, the surface of which was a violently swirling white mist. The blown snow thickened as we ascended until, in a big lateral drift, the jeep sank up to its axles and could go no further. I gave up hope of reaching Qālā-i Nau, and not without a feeling of relief, because the thought of being stranded any further up was fairly frightening; we would obviously have to reverse down the slope.

I had underestimated, again, the heroic determination of the Afghan driver. Just as it seemed unthinkable to go forward, Khalifa ordered us out, took a shovel from the back of the jeep and began digging around the tyres. With his bare hands he fixed chains to the wheels and as half a dozen of the other men pushed in knee-deep snow, the jeep lurched free.

It was paralysingly cold. The wind was lethally sharp and cut unprotected skin like a blade. It seemed quite likely we would not survive the night if stranded, yet incredibly Khalifa battled the jeep forward. The whole thing took on a quality of the surreal. From one side a passenger held his hand against the windscreen to melt a tiny patch of ice for Khalifa to glimpse the way ahead; from the other I tried to do the same, and my hands burned until they were numb. We sank again into a drift, scrabbled frantically at the snow around the wheels, pushed until we were free again and then, half a mile further, lodged so deeply that nothing could get us out. It looked hopeless; we went into battle with the snow again, but the wheels spun uselessly, and by now we were exhausted. It was then that, with a sense that bordered on the miraculous, we caught sight of a blurred dot descending towards us: a jeep travelling in the opposite direction.

It pulled alongside, the driver having suffered similar trials further up. A row of thick icicles hung from the bumper; incongruously pink curtains hung over the windows. It manoeuvred into place and we were hauled out at the end of a metal chain.

'If it were night,' chuckled the man next to me as we got going again, 'we would have died.'

*

At the pass a new world opened before us. The sky had suddenly regained its cyanic intensity, lightening to violet above a northern horizon so distant it gave the impression of tracing the curvature of the earth. Beneath us the mountains had been sucked back into the land. Several thousand feet below a broad valley stretched for fifty miles, enclosed by a thousand-foot escarpment whose flat surface dissolved into the distance. Below its snowy rim ran parallel bands of purple rock. To the west was a sinking wall of rusty mesa-like crenellations buttressed by pine-sprinkled ravines. The route down was gentle but treacherously slippery. Twice we passed trucks that had fallen from the road earlier in the day; both had been lucky enough (or unlucky enough) to have slipped into relatively shallow ravines, but the skewed frames and scattered cargoes told of their somersaulting descents. At one a procession of ant-like men was winding upwards with sacks of salvaged cargo on their backs, which they piled at the side of the road. At another the owner was sitting on his *pattū* on the snow, staring head in hands at the wreckage of his truck.

We crept downwards. At the extremities of the hairpin bends we noticed cairn-like pyramidal structures, built not of stones but scrap metal, salvaged from the carcasses of other vehicles in the ravines below. Old engine blocks and axles formed their bases; there were rusty wheels and camshafts in their midsections, and atop a differential or twisted tailpipe, a door handle or severed wing mirror.

After a cautious descent we stopped at a checkpoint on the valley floor. A tank nestled in a fold of rock, its barrel trained on the road behind us. The jeep was searched briefly as we stood by. I heard the sound of a rifle being cocked and turned with a shudder, wondering if I was about to witness an execution. But the rifle's sights were on a solitary fox trotting across the snow a hundred and fifty yards away. There was a bang that left our ears ringing and a little white fountain went up a few inches in front of the fox, and it galloped away.

The road was a twisted river of ruts and ridges, all expertly negotiated by Khalifa. In the village of Chamān two wiry old men who had been crouched in the very back of the jeep clambered out. I watched them walk away under a canopy of trees drooping with glazed snow; a sight which, if the Afghans celebrated the event, they would have put on a Christmas card.

In some villages we were chased by furiously barking sheep dogs as big as St Bernards. As it grew dark each settlement seemed ghostly and abandoned. Several times we forded swiftly flowing rivers; I wondered how far Qālā-i Nau could possibly be, because it had looked so close and easy on the map. But it was four more hours' drive in darkness before we reached our destination and I had an old feeling of worry because I had expected to arrive in daylight and to be able to find one or other of the foreign missions there.

Then came that sinking moment when we drew finally to a stop, the engine died, and the passengers disappeared with the usual swiftness. The man I sat next to agreed to escort me to what he thought was a place where he had seen other foreigners. We walked through a maze of walled streets in the blackness and stopped briefly at his house, where he greeted the wife he hadn't seen for three months. A few minutes later we were at a gate where there was a UN sign. A *chowkidar* emerged with an oil lantern and stared at us. There were no foreigners there at the moment, he said, and he didn't have permission to put up guests.

We walked back towards my friend's house, and just as we were passing a high wall I thought I heard, from behind it, the hallucinatory sound of a man's voice speaking English.

It was too strange to be true: then I had a sudden memory of the mention, back in Kabul, of an English couple living 'somewhere in the north'. Perhaps this was them.

'Let's try here,' I suggested to my wide-eyed friend, and we banged on the door. We heard a bolt being drawn back. The door swung open, and the face of an anxious-looking man appeared.

'What is it?' he asked in Persian, with an almost irascible note.

For a moment I was too surprised to answer. He looked rather as I imagine Aristotle might have looked. He was tall and lean and his broad brow, furrowed, I guessed, by fifty years, suggested a powerful intellect. His cheeks were drawn and his mouth had a look of aristocratic severity which was softened by the unbrushed silvery curls that caught the light of the lantern as he peered out at us.

I introduced myself and his big eyes blinked like a pheasant's as he asked how I had found the house. His voice had a melodious ring of erudition and heightened the impression of a scholarly asceticism; and it seemed to me he wore a toga-like *pattū* – but perhaps I have added this later from my imagination.

He blinked again as if he was deciding what to do, then looked at me, and said, 'Well, you had better come in then.'

I thanked my Afghan friend, who was as surprised as I was at the sheer improbability of the encounter, and we said goodbye. I had a new host. He held up the lantern and led me across a grassy yard. We went inside a single-storey building, where the floor was littered with children's toys and the walls lined with tall bookshelves. As we passed, he called out, 'Darling, we've got a visitor.'

The first, it turned out, for about a year. Afghans came to see them, of course, said Nick, but their foreign friends in Herat had not passed by for ages; heavy snows and the general deterioration in the road discouraged outsiders.

We sat cross-legged on cushions in a living room strewn with Afghan carpets, and were joined by his very unassuming and attractive wife who, like Nick, was a teacher.

It's true we don't have many visitors,' said Deborah matter-of-factly, as she lifted a tea cosy from a china pot, 'but we're generally too busy to be lonely.'

They were very friendly and soon we had forgotten our earlier sense of surprise: theirs at an English guest arriving unannounced on a midwinter evening, and mine at how this charming couple and their children had ended up living in a village at the tail end of the Hindu

Kush. They were both working with Afghan staff at the local school to design a syllabus that might serve as a model elsewhere in the country.

I asked how often they got back to England. They had been only once in the past couple of years, after the town had been bombed by jets; it had seemed better for the children. But the experience had left them thoroughly disenchanted. Visiting her native Bromley, Deborah had been glad to see her family but appalled by the number of new shopping malls, the accelerated commercialism, and the general unfriendliness of people.

'It was awful. I wanted to run straight back here,' she said.

'England's insidious,' said Nick. 'Media's rubbish too. *Spectator* used to be good, now it's just like the others.'

'It's got no vocabulary at all,' said Deborah.

'Waste of time.'

'We used to listen to the world service,' said Deborah in a thoughtful tone.

'Now it's just as bad, totally superficial.'

'And what about that Danziger chap everyone goes on about?' asked Deborah. 'I mean, what's all the fuss about? It's such selfish writing.'

'A nonsense,' nodded Nick.

He asked if I'd seen the satellite television beamed to the region, and told a story of the hereditary chief of the Sufis in a nearby village: on his succession his first priority had been to ask Nick's help in installing a satellite dish on the roof of his home.

'The satellite programming is absolutely criminal,' he said. 'Should be banned.'

*

I stayed the next day. In the morning we washed up dishes together, while Deborah fed the animals in the yard: a goat and chickens. They didn't believe in having paid help, but the sheer level of physical work was more than they had expected, and didn't leave them much time for anything else. There was a weary note in Nick's voice as he spoke.

While the children were being taken to school, I scrambled up a muddy track skirting the hill that overlooked the town, and at the top found a series of eroded ramparts linked by slit trenches where a battery must have stood during the war. Only after reaching it did I curse myself for ignoring the danger of mines.

From the top I looked down over the village. The single-storey homes were flat-roofed and spread along grids of interlocking walls and courtyards dotted with leafless trees. There was a low hill like a collapsed volcano in the east, and beyond it, a range of snow-streaked hills trailing into the haze. The airport was a mile away to the north: I could make out the usual wrecked transport aircraft lying beside the runway, half a dozen dug-in tanks and, on the ridge above, a cluster of military microwave antennae like the petals of Venus fly-traps. To the south and west the fields below were dusted with snow like icing sugar and across them ran long branching lines of tracks like the traces of atoms in a particle accelerator. The hills were beautiful and oddly shaped, like the peaks of freshly beaten egg-whites.

Afterwards I went with Nick for a tour of the village – by Afghan standards it was a town – and in a shop he seized upon a few cans of ravioli as if they were gold dust: supplies like these were hard to come by, he said.

We looked through some of his rare books on the art and archaeology of Afghanistan. He told me about the sites of ruins in the region that were not on any maps, and how from time to time he was offered odd treasures by Afghans who had dug them up in their fields. I regretted not being able to stay longer.

He was gloomy about England: I said there were worse places to live.

What about America? he asked on a more hopeful note, when I mentioned that I had lived there. 'Are there still places where you can get away from all that madness?' I said I thought there were; but that with children one couldn't evade the local culture anywhere.

'But you have the choice,' he said passionately, 'you don't have to watch TV.'

It wasn't that simple, I suggested; one's children would naturally watch television at their friends' homes, and look upon their parents' puritanism as freakish; or else they would grow up unable to cope with the outside world.

'Not in a community of like-minded people. There must be thousands of people in England who are fed up with the way things have become.'

I didn't doubt that.

Though I was tempted to stay, I had to leave the following morning: with the pass only just manageable and the road to the north closed, I might be stranded there for months.

We found a jeep heading back towards Herat and I said goodbye to Nick. We parted with that same no-nonsense absence of emotion that had characterized our meeting and I wondered how long they would weather things in Qālā-i Nau: I think of them often.

*

Soon a shout went up; the jeep was ready to go. The roof was a quilt draped with plastic sheeting in which a hole had been cut to fit the windscreen. It was tied down with rope like a parcel; the doors were tied with more rope, and the whole jeep looked as though it was held together with rope. Eleven men clambered in. I squeezed into the back next to a man wearing a black fur hat who offered me a handful of pumpkin seeds.

We ricocheted at speed along the route I had taken two days before, weaving between intersecting spurs the colour of lavender, following the glittering grey snake of the river. The driver was possessed, driven in turn by some unfathomable demon, which made him push the jeep to its limits. On a gravel-strewn section of road we went into a long, lurching skid from one side of the road to the other and back again. I remember it was long and serious enough for some of the men to cup their hands heavenward and begin muttering prayers. Seeing the gravel riverbanks rushing towards us I remember thinking selfishly that I might not fare too badly in the crash, being protected by several bodies on either side. But the driver managed to get the jeep under control and we moved on, more cautiously now.

We forded a river where a bus was trapped midway in a rut. On the far side a jeep was waiting to tow it free, and between the two waded a biblical-looking old man clutching one end of the towrope, breaking the ice with his shins as he went forward.

Sometimes the way was blocked by flocks of sheep and dusty old men driving their donkeys forward with sticks; once we were brought to a stop by some nomad families travelling in the opposite direction on a string of camels. They were led by hardy, straight-backed men; the women were draped in black and flashed with jewellery, and the daughters were of unworldly beauty.

Then, at the foot of the pass, we clambered out while the driver put chains around the wheels. We walked upwards across the snow. I soon fell behind the others, slipping on the ice, lungs reeling in the thin air. It was a gruelling hour; the others skipped ahead as though they were on a picnic. As I neared the top I saw a trio of standing silhouettes, and heard their cheerful shouts floating downwards:

'Come on, it's not that hard!'

'What's the matter, something wrong with you?'

'Not tired are you?'

Soon we were winding down again out of the snow, and stopped in the same village as we had on the way. We ate rice and drank tea in a roadside *chaikhāna* set in a cluster of tall silver birch, and a passing blind man led by a small boy began to sing. The melody was deeply stirring and sad and touched us all, as if a portion of the blind man's world had been brought down on us. No one moved until he had finished and began to wend his way forward up the hill.

Gradually the mountains loosened their hold on the route as we descended. Karokh, the largest village on the gently tilting plain, had a solitary beauty. The homes had earthen roofs the shape of young women's breasts, and I could make out courtyards built around groves of oriental pine; the place looked utterly peaceful.

*

Herat was cold and overcast. I walked to the mission, but the gates were locked so I wandered a little further along the street where there was another mission residence, hoping to find someone who could unlock the gate. The *chowkidar* let me inside the compound and apologized that there was no one else about. Seeing how tired I was, he brought me into his cabin-like quarters and fussed over a teapot, stoked the stove, and offered me his bed to rest for a while. We talked a little until I felt my eyelids pushing downwards as irresistibly as suspension bridges. I have no recollection of our actual conversation, but perhaps because of the feeling of exhaustion, and that strange quietness of mind that sometimes accompanies it, I remember the delicious warmth of that little room and the *chowkidar's* care with a tender vividness.

I slept for a couple of hours and woke up just as it was getting dark. At the mission, the gates were still locked. I was beginning to worry about where to stay, and at dusk swallowed my pride and went back to the Red Cross, hoping for a roof for the night and prepared this time to beg for it.

Walking into the garden I saw, to my astonishment, a half-naked and steaming man with a towel around his middle.

'G'day, mate!' he called out as he saw me. 'Fancy a sauna?'

He was a friendly Australian who ran a relief agency in the city, and he invited me inside. We swapped stories in the makeshift sauna – a tiny converted storeroom fitted with a stove and a dim red bulb. He confessed to being worried about his female staff, who since the Tāleban's arrival were growing too scared to come to work. And a few evenings ago, well before curfew, a Tāleb soldier had shot at his jeep as he drove home.

We were joined a few minutes later by the melancholic Frenchman I had sat next to on our way from the airport. His Swiss colleague, whom I had earlier met, was in Kabul for a few days, and he had been left in charge of the place. He spoke very little, but sat opposite and watched me with uncomfortable intensity as the sweat trickled over the simian ridges of his eyebrows. His name was Pierre-Luc.

The Australian left to cool in the garden, and for a few minutes we were alone. I had not put to rest the events of a few days before, and dredged up his boss's decision to refuse me accommodation while allowing Antoinette to stay. If they had a policy on visitors, I suggested, it should be consistent. He looked away and dismissed the issue with an infuriating Gallic shrug. I persisted.

'*Eh bien, c'est vrai,*' he conceded finally. Then he said: 'We think perhaps you are working for ze intelligence organization.'

So that was it – I was a spy! A concern for security was legitimate enough. But had it occurred to him that a spy might have adopted a more substantial camouflage? Antoinette, I suggested, at that very moment a few rooms away, and with the professional cover of a journalist, was a far more likely candidate.

'*Peut-être.*' He shrugged the suggestion away as if it were irrelevant.

So what, I asked, had influenced Beat's decision?

'Ze problem with you,' he answered, 'is that you have been here and you have been there, you have seen zis and you have seen zat – and you know too much.'

I asked him if he knew what spies really did, and how they did it. He didn't. We both left it there. Or so I thought.

We showered and dressed, and shared stories over a beer in the main room with the Australian and Antoinette. It was half-past eight. Curfew began at nine and it seemed obvious we would all spend the night; even after seven people were reluctant go outdoors. The others wandered out of the room and I was talking with Antoinette when, through a small grille in the wall, I heard voices hushed with conspiracy from the hallway. I thought I heard my name, and put my ear to the grille, catching snippets of the Frenchman's voice: '. . . iz a question of *sécurité* . . . wiz you it is different . . . cannot allow him to stay . . . intelligence organization.'

I would have laughed but time was against the humour of the moment. That I was a spy in his overheated imagination was in itself a joke, except that he would ask me to leave for the sake of this fantasy, and it was now twenty minutes to curfew. There was barely enough time to get back to the mission, and I had to leave at once.

I was already putting on my jacket when he came back into the room. I did not want to stay to hear his reasons. By asking me to leave he was deliberately putting a life at risk and I admit I have found it hard to forgive.

'*Désolé,*' said Pierre-Luc and shrugged his shoulders.

'*Moi aussi.*' I was too proud and too angry to speak. There was a bottle of vodka on the table. I poured a measure into a glass and drank it at a gulp. The others were dumbstruck but said nothing: such is the solidarity of foreigners abroad.

I said goodnight, and went out into the freezing air.

Immediately I regretted my foolhardiness. There was no moon and I had no torch. I began to think of all the clever things I might have said, but it was too late. At the gates, an astonished *chowkidar* let me out, asking me where my car was, and did I know what time it was? I lied and said I was going nearby, but the look of worry on his face again prompted the urge to return to the house and plead to be allowed to stay. But by then my pride had already grown in proportion to the danger and I had fifteen minutes to make a half-hour journey.

I knew that in the darkness the route would take longer than in daytime, and cast off from the comfort of the light that shone by the gates, into the main street. It was silent and utterly black. I knew too that there were men with orders to shoot anyone on the streets and felt a familiar sensation of panic, a kind of breathless nausea spreading like a stain through my abdomen.

I cast off into the blackness, trying to picture the likely places where soldiers would be posted along the route. If I could get back to the mission in one piece there would be nothing to compare to it; and I can't deny having felt a contrary urge, equal to the fear, to cheat the odds, the Frenchman and the Tāleban's sentries all in one go.

*

For a hundred yards, deprived of all bearings, I walked down a narrow lane leading from the main road. Turning a corner I saw a pool of yellow light from a single oil lantern, and hurried towards it, stumbling against muddy bumps. Then came a dreadful scream of challenge, and the unforgettable metallic clambering of a bullet into the breach of an automatic rifle.

'All right, all right,' I muttered, and put my hands up. I was scared stiff and heard the unnaturalness of my own voice as if it wasn't mine. In a gateway there were three men; one shone a torch in my face, another pointed his rifle, loaded and cocked, at the middle of my chest, and a third came forward to search me.

A gruff voice asked where I was going at this hour.

'I am so sorry,' I said as I walked up, my heart roaring like a tide at every beat, 'but my vehicle has broken down and I am obliged to walk home. It's not very far.'

What I meant, of course, but my Persian would not stretch to it, was: 'Don't shoot, for fuck's sake!' If they wanted to shoot someone, I could think of no one better than that nameless, *mal baisé salaud* of a Frenchman who had turned me out of his house just before curfew.

A dark, unsmiling pair of eyes framed by a black turban and thick beard drew into the light, and I felt a hand sweep over my pockets.

'Any weapons?'

'No, no weapons.'

'What's this?' He drew back with a start, and the man with the rifle tensed. The barrel, two feet away, seemed to bore like a lance of infinite length into my chest. Very gingerly, I drew out a camera lens.

'And this?' The hands came to a second lump, equally the size and weight of a grenade. He tensed, the barrel jerked, and I shuddered again.

'A rock,' I said. 'From the shrine.'

His eyes betrayed a moment of puzzlement; perhaps all foreigners carried rocks and bits of camera in their pockets.

'Go on, then,' said the voice, and the rifle came down.

'Thank you, brother. Is it safe ahead?' My mouth was dry.

'It's late,' came the stern reply.

Further on I heard the sighing of pines high above me in the blackness. There was another pool of light ahead and I could make out the shapes of men near it, one standing and two sitting. I avoided it, turning down tiny streets. One was a dead end. Eventually I came out on another main road, my fear swelling as the minutes ticked by. There was another pair of sentries I could not avoid, so I walked up and greeted them boldly. They were too baffled, I think, to challenge me, and waved me on without a word, as my apologies trailed away in the dark.

It was nine o'clock and the *mullā* Nasruddin story about curfew went round and round in my head with horrid vividness. I crept a hundred yards, pausing every minute, to listen from behind the trunks of the pines that lined the road. I skirted another checkpoint. What if some Tāleb on a rooftop saw me skulking along the road and began to shoot? My mind raced with the possibilities.

Further on I saw the last post, a shed with a lantern and two armed men sitting outside. I tiptoed through the shadows until I was opposite them, but directly ahead was a broad crossroads which I couldn't hope to cross without being seen. An electric light shone like the sun from a building nearby; it was the Iranian embassy.

Suddenly I was struck with the thought that, if I were seen and challenged, I had no idea what to call out; my Persian had abandoned me completely. For a few minutes I cringed behind the tree, wondering whether to dash across or to step boldly from the shadows and announce myself to a group of armed men whose job it was to shoot me. These are things which, before and after the event, one works out coolly and sensibly. But at the time, I was aware of my imagination working with unnatural vividness through a whole range of possible scenarios, all amplified by fear.

Just then, with all the timeliness of bad fiction, the throb of a motorcycle engine came to my rescue. There was a sudden clatter of loading rifles and a third man rushed from the shed, tripping over himself in the process. He got up and raised a lantern while the others trained their weapons on the approaching headlight.

Dear God! I thought, they will shoot him and by his death I will be able to cross the road. It was an excruciating moment. But a fellow Tāleb loomed into view, and while they all exchanged greetings I padded across the open stretch and slipped gratefully into the incomparably sweet embrace of the shadows beyond.

Five minutes later I was at the mission gates, where I climbed the wall and dropped into the garden, feeling more than a little pleased with myself and full of the exaggerated confidence that comes from having cheated danger. But inside I realized that the Good Lord, all the way from Kansas, had received word of my pride. Before I could disappear into my room, Dorothy cornered me in the hallway and ushered me into the living room, where she and Herb, in a show of devotion to put the Tālebān to shame, had been reading from holy books. I could only think that if these good people wanted to deepen their prayers, they could do no better than walk home after curfew a few times a week.

I tried hopefully for small talk, but once again my religious credentials were under scrutiny. Dorothy picked up a Bible like a traffic warden about to issue a ticket.

'Do you have a favourite passage?' she asked, in a voice sweeter than candy floss.

Twelve

Mīgozārad

(It will pass)

Graffiti on a teahouse wall in Faizābād

LIKE PRISONERS IN A LATTER-DAY tale of Scheherazade, we made our escape the following afternoon. Our enchanted stallion was the Red Cross flight, and the city of our heart's desire, Kabul. The plane swooped down through a veil of drizzle and soon we were skimming effortlessly over a sea of snow-cloaked ridges that stretched to the horizon.

Not without regret. I felt a familiar heartache at having intruded frivolously into the troubled life of Herat, and at having abandoned it with a facility of which its inhabitants could only dream. Superimposed on the ice-glazed plateaus and ravines I seemed to see a crowd of anguished faces waving in front of my eyes, and couldn't shake the image.

We came down, as a ghost sinks through a wall, beneath a canopy of sculpted cloud, and circled the magnificent cradle of mountains surrounding the Shomāli plain in the absinthine light of the setting sun. It flashed as we spiralled downward, first over the right wing and then the left, like a luminous and gigantesque gold coin. From it a final volley of long light-filled lances flew earthwards between the crenellations of the upper ridges, and under their gilded trajectory, clusters of tiny settlements glinted from the snowbound fields below like the illuminated letters of a parchment.

A bus took us back to Kabul. Passing through the shattered outskirts of the city I felt a sense of relief and homecoming: it was, despite the destruction, a beautiful setting, which years of war had been unable to corrupt. Or perhaps I should not say despite; perhaps, reminded again of the frailties of glass and concrete and asphalt, a sense of the indestrucible serenity of its natural surroundings was thereby renewed.

Tim had left, and the house where I had stayed was locked. I walked to the BBC residence to enquire about accommodation, and was recognized by the elderly and toothless cook. He ushered me inside, clucking with delight, as if I were his own son. In the main room a satellite television was showing a travel programme about the Carribean, and women in bright and scanty bathing suits were sipping cocktails around a glittering swimming pool.

The new correspondent, Alain Pearce, had arrived recently from the Far East. He was settling with relish into his new posting, and recounted with pride his achievements to date: appalled at his predecessor's lack of curtains, he had found some material at an excellent price in the fabric market and had new ones put up a few days before; he was also instructing the cook how to make a decent *bolognese*.

In the hallway was a pile of bullet-proof vests, of which he was faintly scornful; his real pride was a camouflage jacket of Swiss army manufacture, with enough pockets to fit all his bits and pieces when in the field. Its colouring, dominated by irregular red blobs, made it unique in Kabul, and among Afghans a valuable conversation-opener. It had the added advantage, were he ever to find himself crawling under fire through a strawberry patch, of providing perfect camouflage.

He made coffee with a splash of rum, and offered me sanctuary upstairs, apologizing for the lack of glass in the windows. But there was an open fire in the main room, from which, as things turned out, we were never far.

As we swapped news he pointed to a weighty volume beside the fireplace: it was a copy of Margaret Thatcher's *Downing Street Years*. I passed it to him; he tore out half a dozen pages and stuffed them under the kindling. Then he coaxed some logs into place with the tip of a Russian bayonet, and before long our eyes were fixed on the heart of the dancing flames.

*

For several days afterwards I carried with me a kind of mental after-image of leaving Herat, and relived the drive to the airport like the ending of a sad film. With Antoinette I had made a last-minute visit to the glassmakers' shop by the central mosque, and hurriedly bought a pair of turquoise vases before catching a taxi to the airport. Then we had bounced along the shattered road and watched through the drizzle the shopkeepers and passers-by at their run-down and ill-stocked stalls with, for my own part at least, a hopeless feeling of abandonment. A few workmen at the airport watched us as we listened for the comforting drone of the approaching plane, and I could hardly bear to meet their eyes.

Now, like looted icons, the vases sat in my room among a private orphanage of souvenirs: a trio of shell-casings in different sizes like Russian dolls, some fragments of green and turquoise tiles, a jagged piece of shrapnel and the split-open fuse cone of an artillery shell, a kidney bean blessed by the dervishes in Mazar, several lumps of lapis lazuli, the jade pot given to me by Hamid for my daughter, an embroidered pair of children's slippers rimmed with rabbit fur, a ripe head of cotton, a book of Afghan short stories, and a bundle of green 50-Afghani notes.

*

After the restricted atmosphere of Herat, Kabul had the air of a place of licence and liberty. I fell back readily, among familiar faces again, into the foreigner's peculiar longing for release. It is only in a country where the consumption of alcohol is not the norm that you realize how deeply the rituals associated with grape and grain penetrate elsewhere into daily life. All of a sudden, there is no cocktail hour to lubricate the motion of social gatherings or after-dark tricklings to erode the barriers of formality; no anticipatory colluding of tumblers around the volatile contribution of a guest, no swirlings of the tongue through favoured vintages, or admiring glances at the parabolic trailing of glycerous legs; no wee drams or just-a-drops; no toasts or tipples, nightcaps or noggins, no valedictory downings at a gulp or ones-for-the-road: for the road is vigorously sober, and the individual who has leaned even lightly on these habits is apt to totter in their absence.

Only the tiniest proportion of Afghans – that is, Afghans in their own country – drink alcohol; outside the biggest cities, consumption is virtually unknown. It is as rare to see an Afghan drink as it is to see a European chewing betel nut. Until the turn of the twentieth century, when their region was converted to Islam by Abdur Rahman, the tribes of Nuristan are said to have produced wine, and before the Soviet period there were some foreign wine-producers in Kabul.* But since then the supply, other than in foreign circles, has matched the demand. There was, while I was in Kabul, rumour of some locally distilled moonshine, but curiosity was dampened by tales of blinding – the curious and irreversible effect of methanol on the human optic nerve.

The religious prohibition on alcohol in the Islamic world has, of course, its adaptations, and shades of stricture vary across the spectrum of the cultures it subsumes. Often I have watched with delight the magical clouding of a raki-shot in a Turkish *lokanta* above the Bosphorus, or stretched out a cooling evening beneath the swaying date-palms of Tozeur as another cupful of pleasantly effervescent elixir has been handed down from the uppermost branches; I have even tried the *khoumiss* – fermented mare's milk – of a Kirgiz farmer from Alma Ata (although, I admit, he was living in Washington at the time).

But in general in Moslem countries it is only among the most worldly – the definition is ambiguous – that the more felicitous by-products of fermentation are genuinely enjoyed; among others there hangs over any drinking session a guilty air that utterly subverts any hope of conviviality.

Sometimes the pursuit of the forbidden takes on a sordid flavour. In neighbouring Pakistan, an officially 'dry' state, the drinks cabinets of the wealthy jostle with illicit distillations, whose consumers, between the plop of ice cubes, heartily affirm their religiosity. On the street, or in the lobby of your hotel, mention of the stuff takes on a more pathetic tone, especially from the lips of grown and otherwise dignified

---

* Peter Levi describes a 'good, brisk tablewine' produced by Italians, and also reports that the native stock of Afghan vines was used for the foundation of the Californian wine industry. Dupree cites another little-known culinary discovery of Afghan provenance, namely one-minute rice: 'In 1941 Mr Ozai-Durrani walked into the offices of General Foods Corporation, set up a portable stove, and cooked a pot of rice in approximately sixty seconds. His discovery made Mr Ozai-Durrani a millionaire.'

men; sometimes it takes the form of an offer (*'You like...?'*), or more often a plea (*Please, mister, you have...?*), but never without that talismanic invocation, 'Johnny Walker.'

Mercifully for our foreign ways, the habit was amicably tolerated* by the government, and no limit was placed on the visitor's quota. These imported stocks only rarely fell short. I found personally that so long as I kept company with foreign friends the momentum of our ritual homage to Bacchus was untroubling; beyond it though, among Afghans, there was no place for it, and this inconsistency, partly my own and partly that of circumstance, became a burden. But making my way one evening to Number Eight, the house in Wazir Akbar Khan which served outsiders as a communal watering-hole and clearing-house of rumour and exchange, such distinctions were easily overruled. Here a fairly regular crowd gathered in the evenings, let in and out by an Afghan *chowkidar* who kept freezing vigil at the door. The bar was in the basement; you walked down a flight of stairs, not without a faint sense of depravity at the descent, and banged your head on the lintel at the entrance.

To one side, I noticed when I first went, was a room lined with mattresses and cushions of garish red; down the centre ran a series of low, lacquered tables on which stood small electric lamps in tulip-shaped shades of red frosted glass. The decor suggested opium pipes, oriental-looking women in iridescent silk pyjamas, or both. But the effect was, of course, only the result of a bad choice of fabric, and the impression so off-putting that hardly anyone ever went in.

People gathered instead around the bar in smoky circles, talking above the din of music. There I met an Italian photojournalist with a flamboyant air and a weakness for tall stories. He told how he had been in Bamiyan when the government had been driven out, and managed to escape on the back of a fleeing tank; on the way it had

---

* Following the entry of the Tālebān into Kabul, thousands of bottles of wine and spirits were rounded up, mostly from the cellars of the Intercontinental Hotel, and in a frenzied display of puritanism, ritually crushed in public beneath the treads of a Russian tank; a cruel sight, I'm told, by friends left behind to watch it.

accidentally run over a woman, from whose arms – he made a cradling gesture – he had rescued a baby. He described, with studied noncha- lance, his secret meeting with a highly placed intermediary in Pakistan who brought together buyers and sellers of pillaged Afghan artefacts; he had been shown, among other treasures, a Buddha of solid gold destined for the hands of a Japanese art dealer. Then there was the time he had negotiated with the CIA for the return of their remaining Stinger missiles . . .

For all this he did not have the air of someone who was consciously lying, but merely found the separation of fact from fiction an unnecessary challenge. I went along with the performance, and we came to like each other, though perhaps for different reasons. Fired by his storytelling I saw an airport-bookstore novel take flight, with an Anglo-Italian search at its heart for the lost Dipankara Buddha with ruby eyes: their success betrayed by a deranged Frenchman, the intrepid couple are captured by drug-crazed, Yataghan-wielding Hazāra tribes- men, but manage to escape in a tank, rescuing a baby on the way – before shooting down the Frenchman in his helicopter with a Stinger missile bestowed (along with a pair of dusky-eyed concubines) by the infant's grateful father . . .

But some time later I saw the photographs he had taken from the top of the fleeing tank, and wondered if I had not been too complacent in my judgement of him.

*

It was a mixed array of souls that evening. There was a Scandinavian doctor recounting the fighting in Kabul in 1994: he had had to abandon his patients and cower in a storeroom with other staff as bullets smacked off the walls outside, pondering whether the lot of them would be slaughtered.

I remember too a young Frenchman, getting quietly drunk on his own. Our paths crossed; he looked at me, and blinked a few times before he spoke. Then, swaying gently, he asked how I would define the Afghan character. I'd been trying for ages without success, I told him.

'Well,' he replied, as his glass traced faltering spirals between us,

'I'll tell you then.' The Afghans, he said, were *un people qui reste debout* – a people who stay standing upright – and he described the event that had left him so visibly troubled. He worked for the ICRC: earlier in the day he had been to inspect one of the city's prisons to check on the conditions of the prisoners. After their names had all been verified, he noticed a door which had remained unopened for the inspection. The prison guard had been reluctant to open it; behind it was just an old man in solitary confinement, he had said. But it was the Frenchman's job to count the prisoners, and he insisted on being shown inside.

When the door was opened, he caught sight of a half-naked old man in the freezing and windowless cell.

'And what do you think he did then?' he asked, as the emotion welled up in his eyes. The old man had tottered to his feet, lifted the scrap of cloth on which he sat, brushed the dust from it and stepped back, smiling, to offer the space to his guest.

'*Et moi,*' he reflected, '*je n'ai jamais cru en rien, moi. Mais là, je me suis demandé* ... As for me, I've never really believed in anything. But just then, I began to wonder...' His voice trailed, and he turned inconsolably towards the drifting coils of smoke around the bar.

*

My old friend Rafiq arrived later and, once we had caught up with each other's news, manoeuvred skilfully into position beside a French nurse sitting at the bar.

'Do you believe in the unity of man and woman?' I heard him ask. When his victim's eyes began to roll, he would feign an ingenious retreat.

'Does it make you feel uncomfortable? I'm sorry. We can speak about something else. *Enfin* ... what would you prefer to speak about? *Life is an experience...*'

I felt a deep sense of relief when, looking like the leader of a trans-polar expedition, a man came down the stairs and strode into the room. It was Bob McKerrow.

Soon we were talking about climbing. During his time in Afghanistan he had made expeditions to the high summits of the Panjshīr and Paghman ranges, and even skied there (assured by a friend and former soldier that the danger from mines was lessened when on skis). He predicted wistfully that soon enough, when the war was sorted out, and the government laid claim once again to the movements of foreigners, you would need guides and permits to make mountaineering expeditions, and the whole spirit of such endeavours would be ruined as it had been in so many other places. Afghanistan was one of the last territories where you could set off for a great mountain, many of them still unclimbed, without any bureaucratic interference and – his hand glissaded towards an unmarked frontier in Tajikistan, Chitral or China – just drop down into a different country the other side. The risks were one's own.

He had in mind for the coming spring a trip to the highest summit in the country, the 25,000-foot Naoshaq near the border with Pakistan. But it wouldn't be a commercial expedition, he explained; there would be no hierarchy, no budget, no flags, no rigid schedule; just a group of dedicated friends who wanted to share in the joys and perils of the mountain. I was very touched when he invited me to come along.

'Someone in the government even asked if I wanted to be the minister of tourism,' he mused. 'I said I wasn't Afghan. "Never mind," they told me, "you *look* like an Afghan."'

As we were talking, something reminded him of a poem he had come across. He took a sheet of paper from his pocket and unfolded it. The title was 'Wanderer'; I had no idea of the author.

'You could read it out if you want,' he grinned. There was a pause in the music; the atmosphere was pleasantly raucous, and we were caught up in the spirit of the moment. I stood up on a chair and read from the sheet in front of me.

' "I have always wanted to sail the south seas, but I can't afford it," ' I began. A few questioning heads turned lazily upwards from their drinks. I read on:

'What these people can't afford is not
to go. They are enmeshed in the cancerous discipline
of "security", and in the worship of security we
fling our lives beneath the wheels of routine – and
before we know it our lives are gone.

'What does a person need – really need? A few
pounds of food each day, heat and shelter, six
feet to lie down in and some form of working activity
that will yield a sense of accomplishment. That's
all – in the material sense. And we know it. But we
are brainwashed by our economic system until we
end up in a tomb beneath a pyramid of time
payments, mortgages, preposterous gadgetry, playthings
that divert our attention from the sheer idiocy of
the charade.

'The years thunder by, the dreams of youth
grow dim where they lie caked in dust on the
shelves of patience. Before we know it the tomb
is sealed. Where then lies the answer? In choice.
Which shall it be; bankruptcy of purse or
bankruptcy of life...?

There was some desultory clapping. The music went back on. I
stepped down; Bob was grinning as he handed me a refilled glass.
'I like that bit about the years thundering by,' he mused. '"Where
then lies the answer?"' He raised his glass; we stayed a little longer,
then walked back to his house.

A *chowkidar* opened the gate and with a raised lantern, lit our way
to the door. Bob mentioned that, on occasions when he'd had a few
too many, his staff planted candles along the borders of the path to
help guide his way back inside.

'Right,' he said at the door, 'let's go and have a whisky, while these
poor people starve,' and showed me inside.

*

Maps, charts, photographs and fragments of manuscript began to swell
across the table. The high summits of Afghanistan had captured his
heart and he was writing a book about them, working just then on a
chapter about the Jesuit Benito de Goes, who visited Kabul in 1603 at
the end of a six-month walk from Lahore. '*Give me a man to match my
mountains...*' said Bob, quoting Blake, I think. He had a soft spot too

for the English poet James Elroy Flecker, who served as a diplomat in the Middle East before his death in 1915 at the age of thirty. It was Flecker (I now discovered) who wrote the well-known lines:

> We travel not for trafficking alone;
> By hotter winds our fiery hearts are fanned:
> For lust of knowing what should not be known,
> We take the Golden Road to Samarkand.

This same lust had propelled my host, as a teenager, onto a transpacific freighter in the hope of joining Che Guevara (the disappointing news of whose death he had received en route); later an unquenched restlessness had taken him through Polynesia, Vietnam, Ethiopia, Antarctica ... but in Afghanistan, he said, he had found his spiritual home. This was his third winter in Kabul. He would write for a few hours from dawn, then go from his desk to his duties with the Red Crescent, supervising a variety of relief projects around the city and beyond.

He also found himself drawn, like so many others who had spent time in its ancient heartland, to that great soul-magnet of Sufism; he was the only other foreigner I met fond of quoting the antics of the *mullā* Nasruddin. He organized care for the blind of the city, and mentioned a congenitally blind couple with three children, two sighted and one born blind. They did not go out much because they were taunted by children, and Bob made regular visits to see how they were faring.

That reminded him: had I heard the Nasruddin tale about the blind man? I hadn't, and he recounted it with typically warm-hearted irreverence.

There was in a village a blind man, very happily married, but to an ugly woman. One day a healer arrived, and offered to cure the man's blindness. A council of the village elders was convened to decide on the matter, and a vote was taken in favour of allowing the healer to do his work — until a voice of dissent was heard from the back of the room.

'Pray reflect on the following, respected elders!' cried Nasruddin. 'Which is better: to see, or to be happy?' And the healer was sent on his way.

'What does one do with all this experience?' sighed Bob. We sat by the fire as the level of the bottle sank gradually lower, and talked well into the night.

*

In the morning he was gone; there was a note pushed under my bedroom door with an invitation to stay for breakfast and an introduction to his housekeeper.

She was on the landing, ironing a shirt, and smiled very sweetly and without a trace of surprise as I emerged, nursing a tender cerebellum.

Her sandy hair was drawn back in a flowered headscarf, accentuating the gentle features of a perfectly oval face. Her every gesture, look and word seemed an extension of that gentleness; once again I felt rooted to the spot.

We chatted for a few moments, and she asked:

'But why didn't you stay here?'

I stammered something about having made other arrangements.

'A shame,' she said, 'but you could come back and live here.' She looked up and smiled boldly. 'I could iron your shirts. Or even sow you one like this –' and she pointed to a man's blouse embroidered exquisitely in delicate geometries of silk. I had bought one like it years ago; so precise and intricate was the stitching that people I had shown it to refused to believe it was not made by machine.

*

Bob had suggested an outing to the Salang Tunnel, in the mountains to the north of the capital, and we met again the following morning. It was an enticing destination. The tunnel itself, we knew, was closed, being the limit of government-held territory; there were constant rumours of its having been blocked by Massoud's troops to prevent the advance of Dostum's forces towards Kabul. I pictured it as a volatile and active front line, and thought it unlikely we would get very far before being turned back.

The tunnel was built by the Soviets in the days of their huge aid projects in Afghanistan, and is one of the engineering feats of the era.

At eleven thousand feet above sea level it is one of the highest motorable passes in the world. For two miles it bores through the upper slopes of the Hindu Kush, linking the precipitous and cliff-shadowed loops of road that scar its northern and southern flanks. It cost over six hundred million dollars to build and opened after six years of work in 1964, eliminating in the process the long and unpaved route over the mountains further west via the Shibar Pass, and shortening thereby the route from Pakistan to the Soviet Union to the length of a single day's drive.

Its name now had a legendary ring. Fifteen years after its construction, it became the logistical jugular vein of the Soviet invasion. Through it had flowed the long columns of invading armour and the greater part of the army's fuel, food and supplies. For years there had been heavy fighting up and down the pass. Along the road leading to the tunnel, the villages on either side had been cruelly subdued to deny the mujaheddin hiding-places for attacks on the creeping enemy convoys. Its flanks are today littered with the hollow carcasses of armoured vehicles, and desecrated monuments to Soviet soldiers who fell in uncounted ambushes.

It was a bright and sunny morning as we left, chauffeured in a Red Crescent jeep by an expert Afghan driver. Some forty miles north of Kabul we left the plain and followed the road beyond Jebel as-Serāj. The villages thinned, growing smaller, and a river sparkled to our left as it wound alongside the road. The mountain walls tightened towards us. We stopped once to photograph the view ahead between steepening intersecting spurs, beside a lonely ruined tank glazed with snow. The road began to twist in narrowing bends and the fresh snow on the terraces grew deeper as we rose. Soon the surface had turned white; there was not a single other vehicle, and gradually we climbed into a freezing alpine world bisected by narrow ravines with tumbling torrents.

Then came the first in a series of long galleries that overhang the road and shelter it from avalanches and landslides. A strong wind was driving the snow between the concrete pillars of the galleries and piling it in wild drifts on the exposed side. It was spectacularly lonely and it seemed likely we were the only human presence along the entire length of the road. We began to wonder how far up we would get. The faded signposts in Cyrillic characters and bullet-pocked bollards lent an eerie quality to the route, and our conversations faded.

Then, unexpectedly, around a final, rising bend we were at the open mouth of the tunnel itself. Vaguely I had imagined that, as the vital dividing-line between the territories of north and south, it would be blocked with wire and barricades. Yet it seemed utterly unprotected, and I was amazed that we should have driven unopposed to such a strategic point. It was only later that we were told, with expressions of disbelief at our folly (and, presumably, our luck), that both road and tunnel were mined.

We stopped and got out briefly to look back at the route. The road looped down the mountain walls like a collapsible ruler, half-extended, in a dizzying descent of hairpin bends. Again I had no doubt which side I would have chosen to be on in the days when Soviet convoys had rumbled up and down the virtually indefensible slopes below us.

Then we drove into the bunker-like entrance, and the whiteness fell away behind us. For the first few minutes the dark was expected and bearable, but we went forward for what seemed like an age with no hint of light ahead. I looked behind; the light had disappeared, and my loathing of tunnels rose on a tide of nausea.

Nearing the northern end, the smooth surface of the road broke up without warning; the driver had been going too fast, braked too hard, and we went into a lurching skid. Had we not recovered from it, and lost the use of the jeep in an accident, our fates would have been sealed there and then.

'Gently, now,' said Bob to the driver, unflappably, with a calming motion of his hand. We went forward more slowly, like potholers, staring with grim fascination into the beam of the headlights. Severed cables dangled like creeping snakes and the broken lamp housings above lent the tunnel the derelict feel of an abandoned mine. The walls were scorched with smoke, and I remembered, with a shudder: the Soviets had suffered one of their worst accidents of the war in just this spot.

In November 1982 a fuel tanker had crashed inside the tunnel, causing panic along the length of the convoy. Guards at either end suspected a mujaheddin attack and sealed both ends as fire broke out within; in the resulting chaos 400 Soviet and 700 Afghan troops are thought to have died.

Whether it was this knowledge alone, working away at the back of my mind, or whether the very walls still carried in their molecules the remembered horrors of the event ... it was a solemn and intimidating place.

We pulled up at the far end of the tunnel: it was sealed with a half-inch plate of steel. But at its base there was a small door, framed by a crack of light. Incredibly, it came open at a tug, and we walked out, as if into a Narnia. Beyond us lay a colourless world: we seemed to have emerged into a frozen cloud. The only recognizable shapes were the concrete semicircle of the tunnel entrance and the faded Persian lettering at its apex. All else receded into the numbing whiteness. Somewhere further along the road were the enemy's forward positions, but how far away, we could only guess.

It was too cold to stay for more than a few moments; my camera shutter had frozen, and we were buffeted by a furious wind, which took the heat from our bodies with frightening swiftness. We drove back through the tunnel to the entrance, awed by the solitude and the cold, and stopped for a final look at the view. Then while the jeep looped around a nearby bluff we took a short cut on foot to the road below. It was not snowing but a vicious wind whipped up the surface snow which was like powdered ice, and flung it in searing waves through the air. The wind howled over our ears; my hands, even clenched in my pockets, went numb, and back in the car I sat on them until the feeling returned, some ten minutes later, with a pain like a fire.

'A little longer out there,' mused Bob, 'and we'd have had the beginnings of frostbite.' It was the coldest and the eeriest place I had ever seen.

*

As if the journey had taken months we drew back into the city with a sense of wonder. It was only for a matter of hours that our senses had been taken captive by the snow and wind and the remoteness of the pass; but there as elsewhere the captivity had been so complete it seemed unlikely, as we entered the grip of the familiar world again, to find a city so close by. I was reminded that the proper rhythm by which to measure one's pace through the country was on foot or horseback, so dense was the place with impressions. We were chastened, too, by the numbers of ruined tanks and vehicles we had seen all the way. An unforgiving road.

*

The days were cold and luminous. Some mornings I would wake to the weary cry of a rag-and-bone man wheeling his barrow in the street below my room, his call almost indistinguishable from the one you still hear in parts of London. Kites danced above the streets. Often from the roof of the house I would see a small boy, with the determined agility of a young tom, balanced on splayed limbs in the slender branches of a tree, reaching towards the downed and tangled victim of a competition.

Conditions were against visits to sites beyond the city. I thought of Paghman, once a royal playground where Amānullah had built the oval racetrack around which elephants were made to run, and where the wealthy had planted their villa gardens with orchards fed by mountain streams. Paghman was a centre of resistance during the Soviet period and had been heavily bombed. A Hazāra driver I asked to take me there refused, saying it was too dangerous. I teased him, saying I'd protect him, regretting this flippancy only later when I was told Paghman had become the headquarters of the faction with more Hazāra blood on its hands than any other.

I was given permission to cross the lines in order to visit the village of Chakaray where I had lived with the mujaheddin years before; but after many attempts, I gave up trying to find a vehicle going in the right direction.

Discouraged by the restrictions and city-bound, I did a lot of walking instead. Sadly the most interesting historical sites, such as Bābūr's shrine and the Bala Hissar citadel lay in lawless and dangerous areas beyond the orbit I was prepared to trace; and of the once-famous

449

ancient covered bazaar, which was destroyed by the retreating British, there was no sign.

I would make a regular detour via the offices of the Red Cross, to check the message box down by the radio room in case of news from home. The radio operator, Amān, had visited England twenty years before to attend a course with the Civil Aviation Authority. The yellowing diploma hung on the wall above his desk and the blinking consoles of the radio equipment. During the war he had worked as an air traffic controller at the Soviet airbase in Qunduz.

'The English are a good people,' he said. He told how he had been in London and got lost on his way to Piccadilly Circus: an English couple had stopped and given him a lift.

'We Afghans don't forget that sort of thing,' he said. 'That was the trouble with the Russians. They never understood our way.'

One morning, in Chicken Street, I met the shopkeeper who had sold me a lapis necklace on my first brief foray into the city four years earlier, when the mujaheddin had finally chased the communists from power. He ushered me inside his shop, despatching a small boy for fresh tea, remembering the exact cost and the cut of the stone I had bought. I asked how he had fared in the meantime; it had been difficult, he said, and looked away. As we were talking the door opened: 'Peace be to you,' called a dignified voice, and my host jumped up.

'And to you, commander,' he replied.

The visitor was a handsome-looking man in his forties, with a long black beard. He wore a *pakoul* and a black leather jacket, and stood about four foot tall; over his right shoulder dangled a Kalashnikov, the barrel of which reached his ankle.

The shopkeeper recounted in detail the event of our meeting as we went into the back of the shop to talk, then excused himself for having to discuss an urgent matter with the commander, who rested his rifle against the wall, tucked his feet under him on a chair, and listened.

It turned out to be a complaint, which swelled into a plea, the details of which were recounted with such vehemence I caught only the barest fragments; he gave the impression of having been cheated, and was appealing for the commander's intervention; there was talk of money and a passport, and a litany of related difficulties.

I began to feel uncomfortable. The shopkeeper, a slightly built man whose manner, from what I had seen of it, was quiet and deferential, had worked himself up into a near frenzy. Then with shocking suddenness his hand flew under his seat and an unsheathed bayonet flashed from its hiding place, menacing the adversary of the story as if he were inches away from the point of the blade. It was a frightening transformation. The commander continued to listen and, sage-like, unruffled, gave him some practical advice in a measured tone.

I thought: it is not every day one is invited to drink tea in the company of a bayonet-wielding lapis dealer and a dwarf with a machine gun. But the show of anger left me unsettled, and soon afterwards I made my excuses and left. I was not sure if I understood their way, either.

✻

All around this part of the city there are shops behind whose dusty windows you glimpse pleasantly disordered arrays of unfamiliar and enticing shapes. They are – depending on your definitions – antique shops, curio shops or junk shops, but they all have the air of an Aladdin's cave and awaken a strange yearning in the eye, a feeling that you will surely be the lucky one to uncover some rare prize from the city's past.

Some favourites dominate the displays: huge brass samovars, their tarnished lids and sides bearing Czarist coats-of-arms, loom with an unwieldy and misplaced air like portions of dismantled steam engines. Beside them, with characteristic incongruity, you see the severed horns of mountain beasts; usually the ribbed curves of an ibex' horns, and occasionally the magnificent spiral from the head of a Marco Polo sheep. Sometimes the head itself has been preserved intact, and the lidless eyes stare numbly from an all-but-forgotten penumbra.

I found myself in front of one such shop and the temptation to enter too much to resist. I went in and was relieved when the owner let me wander about without a fuss.

'Take your time,' he said.

My eyes roamed over the shelves and piles of accumulated treasure, feasting on the unaccustomed shapes. Then gradually, like faces across a darkened room, things began to emerge. The first were giant wooden pestles in narrow mortars three feet high, their rims smooth from generations of labour. Around them crowded families of krater-like vessels of clay and metal, witches' cauldrons and, in a dusty alcove, an exiled community of smaller samovars. There were brass and copper trays and ewers engraved with concentric swirls of fluid calligraphy, clay jugs and blackened ladles and Gardener teapots made in St Petersburg; water pipes with the cobalt glaze of Istalif and oil lanterns whose design had not changed for millennia. Hanging above them were belts and buckles and stirrups stained and cracked with age, whips, gourds, pouches and multiplicities of bags; beads of bone and amber and lapis, trinkets, amulets, and charms sown into leather pouches. There were Turcoman shoes with toes that curled like the inverted proboscis of a moth, multicoloured silk gowns, long bands of embroidery that had once adorned a nomad tent, shawls, tasselled sad 'le-bags, statuettes with demonic faces in wood like the outlawed deities of Nuristan, and mythological animals in stone and marble. A variety of guns filled the spaces; muzzle-loading *jezails* with five-foot tapering barrels, slender arquebuses, their half-moon stocks meticulously inlaid with mother-of-pearl; British officers' pistols, their action still impeccable; even a side-loading Winchester rifle. There were swords – curved, straight, long, short – and pikes, poignards, daggers, bayonets, rhinocerous-hide shields, drums, lute-like *robābs* with topnuts and bridges of ivory, flutes and narrow-necked tambours made from mulberry wood, and even a battered regimental tuba. Above them dangled the pelt of a wolf, a bear and a snow leopard; and everywhere was scattered an encyclopaedic selection of jewellery, the fragments of dismantled clocks, pens, pocket-watches, coins ancient and modern, and banknotes from countries that no longer existed – junk, in short, the lot of it, but I would happily have bought the entire contents.

*

Despite the conditions, our lives were more sociable than ever. Unexpected invitations were the order of the day. Along with the other foreign journalists I even found myself invited to the premier of the first feature film made in Afghanistan since the fall of the communists.*

By late afternoon the life on the streets began to thin, and by early evening they were deserted. The nights were bitterly cold and packs of stray dogs roamed the streets, howling mournfully. I wore my huge wolf-fur hat and long camel-hair gown, whose flared sleeves reached to the knee. No one took much notice. Kabul was one of the few places where you could walk about looking like a Badakh-shāni shepherd from the previous century without attracting undue attention.

With eclectic pockets of friends I took advantage of the foreigner's exemption from curfew and we would walk or drive to follow up on invitations that had come our way during daylight. One evening there was a party at the Indonesian embassy. We pulled up at a house which in the darkness had the incongruous look of a Georgian mansion. An Afghan doorman took our hats and gloves at the entrance. To be in high-ceilinged, carpeted rooms with all their windows intact was faintly troubling. There was a warm hum of conversation from the assembled guests, a white-jacketed waiter shaking cocktails behind a bar, and another circulating with a clinking drinks cart.

I found Rafiq sitting on a leather couch with a trio of French nurses, giggling uncontrollably. I asked what the joke was and he described how a few minutes earlier, a stocky, dark-skinned man had stood near them and smiled.

'Fetch me an ashtray,' said Rafiq to the man, taking him for an

---

* A moving account of the initiatic passage of a village baker into war following the Soviet invasion. There were no professional actors; the film equipment was antique; filming was frequently interrupted by fighting. But the finished product would have held its own at any film festival. *Uruch* ('Ascension') was written by Sadiq Barmak, directed and filmed by Nur Hashemi Abir, and the main character, Mehrdad, was played by Homayoun Paīz. We were deeply impressed.

Afghan waiter. Very graciously, the ambassador had introduced himself.

The most striking sight was that of the two young women who were moving between the rooms with trays of Indonesian delicacies: they were the ambassador's daughters. Graceful, shapely and extremely beautiful, all their visible loveliness was accentuated in a most un-Afghan way by skin-tight black satin blouses and trousers. To judge from the numbers of men signalling for more food when they were no longer hungry, the frequency of longing glances, and of heads turning in abruptly-arrested conversations, they were having an effect akin to the sudden appearance of an oasis among men stranded in a desert.

Conversations were initiated on the flimsiest of pretexts, and when the last of the food had been served, there was a predatory circling of males around the bar, where the daughters had settled, like birds of paradise, on high stools. Someone – I forget who now – was taunting me to introduce myself to them; we were quite nervous. I made my way forward and found myself, rather unexpectedly, between the two of them. They glinted like little jewels and I felt all the thrill of a miner who, after manoeuvring himself along a dangerous and dusty seam, catches a sudden glimpse of a prize between layers of indifferent rock. How far they had come from their palm-fringed home overlooking the coral-pink Jakartan shore where, barefoot and draped in turquoise *batik*, they would walk hand in hand at sunset...

Disguising my nervousness I launched into what I hoped was a suitable rendition of events in Panjshīr.

'I was three hundred feet above the river...' I began, vaguely imagining a duo of oriental sighs from my audience, a demure and fascinated Asiatic cooing. But when they opened their mouths I realized that an upbringing in Los Angeles had exorcised all trace of Eastern promise.

'Oh my *God!*' exclaimed one of them, her brightly varnished nails rising in an extravagant gesture to her cheeks.

'...on a track no wider than my hand...'

'That is *sooooo cooool!*' squealed the other, eyes as wide as saucers.

'And the horse began to stumble...'

'That is *sooooo totally awesome!*' they chorused, then jumped from their chairs, their attention span exhausted, and were gone.

That sinking feeling again.

*

For the most part the methodology of our release was straightforward; for some it had acquired a more personal flavour. One evening, at a loose end for company, and hoping for the chance of a hot shower, I went to find Rafiq. He opened his door with a faintly guilty air, like a schoolboy caught behind a bicycle shed. We went into the main room, where his colleague Rustam was sitting by the fire reading a leather-bound edition of Gobineau's *In Search of Aryan Culture*. He looked up with a contrived and ruminant-like innocence.

'I'm glad it's you,' said Rafiq with a mischievious grin. 'Do you know what we were doing?'

I had no idea; only that they had been doing *something*.

He glanced at Rustam, and said: 'We were — *having a violin lesson!*' And the two of them burst into laughter.

'So . . .' he recovered, wiping tears from his eyes, '. . . I will tell you. Have you ever tried opium?'

He went to the corner of the room and retrieved a paraffin stove from where he had stashed it on hearing my knock at the door. Under his chair was a straightened out coat-hanger; and behind a vase on the mantelpiece, a bent-open safety pin. On its point was fixed a pea-sized pellet of the drug: and we were ready for the ritual.

Rafiq lowered the coat hanger into the flame, nursing it back and forth until it was red hot over a length of several inches, then held the heated portion almost to his lips. Next, Rustam, drawing up the sleeves of his cashmere sweater, sprang into action with the bead of opium, which he drew carefully back and forth over the heated metal. As it melted it emitted a sudden snow-white burst of smoke, the smell of which reminded me instantly of poppies.

'Just like a violin!' giggled Rafiq, his eyes skewed magnetically by the progress of the hissing morsel an inch from his nose. Then with a vigorous suck the smoke was drawn sideways like a tiny serpent, slithering speedily across the void to disappear between his lips.

'In my country,' he exhaled languorously, 'opium is not considered a drug. It is traditional, it is ...' (puff) '... *medicine.*'

As rationalizations go this had a certain charm; what he said was not completely untrue. At the same time, powdered wormwood was traditionally used in Afghanistan for the treatment of syphilitic ulcers, but you didn't see men going about with poultices on their genitals after they were cured.

Rafiq sensed my scepticism.

'*My God, no!*' he shook his head, as his eyes began to acquire a strange translucence. 'I would *never* take *real* drugs; cocaine, heroin ... *never.*'

He went on to explain that the effect of opium was 'cold', and it was essential to drink sweetened tea during a session; sugar was 'warm' and without its balancing influence the shock of the opium induced nausea, which accounted for the tendency of most first-time users to be violently ill.

No, this was not, he remonstrated, the desperate and self-centred narcosis of the Western drug-user. Even Edward Browne, the unimpeachable orientalist, had enjoyed a regular toking during his travels in Iran. The idea was to talk and listen to music and share in – in ...

'... *la vie! Finalement, c'est une experience!* ... life! I mean – life's an experience!'

Then he turned his companion and said: '*N'est-ce pas, Rustam?*'

Rustam's physical resemblance to Salman Rushdie was comically acute. True to his polished urbanity, he quoted something from a French existentialist about the meaning of suicide. Then he grinned contentedly, as if having drawn some irreplaceable jewel from the intellectual treasury of the West.

Rafiq, with a friendly wave of disdain for his companion's cerebral manner, followed up with a couplet from Baha' ūllah. Then the two of them turned to me.

Hopeless in such discussions I looked on mutely; Rafiq chided me for my aloofness. I had indulged my curiosity with the opium, but couldn't say what the effect of Rafiq's medicine had really been; I listened hard for the strains of that Abyssinian maid singing of Mount Abora, but heard only the purr of the flame from the stove. I had burned my lip and my teeth were aching from the quantity of sugar we had drunk.

But perhaps after all there was some effect. Just at the right moment a story bubbled unexpectedly upward from the pool of memory. Were they sitting comfortably? Then I'd begin . . .

*

A certain king was keen to discover who was the most pious man in his land, in order to reward him. So he sent his spies and agents into the country to mingle with the ordinary folk, enquiring wherever they went as to who was the most pious man of the region. Months passed, until the list of candidates was finally reduced to two: a *mullā* and a dervish.

It seemed no one could make a final decision as to their merits, and the judgement was left to the king himself, who summoned the two men to his palace and interviewed them personally.

The *mullā*'s turn was first. In his private chamber the king invited the *mullā* to sit beside him and answer, on his honour, a few questions.

'I have here a sum of gold,' said the king, patting a small bag, 'with which I intend to reward the most worthy candidate. But first I must know this:

'Should this reward become yours, would you be likely to spend any part of it on wine?'

'*Astaghfirullah!*' exclaims the *mullā* at once. 'Heaven forbid!'

'But might you spend it on gambling?'

'*Astaghfirullah!*' exclaims the *mullā* again.

'And what about women?'

'*Astaghfirullah!*' the *mullā* cries, 'I wouldn't dream of it.'

'Very well,' says the king. 'I shall take your answers into account.'

The *mullā* takes his leave respectfully from the king, into whose presence the diminutive dervish is escorted. And the king begins in the same manner, asking:

'If I were to give you this gold, would you be likely to spend it on wine, or other illicit intoxicants?'

The dervish thinks a little, and after a pause says: 'Why not?'

The king is taken aback, but continues.

'What about gambling?'

Again the dervish reflects for a moment, then says: 'Why not?'

'And women?'

'Well,' muses the dervish again, 'why not?'

The king, perplexed, dismisses the dervish, who joins the *mullā* in an adjoining room. Awaiting judgement, the two exchange accounts of their meeting with the king. Then at long last a bearer emerges from the king's chamber and announces:

'His majesty wishes it to be known that the money is hereby awarded — to the dervish.'

The dervish's expression remains unchanged, but immediately the *mullā* jumps up, protesting, 'There must be some mistake!' and rushes past the guards to the king.

'Your majesty!' he implores. 'In all my life I would never dare to spend the reward on the things you mentioned. But this profligate dervish, by his own confession, would not hesitate to spend the money in the most shameful ways!'

'My conclusion precisely,' replies the king. 'His need of it, therefore, is obviously far greater than yours.'

＊

Rafiq laughed and laughed, and sometimes, after a long silence, he would explode again in laughter, mimicking lavishly:

'*Why not? Why not?*'

I had redeemed myself. It was very late. Rafiq offered me a room upstairs. It was actually warm, and between crisp sheets I fell into a sensuous reverie, thinking how readily an outsider, with enough money to live a king-like existence and isolated from the regulating influences of life, might, with the servants and pleasures of his whim, come completely undone here. Conversely the place might also bring out what was most sublime in him. I thought of people I had come to know who had been drawn to both poles, and suffered accordingly; some slipping and others climbing. Here the two extremes presented themselves daily and at a pitch more intense than in ordinary life, and

unsuspecting souls found themselves stretched intolerably by the
tension between them.

*

It was now Ramadan, the Moslem month of fasting. For thirty days
the faithful observe a dawn-to-dusk abstinence from food or drink,
and endeavour to purge the mind of uncharitable thoughts. It is a
month of purification and renewal, in which the individual re-seeds
the furrows carved by habitual sensuality with fresh strivings. The
spiritual enrichment of the fast, and the social cohesion it engenders,
is well known; but it is a difficult ordeal. Now a bitter winter and
widespread shortage of fuel were making it especially hard. Despite
this, the Afghan staff cooked for us without a trace of reluctance, and
once, when I gently reprimanded the toothless Suleyman for cooking
for me, instead of letting me prepare my own food, he laughed out
loud at the absurdity of the suggestion.

'*Wazife-ye mā ast!* It's my duty!' he chuckled. 'You're a guest!' For
hours he would sit alone in the gloom of the kitchen, fussing at
mealtimes over a camping stove, before bicycling home in the icy
darkness.

Later the *chowkidar*, Sultan, a small, wily-looking character whose
reputation suffered unfairly on account of a permanent scowl, would
lock the doors with a gaoler's solemnity. We did not see much of each
other, but once, as I was preparing to leave the house, he signalled to
my door as I headed downstairs.

'Lock your room,' he said dourly. There had been a theft the
month before, and the former correspondent had made the painful
decision to turn his staff over to the police. It had soured things
somewhat.

'Locking is good,' I said, 'but trust is better.'

His face lit up in astonishment.

'*Bī shak!* Good for you!' he chuckled, strode up to me, and hugged
me.

It was the only time I saw him smile.

*

In theory at least, the holy month is also a period of reconciliation, and there was a lull in the fighting. For a time the city was virtually free of the terrifying randomness of attacks, and for several days, walking around its streets, life seemed oddly tranquil and it was possible to imagine the taste of peace. It was a fragile interlude; I don't think anyone believed deeply that it would last.

It did not: the momentum of the fighting was too great. After a week the bangs and thumps began anew, and twice the city was attacked by jets. Alain cheerfully filmed the first of these attacks from the roof of the BBC residence, a rolled-up cigarette dangling from his lip as the house shook from the explosions.

The other time I happened to be in the centre of the city with Rafiq, who I had joined on a shopping expedition to buy a carpet. We drove from place to place in his jeep; it was an almost normal day. Walking out of a shop near Chicken Street we heard a strange, echoing, grating sound that grew so loud it filled the air and made it shake, and everyone in the street stopped in their tracks. Then came the directionless roar of an approaching jet, which grew into a deafening scream. We jumped into a doorway as two almost simultaneous explosions which made the ground tremble, and the shock wave through the air was like a physical blow.

The grating sound was anti-aircraft fire, and echoed from every direction. But the jet tore through the sky, leaving a billowing tower of smoke, which rose from a point several hundred yards away.

Rafiq held his hands over his face and let out an anguished moan.

'Oh, *fuck* this place!' he yelled. 'Oh, *God!*'

I asked if he would quickly take me to the site where the bombs had fallen, but he shook his head sorrowfully and said he couldn't risk getting involved.

'You know –' he said – 'it might be complicated.'

I persuaded him to take me halfway there, and ran the rest of the way, taking wrong turnings and getting lost in an unfamiliar maze of tributary alleys I hoped would provide a short cut. By the time I arrived the smoke had cleared and the flow of traffic and passers-by had returned almost to normal. Two bombs had left car-size craters exactly in line with the Ministry of Defence. It looked as though the pilot had released them a fraction of a second too early: one had fallen on the riverbank a hundred yards short of the ministry buildings, scattering the surrounding houses with mud and shrapnel, the other in a grove of trees just outside the gates of the compound itself. In the road was the shattered glass of a car window and the twisted frame of a bicycle.

A guard was shooing away the men and women who had gathered in a circle around the muddy crater. Several trees had been blasted away to their stumps, and broken sticks and branches were strewn around in a dissolute arc. Then I realized: the crowd was not there, as I was, to ponder the effects of the attack, but to gather firewood.

These disheartening portents were followed by news of a blockade in the south. Prices began to rise, and the most perishable goods grew daily scarcer; meat disappeared from our diet and the selection of foods in shops and stalls grew perceptibly meaner.

As ever in wartime, stories were rife, and tales of the new hardships imposed by the blockade began to spread with grim vigour. One particular tale that had been circulating in Kabul was quoted literally by visiting reporters. It was the story of a widowed woman who had left her house in search of firewood and been taken prisoner and repeatedly raped by rogue mujaheddin, who kept her captive for several days. Struggling home she found her house ruined by a stray rocket, and amid the rubble, the emaciated bodies of her remaining children, who had starved slowly in her absence.

I had not reflected much on how such a story might have evolved until a small but illuminating incident got me thinking.

It was when I went back to the barber I had seen a month before. He greeted me warmly and as he fastened a cape at the back of my neck, said:

'You've been away.' I was not sure if it was a question or a statement.

'Yes,' I said.

'To Herat.'

'Yes, actually.'

His scissors worked their way over my head as I began to puzzle over his remarkable insight. Then he asked again:

'And you went to the shrine of Khwaja Ansari?'

'Yes...'

'And some Tālebs came into the shrine while you were there.'

'Yes, but how——'

'And they were laughing and smoking *chars*,' the general term for cannabis or marijuana. (*Bhang* is, I think, an intoxicating drink made from cannabis; *Teryāq* is opium.) The *chars* was an embellishment, and a provocative one. It was Ramadan and even the smoking of cigarettes was a transgression; to be smoking *chars* in one of the holiest shrines of the country was little short of heinous. Somehow, faster than ants spreading word of sugar, a stranger had heard news of my trip. I asked how he could possibly know.

'I know,' he said with a grin, 'because I heard it on the radio this morning.'

I was dumbstruck! And worried too, lest the broadcast had been heard in Herat and caused trouble for the kindly guardian of the shrine who had let me stay there. All through the rest of the day I thought back to the people I had told about the journey to Herat, realizing eventually who had passed it on. Intact, he claimed, when challenged, and I believed him (and was relieved to discover that the transmission could be heard only locally); someone further down the line, someone working for the radio station, must have added the other bits. It was interesting to see how stories evolved, and how their expression suited the needs of the time, gathering extra detail as they went. Like the grim story of the widow, each separate element had a basis in fact; woven together, the sum of them became a representation of popular sentiment.

*

Then one morning, like the fall of a scythe, I knew the day wasn't far off when I'd have to leave. I had been counting my remaining money, and realized I had barely enough for a few parting gifts. From then on the prospect of leaving hung like a shadow, and in its presence the days were more precious than ever. I felt a sense of panic at all the things I hadn't got round to doing – through my own fault as well as the conditions of the time – and felt little short of dread at the prospect of returning to the complicated world of home.

I had never had a proper of view of Kabul and walked up to the Azāmai hill the following day through mazes of tiny mud-walled alleys, passing children carrying water in clay pots on their heads, and emerged where the military roads snaked upwards. A Panjshīri fighter came out of a bunker to stop me. We chatted for a while, and his radio crackled as he requested permission for me to go up further; but he failed to get through, so we walked up together between rocks at the verge painted red where there were buried mines. He watched in silence as I stood on a big rock and looked out over the city.

All along the northern horizon ran the white-toothed blade of the Hindu Kush. A mile away, in the northeast, I could make out the grid of streets with which I'd grown familiar. Against the sprawl of the whole of Kabul, it was a tiny portion. It would take years to be able to say one really knew the place, and I felt how limited the radius of my exploring had been.

Several miles away, at the edge of the easternmost suburbs beyond the Soviet tumour of Microrayon, I could just make out a trio of structures resembling misplaced rooks from a chessboard. For a while I stared at them, uncertain. Then there was no doubt: *the brick kilns!* At the sight of them, a tentacle of memory reached suddenly forward across eleven years; I could almost feel my feet padding through the dust at their bases, and hear the whispers and rustle of guns and the final tightening of laces and webbing, the barking of a dog, and a man's scream from within a nearby building that had chilled the blood ... for a moment I was there again. It was our first terrifying foray into the city. I had paused there under their moon-thrown shadows with Pål and a troupe of fifty mujaheddin, just before we fanned out among the ruined buildings in a ripple of unclicking safety-catches. I could still hear the bullets zinging above our heads soon afterwards, and remembered Pål's grinning face in the moonlight at the height of the attack as he suggested we send one of the men into the city to fetch us a pizza.

A fighter had dropped into our trench with a jammed rifle, and Pål had cleared a misshapen round from the breach.

'Now don't do it again.'

Its owner, with a breathless and uncomprehending nod of thanks, flew back into the fight, and we had called after him:

'Mine's with anchovies ... and spicy oil!'

'And don't forget the fresh basil!'

And as if in response to this impudence a scarifying volley of tracers had torn overhead. We huddled and laughed, and changed our orders.

*

There was what turned out to be a final party. I had always held back at such events, which I thought of as lonely affairs requiring an unnatural effort to supply the appropriate enthusiasm. Now, for the first time, I gave in to a sense of abandon, and found it unexpectedly pleasant.

There was the usual raucousness, but by the end of the evening it had died down like a fire to a few stubborn coals. The furniture and carpets were in mild disarray, the result of an improvised rugby scrum: English on one side and French on the other, two dozen drunken feet had trampled over a thrown-in watermelon; I forget which side claimed victory. A few of us now remained, sitting around a table strewn with leftover food from the earlier spread, supplemented with private stashes of cigarettes and chocolate ferreted out from bedrooms upstairs.

Franco, the Italian adventurer, was treating me to one of his extravagant tales; something about the time he'd been shot, but happened luckily to be wearing a bullet-proof vest...

A half-bottle of whisky appeared, and a first round was distributed into glasses swaying with reckless quixotism. Someone suggested getting rid of the UN and electing in its place an interim government of outsiders who, knowing nothing about the country, would confound the arguments of the opposition with a commonsensical equinamity:

Scandinavians would work best, they'd do well in the winter too. Richard Branson was put forward to flesh out economic policy. Vaclav Havel, suggested someone else, could draft a new constitution with the help of farmers elected from the various ethnic groups.

As a second round splashed forth, the ravaged capital was being rebuilt by Hekmatyar's former followers under the patronage of Prince Charles; and a new body for religious education was headed by *mullā* Nasruddin...

And as the level of the bottle sank lower, news flooded in of some astonishing acts of magnanimity: Bill Gates had agreed to contribute a year's interest on his fortunes in order to buy every weapon in the country: Peace! The Prime Minister of Pakistan had sold her mansions in England and America and founded a network of schools for mine-crippled children, and her husband was supervising a kite-making workshop in the capital. The Saudis had diverted their funds from the Tālebān to buying trees, of which every man formerly under arms had agreed to plant a hundred; and the Americans, a naturally generous people and cognizant at last of the enormity of human suffering required to maintain low oil prices in their country, had agreed to allow their pipeline across Afghanistan to end not in Pakistan but in Kabul, where cheap fuel was now saving the lives of its freezing populace. Mine-clearing teams, set up by penitent Soviet generals, were being run by former officers of the Afghan secret police, who had returned from hiding in Europe for the purpose; and the condemned British cows, instead of being incinerated, had been flown in by the Red Cross to solve the food crisis, and were now being slaughtered gratefully by hungry families.

Glasses smacked against the table: the bottle was empty.

I was aware all the while of a woman sitting nearby, listening to the conversation; at some point we introduced ourselves. She had striking blue eyes; and as we joked about life in Kabul, I felt suddenly that all the speculation and Pantagruelian talk, which in the party-going conducted our anxieties harmlessly away, was no more than a disguised form of longing. But for what? We hit upon it at the same moment: closeness. Closeness to life, or closeness to others? We wondered. Our theme gathered a kind of momentum. Did she believe, I asked, that closeness was possible without the interference of its demon twin, possession?

'It must be,' she said, 'for some people.'

But that is another story.

Walking home, tiptoeing past the sentries in their nearby hut for fear of being challenged in the darkness at riflepoint, I heard a flute playing inside. The *chowkidar* had taken to sleeping in the living room, and couldn't hear me knock. I scrambled, after several tries, up a tree onto the wall, dropped into the garden, and through the window saw him sleeping by the fire under a mound of bedding. He looked too peaceful to wake up. By way of a drainpipe I made it to my window and peeled back the plastic sheeting. A cat, which darted out as I tried to scramble in, had found a temporary haven in my bed which, as I sank into it, was still warm.

*

Anyone who has spent time against a backdrop of prolonged danger knows something of the protective reorganization that goes on in the senses and which, years later, kicks into action at odd moments. Nerves once stretched over a rack never fully return to their original innocence. In time, these now-fugitive reflexes are consciously suppressed: it's only when you're half-asleep or daydreaming you realize how deeply their roots are still sunk into the system. A door slams and you have rolled from bed with a speed you didn't know you had; walking at night, the sight of approaching headlights has you tumbling into a thicket at the verge; from the corner of your eye you see, across a busy street, a man reaching under his shirt and you whirl — but he's only scratching.

I heard the car while it was fifty yards away, but by the pitch of the engine I knew it was slowing. By the time it was almost behind me, the sweat had already broken between my shoulder-blades.

It was Hāroun, the dashing young Afghan diplomat: did I want a lift anywhere? And why that sigh of relief? I jumped in gratefully. He was on his way to visit his childhood home, which was being redecorated. As we drove along he began rummaging in his midriff.

'Hold onto this for a second, would you?' he asked. I felt something heavy fall into my lap. It was a Russian officer's pistol, and it was loaded. I looked across to him questioningly.

'You never know,' he said.

We passed impoverished street vendors wheeling their barrows to and fro, or pulling down the metal grilles over their makeshift stalls.

'Kabul was never like this,' he said irascibly, 'look at it now.' He shook his head. His wife had recently arrived from America: as they had pulled up outside their home, she had looked at the bullet-chipped walls and sandbags and asked:

'Is this the worst part of town?'

'No, honey,' he had answered, 'it's the best.'

We drove to a quiet street in Wazir, and as we got out of the car, he tucked the pistol back into his belt. 'God,' he grinned, 'if my wife knew I was carrying a gun, she'd have a fit.'

Inside the house, half a dozen workmen were levelling and grouting a new marble floor. 'It's a lot smaller than I remember,' he said, peering into his childhood bedroom. Twenty years had passed since he had fled with his parents. With his brother he was planning to restore, along with the house itself, a sense of home. I thought privately of the precarious task of adapting from life in California to the ways of the troubled country to which he had returned. But he seemed vigorously convinced of the way ahead.

'Come back and live here,' he said, as we sipped tea in the garden. The sun was warm on our faces. 'Life is simple. We make it complicated for ourselves in the West.' He had just been back for a brief visit to America, and shuddered at the recollection.

'I can't go back to that. I'll live here and, God willing, I'll die here. Here we talk, we meet, we pray, we live. It's that simple. I can help you get set up.'

'It's very tempting,' I said.

'What more do you want?' he asked.

What more indeed? It was true that life seemed to have condensed into different concerns, and some of its dreams grown more luminous. I toyed with the idea; it touched a nerve made more tender by the prospect of leaving, and I realized I'd been happier in that shabby capital than for years. Not with the happiness of pleasure, but with that of having really lived. By then it was home that seemed a miserable place: a dreary and unfriendly refuge where no one looked you in the eye. Home. All I could think of was the lemming-like jostling of cars on overcrowded motorways and the prospect of unpaid parking tickets.

It was, as the cliché has it, the small things I would miss, and the sustenance to which they pointed. I would miss the shopkeepers disappearing from their shops to get sweets to go with tea; I would miss the kebab seller whose stall I passed in the freezing mornings, and who without a word would beckon me to warm my hands against the coals of his grill; and the *chowkidar* at the Red Cross who at night would insist on following me a hundred yards down the street to share the light of his torch; I would miss the bookseller at his ragged barrow who, when things were particularly bad, would rub his hands together and hold his palms up to the sun with a chuckle, and say:

'*Khoda mehreban ast!* God's good to us!'

It was the one visible and incorruptible icon left to them: I would miss the light of their sun.

*

Shortly before I left, I was invited with half a dozen friends, together with two visiting European journalists, to an informal dinner with some government officials. Our defence ministry liaison, Amrullah, was there, Hāroun and his wife and brother, and three of Massoud's closest advisers.

We did not mistake our hosts for saints; by means of such events they kept themselves abreast of their guests' opinions, and found generally sympathetic ears for their own; but they were courteous to a fault and it was hard not to be touched by the fact that they had taken time off from running their government, and a war, to treat us to a generous meal.

While the various guests were arriving, a printed document in English on a table caught my eye. It was the report of a foreign development agency which had recently made a two-week visit to the country 'to assess Afghanistan's current and projected aid needs and priorities in the light of predicted future political and security scenarios and recommend a forward strategy...'

The words swam in front of my eyes. 'The review methodology adopted a common framework of explicit assessment criteria and semi-structured interviews with key informants...' I wondered if the Afghan sitting next to me knew that his country displayed 'relative social mobility, extreme political fluidity, and organizational diversity that characterize both the micro- and macro-levels', and felt a pang of sympathy for the men endeavouring to rebuild their government.

The conversation was friendly. But there was a note of frustration when it came to the recent news of America's 'covert' intention to destabilize the regime in neighbouring Iran. America: it was an old and tender theme. Afghans still felt abandoned by their former ally, whom they had supposed would return after the defeat of the Soviets and help rebuild their ruined country. News that Washington had now agreed to sponsor the undermining of a neighbouring government came as a kind of cynical confirmation.

'We see the American logic,' said a thoughtful voice, 'and we see the logic of Iran. We don't support either. But the American action is deeply offensive. It's as if we told the Americans how to live!'

The assembled men were not politically naive but the old vision of America as a benevolent and freedom-loving nation was dying a stubborn death in Afghanistan. Behind this disbelieving tone was, in part, a feeling of having been shunned in their hour of need. Even the government's former adversaries in Russia and Iran had agreed to recognize and support the effort from Kabul to resist the Tālebān's advance. But the Americans had held back, and their reluctance to recognize the government officially was a source of bitter disappointment. Washington had also refrained from expressing disapproval of the Tālebān; an American congressman had even spoken up publicly strongly in their favour, suggesting they were the sole candidates for leadership of the country.

'Positive support by America could have been so good for regional security,' said someone else. 'It needn't have come to this.'

The note of the conversation was not so much hostile as sad. After the meal we sat around the fire; occasionally the windows would rattle as the thump of artillery sounded from far away. We sipped tea. It was a difficult evening if your favourite topics weren't religion or politics.

For a few minutes I talked privately with one of Massoud's closest advisers. He spoke fluent and thoughtful English. Sometimes his walkie-talkie would crackle into life and he would issue a few instructions and return it to the table in front of us.

He had come recently from a meeting with state department officials in the north of the country, to discuss terms by which the Americans would agree to recognize the government officially. The results had been deeply disappointing, the terms impossible to meet. One was the return of the former king, Zāher Shāh, from his thirty-year exile in Italy. It had worked in Cambodia, the Americans said, and it could work in Afghanistan.

He gave an exasperated sigh, as if nothing could be less relevant to the country: what had the king done for them in the last thirty years?

Was he still hoping it was possible, I asked, to build the necessary bridges, in spite of everything?

'Yes,' he said, 'we deal with realities. We want to be a part of the world. But we don't know what we've done to deserve this. If it's for some reason we don't know, we want to look at that. But if it's because we're too independent for them – well, we're proud of that.'

Then half to himself, he said:

'Why have we had to go through this, I wonder? Sometimes I even wish that the Tāleban could take over the whole of Afghanistan – just for a day – to show the Americans how bad it could get.'

It was already bad. I could think of only one positive aspect to things. All the failed efforts of Afghanistan's would-be rulers – of which the Tāleban appeared to be the crowning proof – were evidence that the country was beyond the domination of a single authority. There would, eventually, be compromise. The conflict could no longer be restricted to a local affair, but was part of a violent synthesis in which a greater than ever portion of humanity was implicated. At such moments it seemed just possible that the catastrophes of recent years were the result of something even more implacable than war itself — an organic, supracultural, and ultimately unitive force; not slouching, as in the poem, towards its Bethlehem, but stampeding like an elephant through a jungle, uprooting obstacles violently and drawing together in its wake new strands of culture like stitches over a wound: perhaps, after all, the country was not dying, but healing.

*

Often during those final days, as things turned ever worse from the visible point of view, I was prone to spontaneous moments of burgeoning joy. Even the sight of the crippled and wounded, or news of some particularly tragic event, no longer had the power to bring down that oppressive mantle of grief under which I'd earlier taken shelter. The opposite, in fact: terrible as such things were, they had the capacity to uplift. Something had changed.

For much of the journey I had found myself looking towards positive moments to redeem the difficult ones, and struggled with consolatory explanations for painful events. But the one was a troublesome see-saw of feeling, and the other self-defeating. I had noticed this tendency from the very outset of the journey: this instinctive longing to shunt painful experience towards some form of expression, to clothe it quickly with some kind of action in the feelings or intellect. I had earlier set myself a personal challenge: was it possible to enlarge the space in oneself where the raw material of experience might sit awhile, before being decanted in the usual way? To fashion some intermediary vessel in which to bear the raw impressions of life, like freshly pressed grapes with all their husks and ugly stalks? I was not sure what the outcome might be; a sort of stretching, a deepening of one's ability to stand up to life and absorb it as it happens.

But I now found out that the change had begun to happen of its own accord. Contradictory moments, and the extremes of feeling they evoked, had grown less antithetical, and the distance between them was mysteriously reduced. Now the poles from which they sprang were no longer irreconcilable, but intertwined like the serpents of a caduceus.

Something had definitely changed; I was infected not with the sense of despair I'd so often felt at the beginning of the journey, but with a strange hopefulness.

✻

The following day I checked the flight list, and found my name on it. The Red Cross bus was leaving for the airport the next afternoon. I stripped down my belongings, made gifts of my warm clothes, and hurriedly bought some small presents with my remaining cash. The world was deflating with horrible swiftness and I wanted to get away as quickly as possible.

The wily Sultan caught me at the door as I left.

'I have left you something inside,' I said.

His eyes narrowed. 'Dollars or pounds?'

✻

I watched the mountains sink back into the land as we flew southeast. Half an hour later the little plane had broken from the embrace of light, and began descending.

In the morning I woke up in a capacious bedroom between crisp sheets, uncertain whether I'd dreamed what had gone before or whether I had awoken into a dream. I was in Pakistan. The Red Cross fleet mechanic, a kind-hearted Frenchman, had put me up for the night at his home. I had a vague memory of dinner the previous evening at the American club and, among the foreign guests, a vision of pale faces as sad as those of old men lingering outside betting offices.

Outside it was sunny and humid; the air smelled of exotic plants and dust and diesel fumes: Peshawar again. The sky was heavy and hazy and for the first time since the beginning of the journey, it was warm. I slung my coat over my shoulder and walked for a while alongside the railway tracks, where more than a decade before I had met my first Afghan refugees, and trespassed with such longing on their world.

It felt like spring. Beyond the tracks spread some scattered houses among fields where the vegetation was lush and green and a man was leading a sleek calf along a path. Someone was watering bright bougainvillea in his garden and the water sparkled as it fountained into the dust.

A few colourfully dressed children were playing nearby. It was utterly peaceful. I felt a kind of welling up and, a little further on, sat down by the tracks, and began to weep.